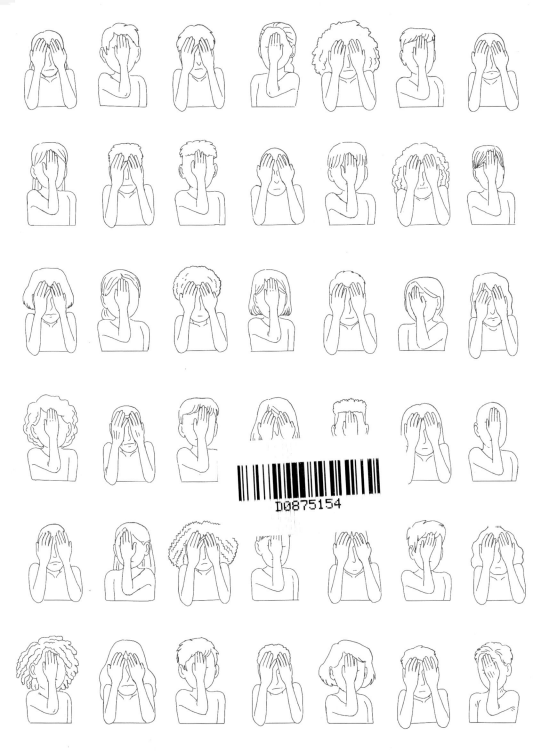

D0875154

OTHER BOOKS BY AMINDER DHALIWAL

Woman World

drawnandquarterly.com
aminderdhaliwal.com

First edition: April 2021
Printed in China
10 9 8 7 6 5 4 3 2 1

Cataloguing data available from Library and Archives Canada.

Published in the USA by Drawn & Quarterly, a client publisher of Farrar, Straus and Giroux. | Published in Canada by Drawn & Quarterly, a client publisher of Raincoast Books. | Published in the United Kingdom by Drawn & Quarterly, a client publisher of Publishers Group UK.

 Drawn & Quarterly acknowledges the support of the Government of Canada and the Canada Council for the Arts for our publishing program.

D
RA
WN&
QUAR
TERLY
PRESENTS

Cyclopedia Exotica

This book is dedicated to those who don't feel seen.

Aminder Dhaliwal
Color by Nikolas Ilic

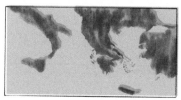

FIG. 01. Map of Cyclops-dense areas.

The Cyclops

AN OVERVIEW
Kingdom: Animalia.

The Cyclops is an exotic subspecies of archaic humans that settled in western Eurasia. They thrived through the extinction of other archaic humans because of a tendency to live and hide in caves. The Cyclops's most recognizable feature is the single eye, which cannot see in stereoscopic vision like other humans.

For a great deal of human history, Cyclopes were asocial. While Two-Eyes lived in communities, Cyclopes preferred secluded islands, and built their habitats into natural structures like caves (Figure 03).

For much of recorded history, Two-Eyes and Cyclopes have been at odds. Many myths and stories recount violence between the two. This violence typically occurred near caves and volcanic regions where Cyclops density peaked.

The modern Cyclops is an equal citizen of the world and cohabitates with Two-Eyes.

The following subsections take an in-depth look into the life, body, and history of the Cyclops.

Greek mythology from Two-Eyes culture portrays Cyclopes as monsters (Figure 02). It also

FIG. 02. Illustration of a Cyclops in cave.

portrays Cyclopes as gargantuan and less intelligent than Two-Eyes.

The "less intelligent" stereotype originates from early Cyclopes' communication skills. The Cyclopian language is concise and specific to herding, and has 13 different terms for sheep of differing temperaments.

FIG. 03.
Early Cyclops
dwelling.

ANATOMY OVERVIEW

This section will cover Cyclopean sight, breasts, and reproductive means. Current information dictates these are the areas where Cyclopes differ from Two-Eyes.

THE EYE (Figure 04).

The Cyclops's most iconic feature is the single eye. The mono-eye covers a wide angle and has a greater ability to function in low light. The Cyclopean eye has many features to ensure it thrives. For example, a large tear duct on one end

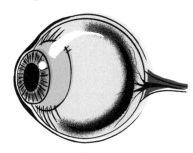

FIG. 04. Cyclops Eye.

pairs with a minuscule secondary duct on the opposing side. Cyclopean eye-lashes are also longer than those of Two-Eyes.

Another peculiar difference is the nose. The nose is flat with minuscule nostrils. This way the nose is not a visual obstruction.

REPRODUCTIVE ORGANS

A two-pronged penis is the main difference in the male Cyclopean

KIDNEY
OVARY
UTERUS
MIDDLE VAGINA
SIDE VAGINAS
BLADDER

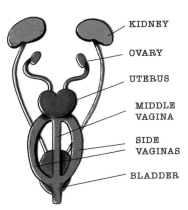

FIG. 05. Cyclops reproductive system.

reproductive organs. The female genitalia include three vaginas and two uteri (Figure 05). This explains the Cyclops's dual pregnancies. In a dual pregnancy, one fertilized egg will grow, while a second fertilized egg remains in stasis. The second egg waits until the first pregnancy has ended.

Another difference is the Cyclops has one breast, although the pectoralis major functions like that of a Two-Eyes (Figure 06).

FIG. 06. Female Cyclops with one breast.

HISTORY

Cyclopes have an ancestry as herders. They domesticated ancient sheep, and used them for milk, cheese, clothing, and food (Figure 08).

Cyclopes lived in isolation, but whether Cyclopes preferred seclusion or if it was a learned behavior is not definitively known. The Hunted Theory suggests Cyclopes isolated themselves because Two-Eyes hunted them for their sheep. Cyclopean isolation also lends itself to the Cave Theory, which points to a correlation between multiple progeny from limited sexual encounters.

Geneticists trace Cyclopean origins to Italy and its islands. Cyclopes thrived in this volcanic region, which created nutrient-dense and arable land for farming and sheep herding (Figure 07).

Cyclopes introduced various sheep products to

FIG. 08. Ancient sheep.

Two-Eyes, such as sebaceous gland extracts in lanolin. Various Cyclopean mutton dishes have also fused with recipes from Western Europe. Records show Two-Eyes trading with Cyclopes as early as the 17th century.

Cyclopes traded sheep, ovine products, and produce. In return they received spices, farming tools, and metals, like nails and hinges. This allowed Cyclopes to move from caves to self-built structures. Early Cyclopean homes were located beside caves. Caves continued to function as holding pens for the sheep at night.

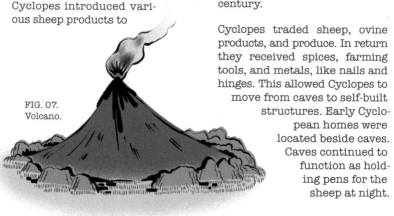

FIG. 07. Volcano.

VIOLENCE

There is a myth that Cyclopes have violent tendencies. Violence against Cyclopes is much more common. Two-Eyes have historically targeted the single eye in attacks (Figure 09).

FIG. 10. An interaction between a Two-Eyes and a Cyclops.

There is a common logical fallacy amongst Two-Eyes that frames Cyclopes as violent (Figure 10). The claim, "If Cyclopes have nothing to hide, then why are they hiding?" assumes that an isolated Cyclops is hiding because it is a monster rather than out of fear.

caught for two decades. The murders spawned many movies, books, and television shows. Cyclomedia produced a documentary about policing biases and Cyclops safety, called *Eye'd Down* in 2009. It won the Oscar for best documentary the following year (Figure 11).

FIG. 09. Cyclops after attack.

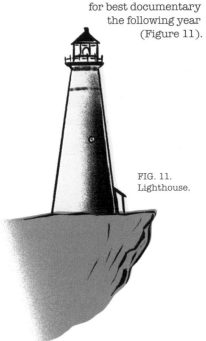

FIG. 11. Lighthouse.

Violence against Cyclopes reached an all-time low in 1980, but it spiked again in 1987, because of a string of high-profile murders in Washington State.

Referred to as the Lighthouse Killer, the murderer was not

WORLDS MERGING

By the late 19th century, Cyclopes integrated into Two-Eyed areas. In some counties, circuses recruited Cyclopes for shows (Figure 12). In other areas, Two-Eyes considered Cyclopes shamans (Figure 13). There were few job opportunities for Cyclopes beyond herding. Publishers turned away Cyclopean authors, while many popular Two-Eyed authors wrote stories featuring Cyclopean leads.

As Cyclopes flocked to cities, Cytown referred to a part of the city with a denser Cyclops population. In Cy-towns, sheep products and mutton dishes, such as Shlamp, were and still continue to be popular. Sheep tongue was another popular delicacy. It fell out of favor when Two-Eyes popularized it as a slur.

FIG. 13. Cyclops fortune-teller.

Although Cyclopean healthcare is almost equal to Two-Eyed care, there are still shortcomings. Until recently, the UK's National Health Service registered Cyclopes as sight impaired. In Italy, an error in paperwork resulted in the Servizio Sanitario Nazionale labeling many Two-Eyes as 'Cyclopes.' This was a clerical error due to those citizens each having a glass eye.

MODERN CYCLOPES

The lives of modern Cyclopes (Figure 14) do not differ from those of Two-Eyes. The divides of the past have faded away. A big reason for this is a 1978 magazine cover (see next section 'Etna').

FIG. 12.
Cyclops clown.

FIG. 14.
Modern Cyclops
on the phone.

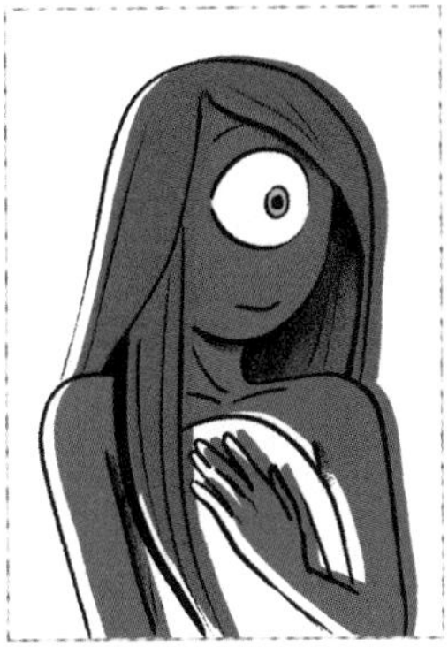

FIG. 15. Etna.

Etna

In 1978, Etna appeared on the cover of a popular nude magazine. She was the first Cyclops to cross this threshold. The company renamed the magazine "Playclops" for the issue. Because of the cover's popularity, "Playclops" spun off into its own magazine five years later.

Etna later dated Clark Staple, a young Hollywood actor. Many Two-Eyes considered the couple scandalous. Because of public outcry, *The Happy Morning Show* canceled Clark and Etna's appearance.

After th
back fr
stead, c
an-

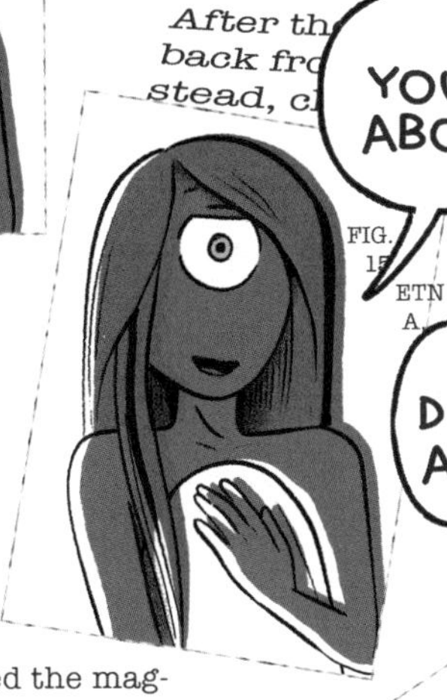
OH...HI! YOU'RE READING ABOUT ME, I SEE.

FIG. 15. ETNA.

See Appendix section, "Etna" for her return to the

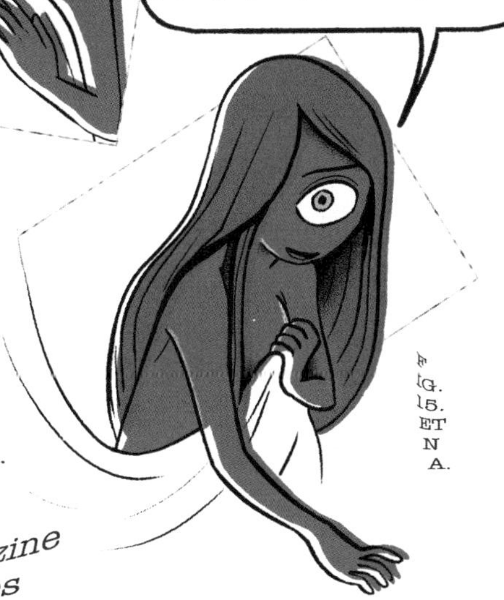
BLEGH! WHAT A DULL WAY TO LEARN ABOUT A MINORITY.

FIG. 15. ETNA.

Many regard Etna as the first Cyclops sex symbol. Etna brought Cyclops sexuality to the mainstream.

The original intent of the magazine was to cater to a growing Cyclops demographic. Yet, surveys show no difference in magazine sales among Two-Eyes and Cyclopes.

CYCLO
PEDIA
EXOTICA

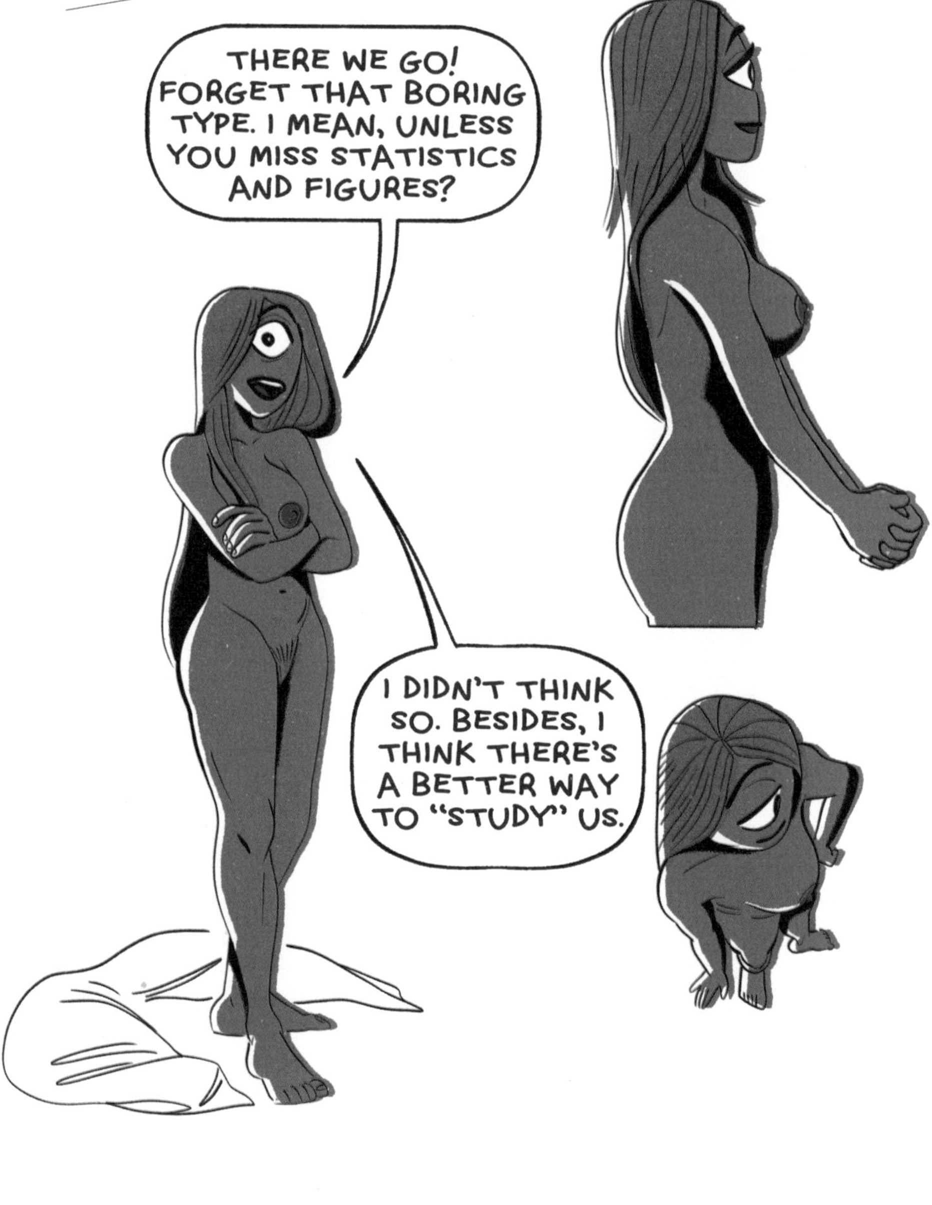
THERE WE GO! FORGET THAT BORING TYPE. I MEAN, UNLESS YOU MISS STATISTICS AND FIGURES?
I DIDN'T THINK SO. BESIDES, I THINK THERE'S A BETTER WAY TO "STUDY" US.

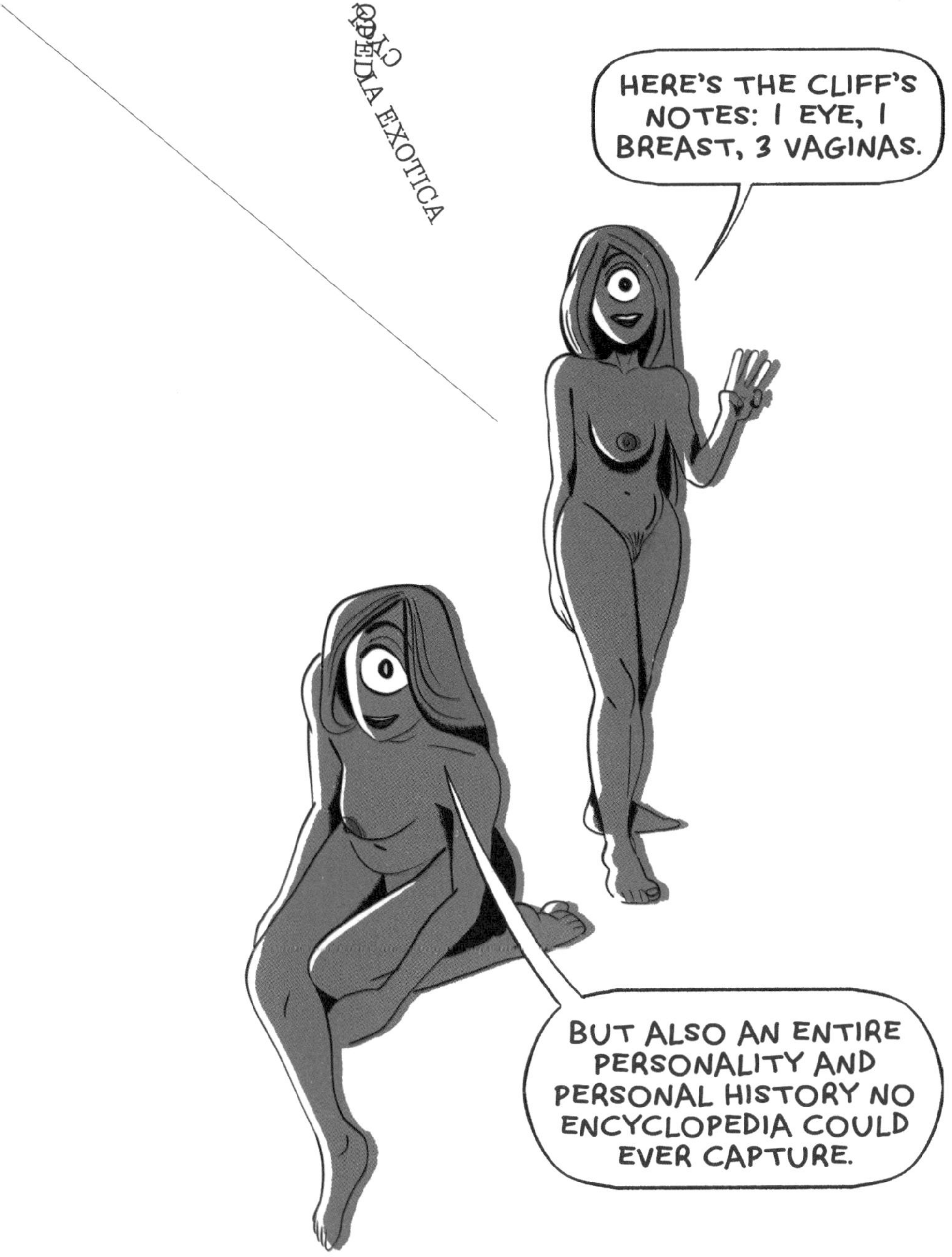
HERE'S THE CLIFF'S NOTES: 1 EYE, 1 BREAST, 3 VAGINAS.
BUT ALSO AN ENTIRE PERSONALITY AND PERSONAL HISTORY NO ENCYCLOPEDIA COULD EVER CAPTURE.

PLAYCLOPS

Latea and Pari shop

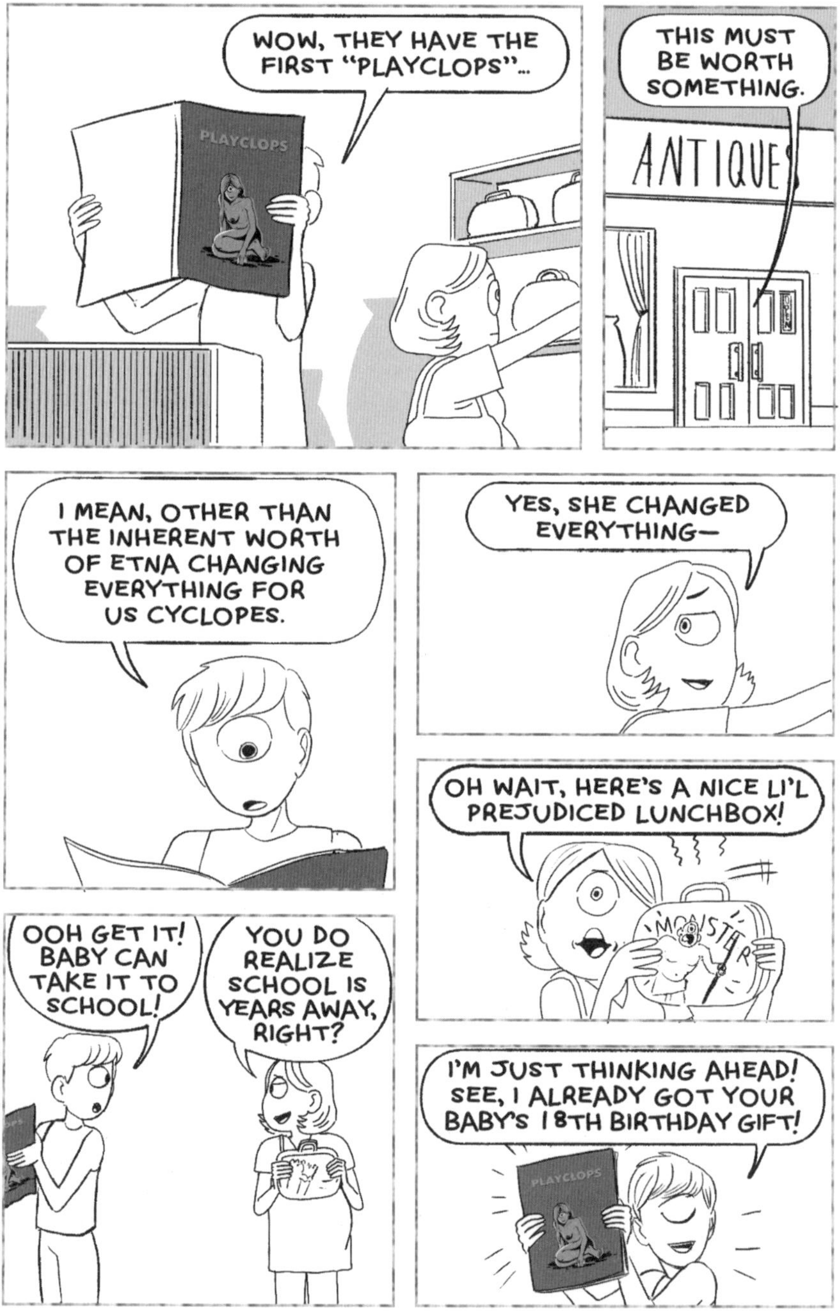
WOW, THEY HAVE THE FIRST "PLAYCLOPS"...
PLAYCLOPS
THIS MUST BE WORTH SOMETHING.
I MEAN, OTHER THAN THE INHERENT WORTH OF ETNA CHANGING EVERYTHING FOR US CYCLOPES.
YES, SHE CHANGED EVERYTHING—
OH WAIT, HERE'S A NICE LI'L PREJUDICED LUNCHBOX!
MONSTER
OOH GET IT! BABY CAN TAKE IT TO SCHOOL!
YOU DO REALIZE SCHOOL IS YEARS AWAY, RIGHT?
I'M JUST THINKING AHEAD! SEE, I ALREADY GOT YOUR BABY'S 18TH BIRTHDAY GIFT!
PLAYCLOPS

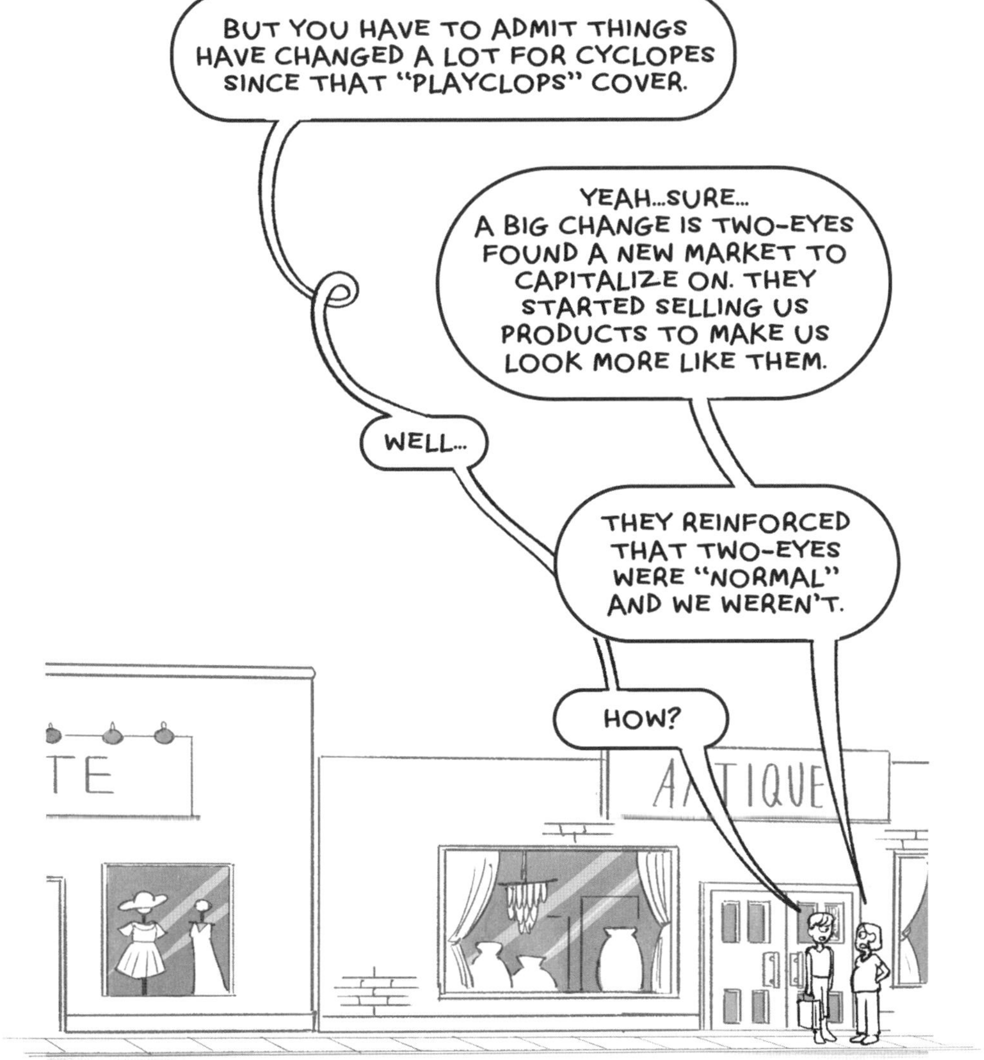
BUT YOU HAVE TO ADMIT THINGS HAVE CHANGED A LOT FOR CYCLOPES SINCE THAT "PLAYCLOPS" COVER.
YEAH...SURE... A BIG CHANGE IS TWO-EYES FOUND A NEW MARKET TO CAPITALIZE ON. THEY STARTED SELLING US PRODUCTS TO MAKE US LOOK MORE LIKE THEM.
WELL...
THEY REINFORCED THAT TWO-EYES WERE "NORMAL" AND WE WEREN'T.
HOW?
ANTIQUE

THOSE EXPERIMENTAL EYE SURGERIES...

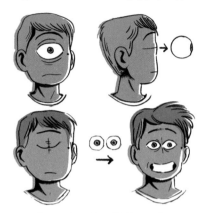

EYE JOB

COSMETIC-EYE TREATMENT

*USES HUMAN EYE DONORS

OR THE SECRET TO HAPPINESS IS A NOSE, OR THE SOLUTION TO DEPRESSION IS A BRA?!

THERE'S NO REVERSE MARKETPLACE. WHAT TWO-EYES WANTS TO LOOK MORE LIKE A CYCLOPS?

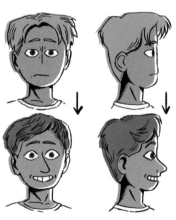

NOSE SCULPTING

POST COSMETIC EYE TREATMENT RHINOPLASTY

*NOSE DOES NOT HAVE WORKING NOSTRILS. FOR AESTHETIC PURPOSES ONLY.

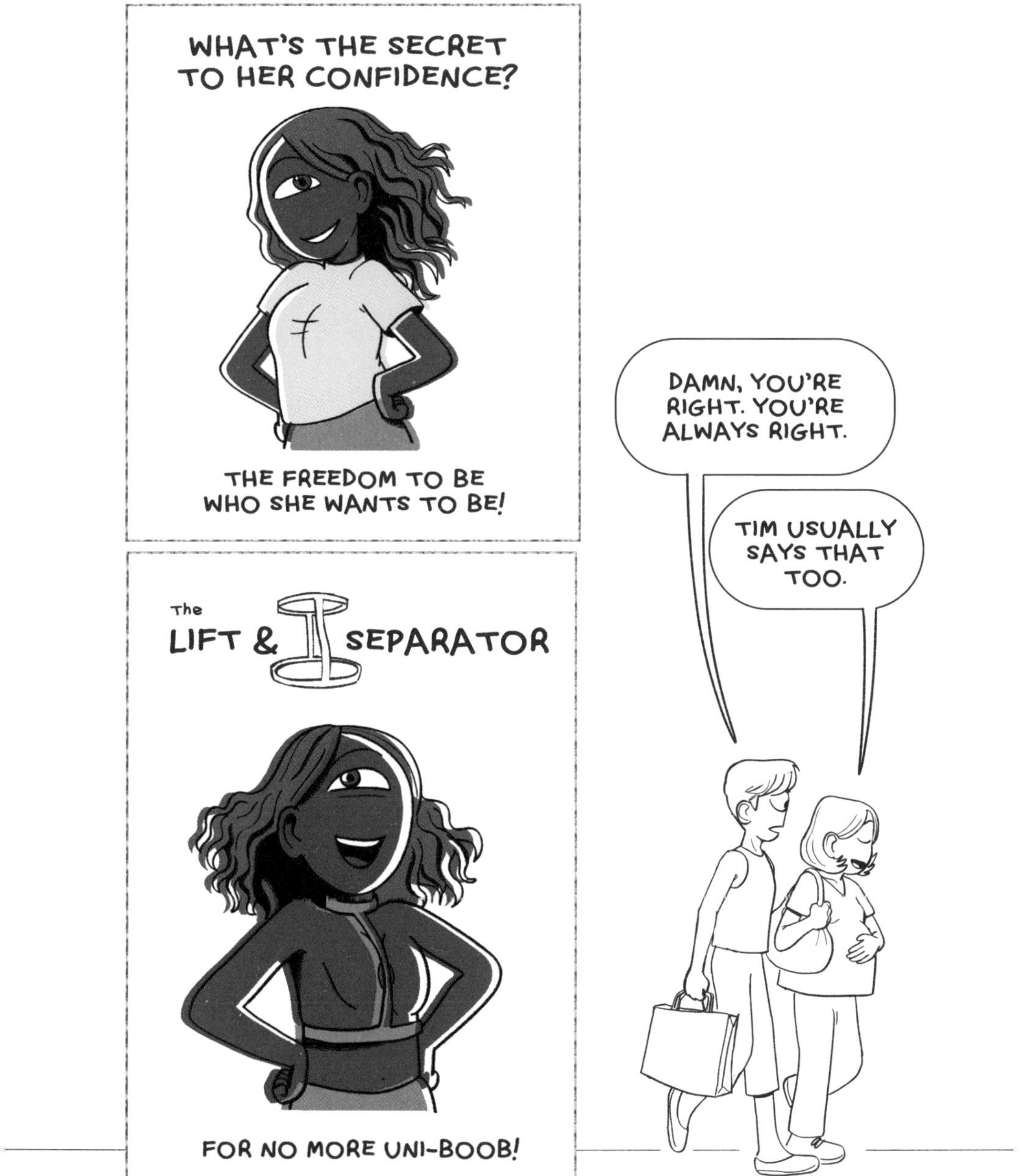
WHAT'S THE SECRET TO HER CONFIDENCE?
THE FREEDOM TO BE WHO SHE WANTS TO BE!
The LIFT & SEPARATOR
FOR NO MORE UNI-BOOB!
DAMN, YOU'RE RIGHT. YOU'RE ALWAYS RIGHT.
TIM USUALLY SAYS THAT TOO.

Pari goes on maternity leave

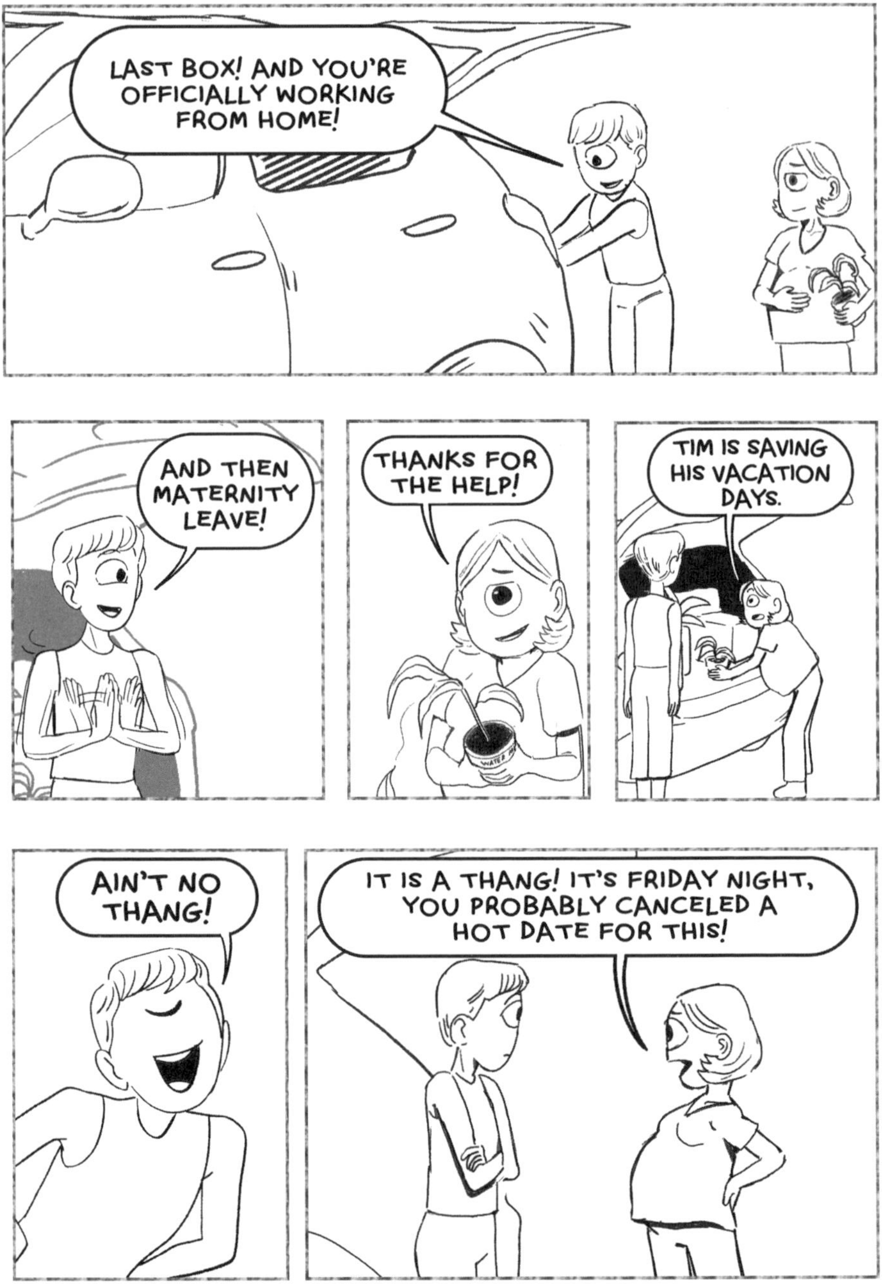
LAST BOX! AND YOU'RE OFFICIALLY WORKING FROM HOME!
AND THEN MATERNITY LEAVE!
THANKS FOR THE HELP!
TIM IS SAVING HIS VACATION DAYS.
AIN'T NO THANG!
IT IS A THANG! IT'S FRIDAY NIGHT, YOU PROBABLY CANCELED A HOT DATE FOR THIS!

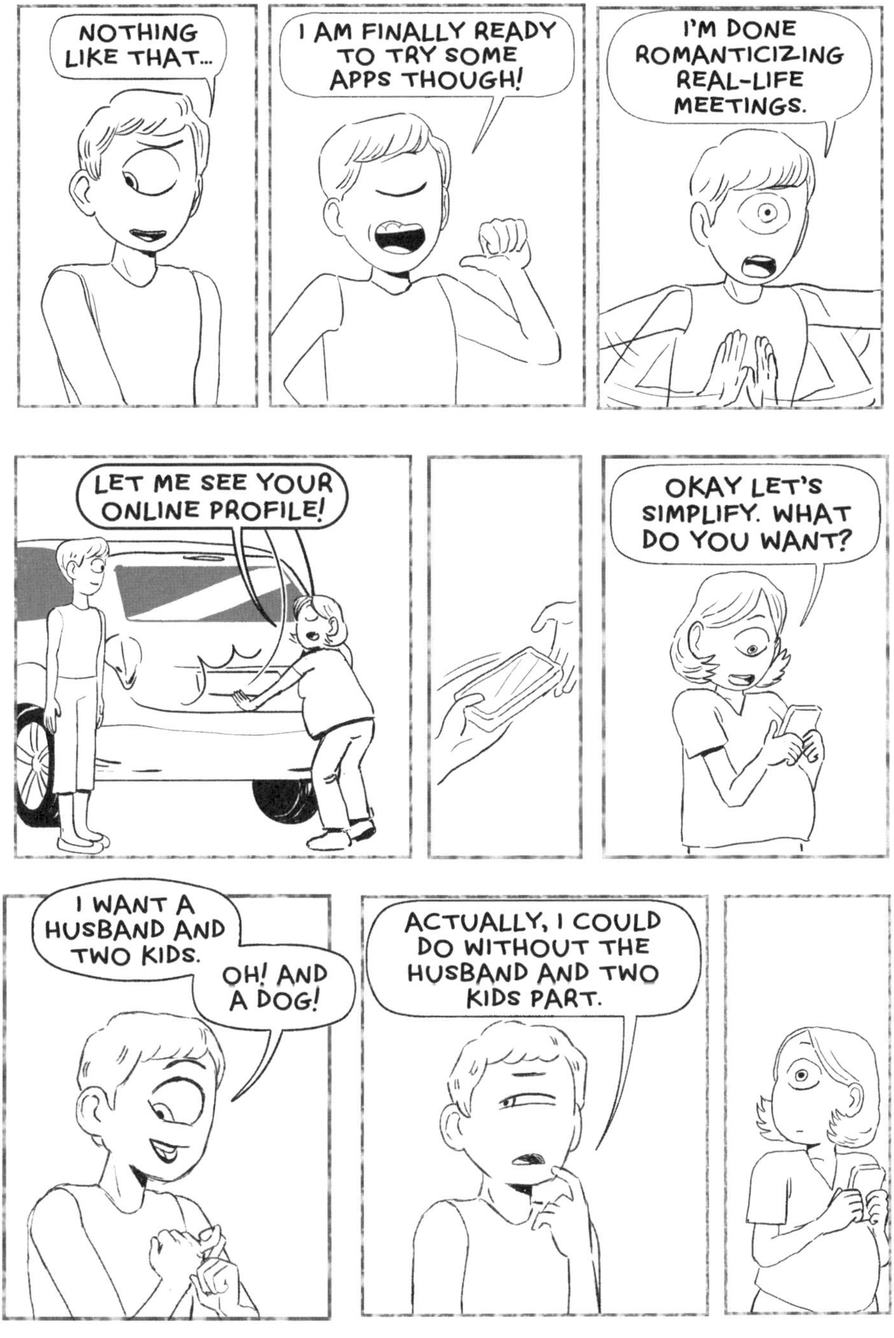
NOTHING LIKE THAT...
I AM FINALLY READY TO TRY SOME APPS THOUGH!
I'M DONE ROMANTICIZING REAL-LIFE MEETINGS.
LET ME SEE YOUR ONLINE PROFILE!
OKAY LET'S SIMPLIFY. WHAT DO YOU WANT?
I WANT A HUSBAND AND TWO KIDS.
OH! AND A DOG!
ACTUALLY, I COULD DO WITHOUT THE HUSBAND AND TWO KIDS PART.

Bron's history

I WAS A SHY KID. INSECURE, I GUESS.

WHEN UNIFEYE™ CAME OUT WITH THEIR EYE SURGERY, I WAS PRETTY EXCITED.

I WAS ONE OF THE FIRST TO SIGN UP.

THE SURGERY WENT PERFECTLY. I WAS SO READY TO FINALLY LIVE MY LIFE.

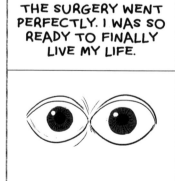

I WAS DATING!

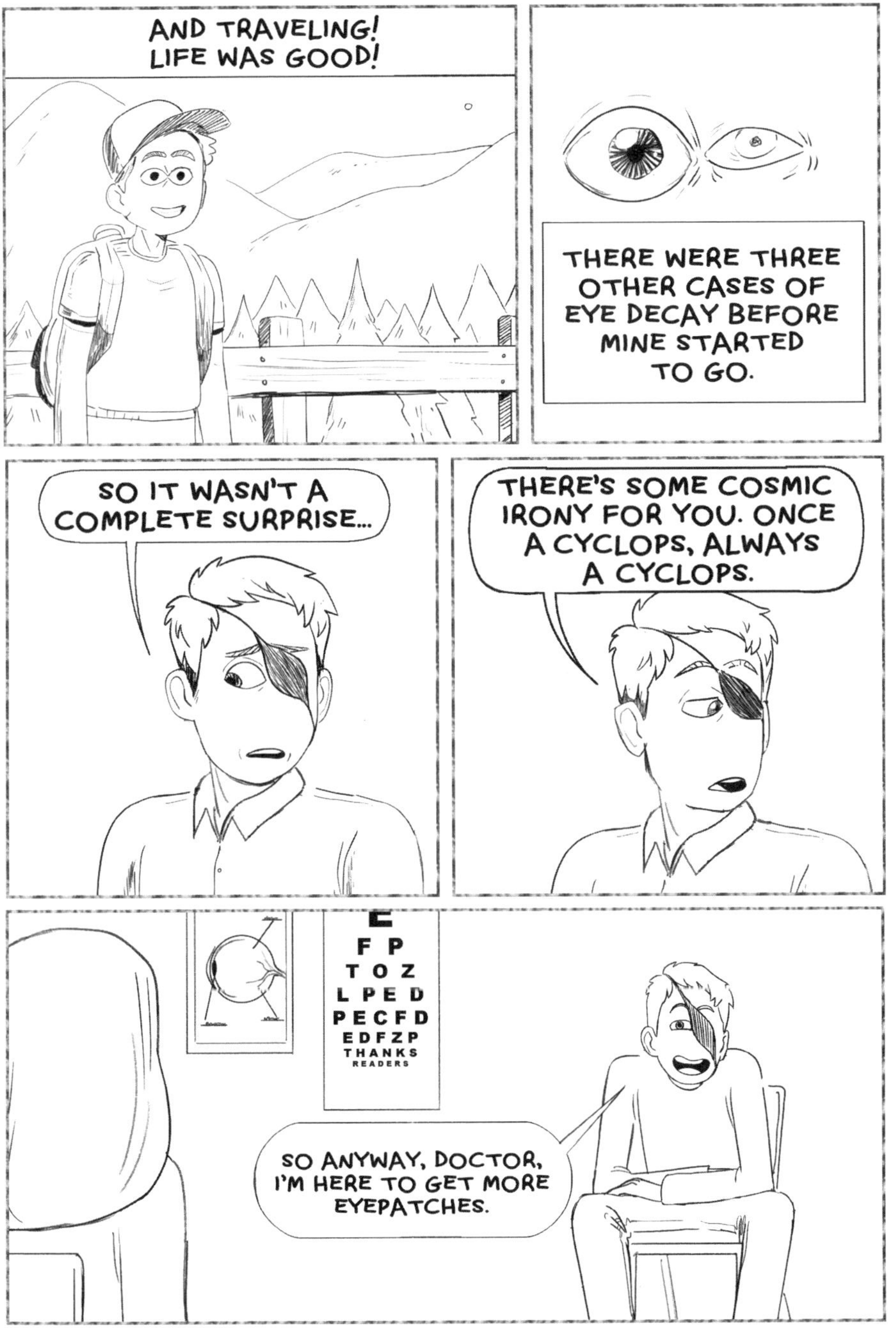
AND TRAVELING! LIFE WAS GOOD!
THERE WERE THREE OTHER CASES OF EYE DECAY BEFORE MINE STARTED TO GO.
SO IT WASN'T A COMPLETE SURPRISE...
THERE'S SOME COSMIC IRONY FOR YOU. ONCE A CYCLOPS, ALWAYS A CYCLOPS.
F P
T O Z
L P E D
P E C F D
E D F Z P
THANKS
READERS
SO ANYWAY, DOCTOR, I'M HERE TO GET MORE EYEPATCHES.

The optometrist

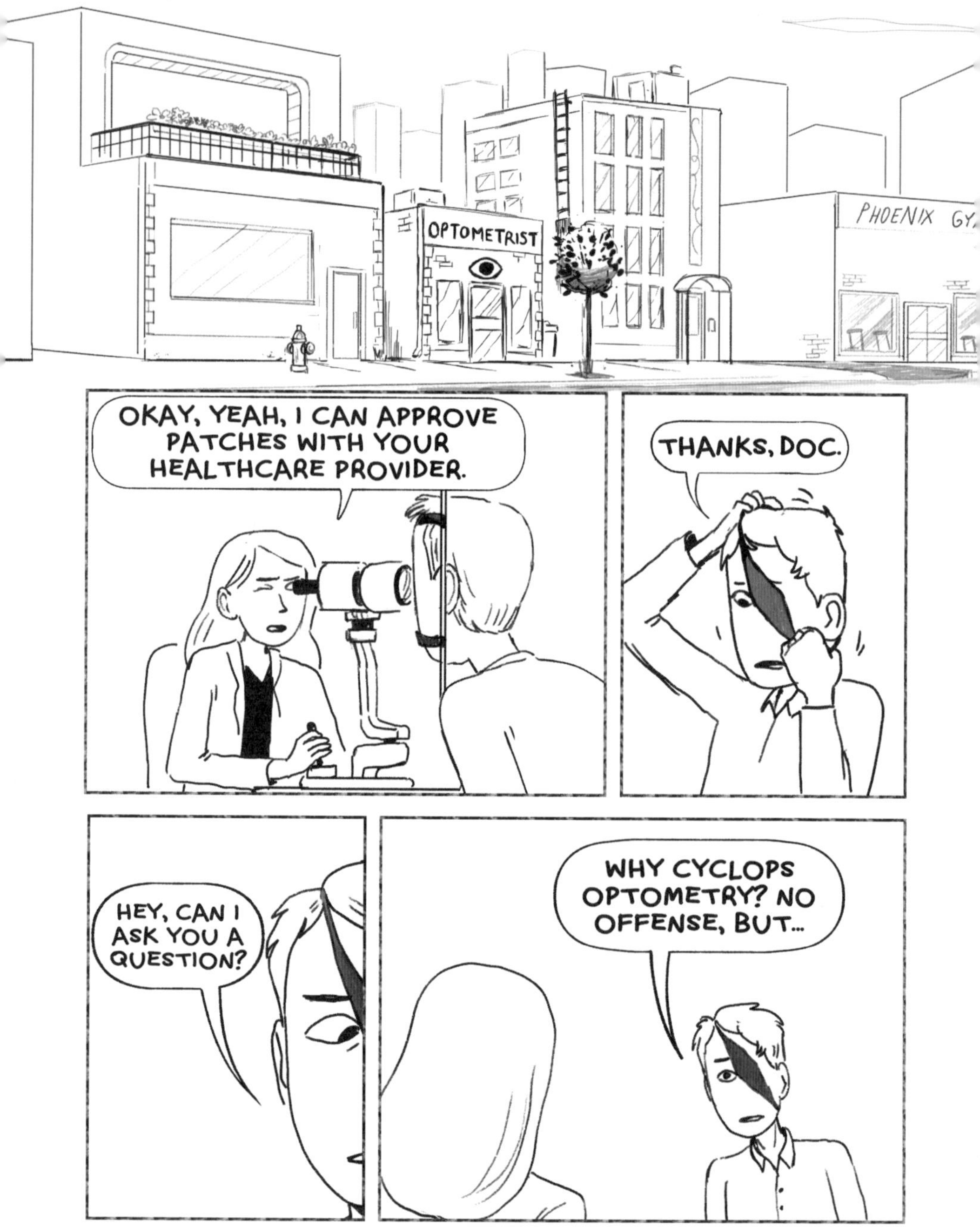
OPTOMETRIST
PHOENIX
OKAY, YEAH, I CAN APPROVE PATCHES WITH YOUR HEALTHCARE PROVIDER.
THANKS, DOC.
HEY, CAN I ASK YOU A QUESTION?
WHY CYCLOPS OPTOMETRY? NO OFFENSE, BUT...

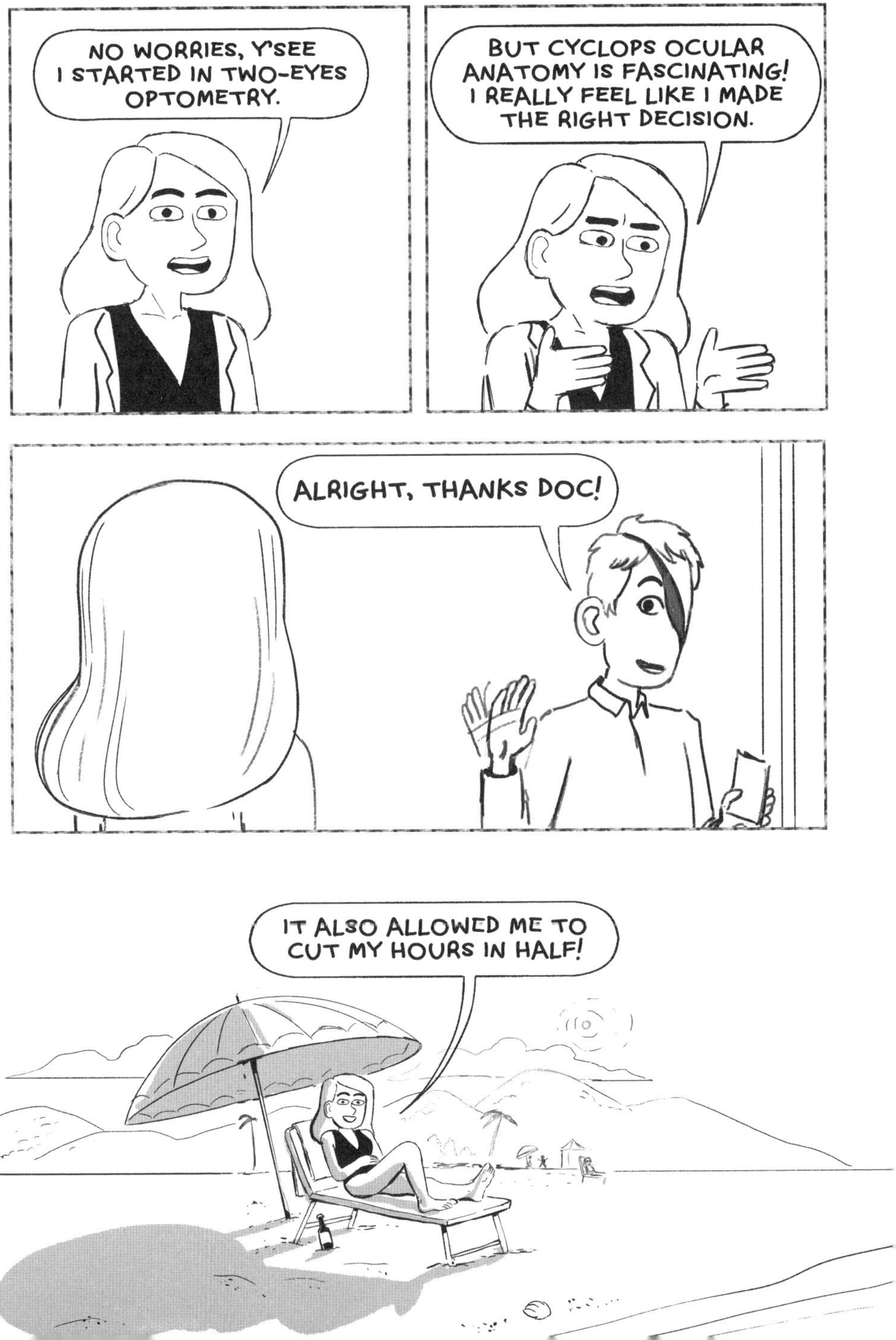
NO WORRIES, Y'SEE I STARTED IN TWO-EYES OPTOMETRY.
BUT CYCLOPS OCULAR ANATOMY IS FASCINATING! I REALLY FEEL LIKE I MADE THE RIGHT DECISION.
ALRIGHT, THANKS DOC!
IT ALSO ALLOWED ME TO CUT MY HOURS IN HALF!

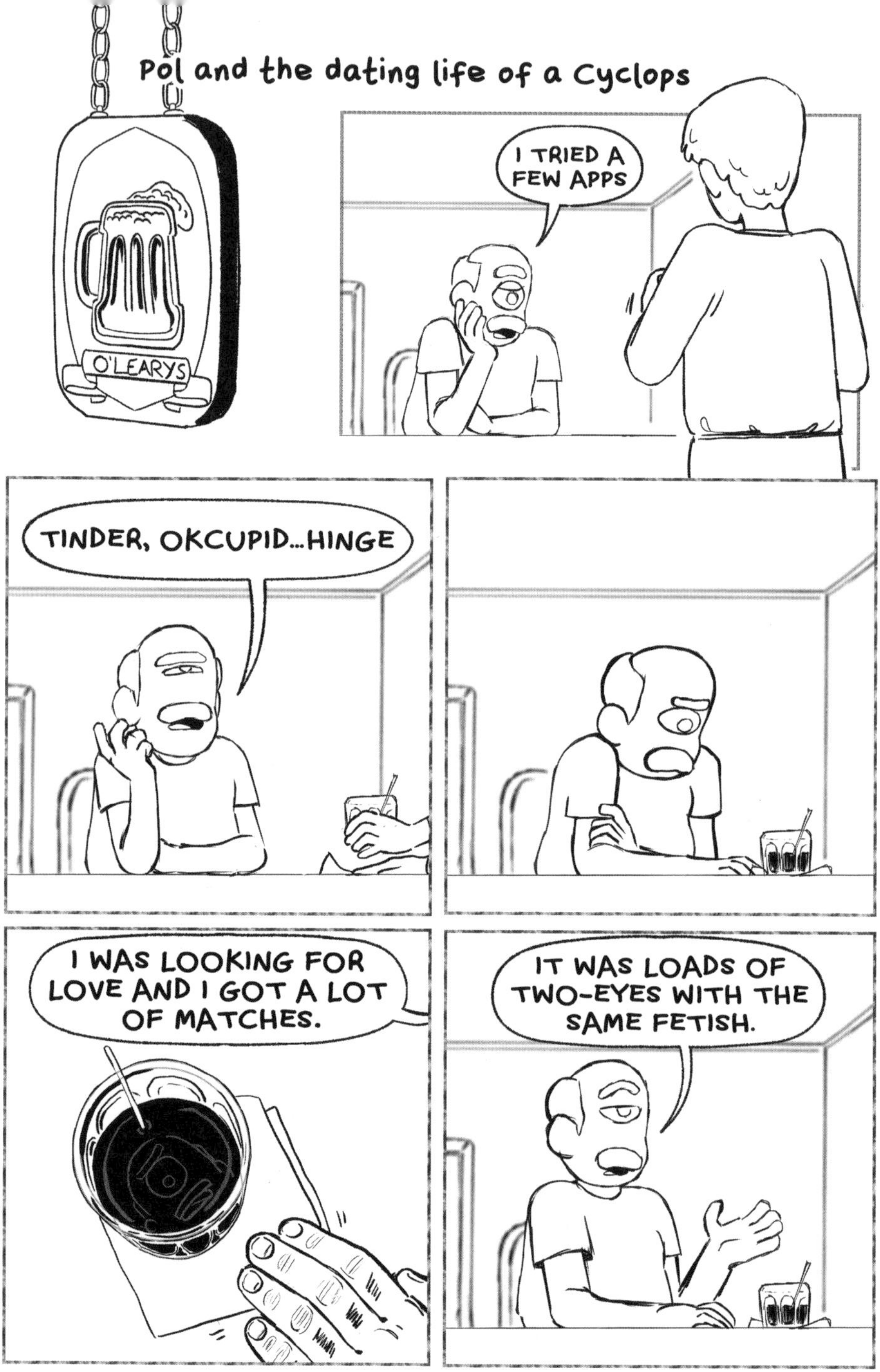

Pol and the dating life of a Cyclops
O'LEARYS
I TRIED A FEW APPS
TINDER, OKCUPID...HINGE
I WAS LOOKING FOR LOVE AND I GOT A LOT OF MATCHES.
IT WAS LOADS OF TWO-EYES WITH THE SAME FETISH.

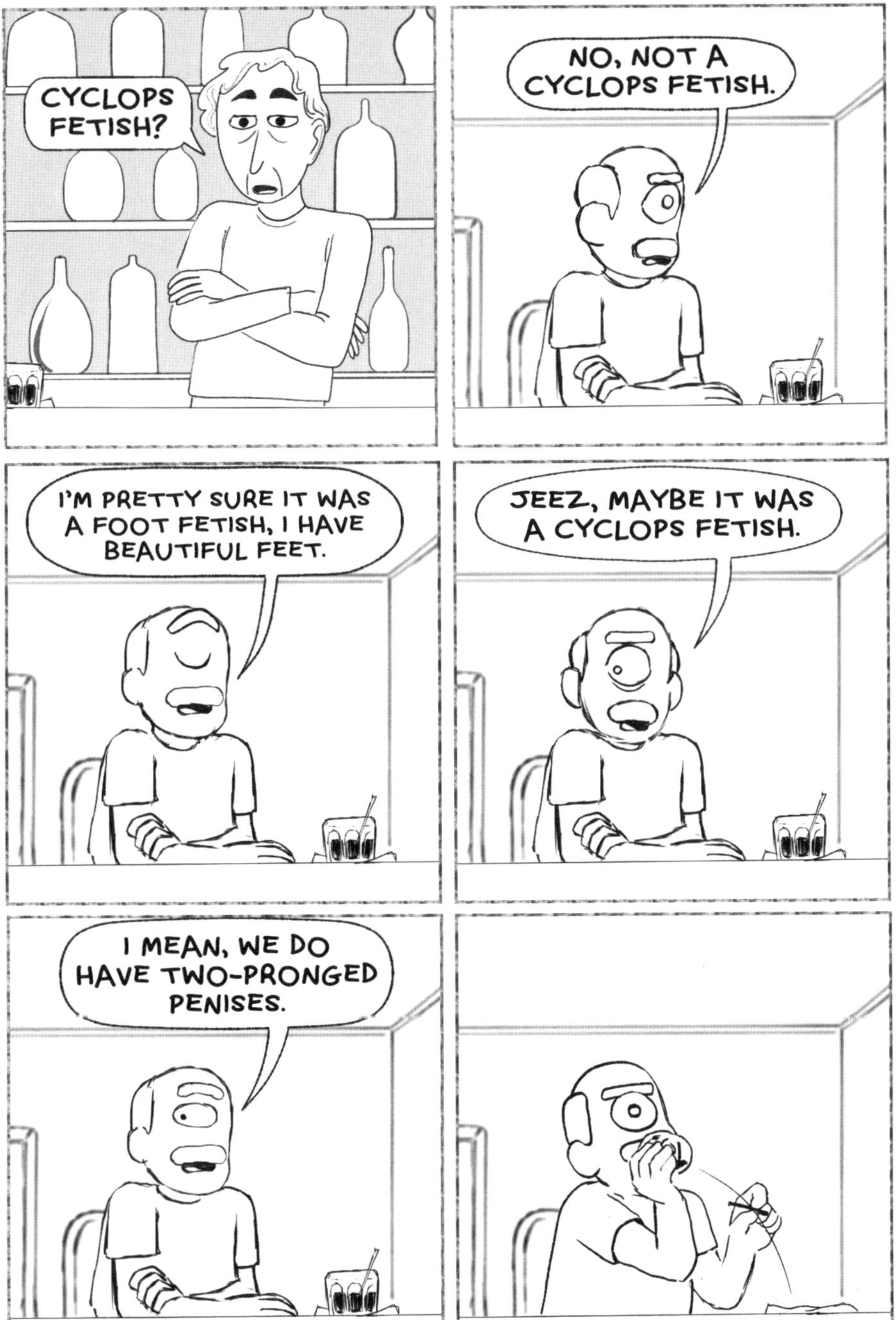
CYCLOPS FETISH?
NO, NOT A CYCLOPS FETISH.
I'M PRETTY SURE IT WAS A FOOT FETISH, I HAVE BEAUTIFUL FEET.
JEEZ, MAYBE IT WAS A CYCLOPS FETISH.
I MEAN, WE DO HAVE TWO-PRONGED PENISES.

I GOT AN OFFER TO MODEL CONTACT LENSES FOR UNIFEYE.

AWESOME, AND YOU'RE GOING TO DO IT?

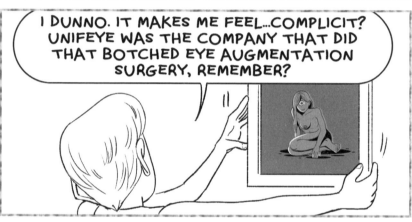

I DUNNO. IT MAKES ME FEEL...COMPLICIT? UNIFEYE WAS THE COMPANY THAT DID THAT BOTCHED EYE AUGMENTATION SURGERY, REMEMBER?

BUT I NEED THE MONEY.

DO YOU WANT ME TO SAY THAT YOU SHOULD DO IT?

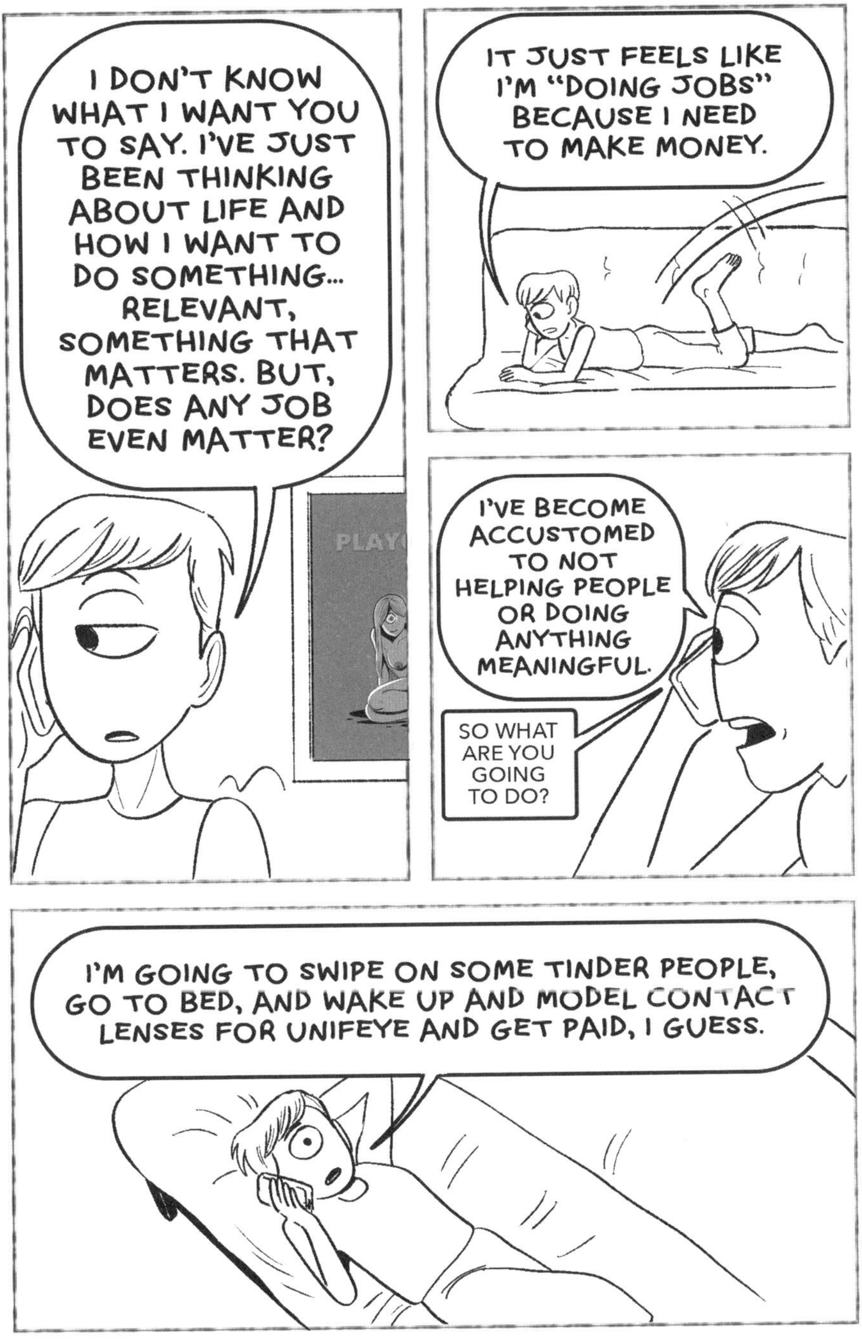
I DON'T KNOW WHAT I WANT YOU TO SAY. I'VE JUST BEEN THINKING ABOUT LIFE AND HOW I WANT TO DO SOMETHING... RELEVANT, SOMETHING THAT MATTERS. BUT, DOES ANY JOB EVEN MATTER?
PLAY
IT JUST FEELS LIKE I'M "DOING JOBS" BECAUSE I NEED TO MAKE MONEY.
I'VE BECOME ACCUSTOMED TO NOT HELPING PEOPLE OR DOING ANYTHING MEANINGFUL.
SO WHAT ARE YOU GOING TO DO?
I'M GOING TO SWIPE ON SOME TINDER PEOPLE, GO TO BED, AND WAKE UP AND MODEL CONTACT LENSES FOR UNIFEYE AND GET PAID, I GUESS.

NEW FROM
Unif Eye

One Quick Drop

Keeps You Fresh*
*may cause psychic visions

PAPA, NO! DON'T TAKE THAT TRAIN!

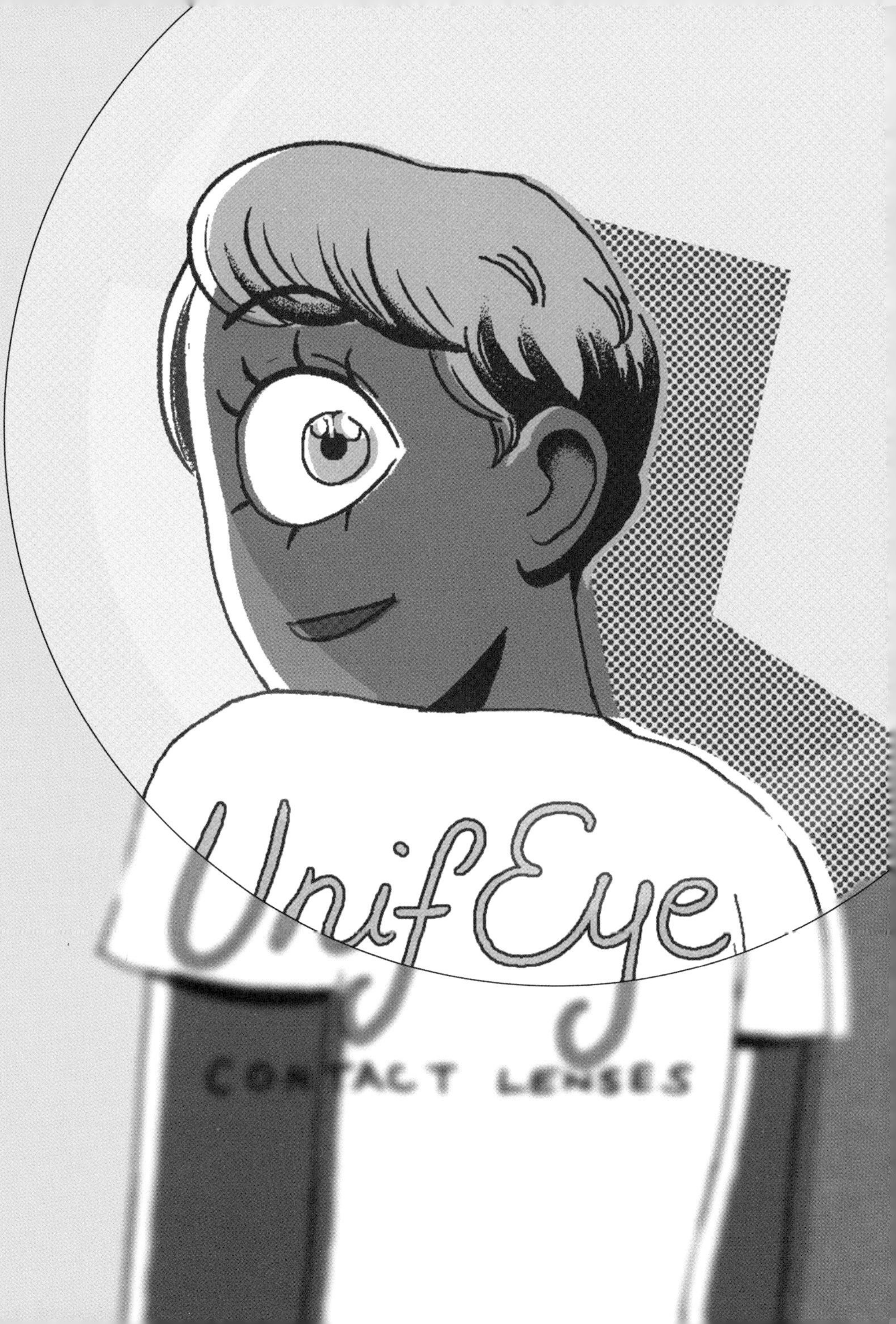

UnifEye
CONTACT LENSES

Pol & Crystal

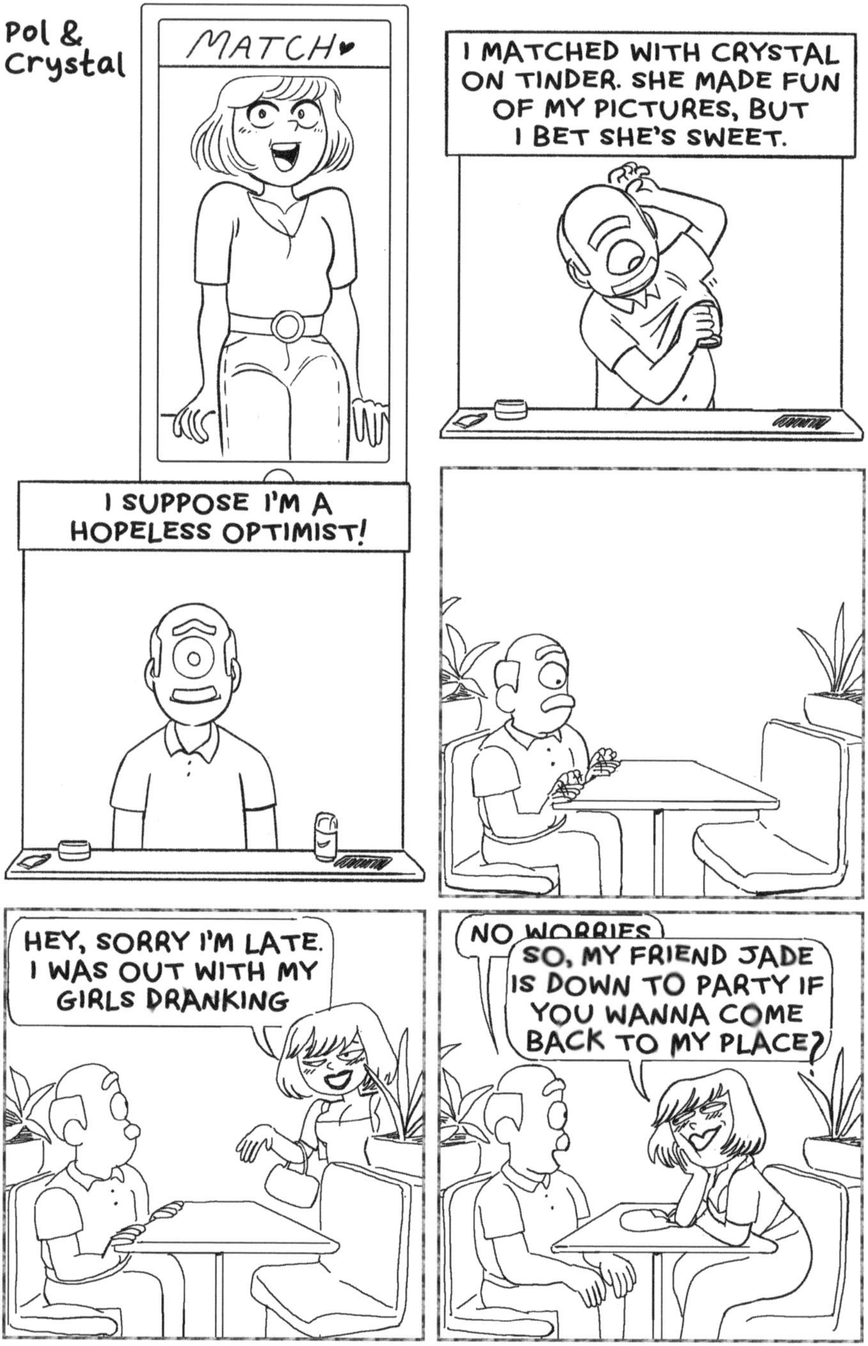
MATCH♥
I MATCHED WITH CRYSTAL ON TINDER. SHE MADE FUN OF MY PICTURES, BUT I BET SHE'S SWEET.
I SUPPOSE I'M A HOPELESS OPTIMIST!
HEY, SORRY I'M LATE. I WAS OUT WITH MY GIRLS DRANKING
NO WORRIES
SO, MY FRIEND JADE IS DOWN TO PARTY IF YOU WANNA COME BACK TO MY PLACE?

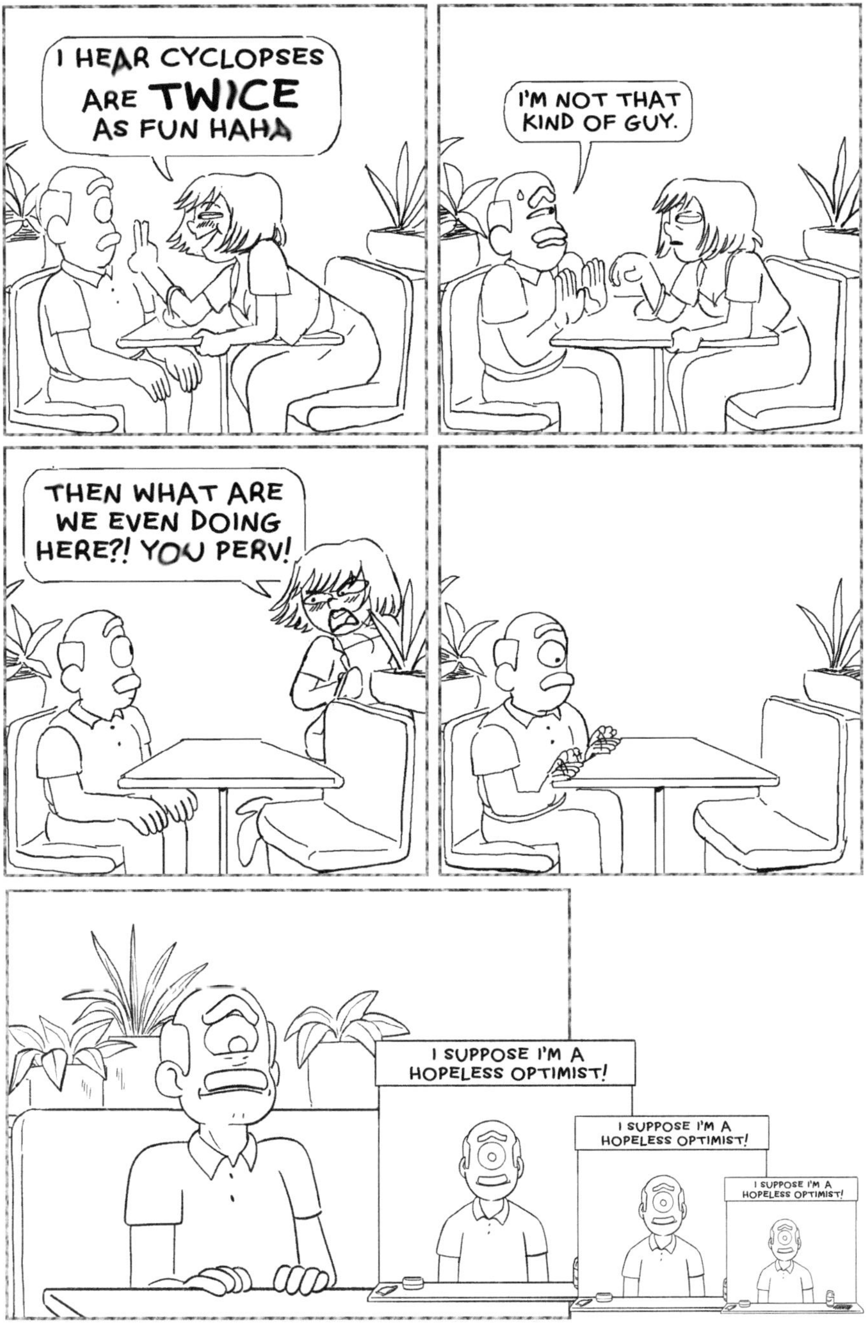
I HEAR CYCLOPSES ARE TWICE AS FUN HAHA
I'M NOT THAT KIND OF GUY.
THEN WHAT ARE WE EVEN DOING HERE?! YOU PERV!
I SUPPOSE I'M A HOPELESS OPTIMIST!
I SUPPOSE I'M A HOPELESS OPTIMIST!
I SUPPOSE I'M A HOPELESS OPTIMIST!

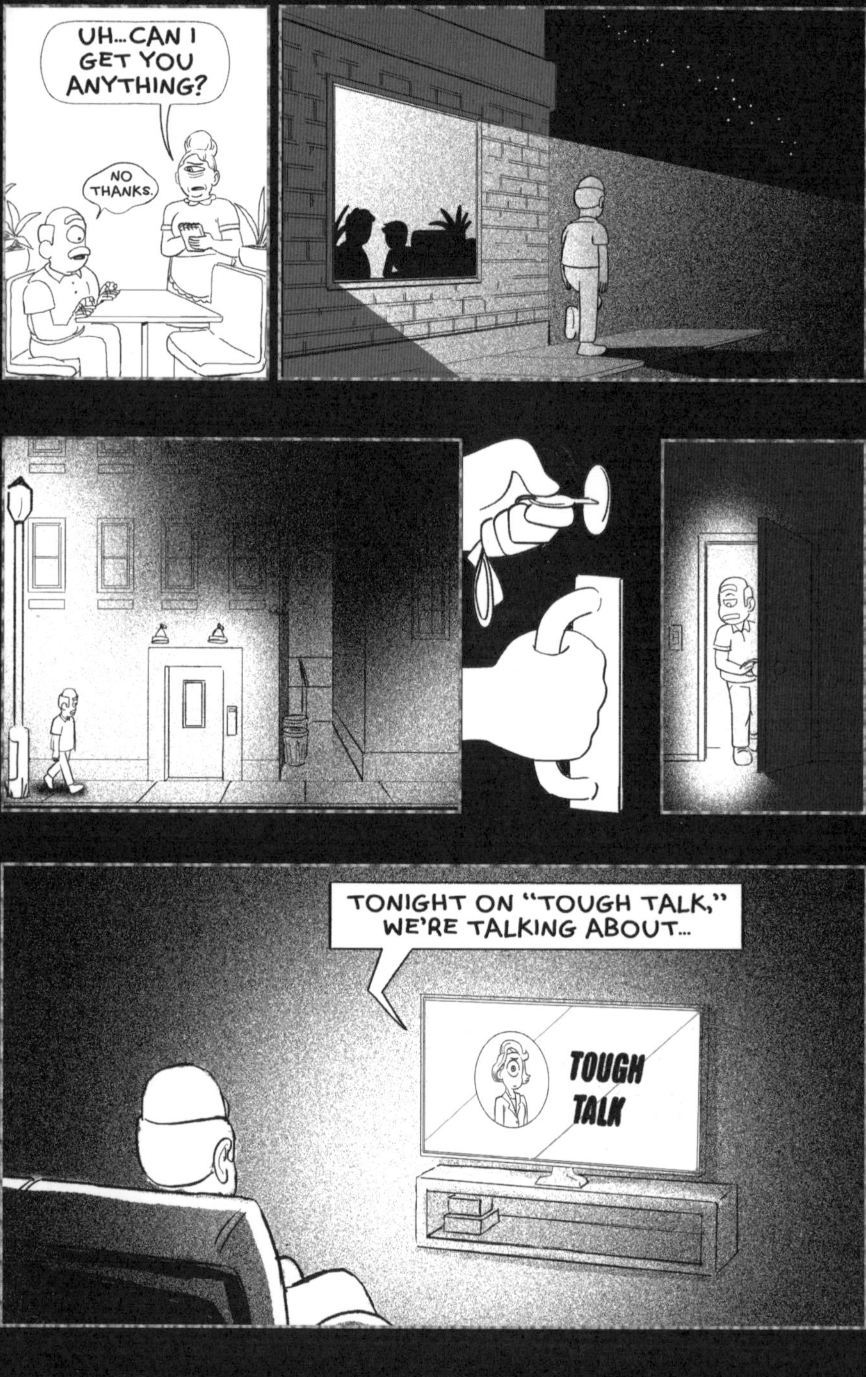
UH...CAN I GET YOU ANYTHING?
NO THANKS.
TONIGHT ON "TOUGH TALK," WE'RE TALKING ABOUT...
TOUGH TALK

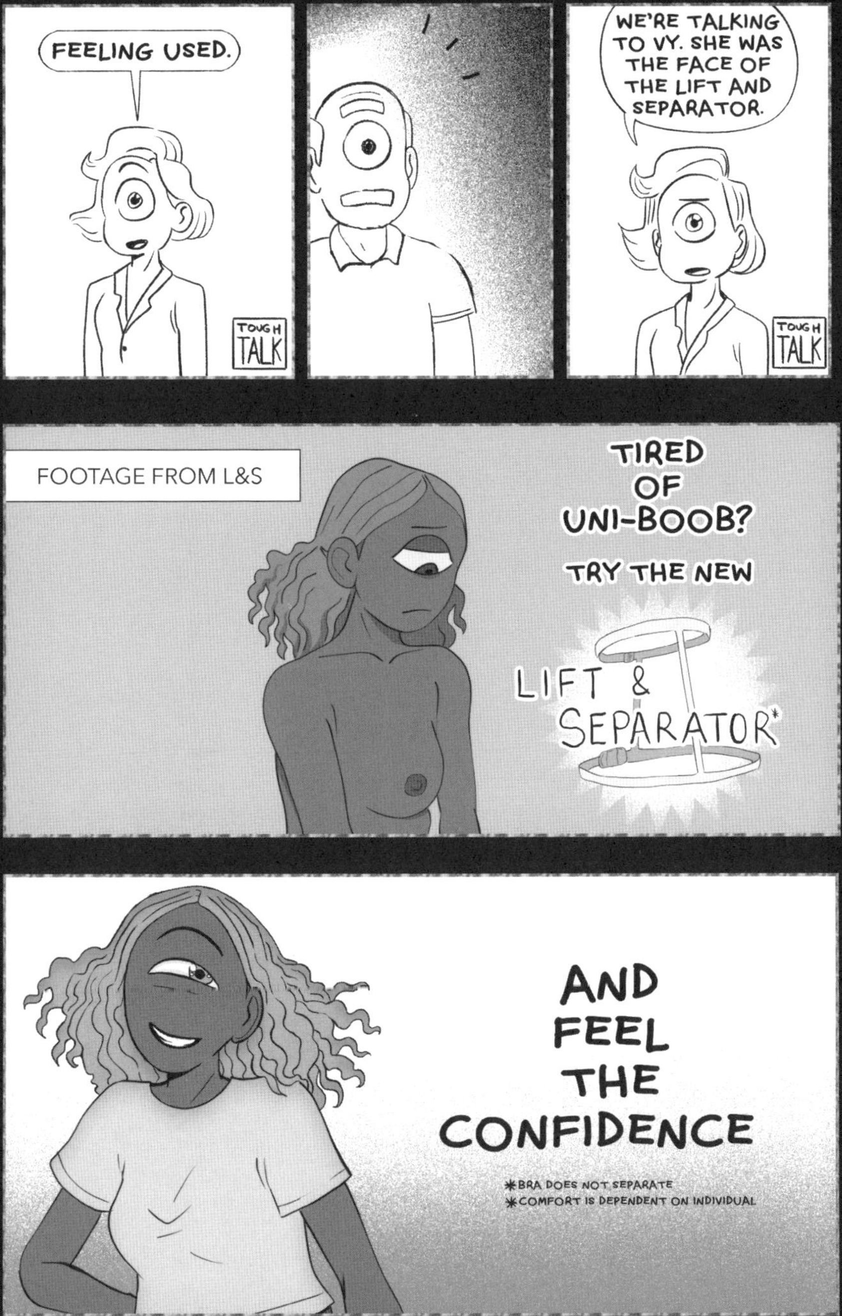
FEELING USED.
TOUGH TALK
WE'RE TALKING TO VY. SHE WAS THE FACE OF THE LIFT AND SEPARATOR.
TOUGH TALK
FOOTAGE FROM L&S
TIRED OF UNI-BOOB?
TRY THE NEW
LIFT & SEPARATOR*
AND FEEL THE CONFIDENCE
*BRA DOES NOT SEPARATE
*COMFORT IS DEPENDENT ON INDIVIDUAL

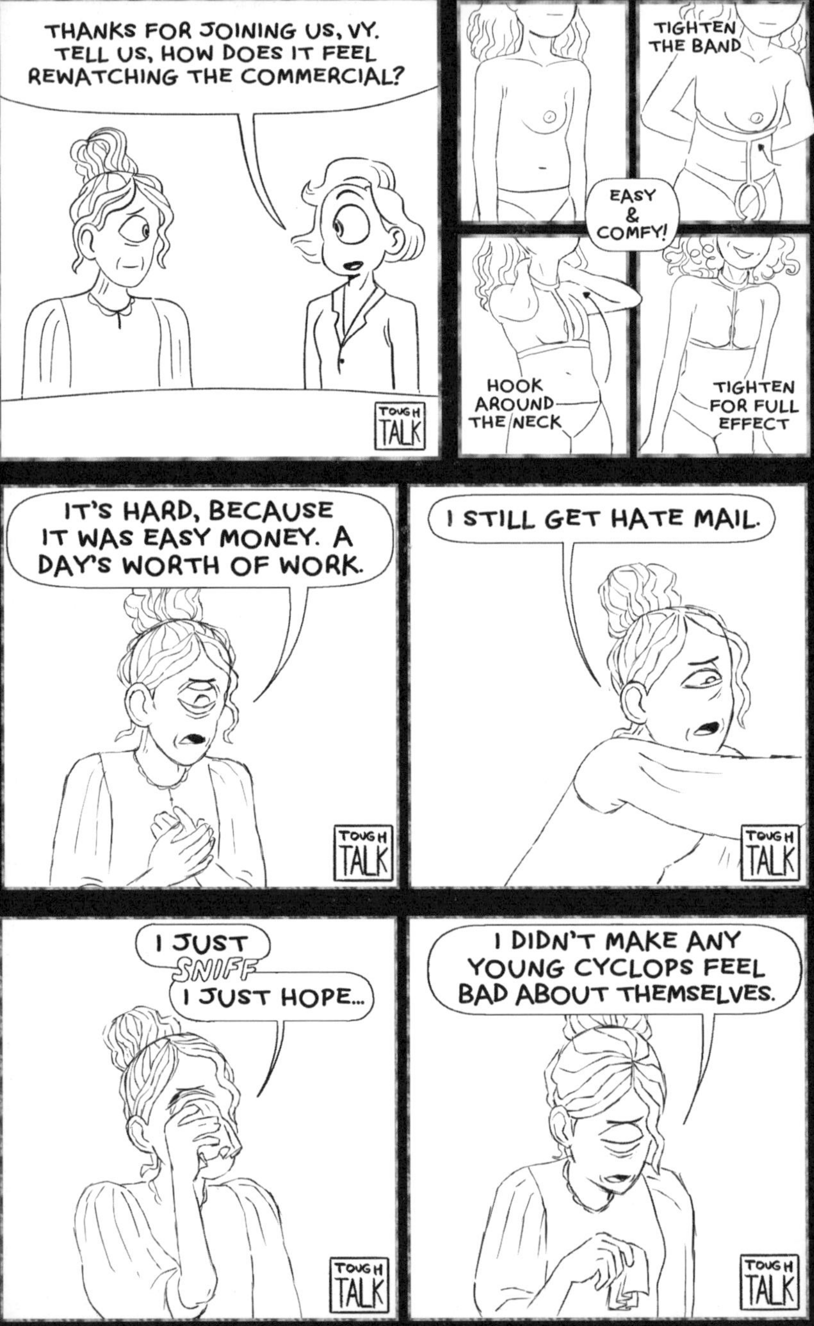
THANKS FOR JOINING US, VY. TELL US, HOW DOES IT FEEL REWATCHING THE COMMERCIAL?
TOUGH TALK
TIGHTEN THE BAND
EASY & COMFY!
HOOK AROUND THE NECK
TIGHTEN FOR FULL EFFECT
IT'S HARD, BECAUSE IT WAS EASY MONEY. A DAY'S WORTH OF WORK.
TOUGH TALK
I STILL GET HATE MAIL.
TOUGH TALK
I JUST
SNIFF
I JUST HOPE...
TOUGH TALK
I DIDN'T MAKE ANY YOUNG CYCLOPS FEEL BAD ABOUT THEMSELVES.
TOUGH TALK

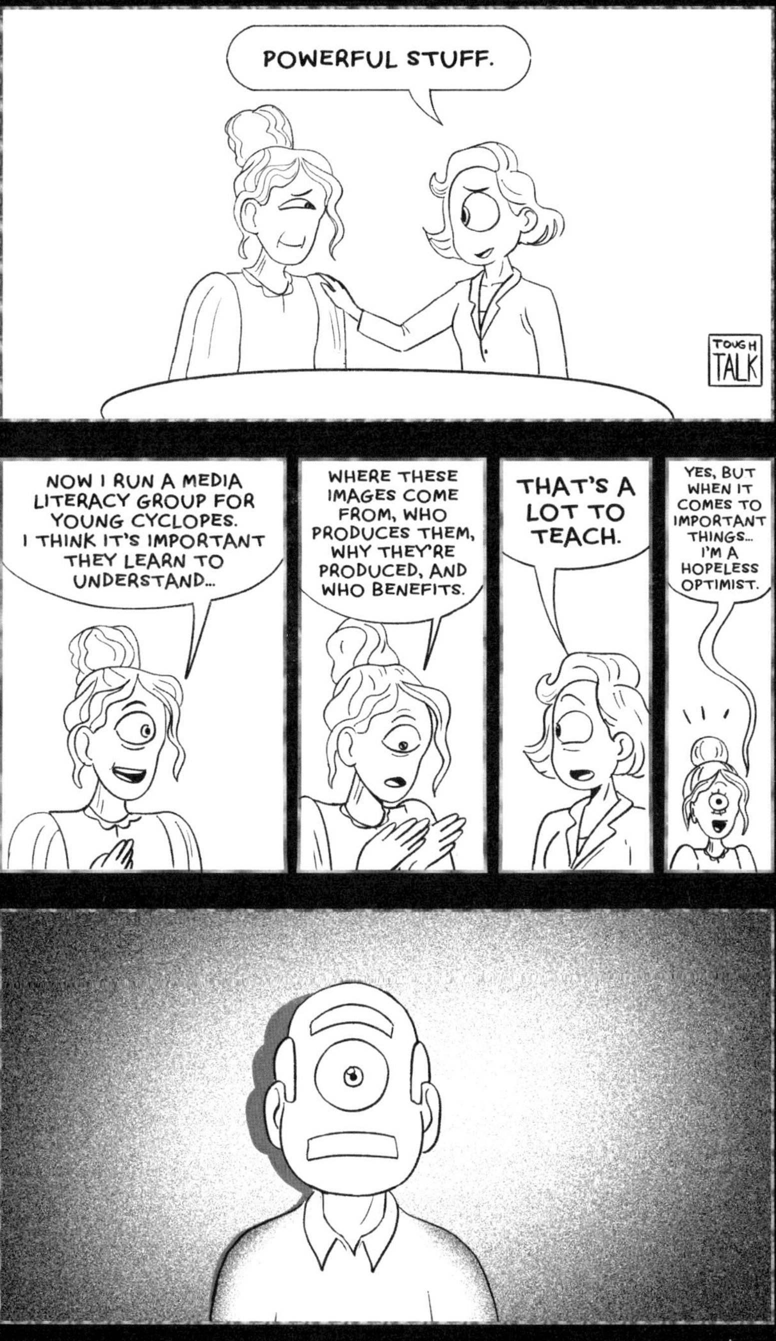
POWERFUL STUFF.
TOUGH TALK
NOW I RUN A MEDIA LITERACY GROUP FOR YOUNG CYCLOPES. I THINK IT'S IMPORTANT THEY LEARN TO UNDERSTAND...
WHERE THESE IMAGES COME FROM, WHO PRODUCES THEM, WHY THEY'RE PRODUCED, AND WHO BENEFITS.
THAT'S A LOT TO TEACH.
YES, BUT WHEN IT COMES TO IMPORTANT THINGS... I'M A HOPELESS OPTIMIST.

Tim and Pari's baby

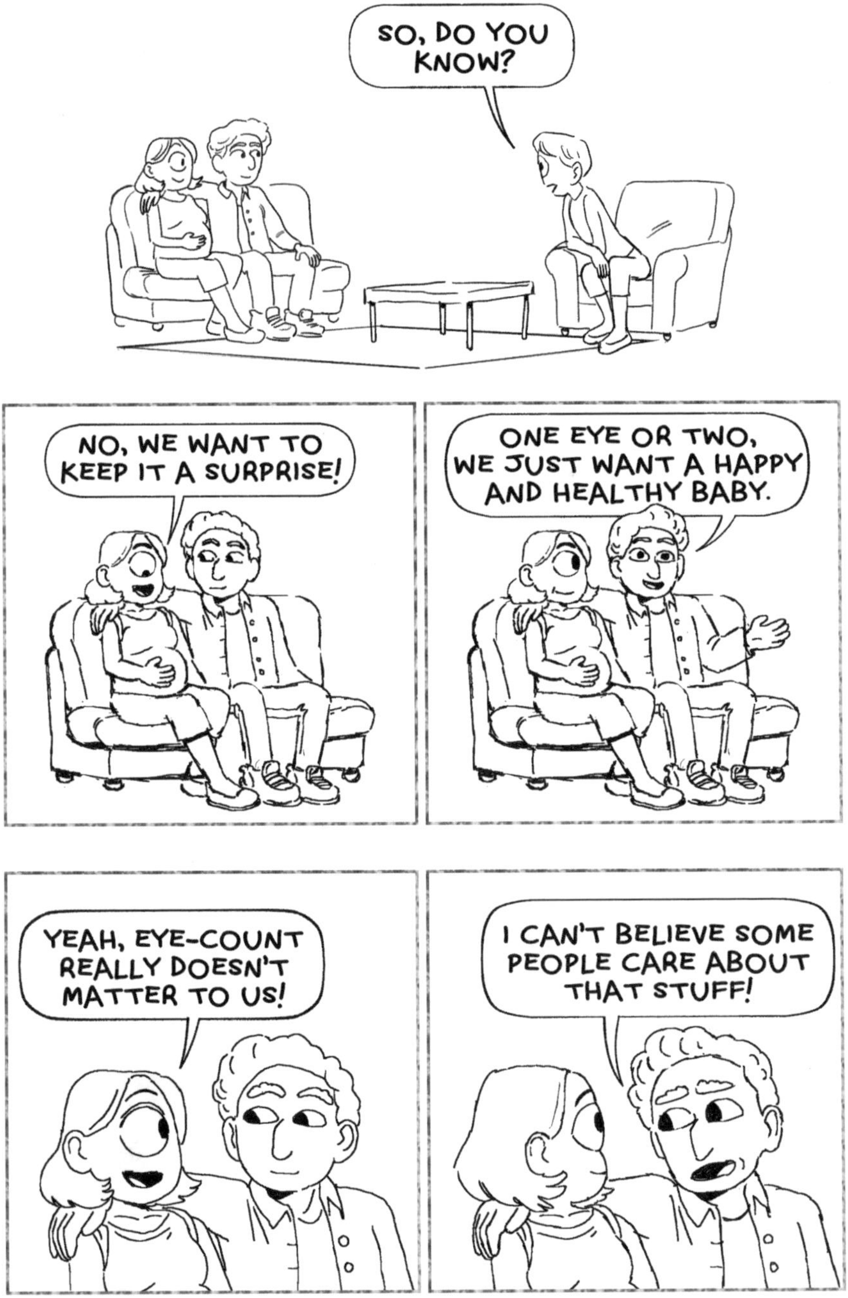
SO, DO YOU KNOW?
NO, WE WANT TO KEEP IT A SURPRISE!
ONE EYE OR TWO, WE JUST WANT A HAPPY AND HEALTHY BABY.
YEAH, EYE-COUNT REALLY DOESN'T MATTER TO US!
I CAN'T BELIEVE SOME PEOPLE CARE ABOUT THAT STUFF!

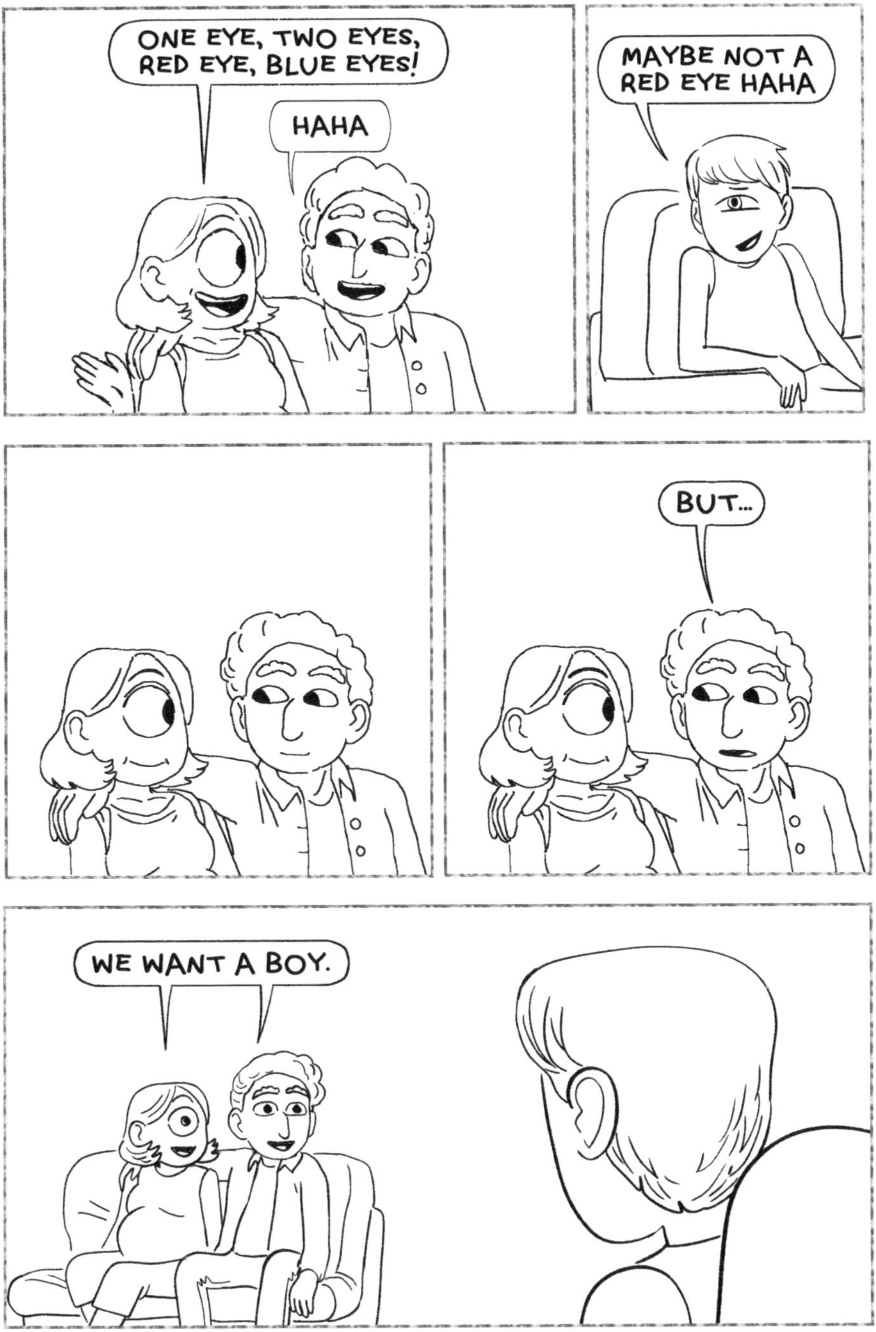
ONE EYE, TWO EYES, RED EYE, BLUE EYES!
HAHA
MAYBE NOT A RED EYE HAHA
BUT...
WE WANT A BOY.

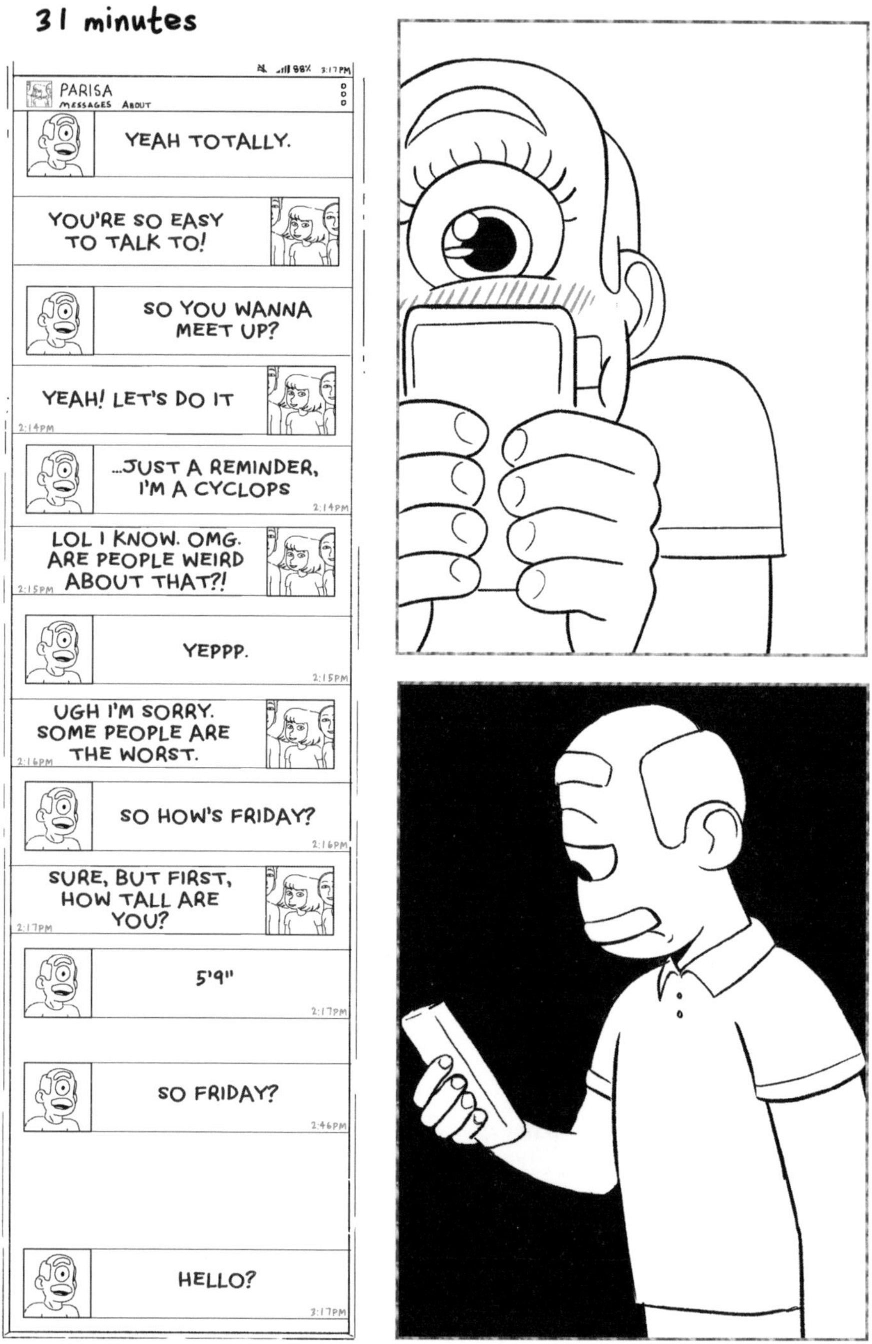

31 minutes
3:17PM
PARISA
MESSAGES ABOUT
YEAH TOTALLY.
YOU'RE SO EASY TO TALK TO!
SO YOU WANNA MEET UP?
YEAH! LET'S DO IT
2:14PM
...JUST A REMINDER, I'M A CYCLOPS
2:14PM
LOL I KNOW. OMG. ARE PEOPLE WEIRD ABOUT THAT?!
2:15PM
YEPPP.
2:15PM
UGH I'M SORRY. SOME PEOPLE ARE THE WORST.
2:16PM
SO HOW'S FRIDAY?
2:16PM
SURE, BUT FIRST, HOW TALL ARE YOU?
2:17PM
5'9"
2:17PM
SO FRIDAY?
2:46PM
HELLO?
3:17PM

Masks

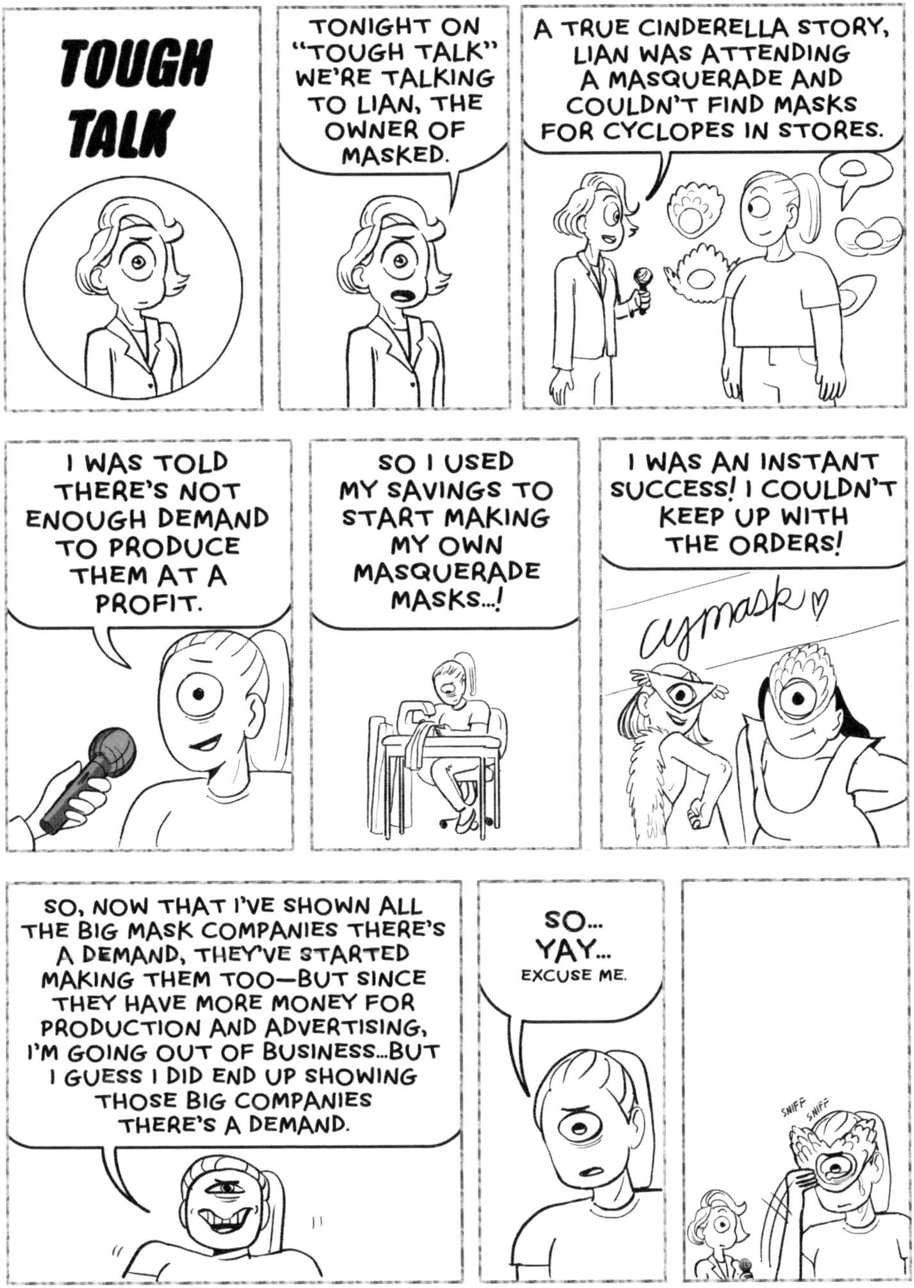
TOUGH TALK
TONIGHT ON "TOUGH TALK" WE'RE TALKING TO LIAN, THE OWNER OF MASKED.
A TRUE CINDERELLA STORY, LIAN WAS ATTENDING A MASQUERADE AND COULDN'T FIND MASKS FOR CYCLOPES IN STORES.
I WAS TOLD THERE'S NOT ENOUGH DEMAND TO PRODUCE THEM AT A PROFIT.
SO I USED MY SAVINGS TO START MAKING MY OWN MASQUERADE MASKS...!
I WAS AN INSTANT SUCCESS! I COULDN'T KEEP UP WITH THE ORDERS!
cymask ♡
SO, NOW THAT I'VE SHOWN ALL THE BIG MASK COMPANIES THERE'S A DEMAND, THEY'VE STARTED MAKING THEM TOO—BUT SINCE THEY HAVE MORE MONEY FOR PRODUCTION AND ADVERTISING, I'M GOING OUT OF BUSINESS...BUT I GUESS I DID END UP SHOWING THOSE BIG COMPANIES THERE'S A DEMAND.
SO... YAY... EXCUSE ME.
SNIFF SNIFF

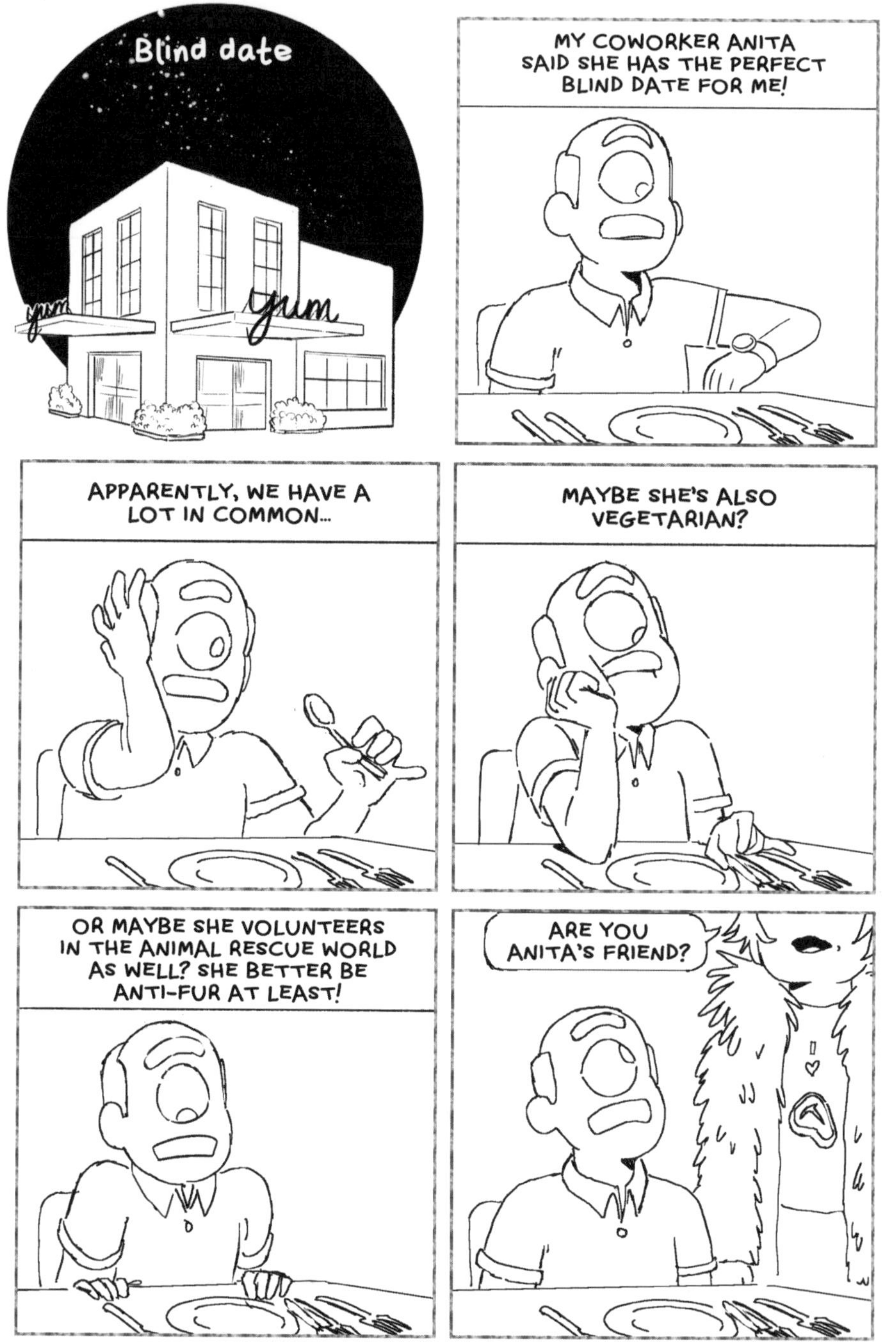

Blind date
yum
yum
MY COWORKER ANITA SAID SHE HAS THE PERFECT BLIND DATE FOR ME!
APPARENTLY, WE HAVE A LOT IN COMMON...
MAYBE SHE'S ALSO VEGETARIAN?
OR MAYBE SHE VOLUNTEERS IN THE ANIMAL RESCUE WORLD AS WELL? SHE BETTER BE ANTI-FUR AT LEAST!
ARE YOU ANITA'S FRIEND?

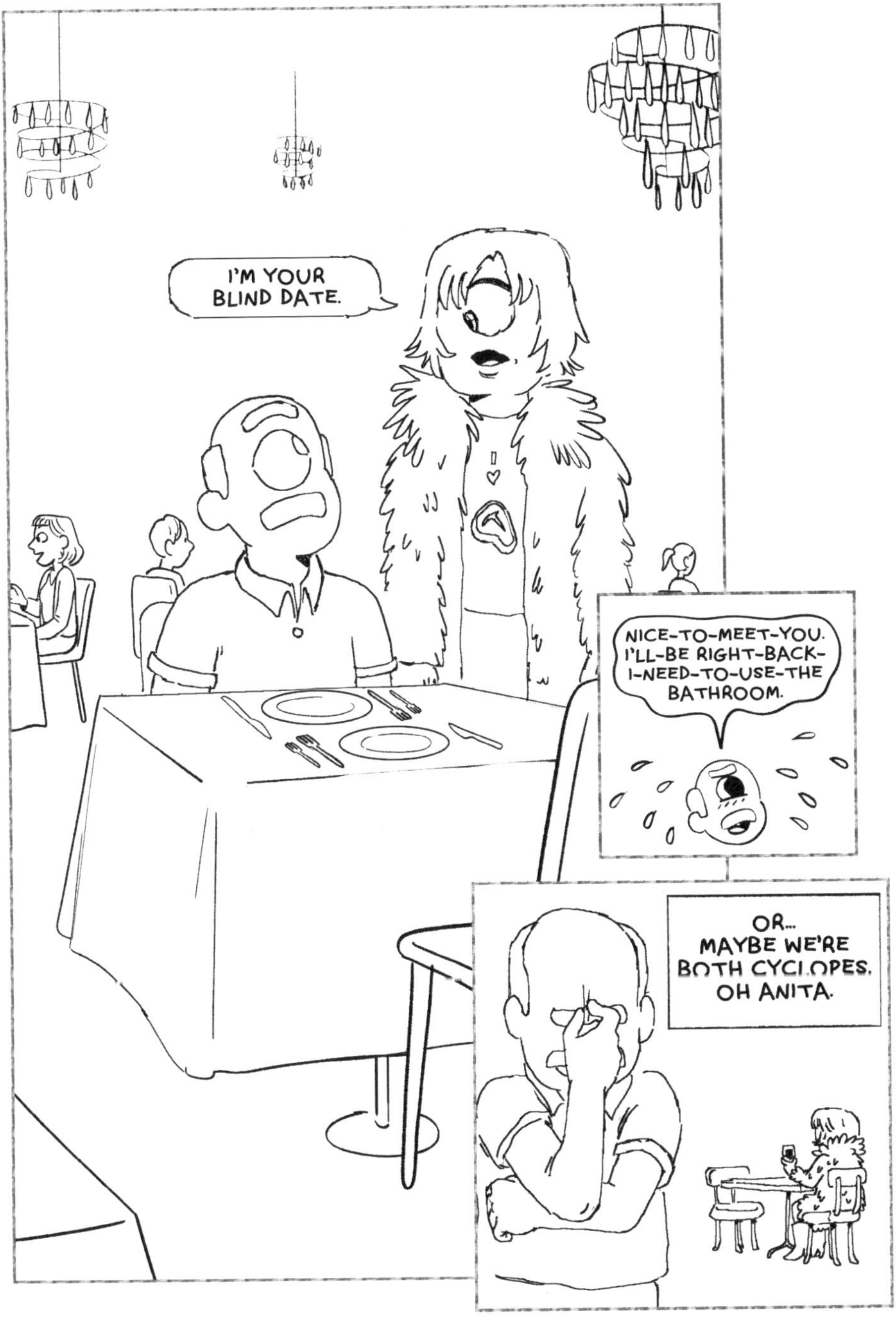
I'M YOUR BLIND DATE.
NICE-TO-MEET-YOU. I'LL-BE RIGHT-BACK-I-NEED-TO-USE-THE BATHROOM.
OR... MAYBE WE'RE BOTH CYCLOPES. OH ANITA.

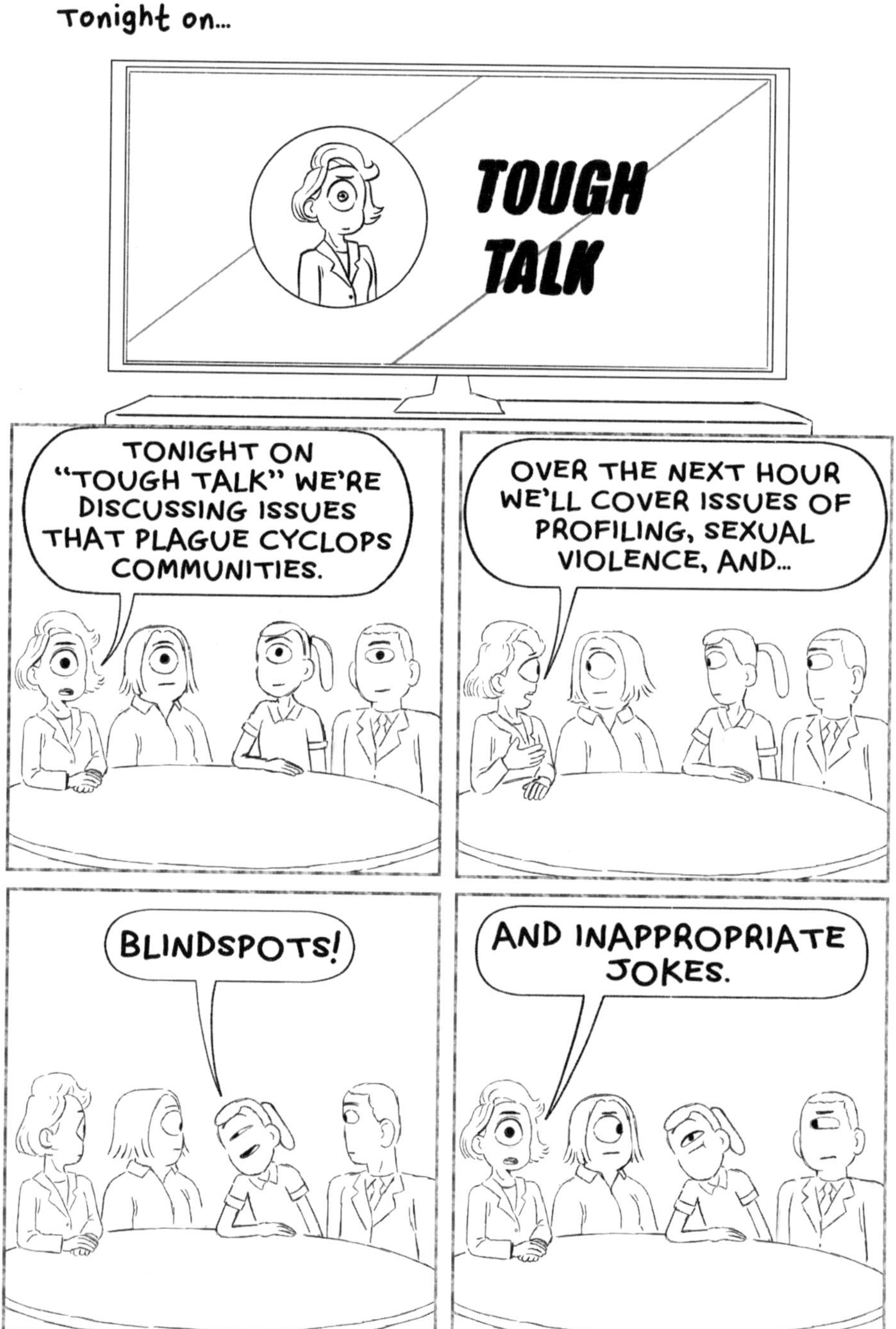
Tonight on...
TOUGH TALK
TONIGHT ON "TOUGH TALK" WE'RE DISCUSSING ISSUES THAT PLAGUE CYCLOPS COMMUNITIES.
OVER THE NEXT HOUR WE'LL COVER ISSUES OF PROFILING, SEXUAL VIOLENCE, AND...
BLINDSPOTS!
AND INAPPROPRIATE JOKES.

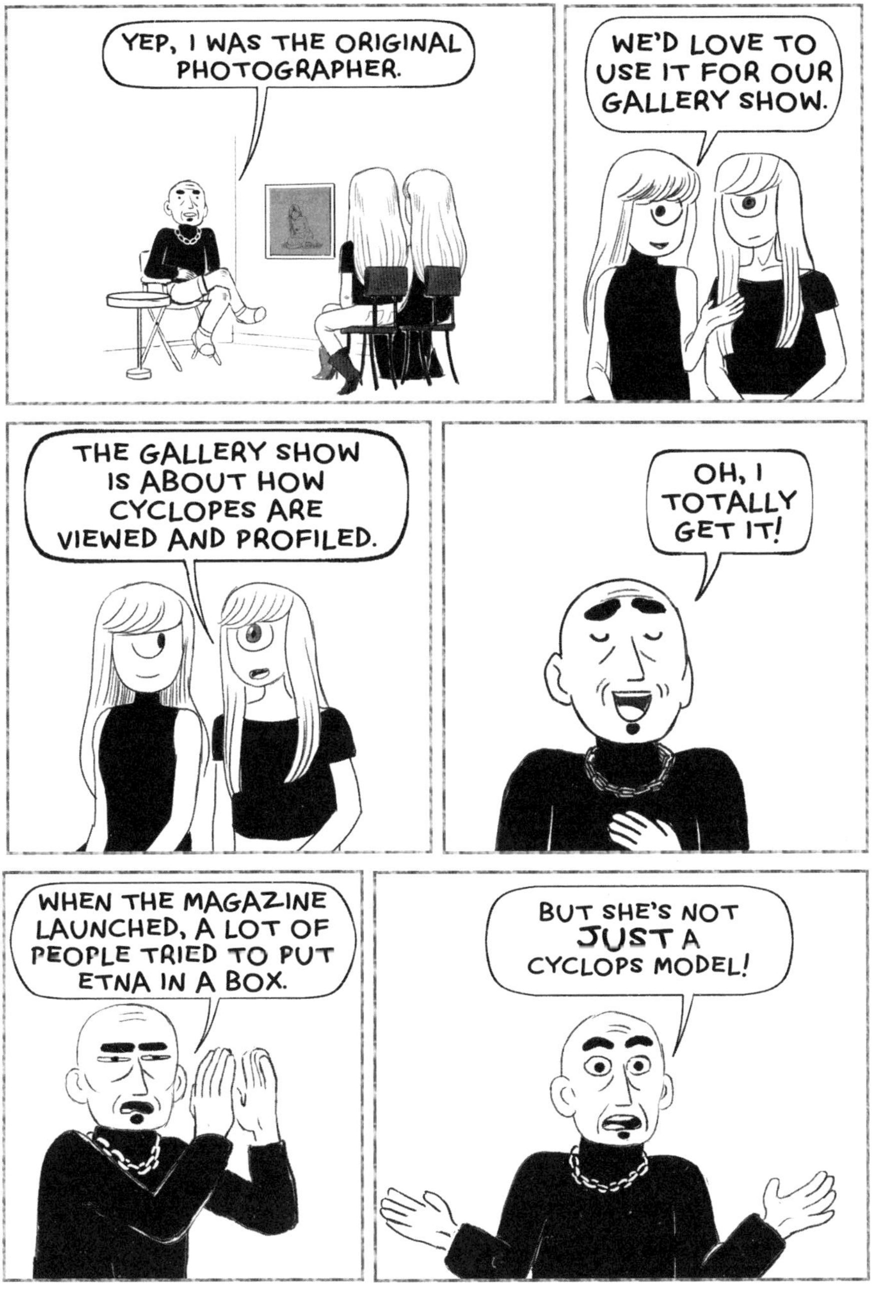
YEP, I WAS THE ORIGINAL PHOTOGRAPHER.
WE'D LOVE TO USE IT FOR OUR GALLERY SHOW.
THE GALLERY SHOW IS ABOUT HOW CYCLOPES ARE VIEWED AND PROFILED.
OH, I TOTALLY GET IT!
WHEN THE MAGAZINE LAUNCHED, A LOT OF PEOPLE TRIED TO PUT ETNA IN A BOX.
BUT SHE'S NOT JUST A CYCLOPS MODEL!

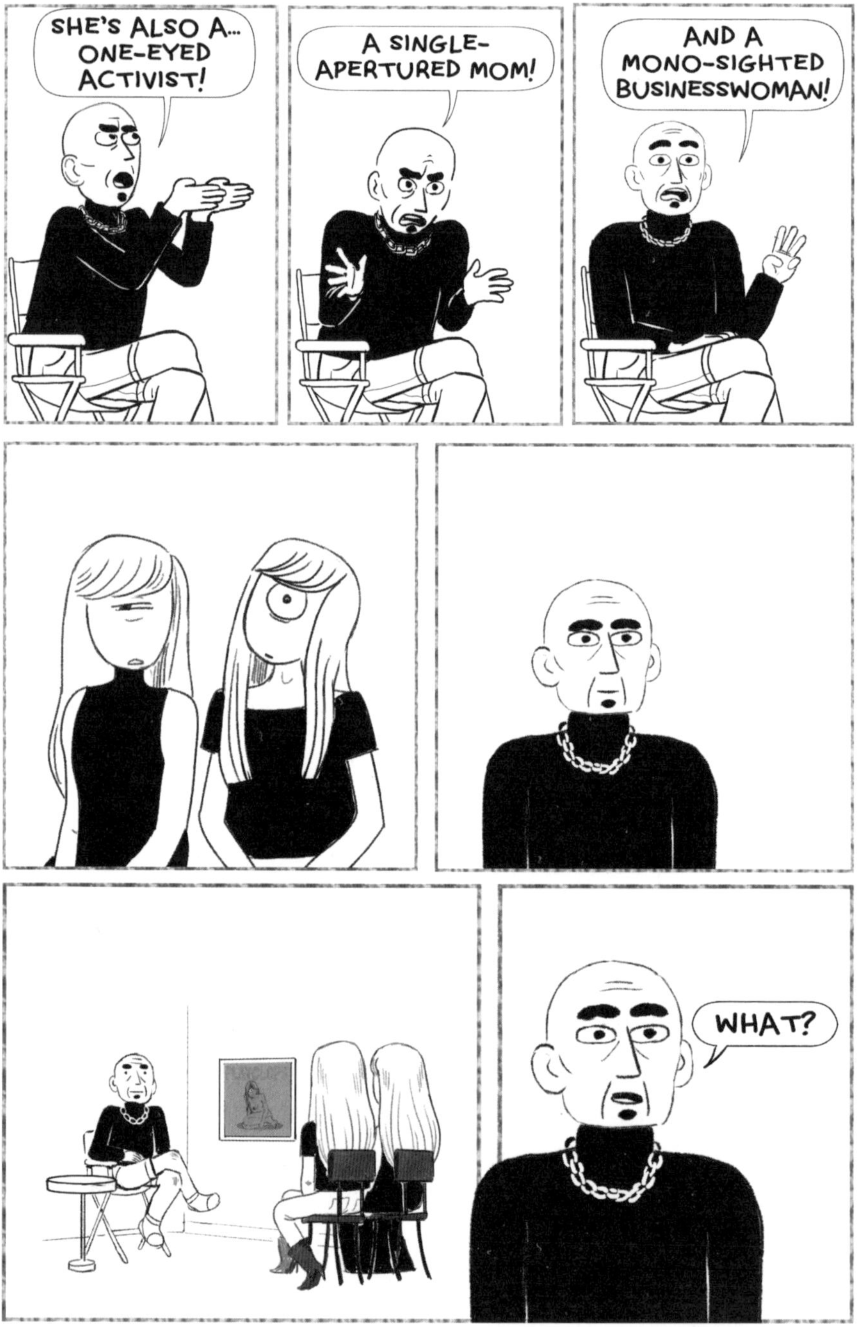
SHE'S ALSO A... ONE-EYED ACTIVIST!
A SINGLE-APERTURED MOM!
AND A MONO-SIGHTED BUSINESSWOMAN!
WHAT?

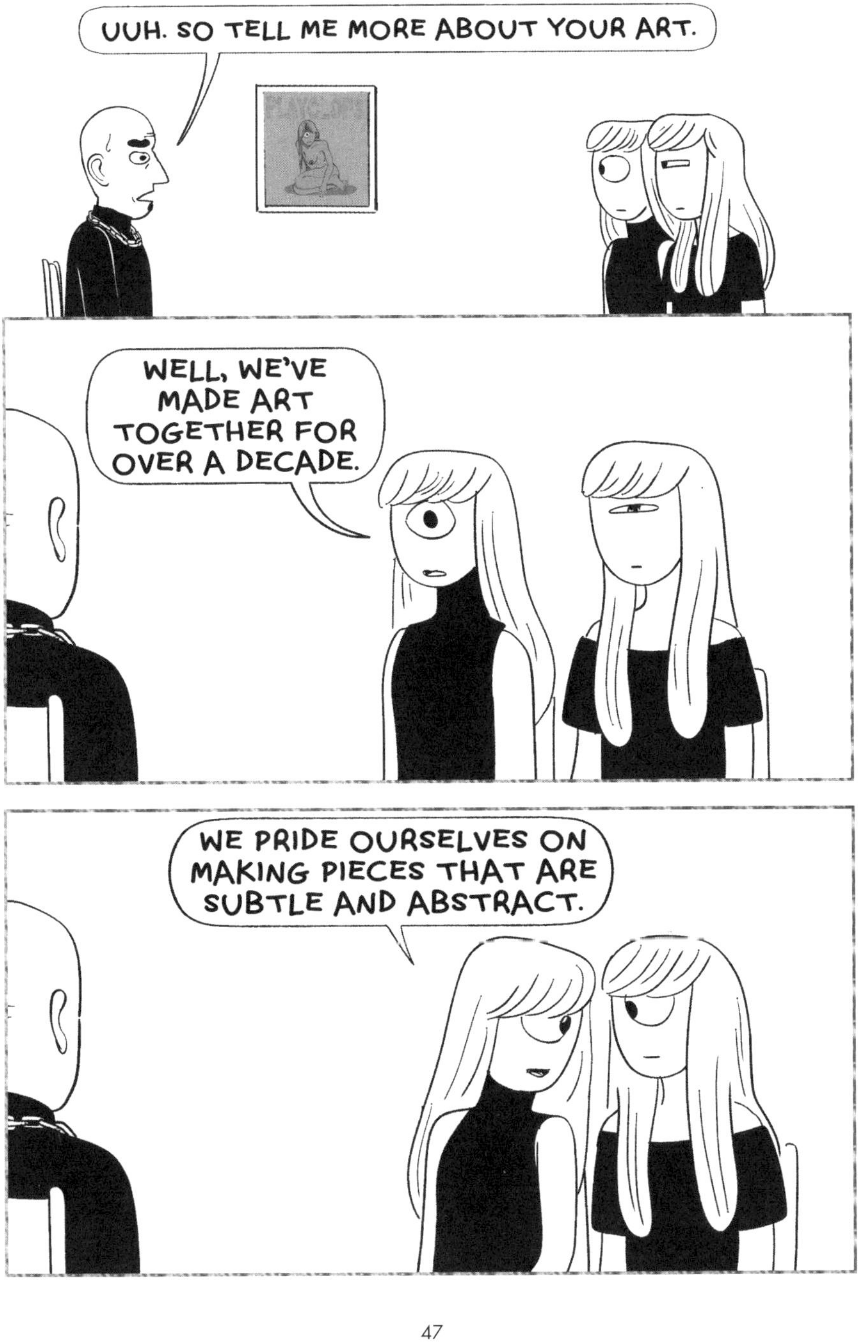
UUH. SO TELL ME MORE ABOUT YOUR ART.
WELL, WE'VE MADE ART TOGETHER FOR OVER A DECADE.
WE PRIDE OURSELVES ON MAKING PIECES THAT ARE SUBTLE AND ABSTRACT.

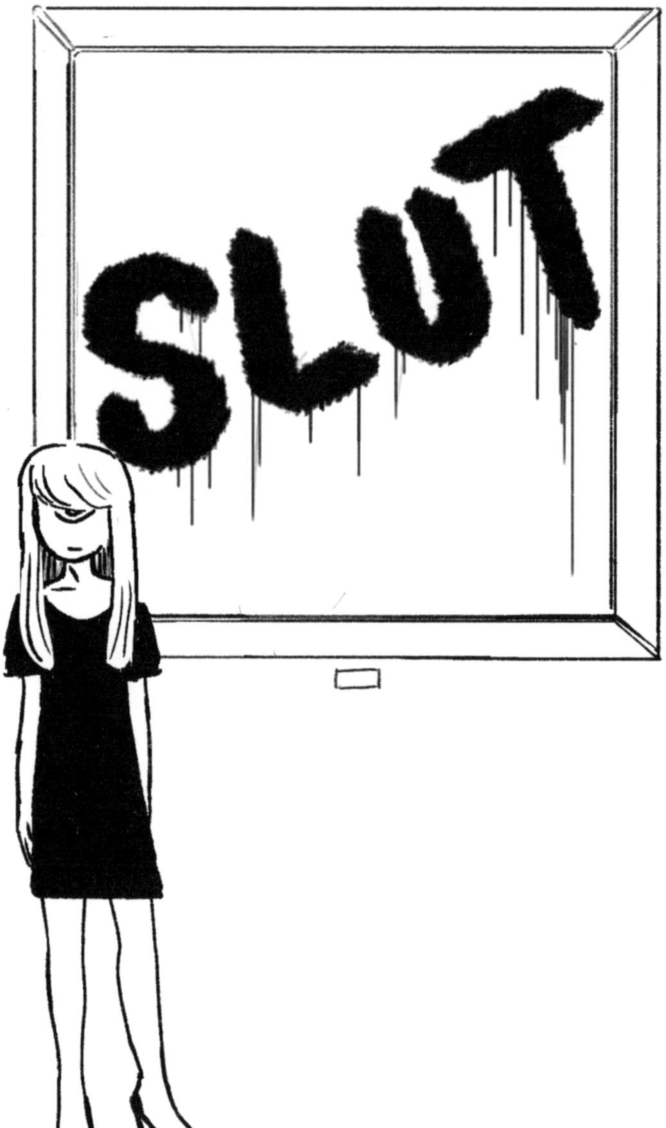
SLUT

Different and proud

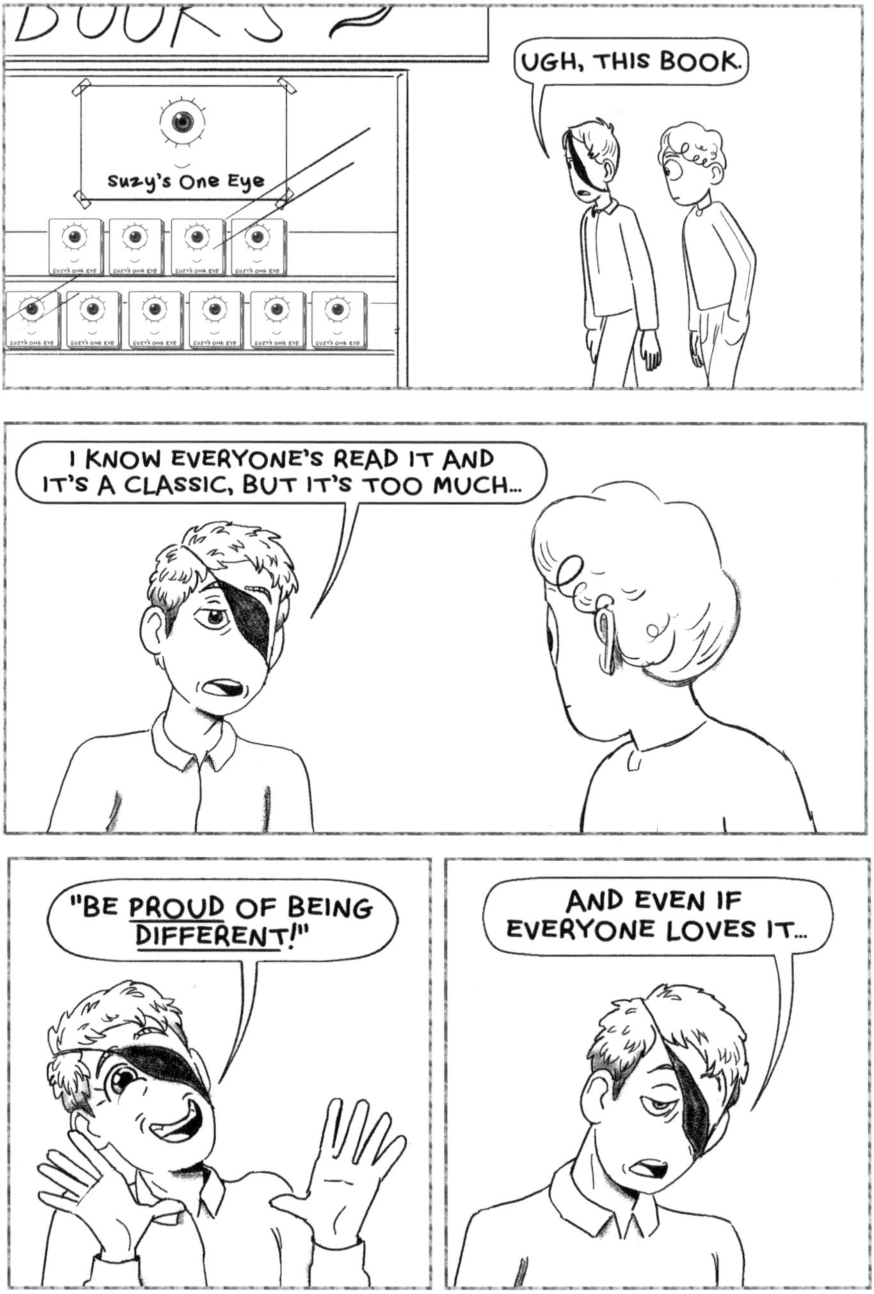

Suzy's One Eye
UGH, THIS BOOK.
I KNOW EVERYONE'S READ IT AND IT'S A CLASSIC, BUT IT'S TOO MUCH...
"BE PROUD OF BEING DIFFERENT!"
AND EVEN IF EVERYONE LOVES IT...

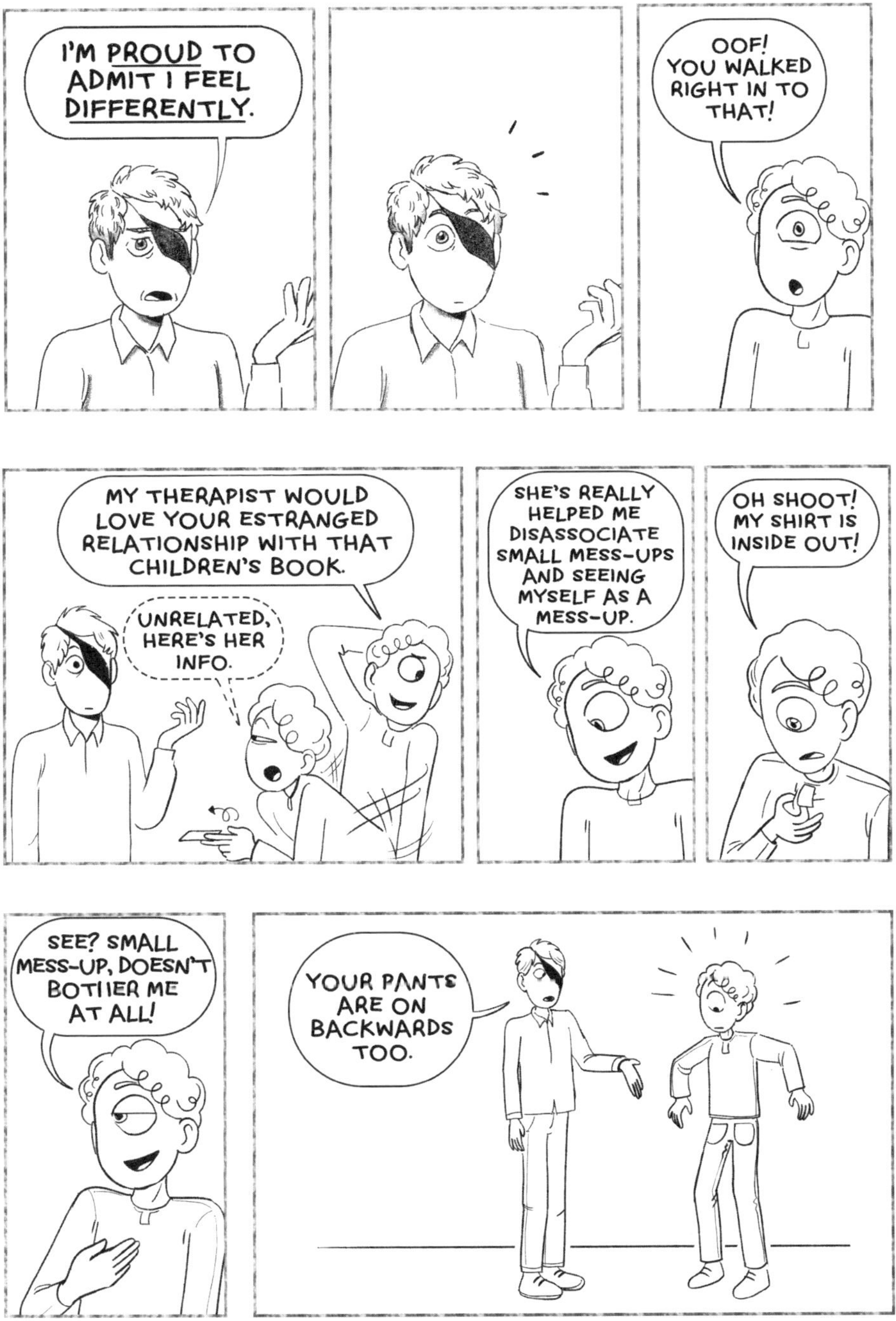
I'M PROUD TO ADMIT I FEEL DIFFERENTLY.
OOF! YOU WALKED RIGHT IN TO THAT!
MY THERAPIST WOULD LOVE YOUR ESTRANGED RELATIONSHIP WITH THAT CHILDREN'S BOOK.
UNRELATED, HERE'S HER INFO.
SHE'S REALLY HELPED ME DISASSOCIATE SMALL MESS-UPS AND SEEING MYSELF AS A MESS-UP.
OH SHOOT! MY SHIRT IS INSIDE OUT!
SEE? SMALL MESS-UP, DOESN'T BOTHER ME AT ALL!
YOUR PANTS ARE ON BACKWARDS TOO.

Arj at therapy

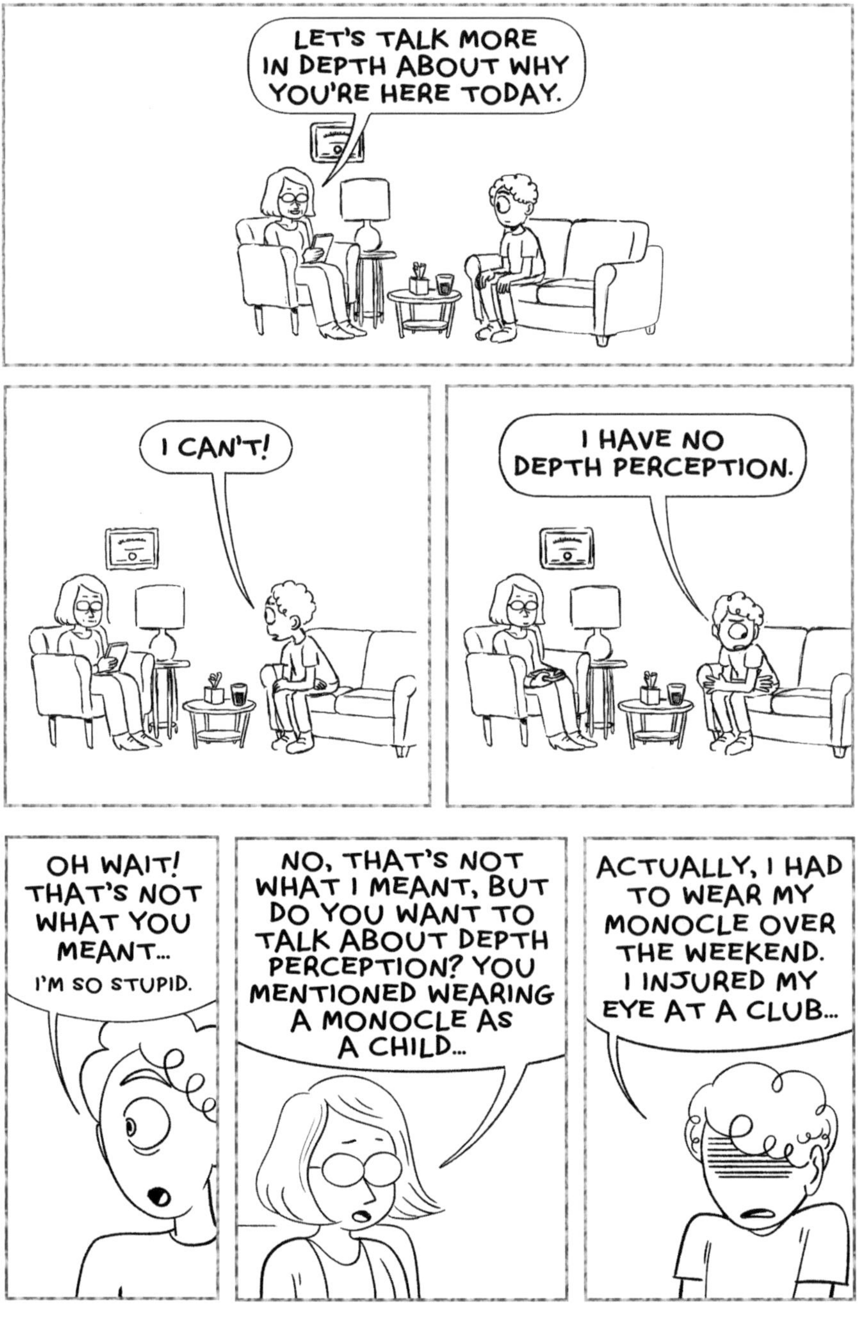
LET'S TALK MORE IN DEPTH ABOUT WHY YOU'RE HERE TODAY.
I CAN'T!
I HAVE NO DEPTH PERCEPTION.
OH WAIT! THAT'S NOT WHAT YOU MEANT...
I'M SO STUPID.
NO, THAT'S NOT WHAT I MEANT, BUT DO YOU WANT TO TALK ABOUT DEPTH PERCEPTION? YOU MENTIONED WEARING A MONOCLE AS A CHILD...
ACTUALLY, I HAD TO WEAR MY MONOCLE OVER THE WEEKEND. I INJURED MY EYE AT A CLUB...

Arj's Friday night

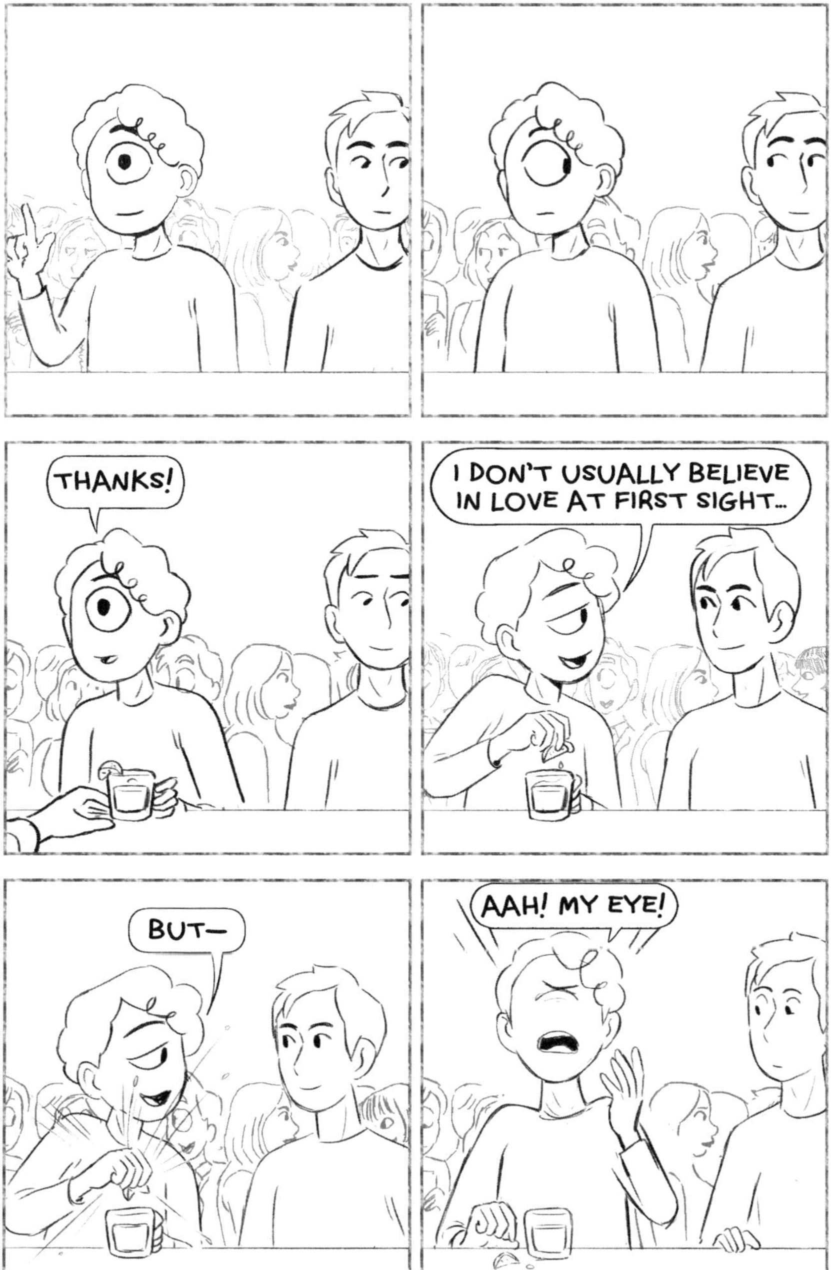
THANKS!
I DON'T USUALLY BELIEVE IN LOVE AT FIRST SIGHT...
BUT—
AAH! MY EYE!

The monocle

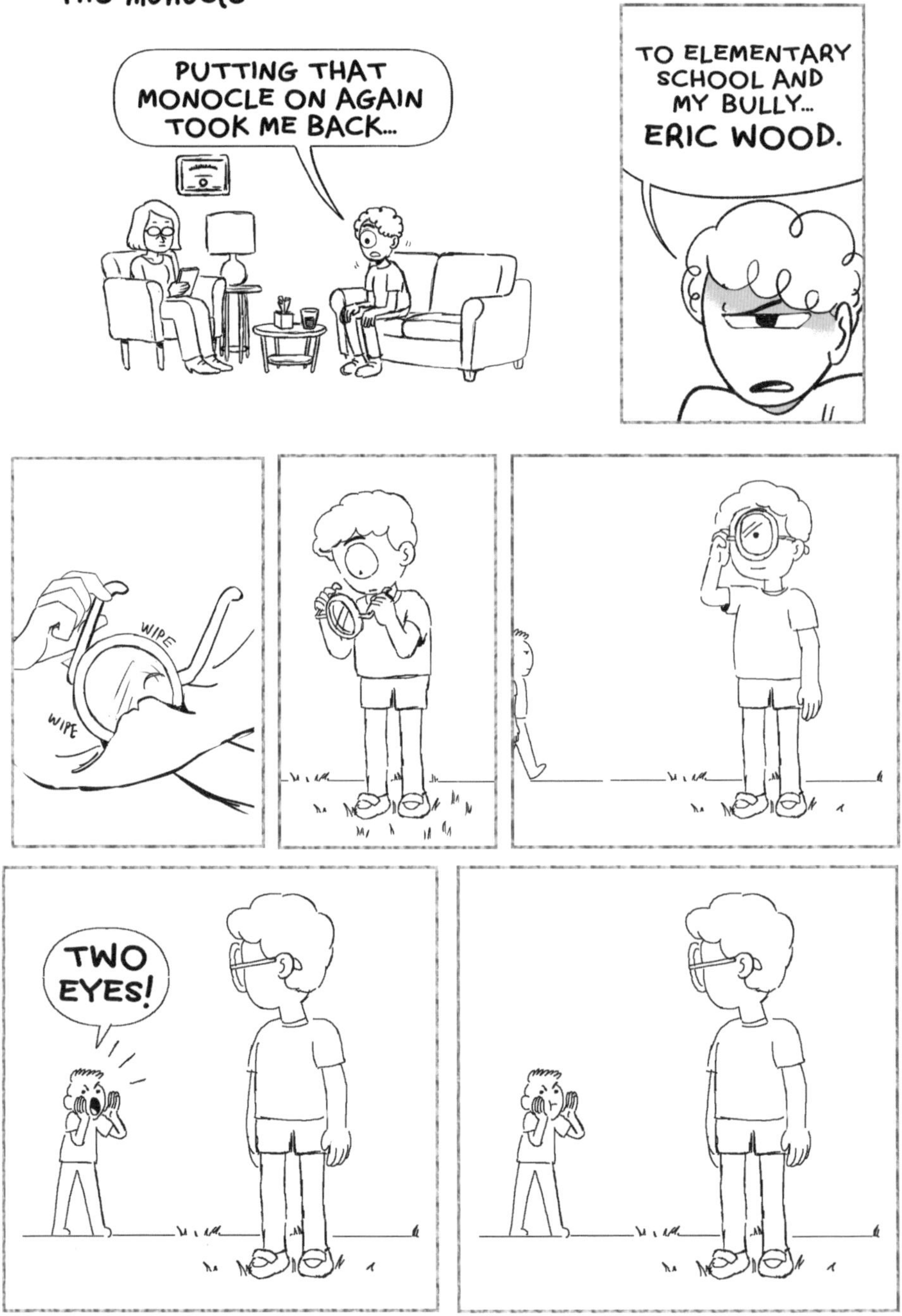
PUTTING THAT MONOCLE ON AGAIN TOOK ME BACK...
TO ELEMENTARY SCHOOL AND MY BULLY... ERIC WOOD.
WIPE
WIPE
TWO EYES!

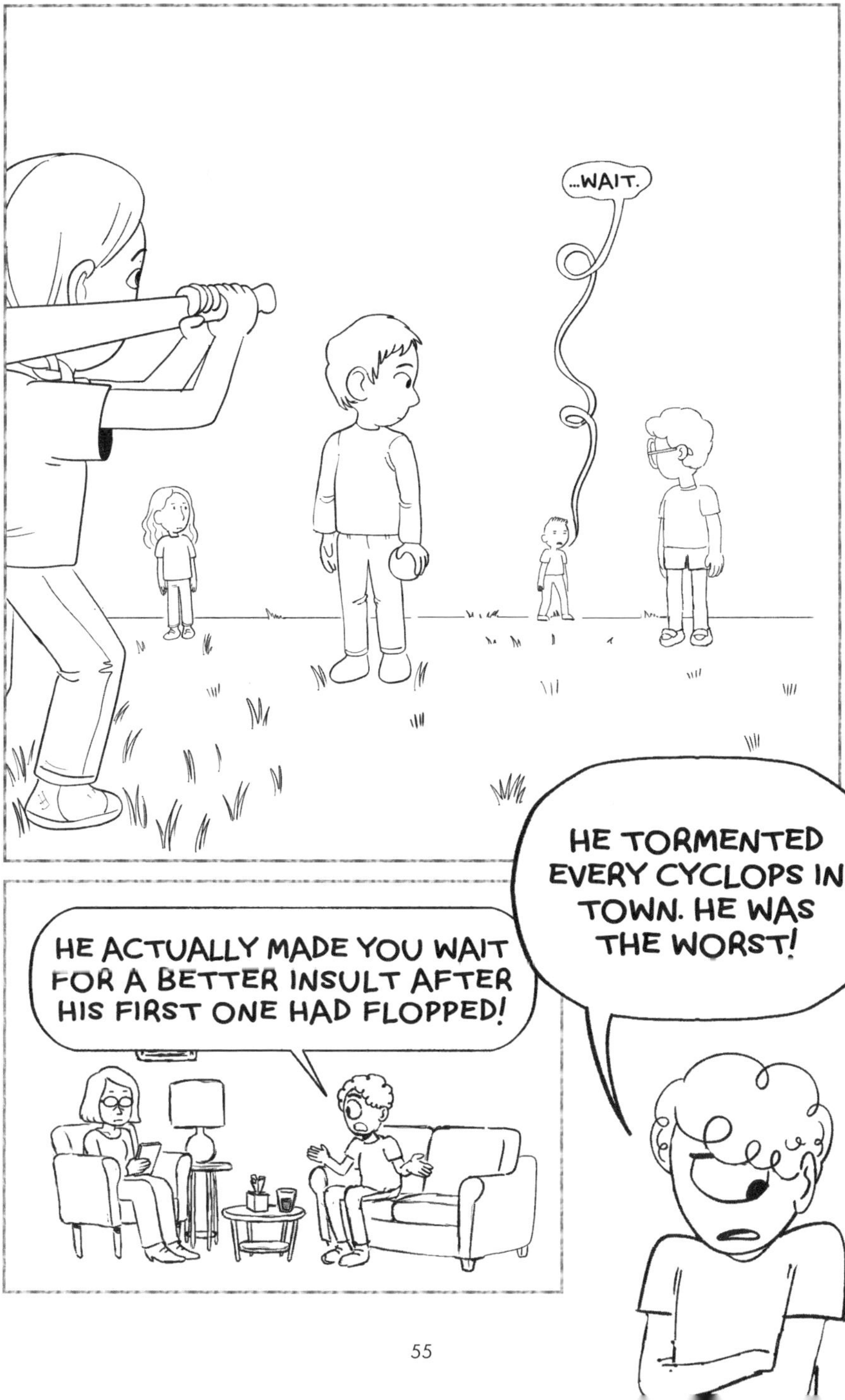
...WAIT.
HE ACTUALLY MADE YOU WAIT FOR A BETTER INSULT AFTER HIS FIRST ONE HAD FLOPPED!
HE TORMENTED EVERY CYCLOPS IN TOWN. HE WAS THE WORST!

The adventures of Eric Wood

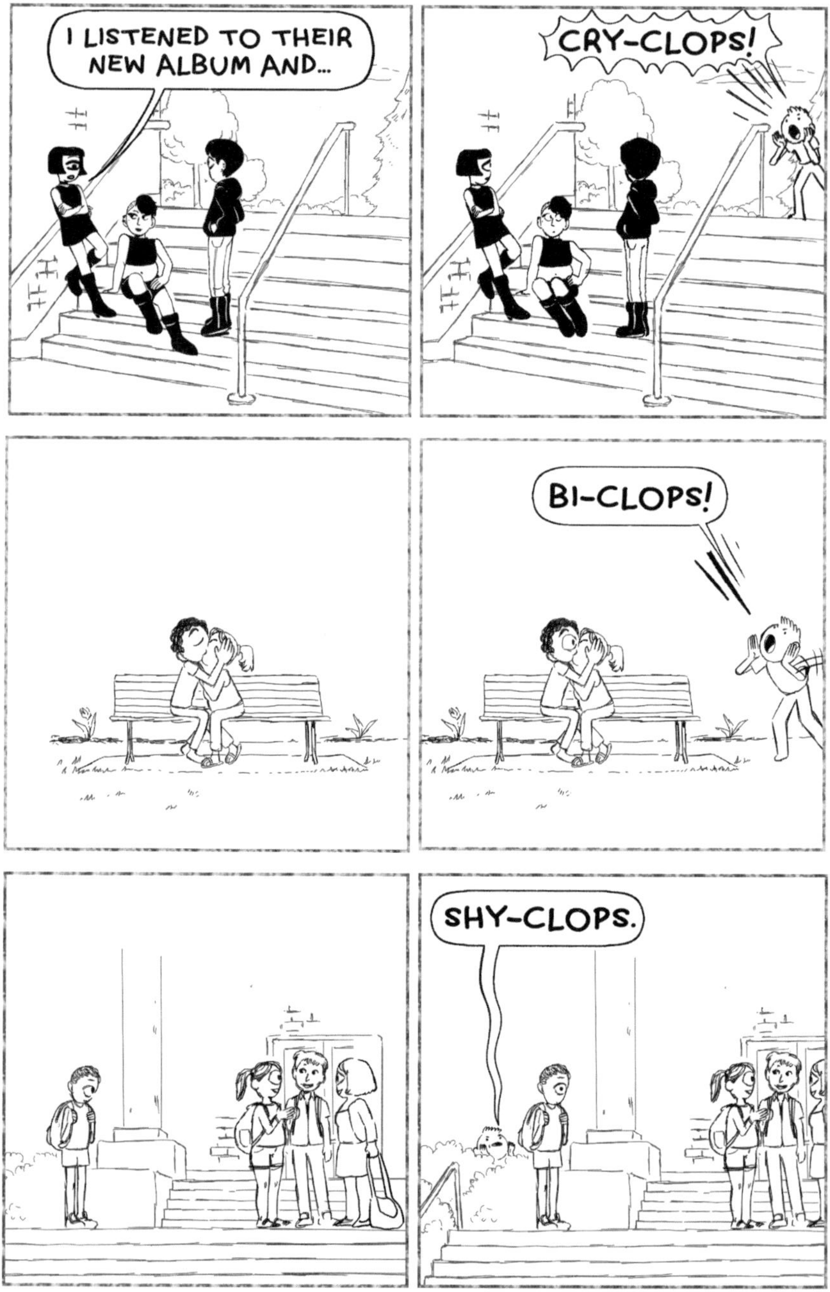
I LISTENED TO THEIR NEW ALBUM AND...
CRY-CLOPS!
BI-CLOPS!
SHY-CLOPS.

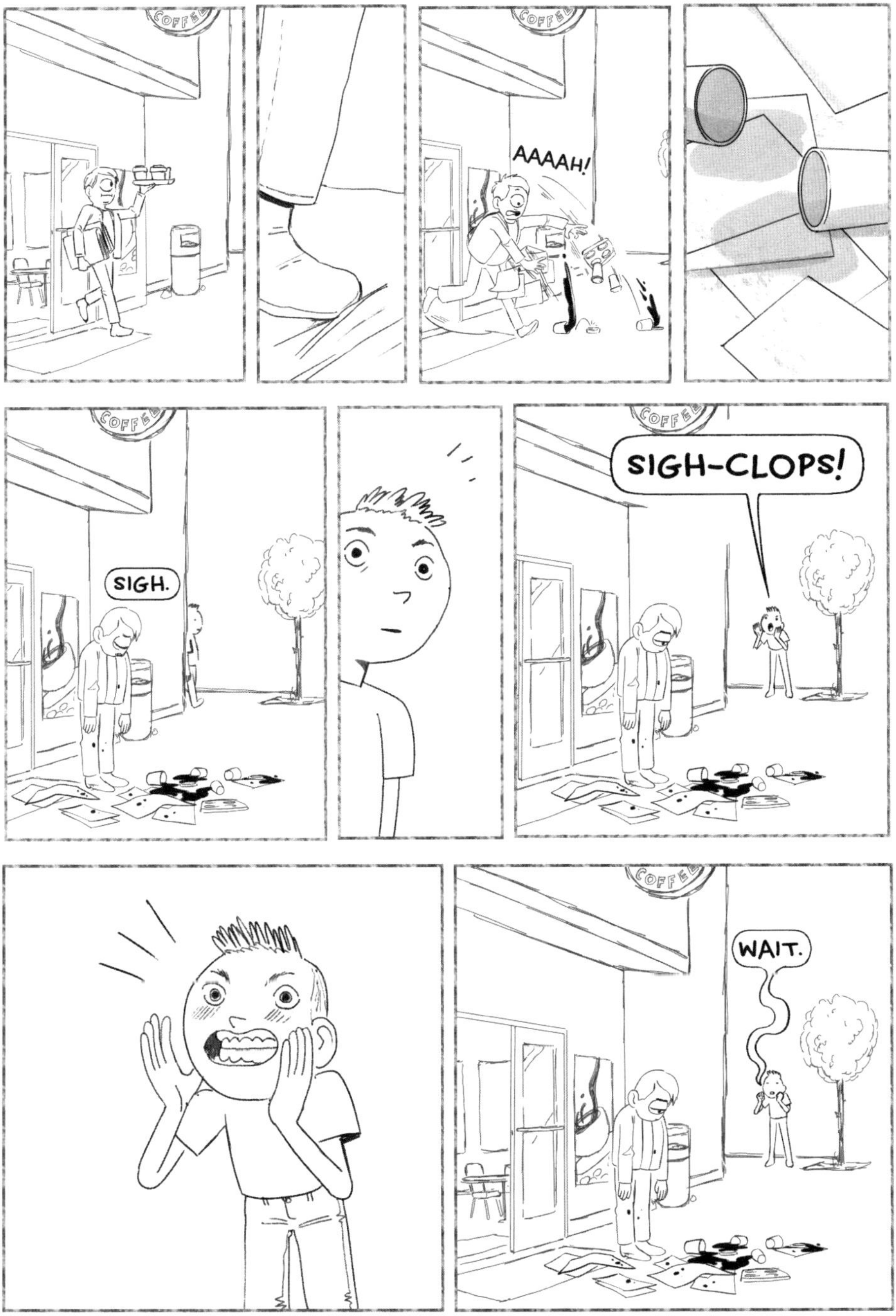
AAAAH!
SIGH.
SIGH-CLOPS!
WAIT.

Cyclopes night

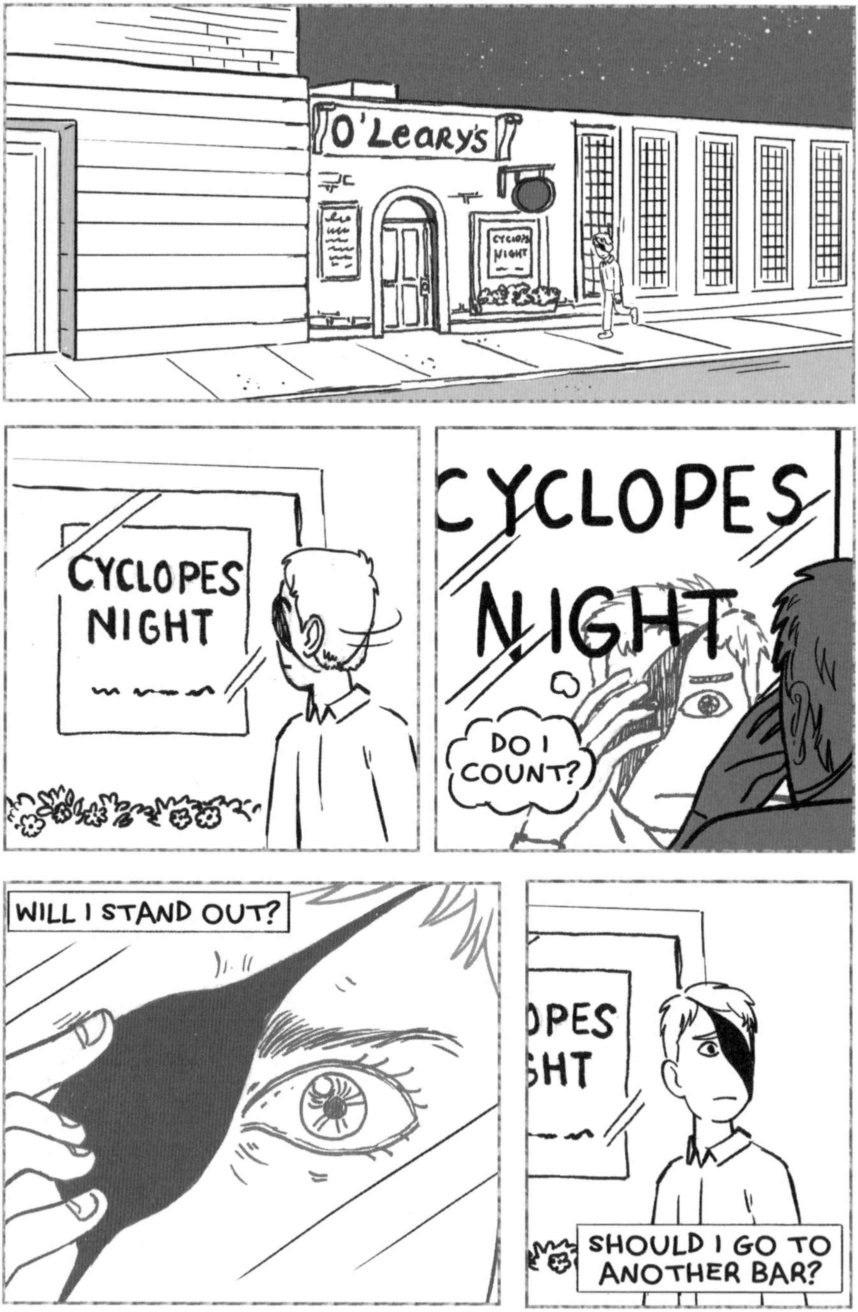
O'Leary's
CYCLOPS NIGHT
CYCLOPES NIGHT
CYCLOPES NIGHT
DO I COUNT?
WILL I STAND OUT?
OPES
GHT
SHOULD I GO TO ANOTHER BAR?

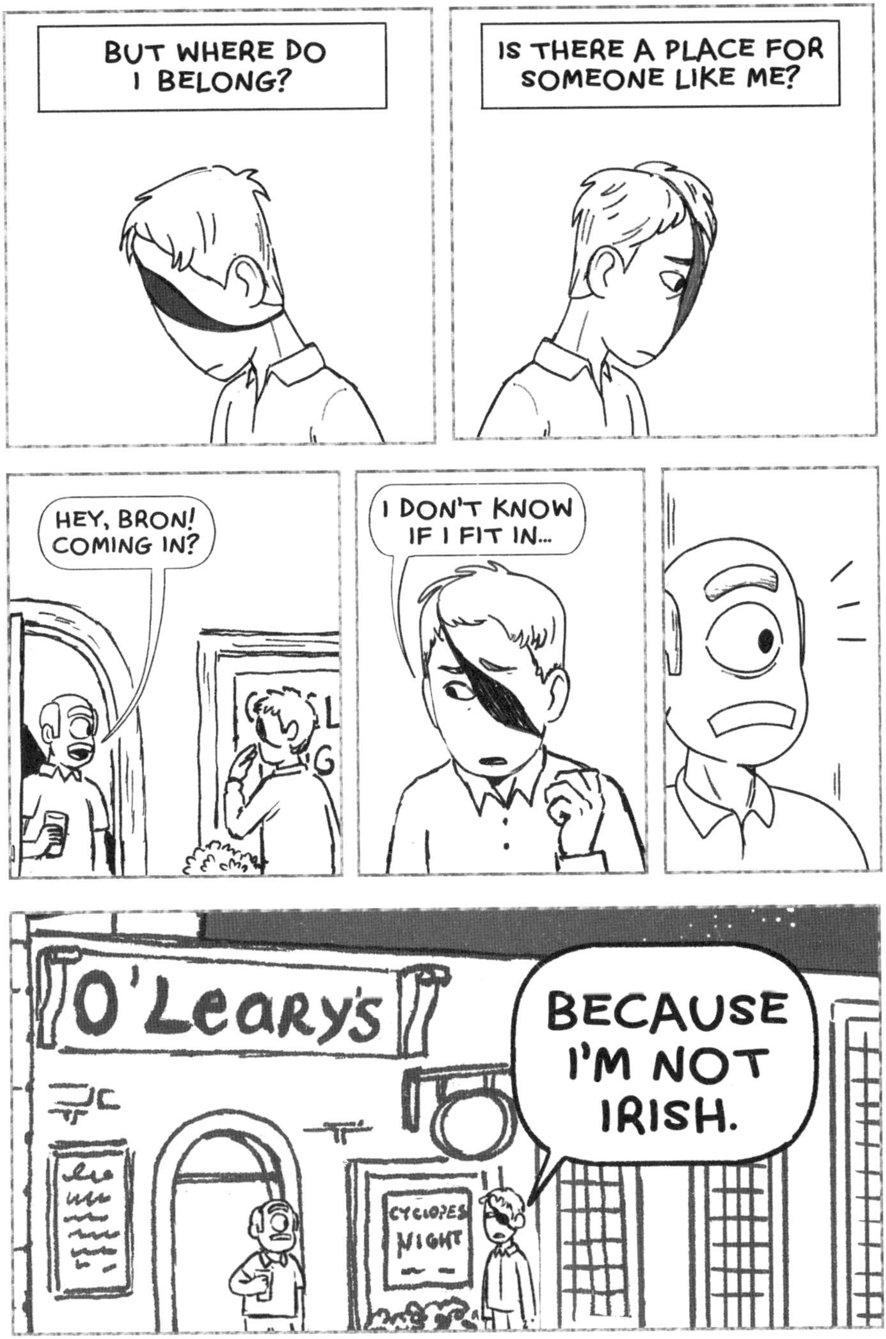
BUT WHERE DO I BELONG?
IS THERE A PLACE FOR SOMEONE LIKE ME?
HEY, BRON! COMING IN?
I DON'T KNOW IF I FIT IN...
O'Leary's
CYCLOPES NIGHT
BECAUSE I'M NOT IRISH.

Bron and Pol

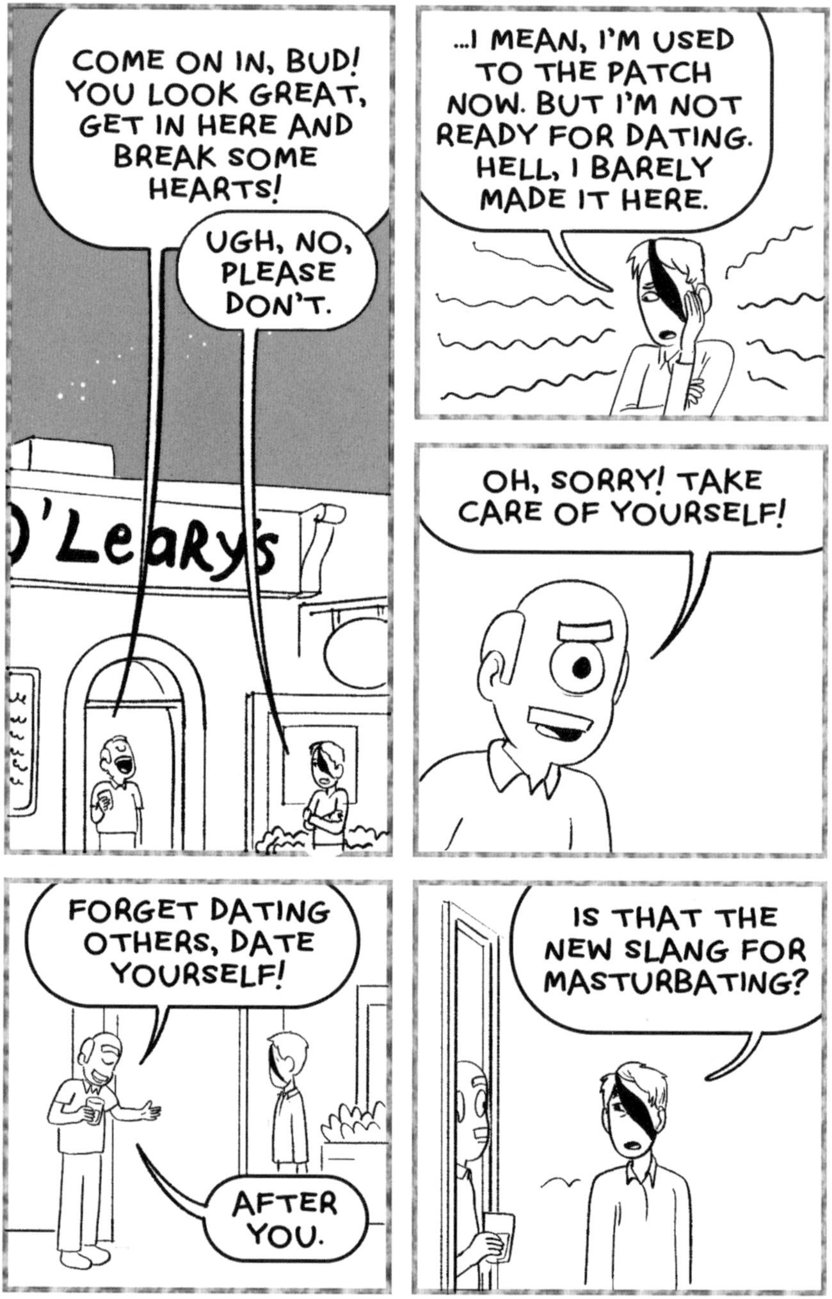
COME ON IN, BUD! YOU LOOK GREAT, GET IN HERE AND BREAK SOME HEARTS!
UGH, NO, PLEASE DON'T.
O'Leary's
...I MEAN, I'M USED TO THE PATCH NOW. BUT I'M NOT READY FOR DATING. HELL, I BARELY MADE IT HERE.
OH, SORRY! TAKE CARE OF YOURSELF!
FORGET DATING OTHERS, DATE YOURSELF!
AFTER YOU.
IS THAT THE NEW SLANG FOR MASTURBATING?

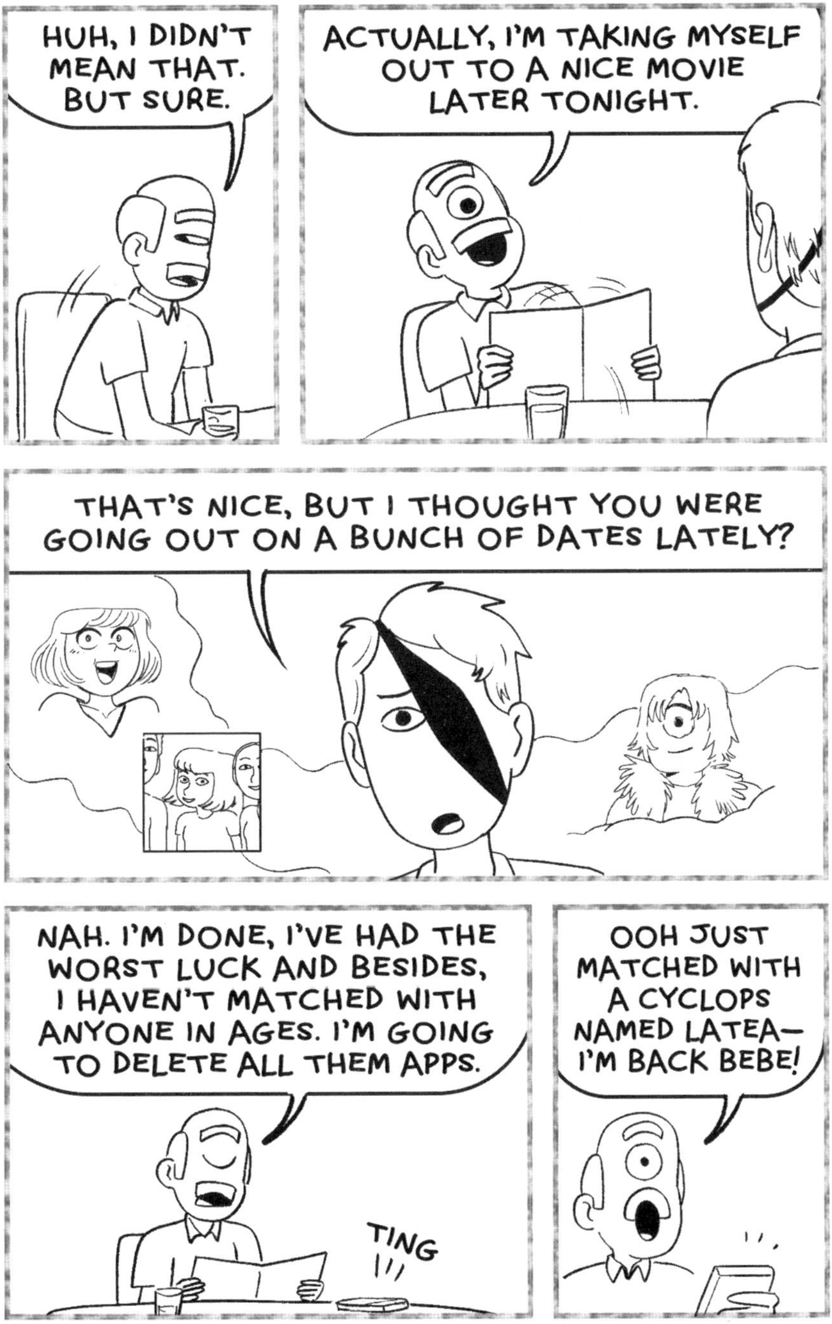
HUH, I DIDN'T MEAN THAT. BUT SURE.
ACTUALLY, I'M TAKING MYSELF OUT TO A NICE MOVIE LATER TONIGHT.
THAT'S NICE, BUT I THOUGHT YOU WERE GOING OUT ON A BUNCH OF DATES LATELY?
NAH. I'M DONE, I'VE HAD THE WORST LUCK AND BESIDES, I HAVEN'T MATCHED WITH ANYONE IN AGES. I'M GOING TO DELETE ALL THEM APPS.
TING
OOH JUST MATCHED WITH A CYCLOPS NAMED LATEA— I'M BACK BEBE!

First date

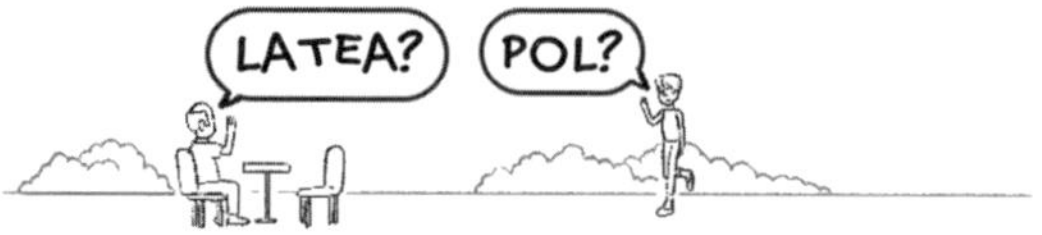
LATEA?
POL?

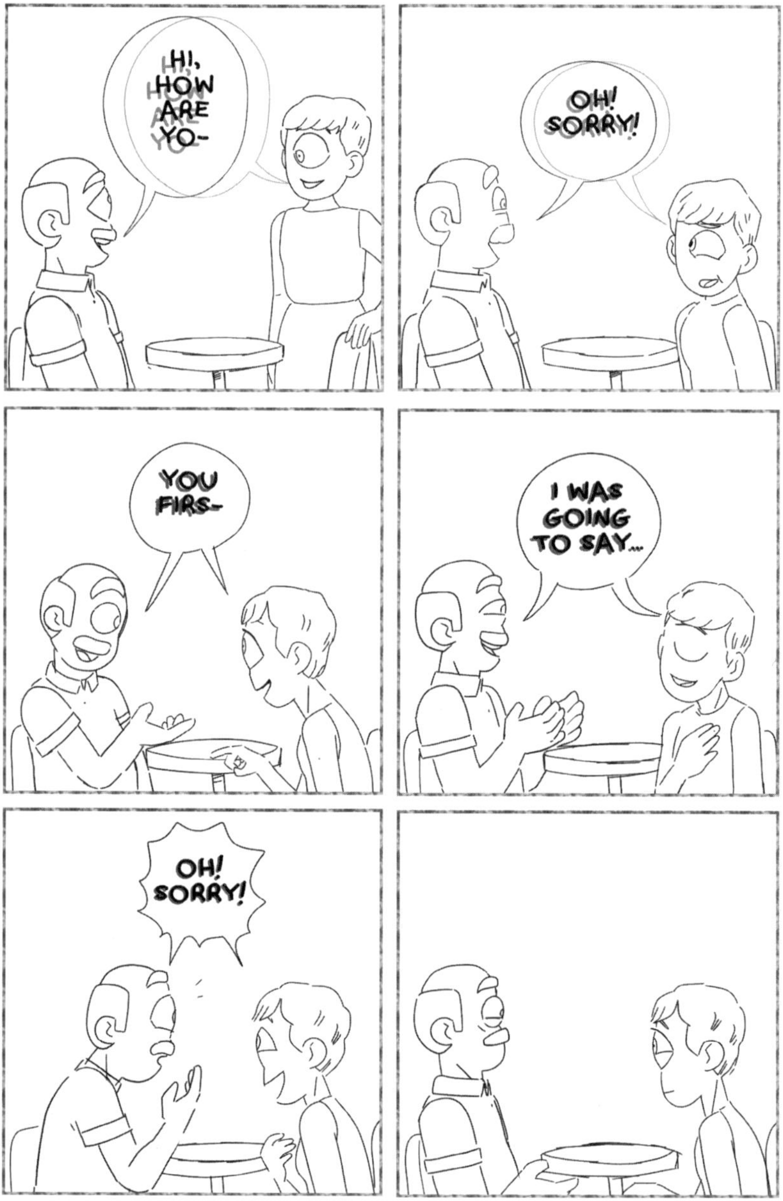
HI, HOW ARE YO-
OH! SORRY!
YOU FIRS-
I WAS GOING TO SAY...
OH! SORRY!

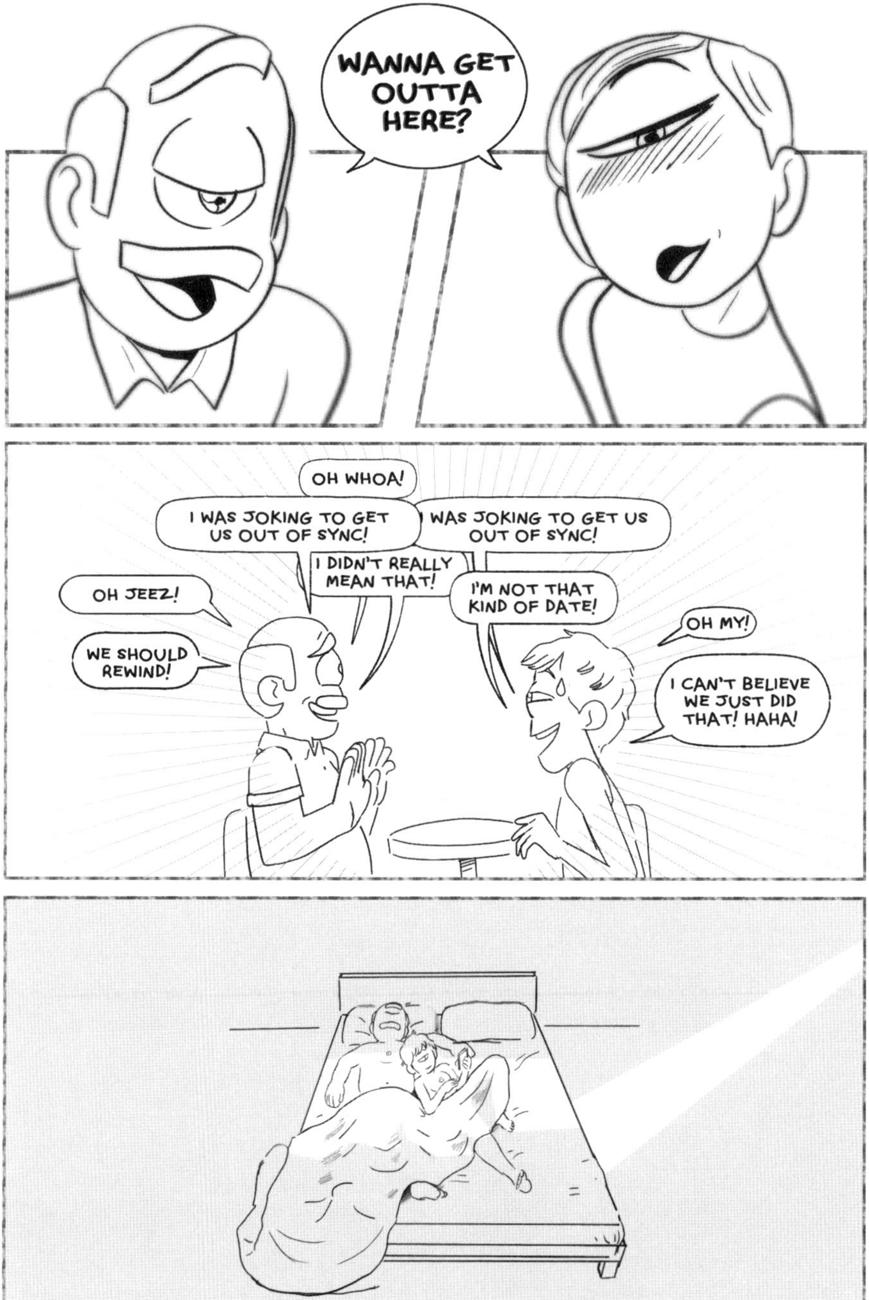
WANNA GET OUTTA HERE?
OH WHOA!
I WAS JOKING TO GET US OUT OF SYNC!
I WAS JOKING TO GET US OUT OF SYNC!
I DIDN'T REALLY MEAN THAT!
I'M NOT THAT KIND OF DATE!
OH JEEZ!
WE SHOULD REWIND!
OH MY!
I CAN'T BELIEVE WE JUST DID THAT! HAHA!

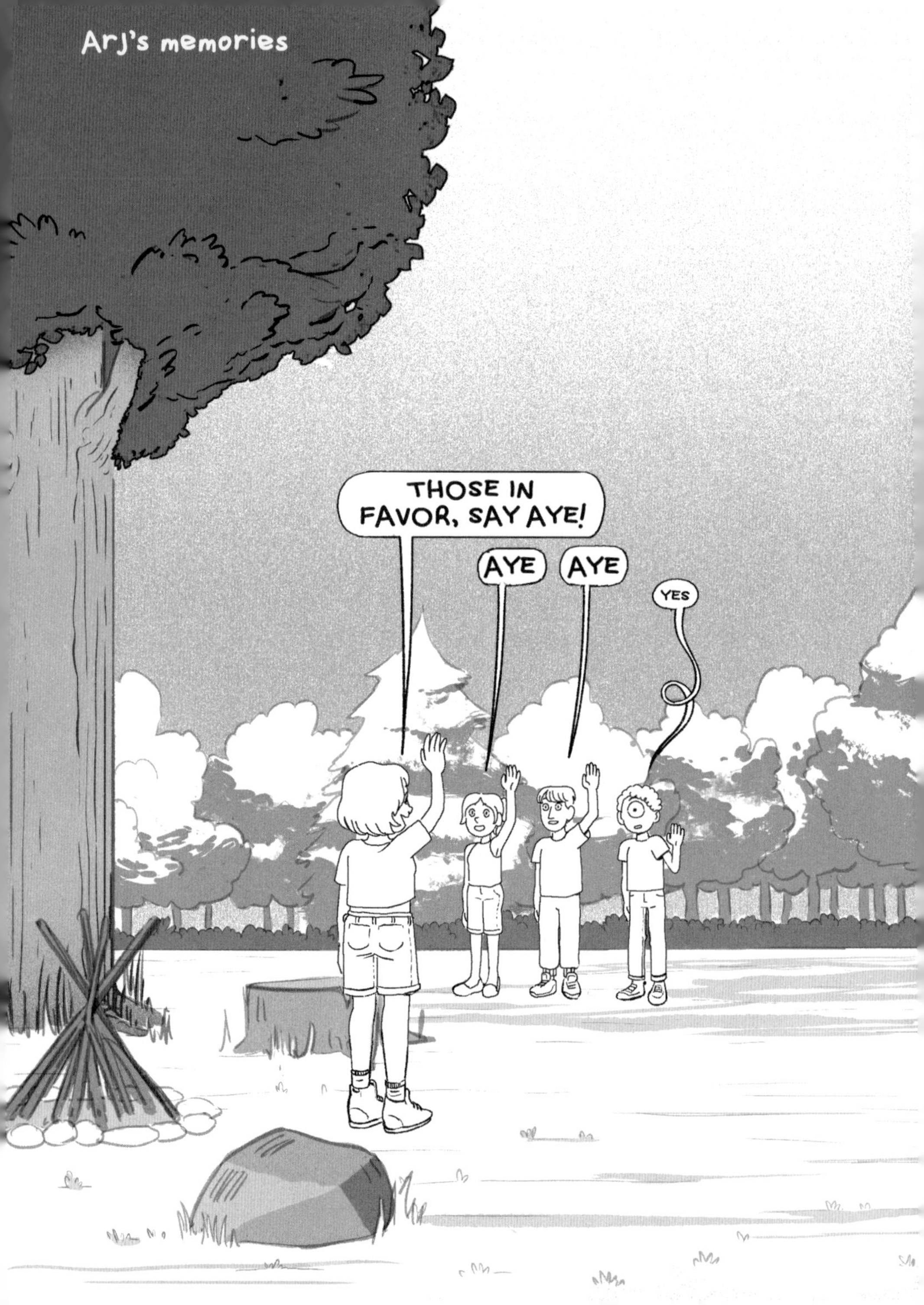
Arj's memories
THOSE IN FAVOR, SAY AYE!
AYE
AYE
YES

Pol and Latea

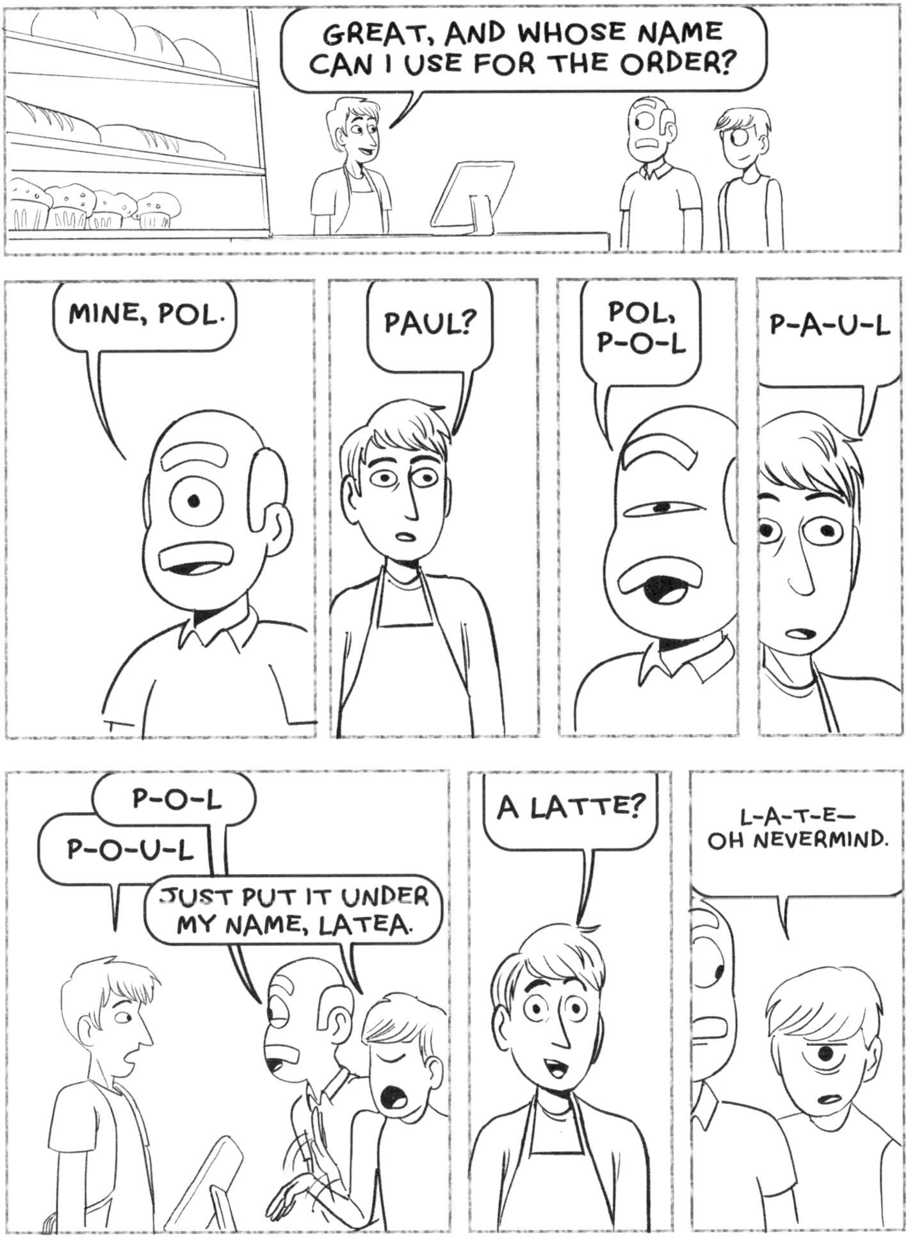
GREAT, AND WHOSE NAME CAN I USE FOR THE ORDER?
MINE, POL.
PAUL?
POL, P-O-L
P-A-U-L
P-O-L
P-O-U-L
JUST PUT IT UNDER MY NAME, LATEA.
A LATTE?
L-A-T-E— OH NEVERMIND.

Unprepared

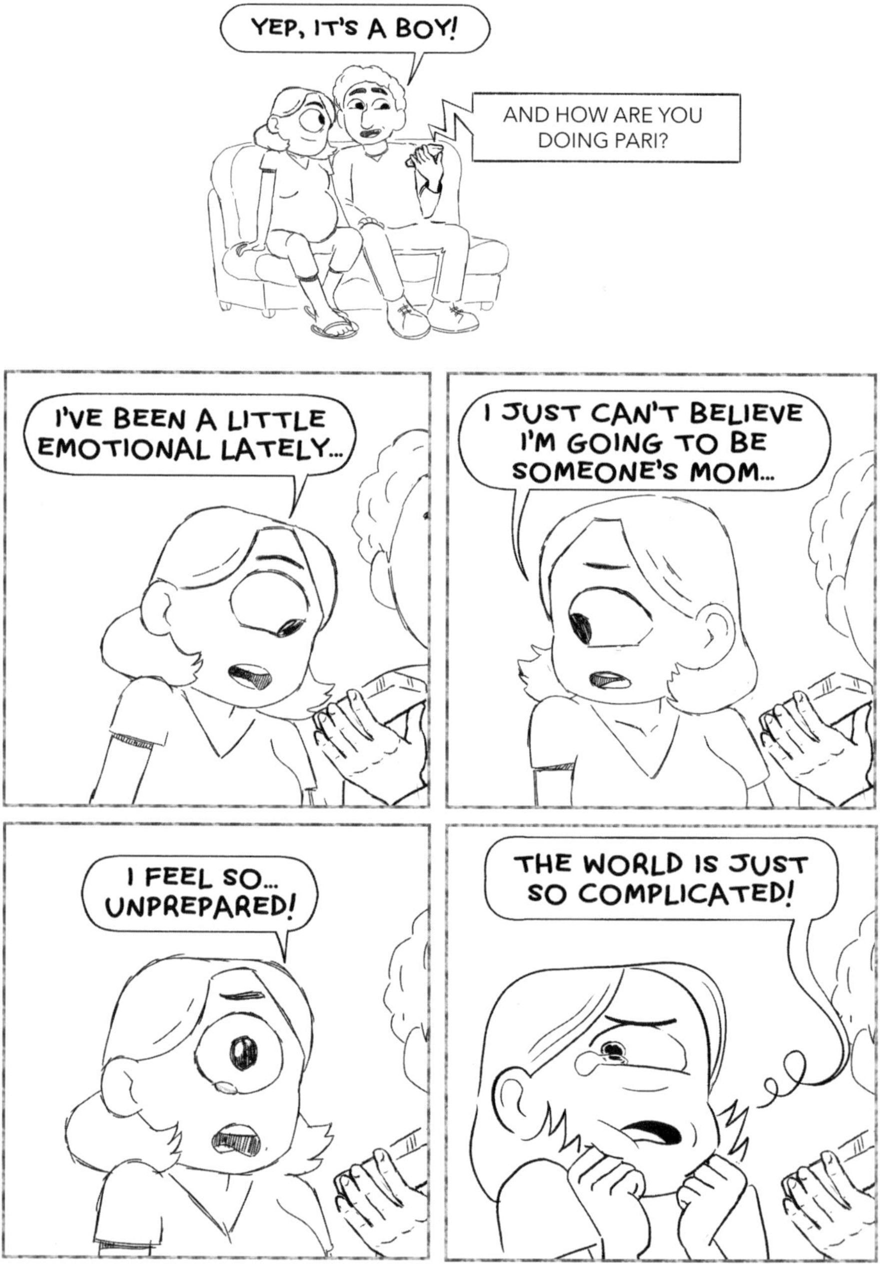

YEP, IT'S A BOY!
AND HOW ARE YOU DOING PARI?
I'VE BEEN A LITTLE EMOTIONAL LATELY...
I JUST CAN'T BELIEVE I'M GOING TO BE SOMEONE'S MOM...
I FEEL SO... UNPREPARED!
THE WORLD IS JUST SO COMPLICATED!

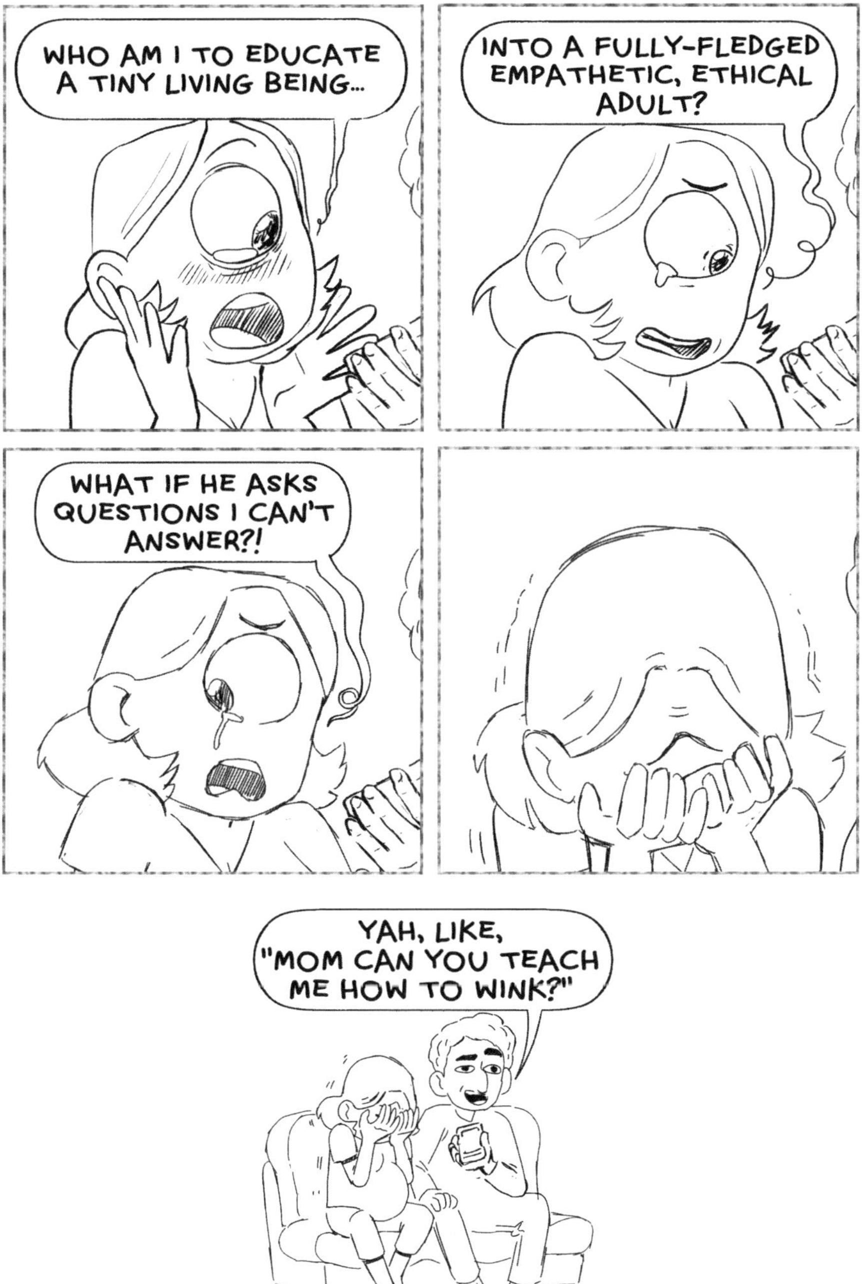
WHO AM I TO EDUCATE A TINY LIVING BEING...
INTO A FULLY-FLEDGED EMPATHETIC, ETHICAL ADULT?
WHAT IF HE ASKS QUESTIONS I CAN'T ANSWER?!
YAH, LIKE, "MOM CAN YOU TEACH ME HOW TO WINK?"

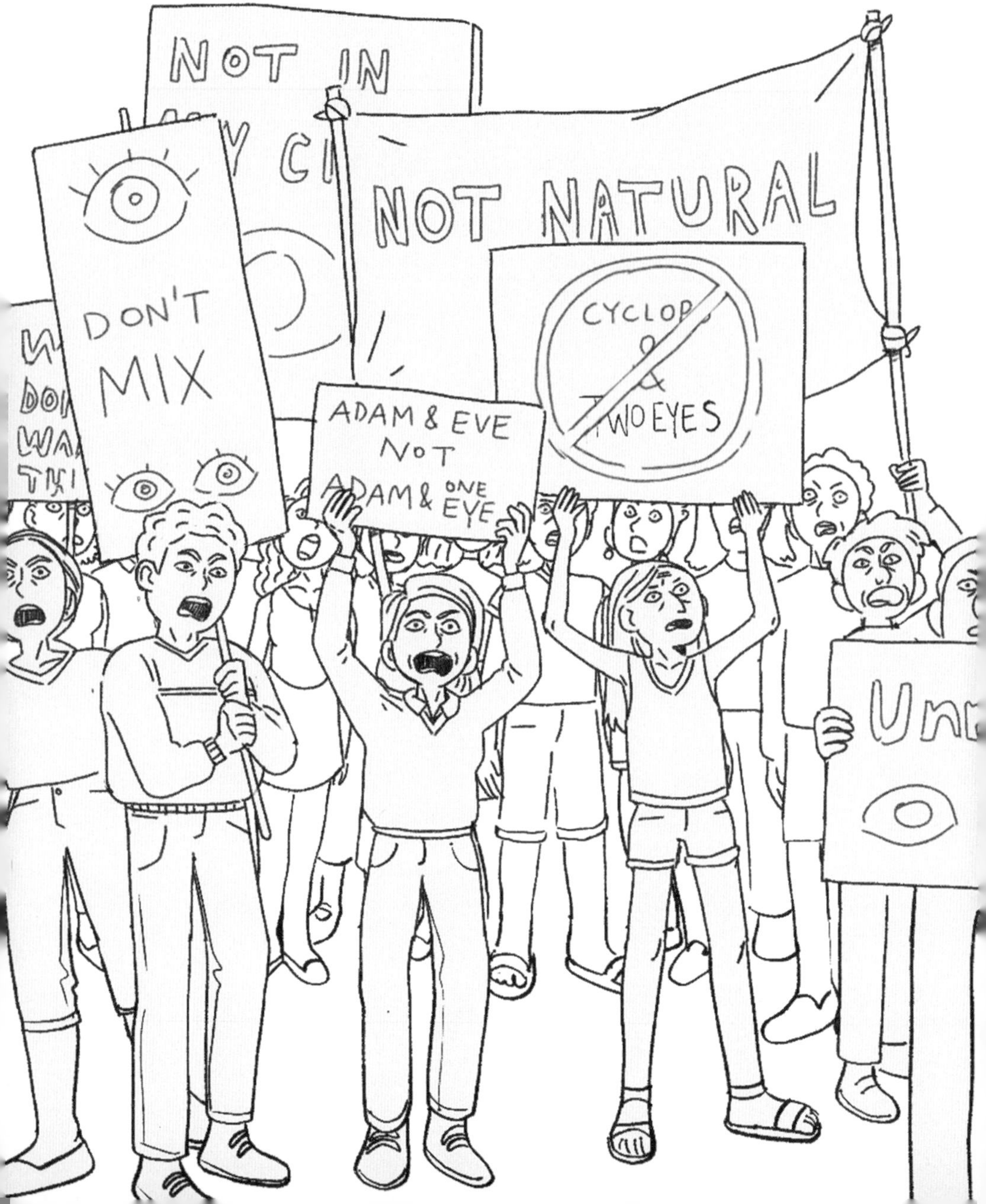
NOT IN
DON'T MIX
NOT NATURAL
ADAM & EVE NOT ADAM & ONE EYE
TWO EYES

Top Searches

1. male cyclops two eyes man

2. female cyclops two eyes woman

3. xxx male cyclops two eyes
   clown costume orgy xxx

4. female cyclops two eye man

5. male cyclosp tow eyes man

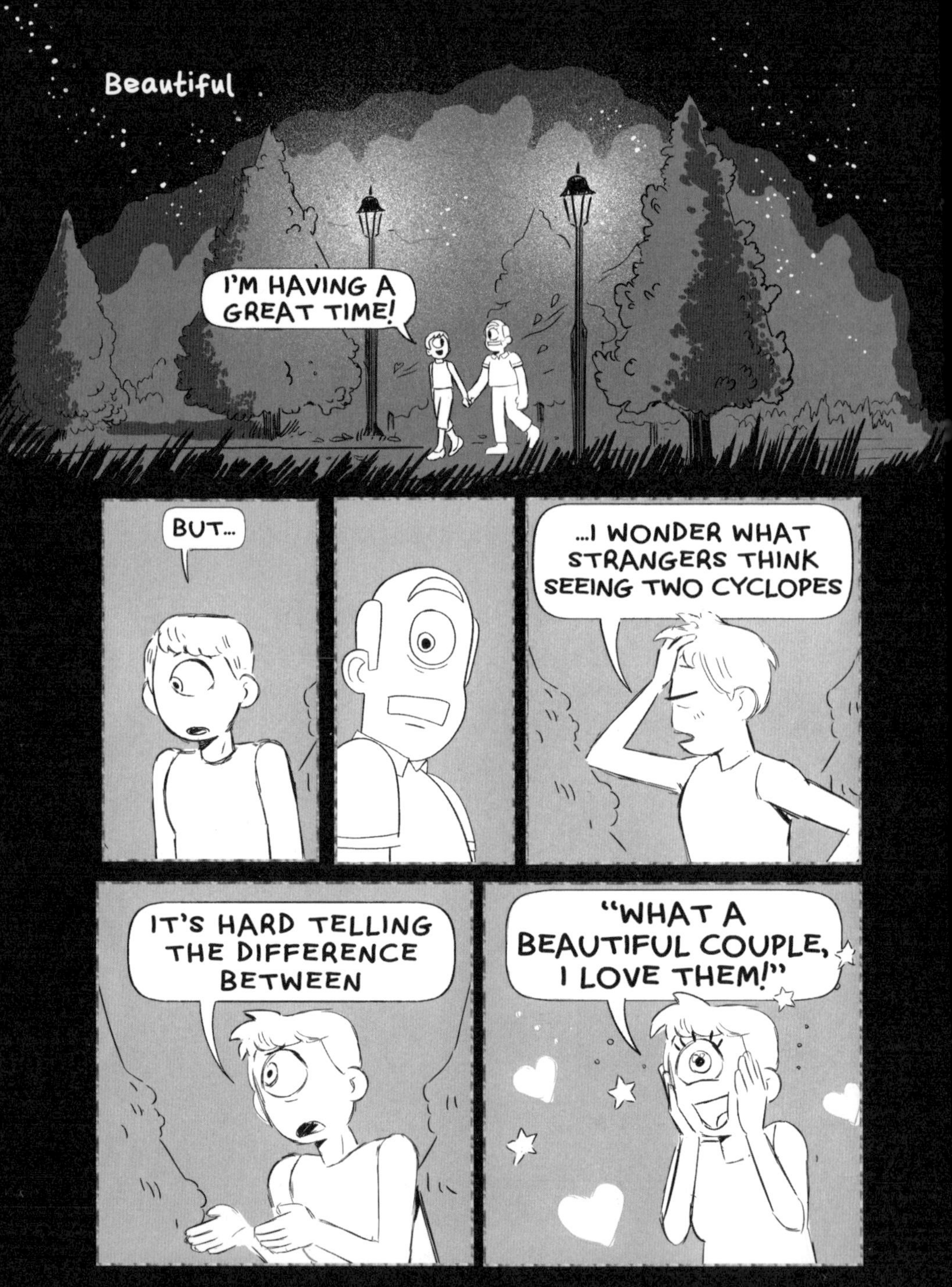
Beautiful
I'M HAVING A GREAT TIME!
BUT...
...I WONDER WHAT STRANGERS THINK SEEING TWO CYCLOPES
IT'S HARD TELLING THE DIFFERENCE BETWEEN
"WHAT A BEAUTIFUL COUPLE, I LOVE THEM!"

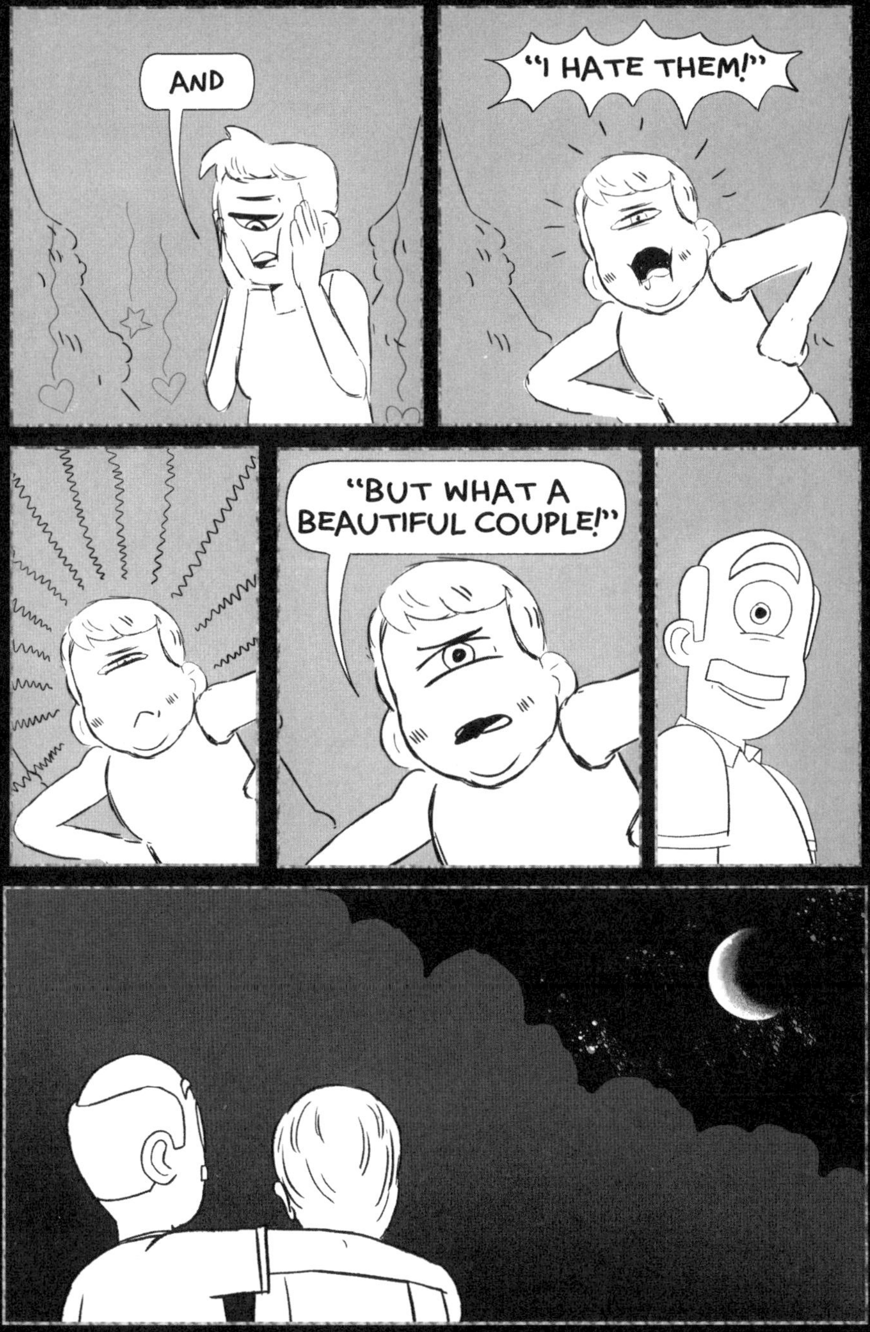
AND
"I HATE THEM!"
"BUT WHAT A BEAUTIFUL COUPLE!"

Cute

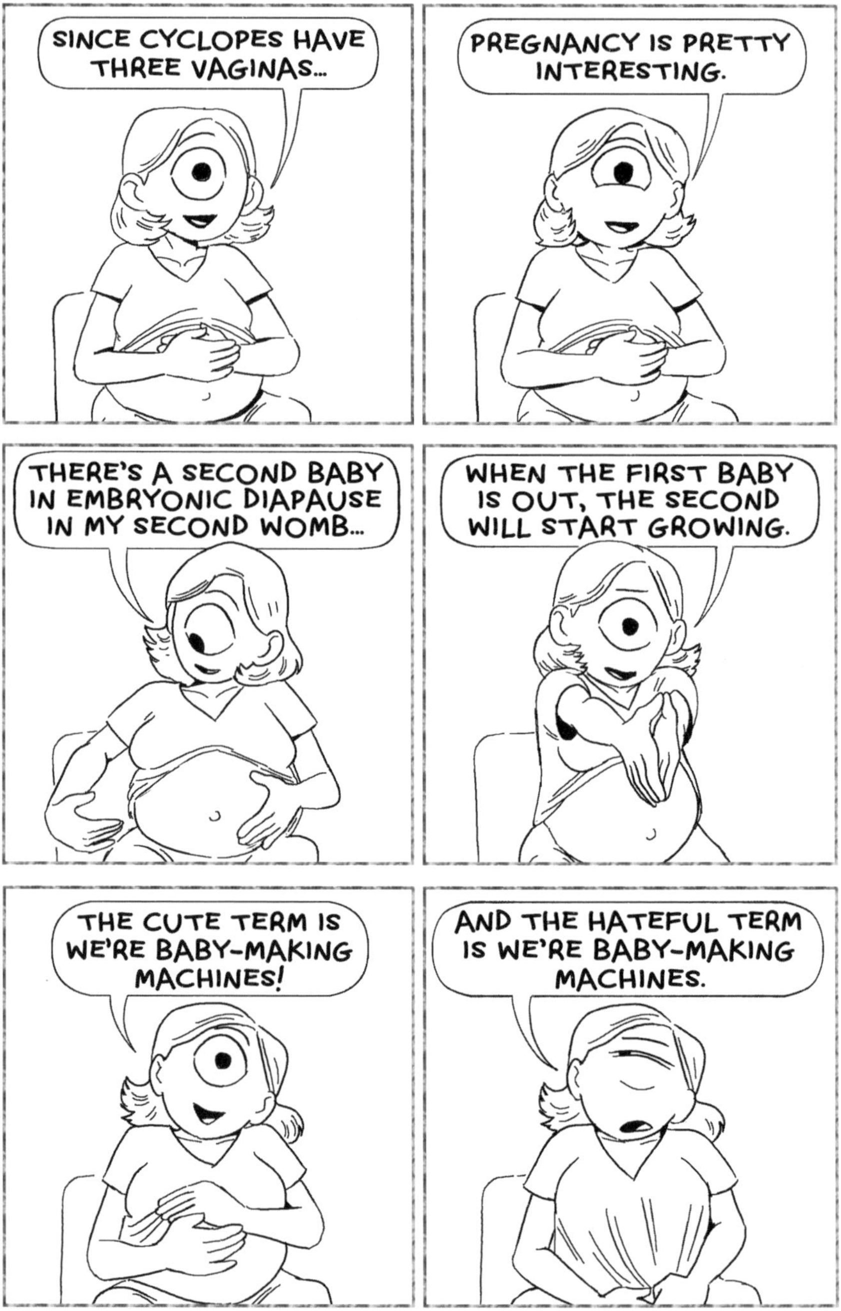
SINCE CYCLOPES HAVE THREE VAGINAS...
PREGNANCY IS PRETTY INTERESTING.
THERE'S A SECOND BABY IN EMBRYONIC DIAPAUSE IN MY SECOND WOMB...
WHEN THE FIRST BABY IS OUT, THE SECOND WILL START GROWING.
THE CUTE TERM IS WE'RE BABY-MAKING MACHINES!
AND THE HATEFUL TERM IS WE'RE BABY-MAKING MACHINES.

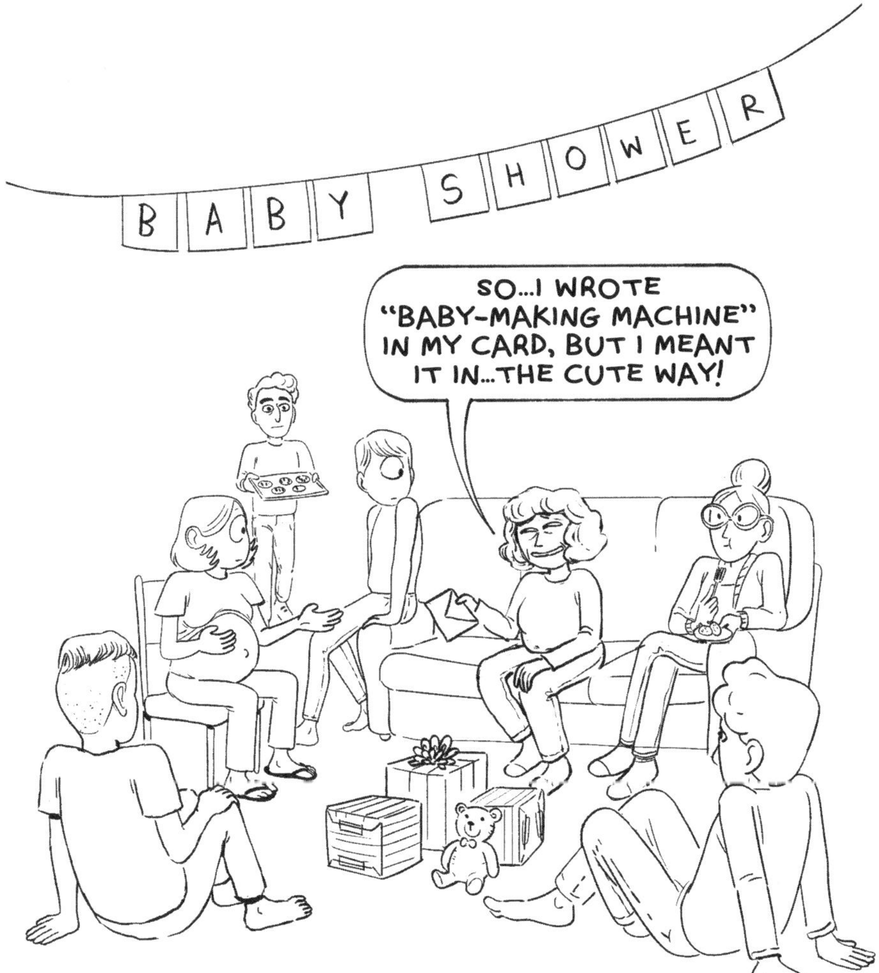
BABY SHOWER
SO...I WROTE "BABY-MAKING MACHINE" IN MY CARD, BUT I MEANT IT IN...THE CUTE WAY!

Latea + Pol

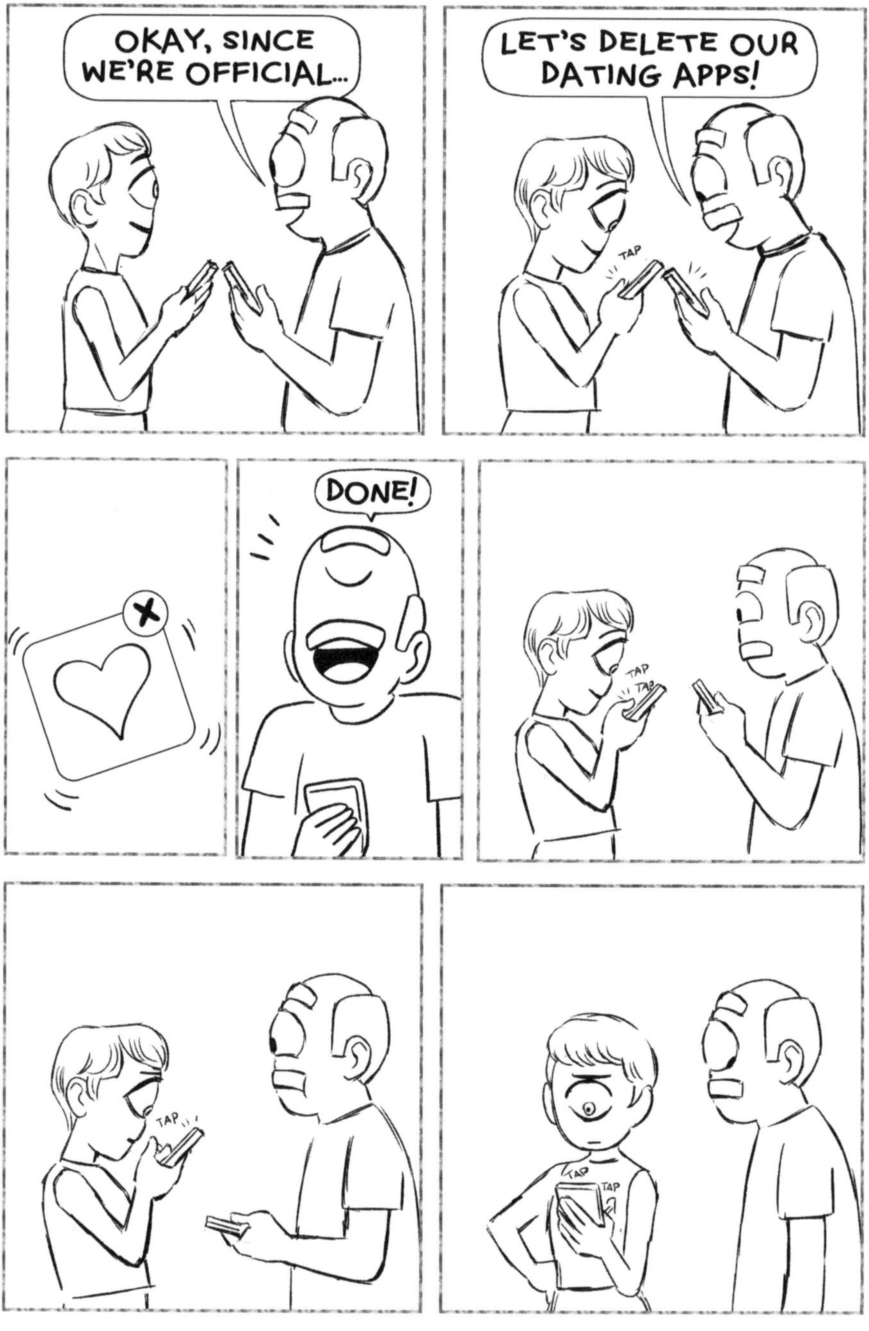

OKAY, SINCE WE'RE OFFICIAL...
LET'S DELETE OUR DATING APPS!
TAP
DONE!
TAP
TAP
TAP
TAP
TAP

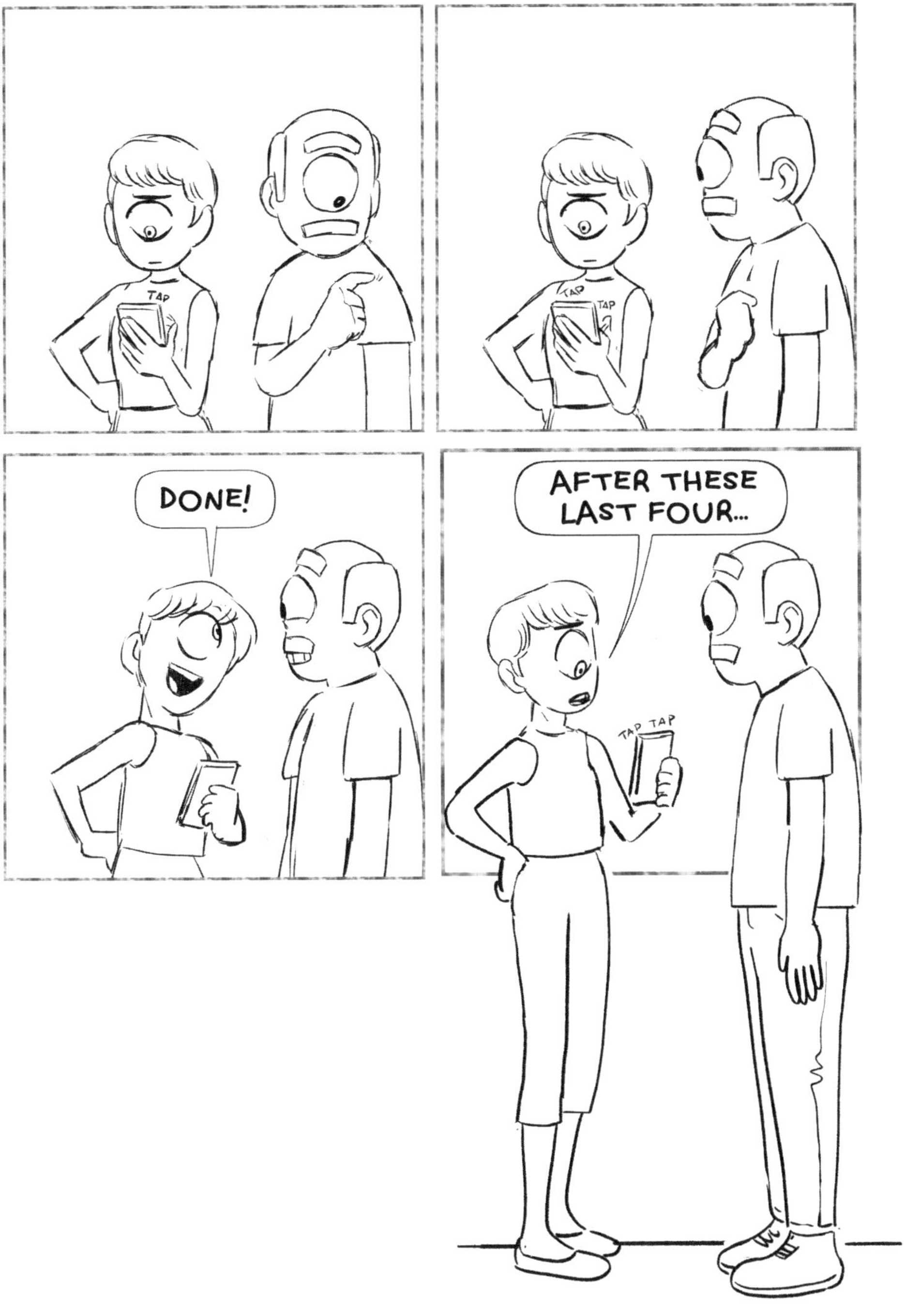
TAP
TAP
TAP
DONE!
AFTER THESE LAST FOUR...
TAP TAP

Cyborg

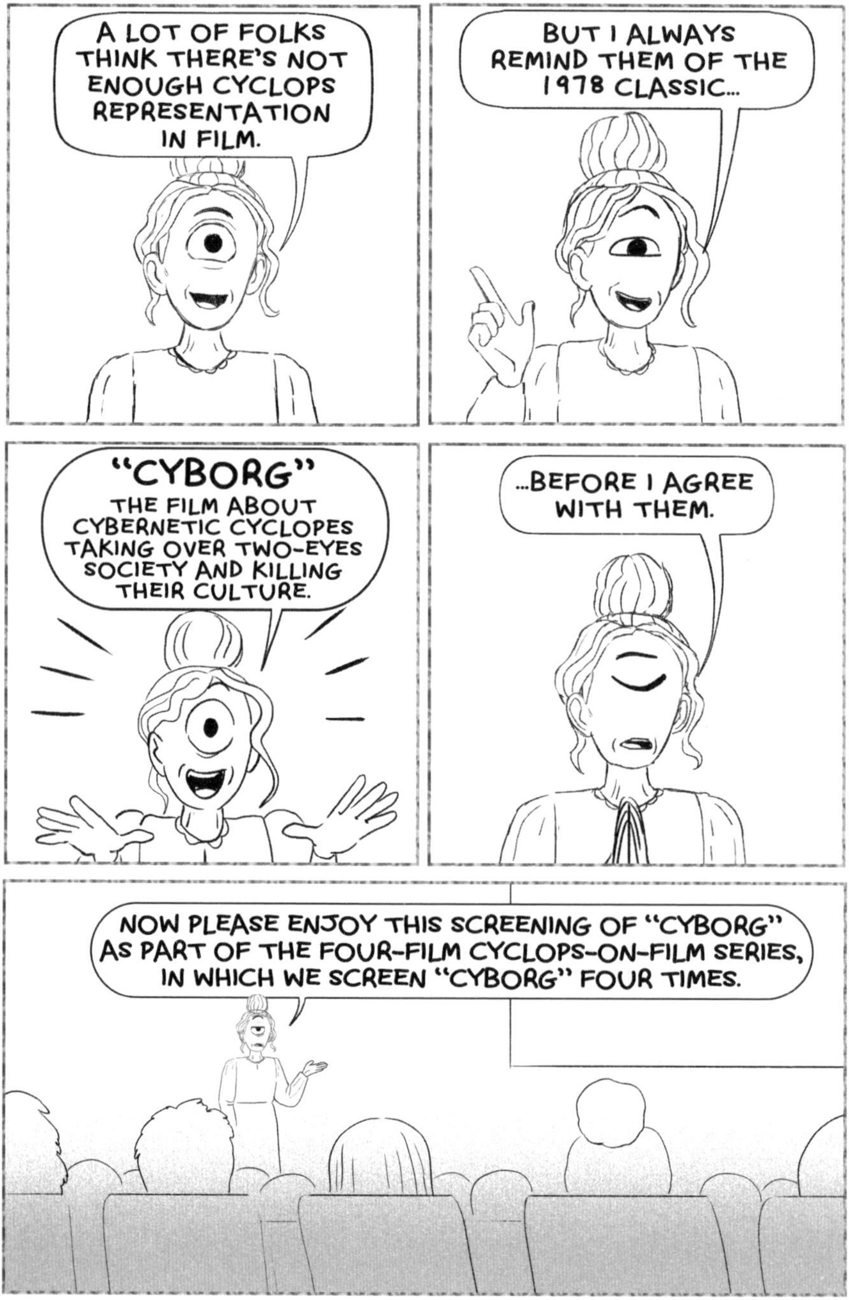

A LOT OF FOLKS THINK THERE'S NOT ENOUGH CYCLOPS REPRESENTATION IN FILM.
BUT I ALWAYS REMIND THEM OF THE 1978 CLASSIC...
"CYBORG" THE FILM ABOUT CYBERNETIC CYCLOPES TAKING OVER TWO-EYES SOCIETY AND KILLING THEIR CULTURE.
...BEFORE I AGREE WITH THEM.
NOW PLEASE ENJOY THIS SCREENING OF "CYBORG" AS PART OF THE FOUR-FILM CYCLOPS-ON-FILM SERIES, IN WHICH WE SCREEN "CYBORG" FOUR TIMES.

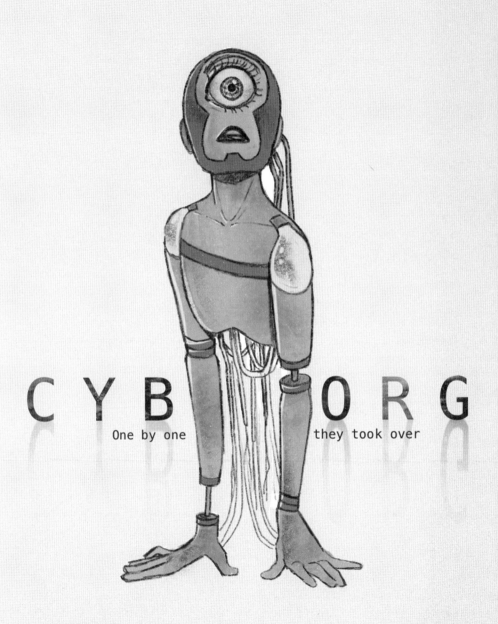

CYB ORG

One by one   they took over

Arj's memories

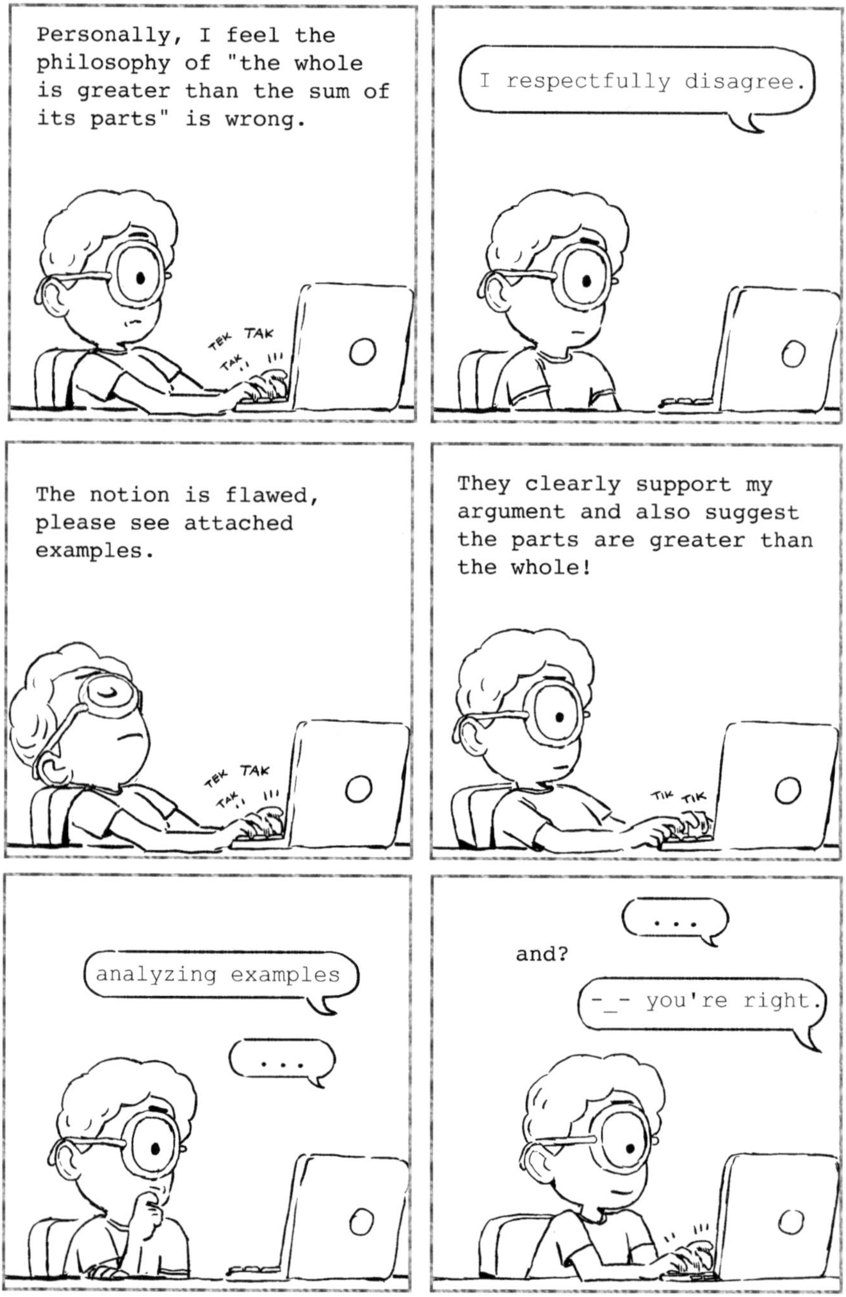

Personally, I feel the philosophy of "the whole is greater than the sum of its parts" is wrong.
TEK TAK
TAK
I respectfully disagree.
The notion is flawed, please see attached examples.
TEK TAK
TAK
They clearly support my argument and also suggest the parts are greater than the whole!
TIK TIK
analyzing examples
...
...
and?
-_- you're right.

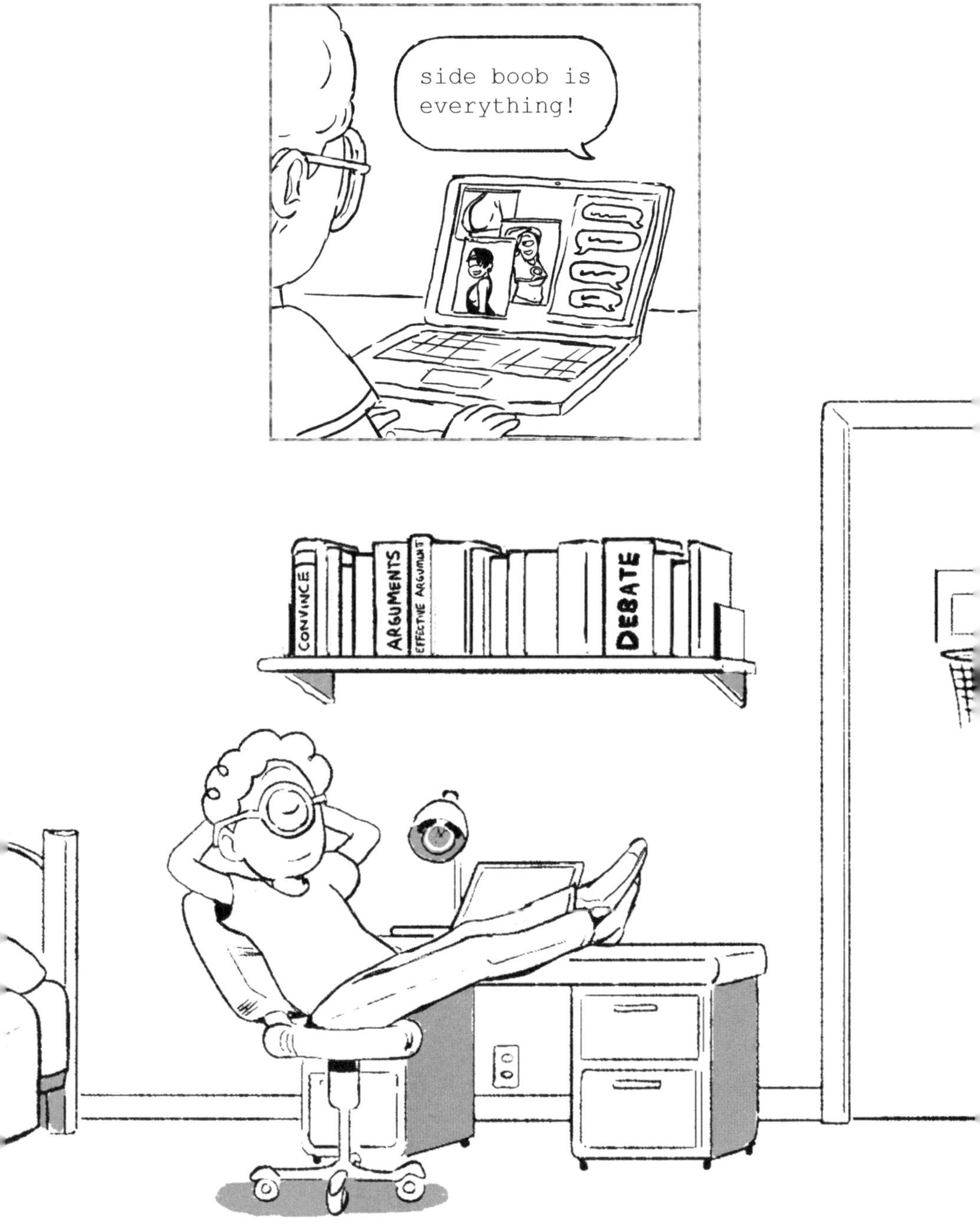
side boob is everything!
CONVINCE
ARGUMENTS
EFFECTIVE ARGUMENT
DEBATE

Arj at therapy

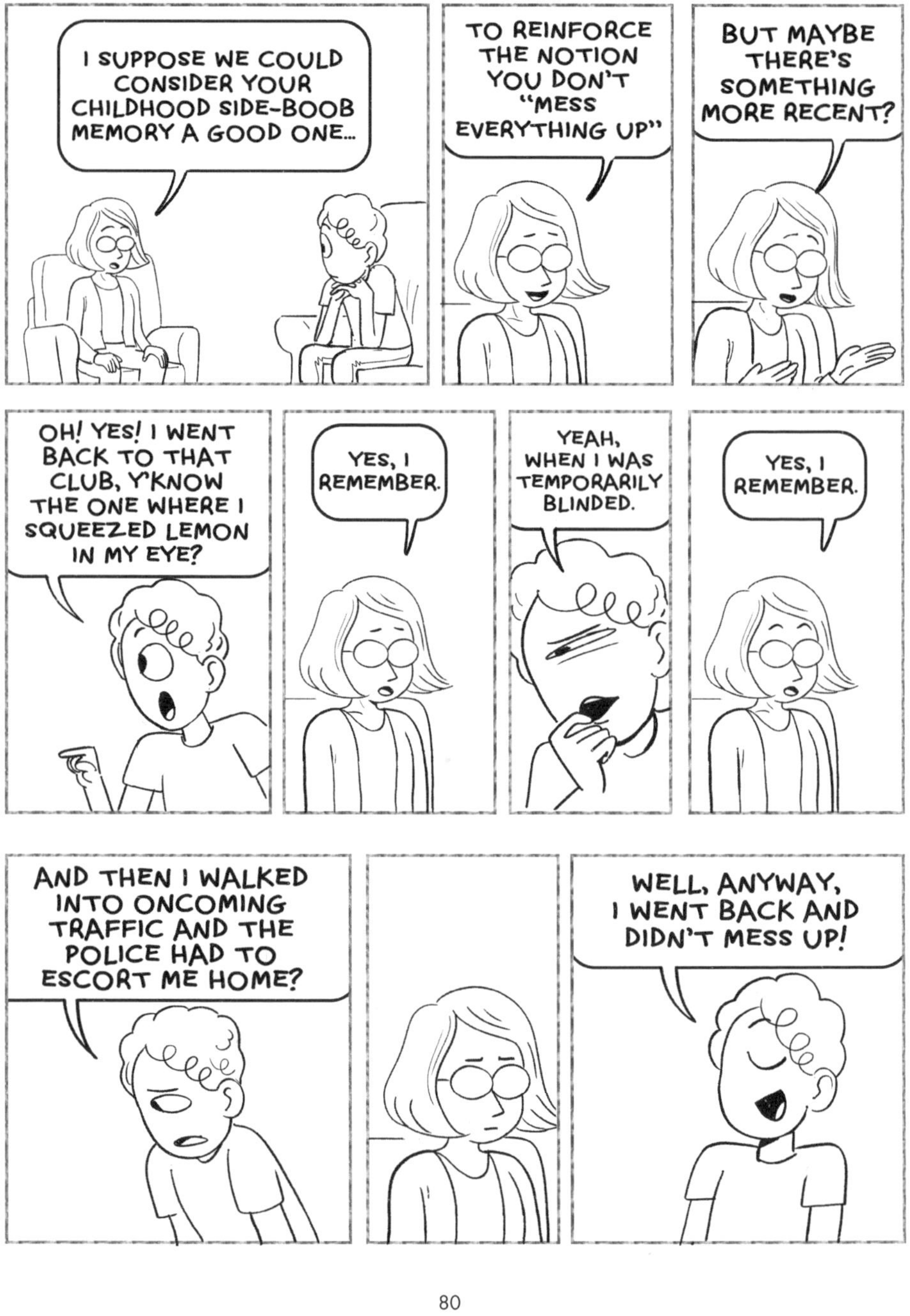
I SUPPOSE WE COULD CONSIDER YOUR CHILDHOOD SIDE-BOOB MEMORY A GOOD ONE...
TO REINFORCE THE NOTION YOU DON'T "MESS EVERYTHING UP"
BUT MAYBE THERE'S SOMETHING MORE RECENT?
OH! YES! I WENT BACK TO THAT CLUB, Y'KNOW THE ONE WHERE I SQUEEZED LEMON IN MY EYE?
YES, I REMEMBER.
YEAH, WHEN I WAS TEMPORARILY BLINDED.
YES, I REMEMBER.
AND THEN I WALKED INTO ONCOMING TRAFFIC AND THE POLICE HAD TO ESCORT ME HOME?
WELL, ANYWAY, I WENT BACK AND DIDN'T MESS UP!

Comic title pending...

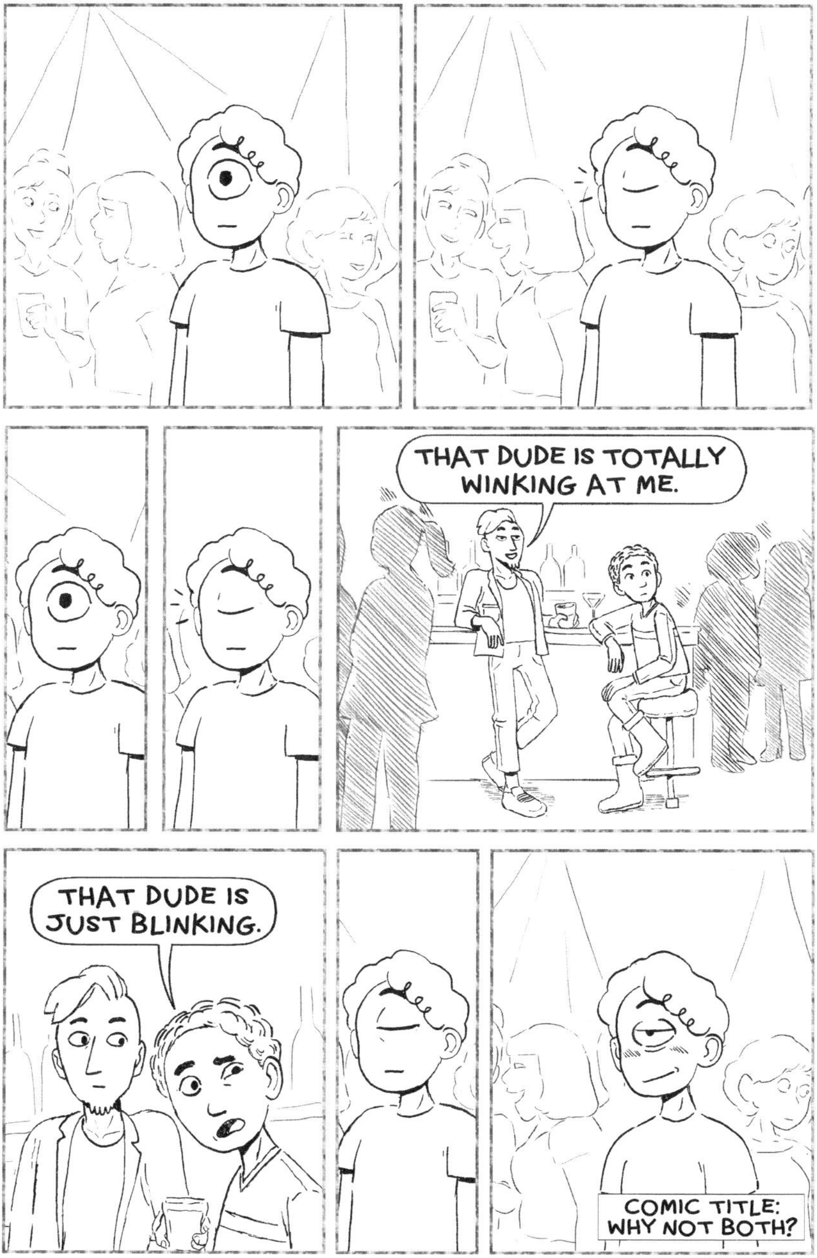
THAT DUDE IS TOTALLY WINKING AT ME.
THAT DUDE IS JUST BLINKING.
COMIC TITLE: WHY NOT BOTH?

Tote-al mistake

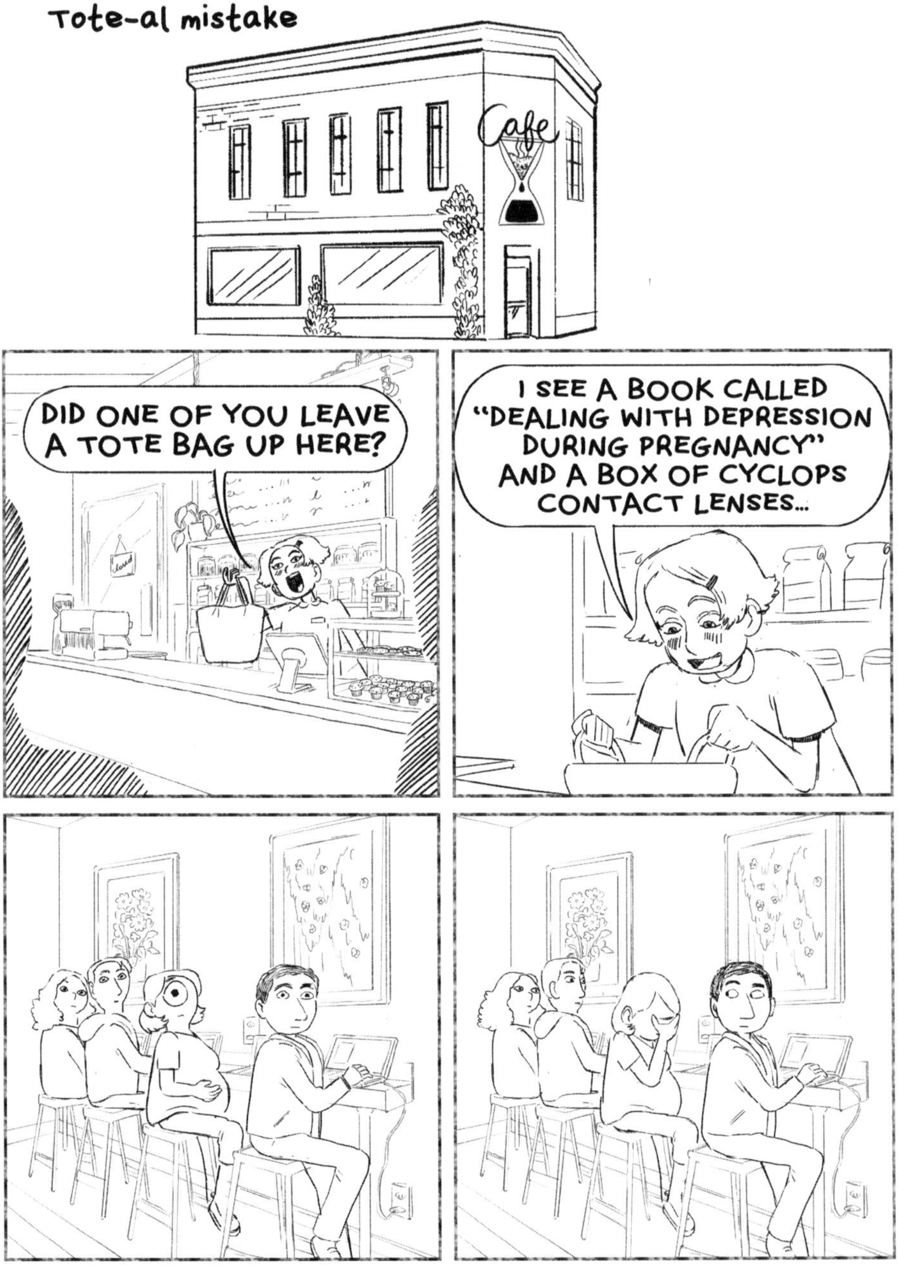
Cafe
closed
DID ONE OF YOU LEAVE A TOTE BAG UP HERE?
I SEE A BOOK CALLED "DEALING WITH DEPRESSION DURING PREGNANCY" AND A BOX OF CYCLOPS CONTACT LENSES...

This Week's Children's Pick!

"Cartemis is a visionary."

"No one else can capture the voice of a young Cyclops girl in a Two-Eyed space!"

"No one can write the story of a young Cyclops girl and her friends better than Cartemis!"

SUZY'S ONE EYE

SUZY'S ONE EYE
SUZY'S ONE EYE

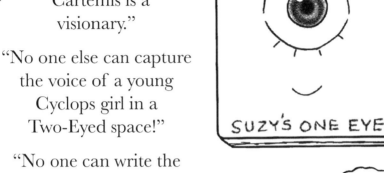

Dr. Leonard Cartemis (68 years old) pictured at his private ranch where he resides alone.

Patches

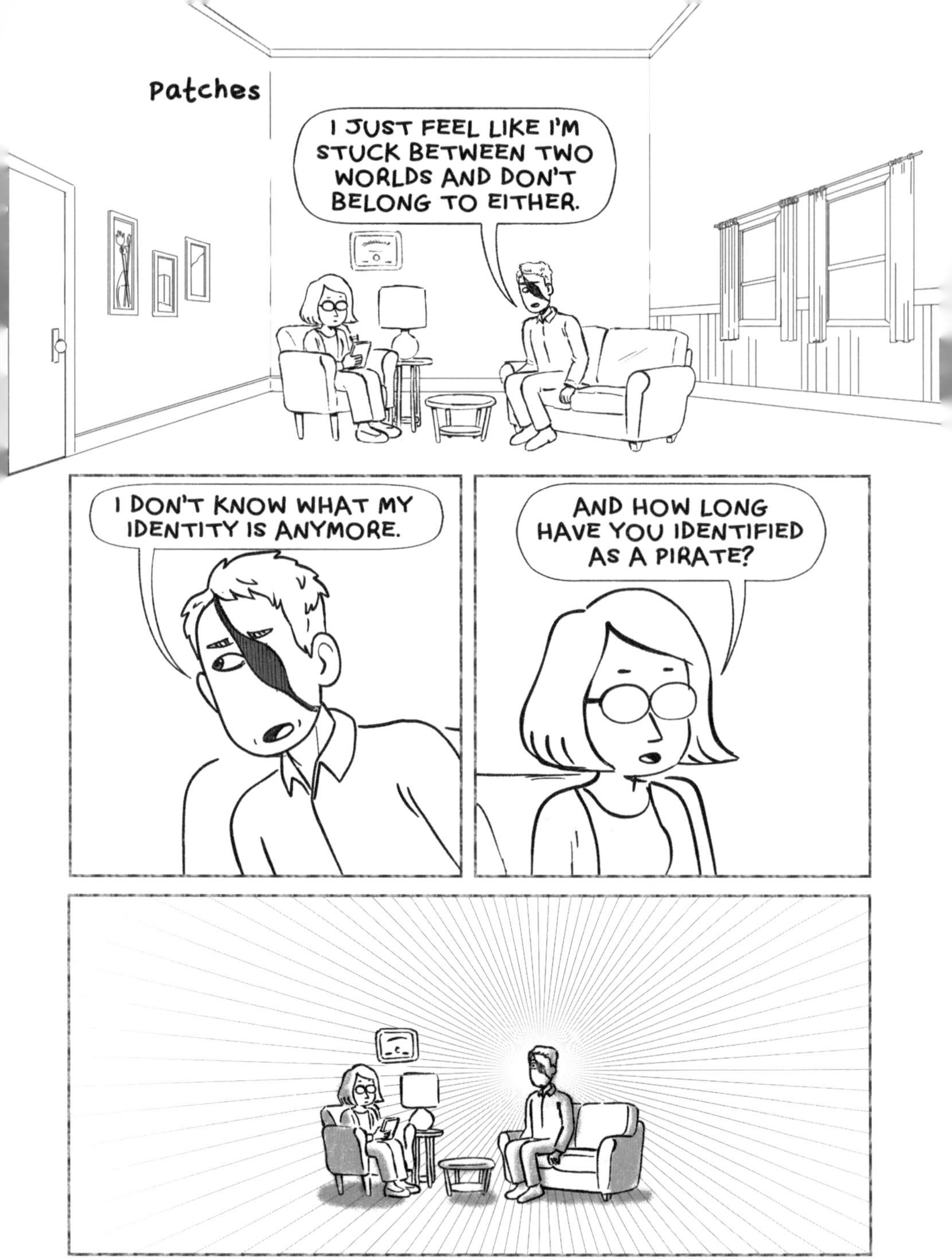
I JUST FEEL LIKE I'M STUCK BETWEEN TWO WORLDS AND DON'T BELONG TO EITHER.
I DON'T KNOW WHAT MY IDENTITY IS ANYMORE.
AND HOW LONG HAVE YOU IDENTIFIED AS A PIRATE?

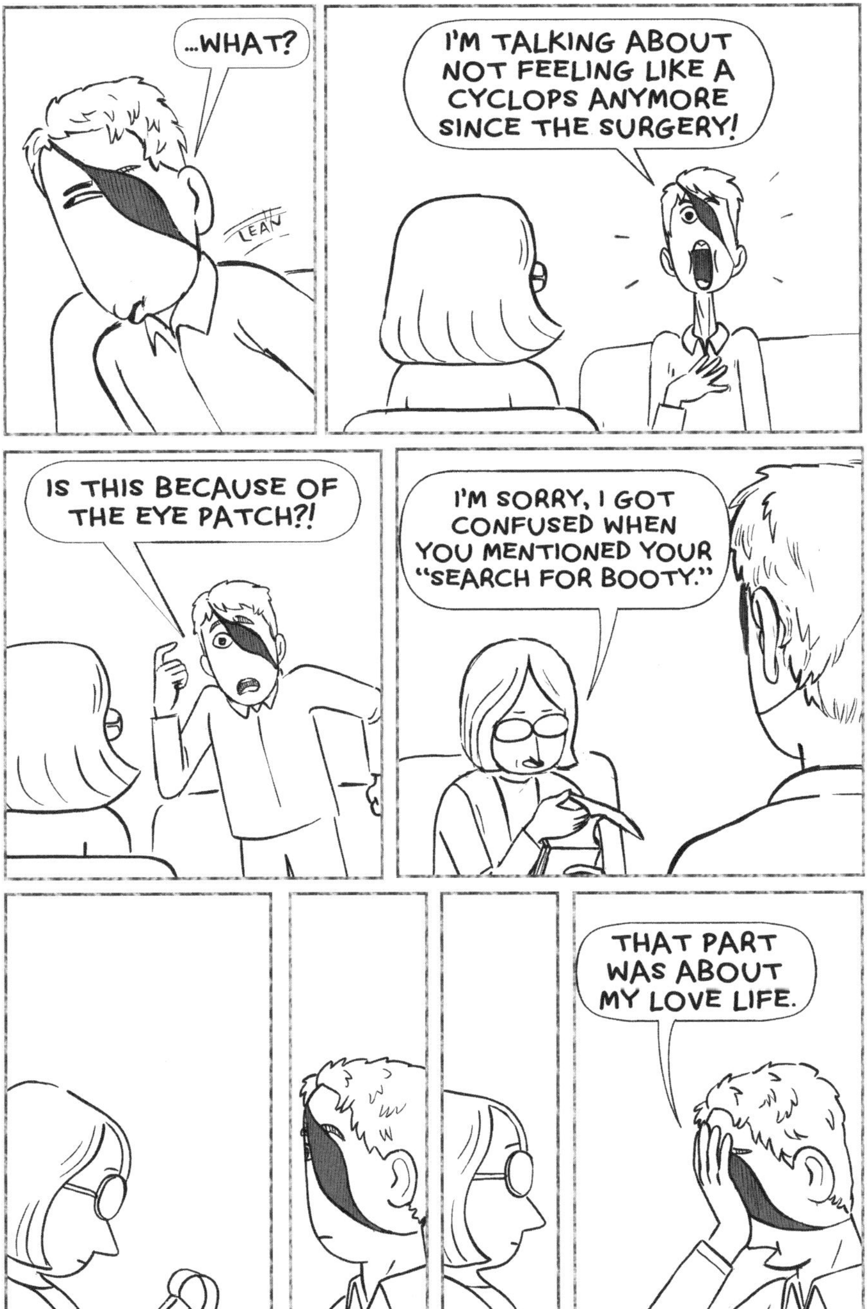
...WHAT?
LEAN
I'M TALKING ABOUT NOT FEELING LIKE A CYCLOPS ANYMORE SINCE THE SURGERY!
IS THIS BECAUSE OF THE EYE PATCH?!
I'M SORRY, I GOT CONFUSED WHEN YOU MENTIONED YOUR "SEARCH FOR BOOTY."
THAT PART WAS ABOUT MY LOVE LIFE.

Texts

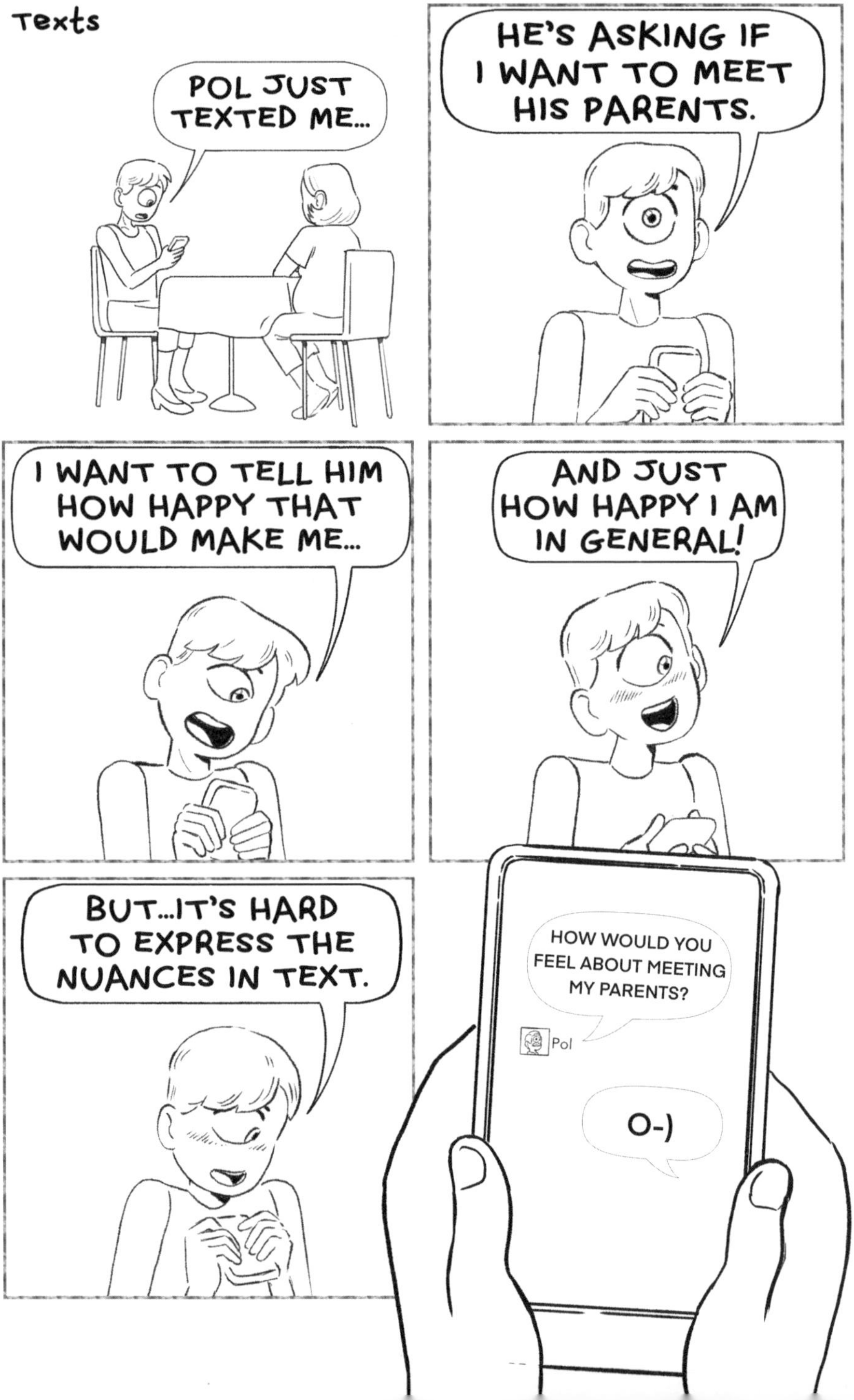
POL JUST TEXTED ME...
HE'S ASKING IF I WANT TO MEET HIS PARENTS.
I WANT TO TELL HIM HOW HAPPY THAT WOULD MAKE ME...
AND JUST HOW HAPPY I AM IN GENERAL!
BUT...IT'S HARD TO EXPRESS THE NUANCES IN TEXT.
HOW WOULD YOU FEEL ABOUT MEETING MY PARENTS?
Pol
O-)

Bron's dream

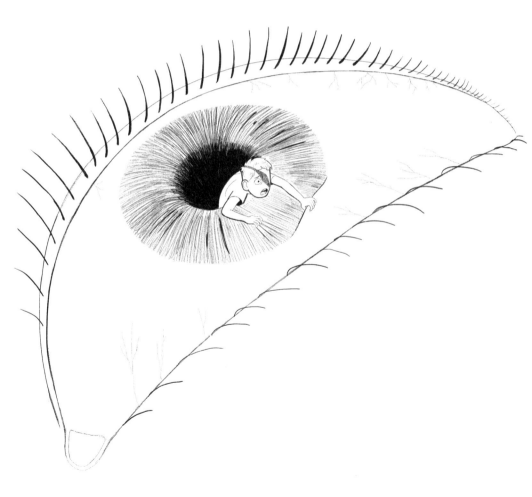

Tones

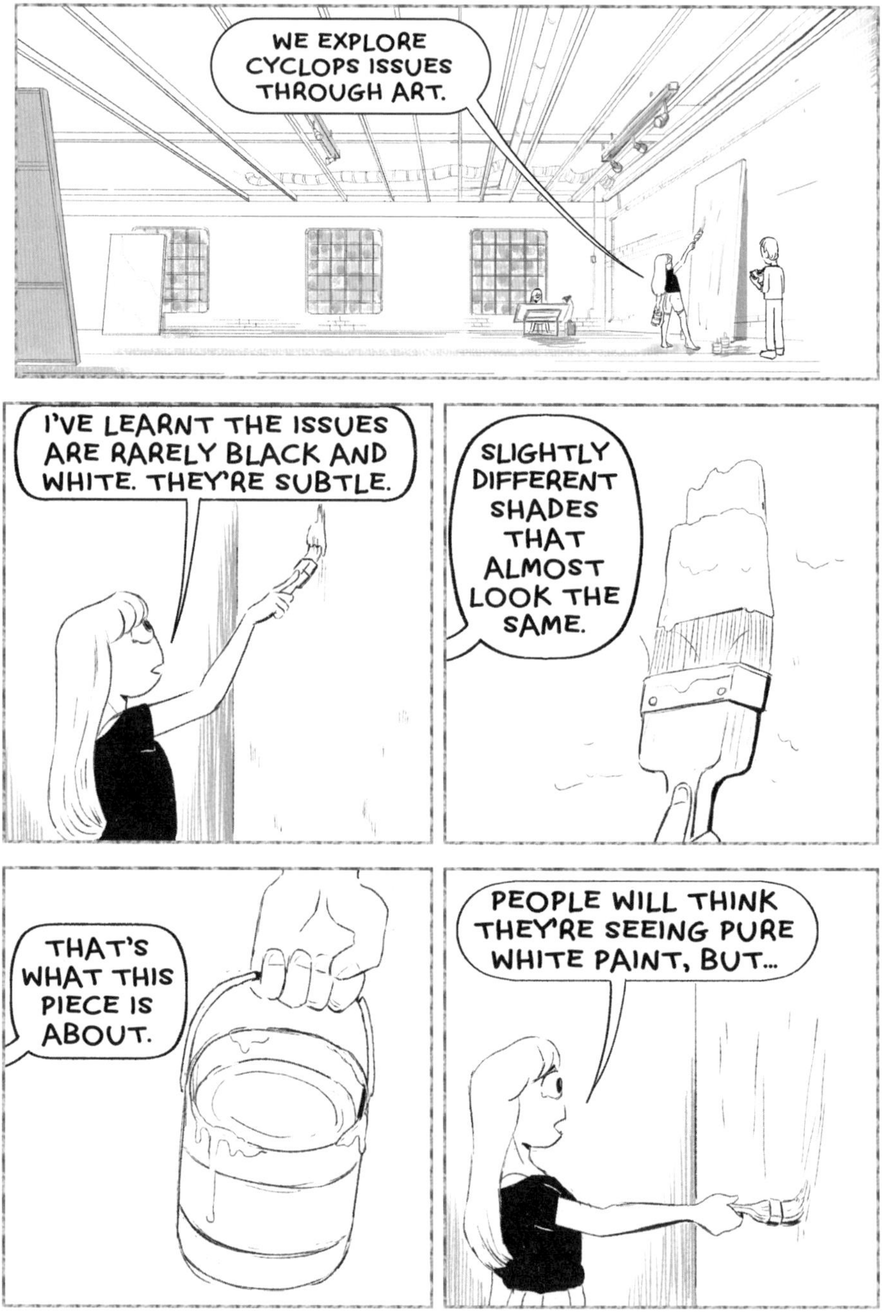
WE EXPLORE CYCLOPS ISSUES THROUGH ART.
I'VE LEARNT THE ISSUES ARE RARELY BLACK AND WHITE. THEY'RE SUBTLE.
SLIGHTLY DIFFERENT SHADES THAT ALMOST LOOK THE SAME.
THAT'S WHAT THIS PIECE IS ABOUT.
PEOPLE WILL THINK THEY'RE SEEING PURE WHITE PAINT, BUT...

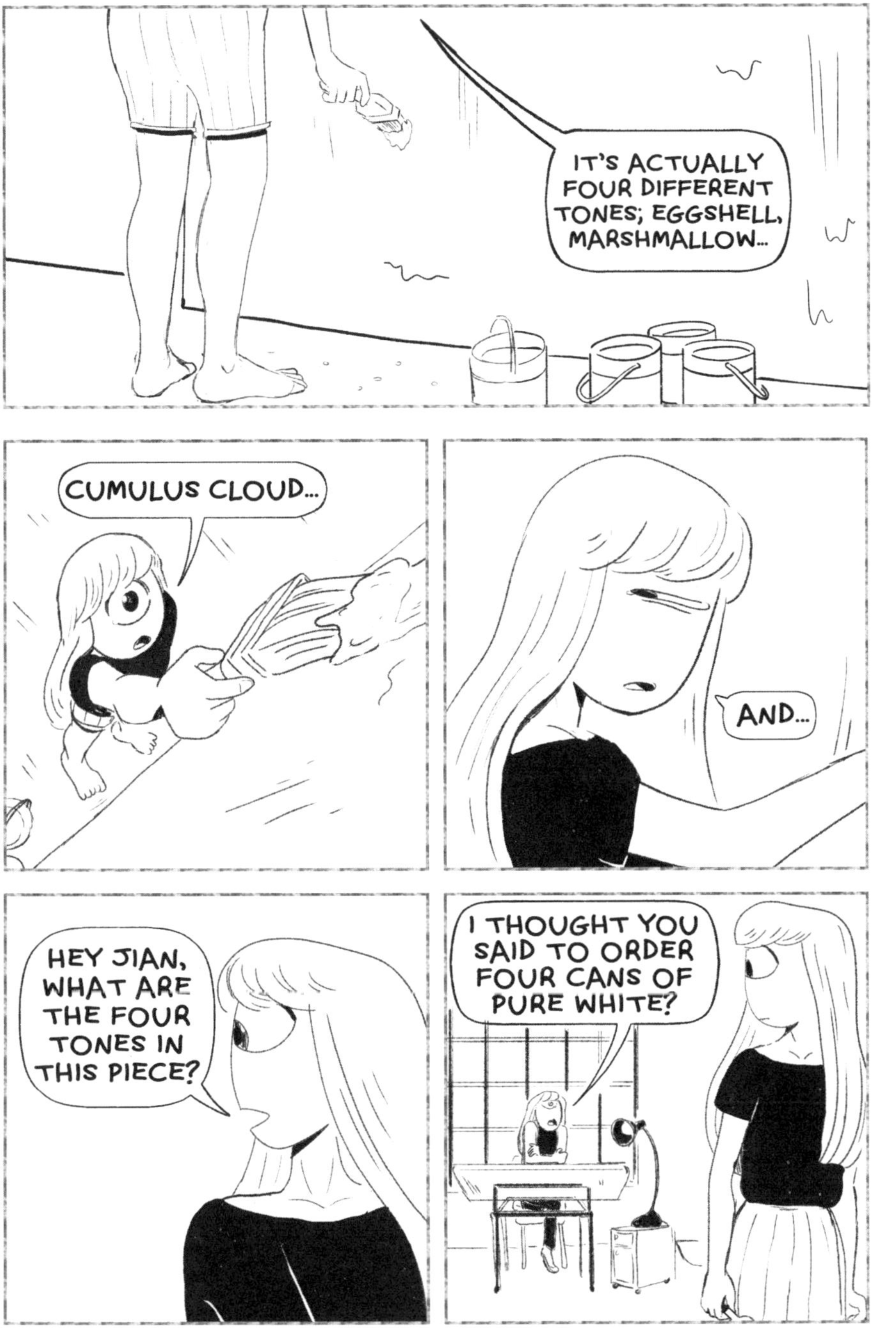
IT'S ACTUALLY FOUR DIFFERENT TONES; EGGSHELL, MARSHMALLOW...
CUMULUS CLOUD...
AND...
HEY JIAN, WHAT ARE THE FOUR TONES IN THIS PIECE?
I THOUGHT YOU SAID TO ORDER FOUR CANS OF PURE WHITE?

Informative

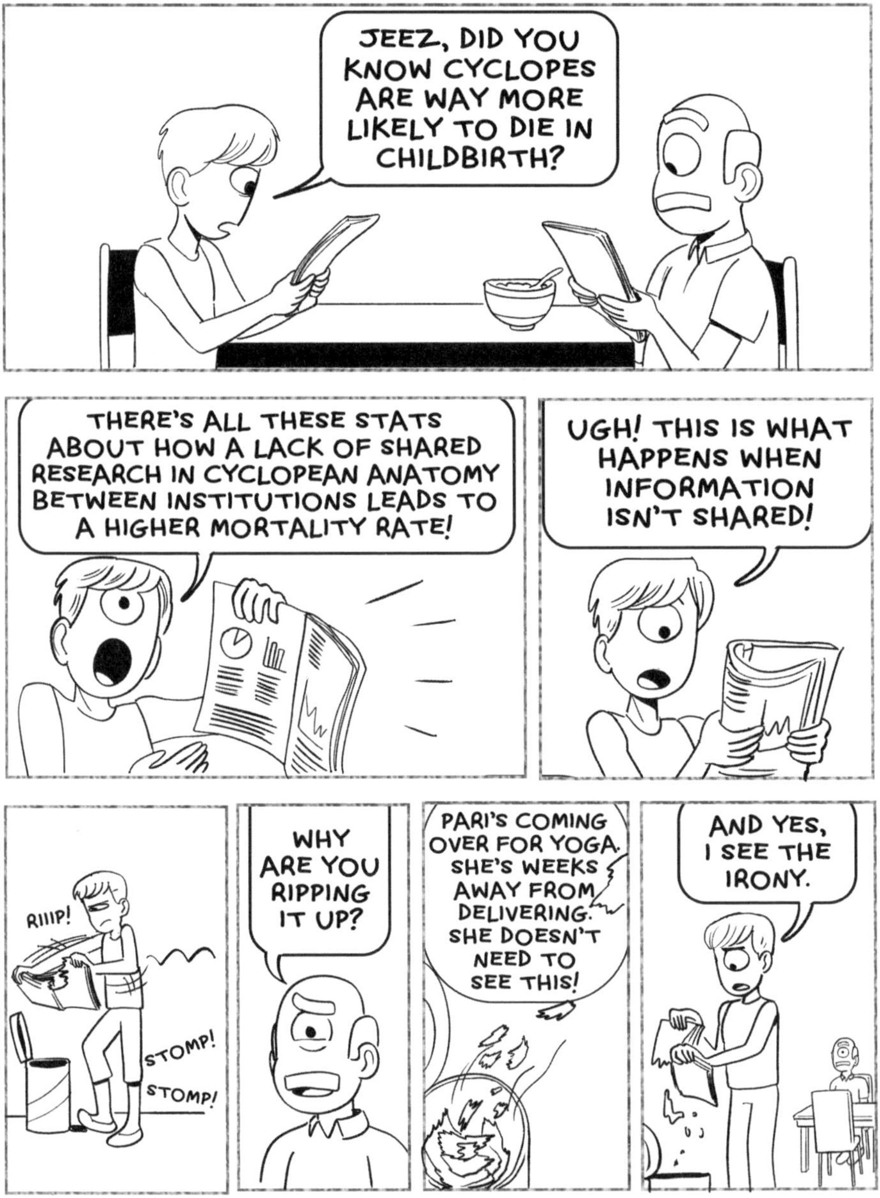
JEEZ, DID YOU KNOW CYCLOPES ARE WAY MORE LIKELY TO DIE IN CHILDBIRTH?
THERE'S ALL THESE STATS ABOUT HOW A LACK OF SHARED RESEARCH IN CYCLOPEAN ANATOMY BETWEEN INSTITUTIONS LEADS TO A HIGHER MORTALITY RATE!
UGH! THIS IS WHAT HAPPENS WHEN INFORMATION ISN'T SHARED!
RIIIP!
STOMP!
STOMP!
WHY ARE YOU RIPPING IT UP?
PARI'S COMING OVER FOR YOGA. SHE'S WEEKS AWAY FROM DELIVERING. SHE DOESN'T NEED TO SEE THIS!
AND YES, I SEE THE IRONY.

Hold and release

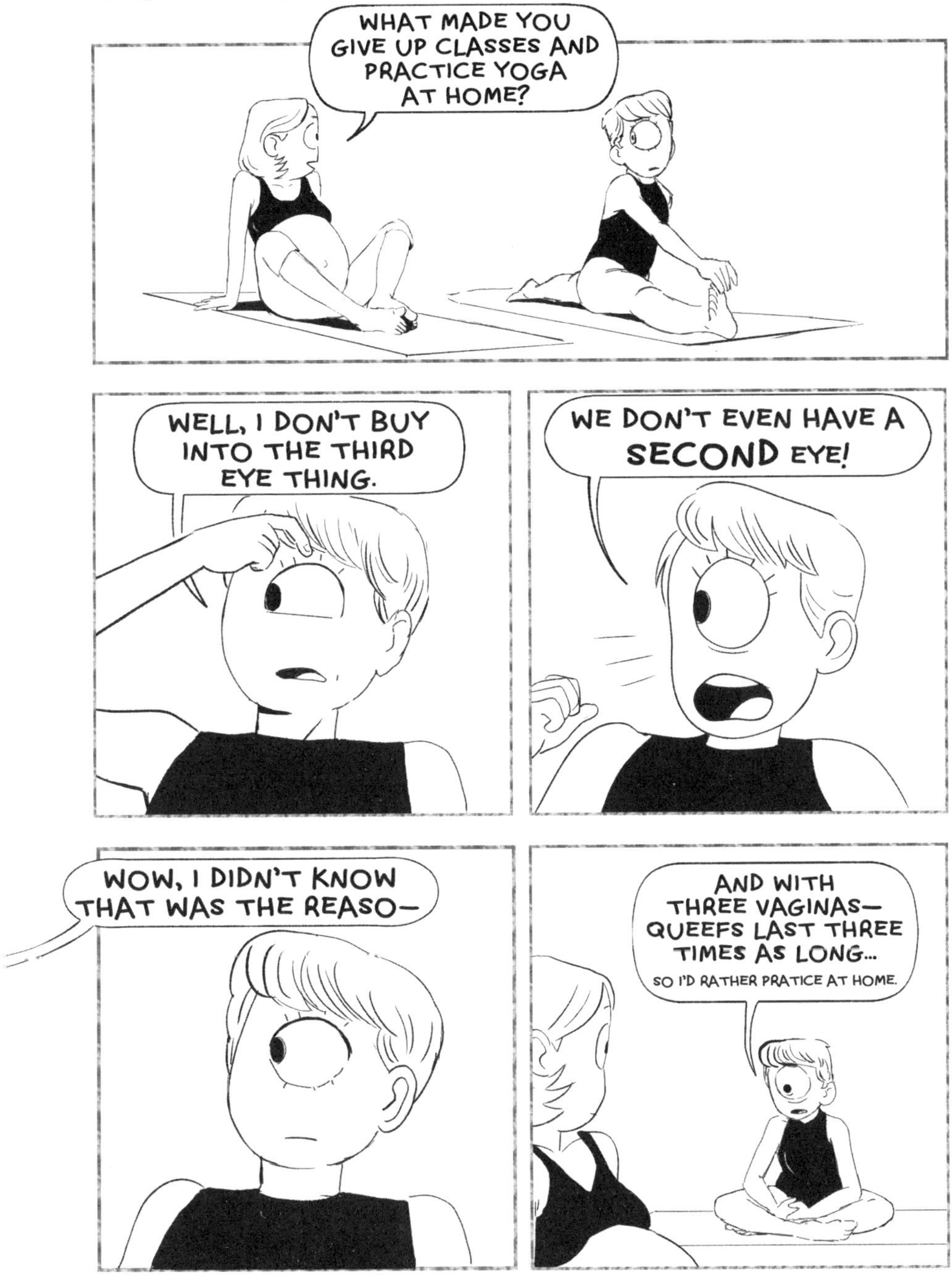
WHAT MADE YOU GIVE UP CLASSES AND PRACTICE YOGA AT HOME?
WELL, I DON'T BUY INTO THE THIRD EYE THING.
WE DON'T EVEN HAVE A SECOND EYE!
WOW, I DIDN'T KNOW THAT WAS THE REASO—
AND WITH THREE VAGINAS— QUEEFS LAST THREE TIMES AS LONG...
SO I'D RATHER PRATICE AT HOME.

seeing clearly

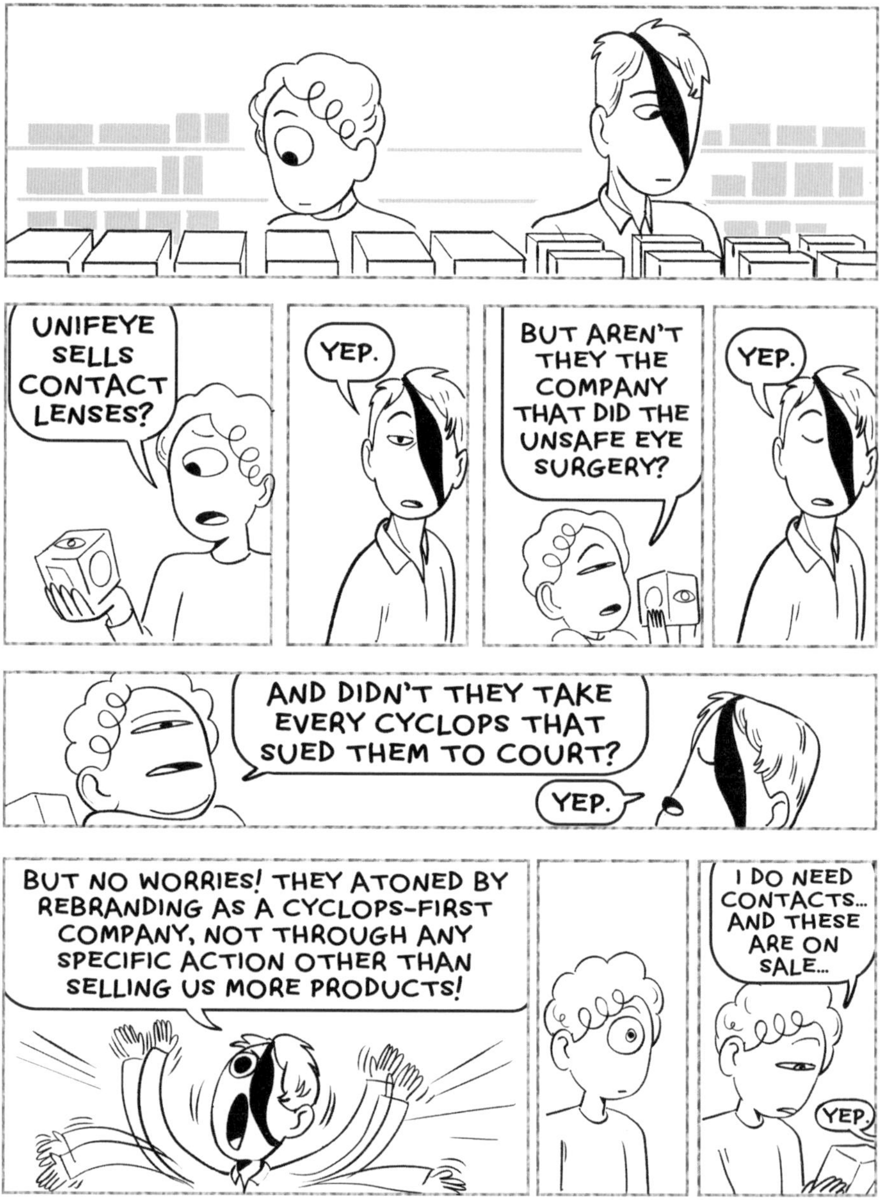
UNIFEYE SELLS CONTACT LENSES?
YEP.
BUT AREN'T THEY THE COMPANY THAT DID THE UNSAFE EYE SURGERY?
YEP.
AND DIDN'T THEY TAKE EVERY CYCLOPS THAT SUED THEM TO COURT?
YEP.
BUT NO WORRIES! THEY ATONED BY REBRANDING AS A CYCLOPS-FIRST COMPANY, NOT THROUGH ANY SPECIFIC ACTION OTHER THAN SELLING US MORE PRODUCTS!
I DO NEED CONTACTS... AND THESE ARE ON SALE...
YEP.

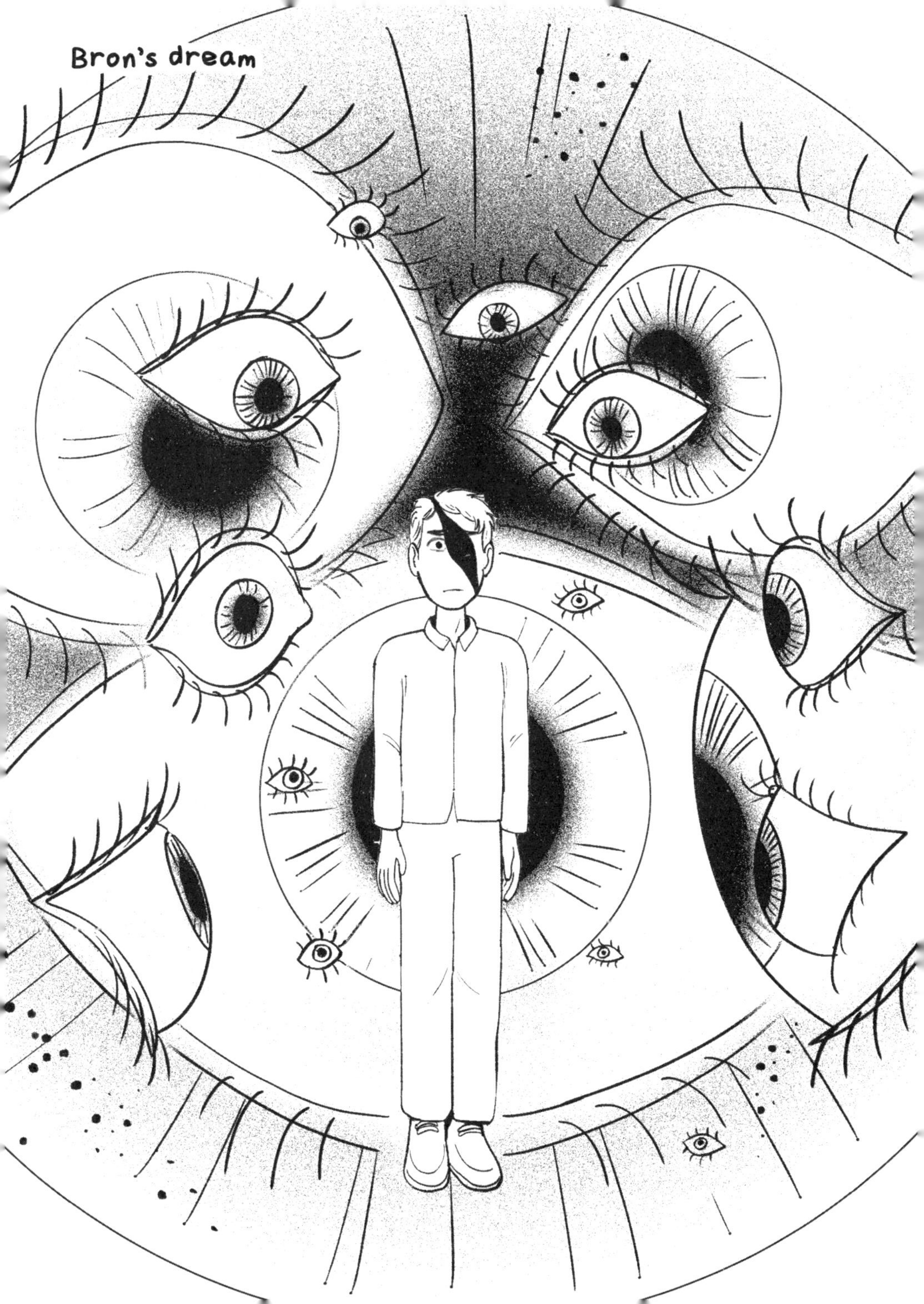
Bron's dream

Back to work

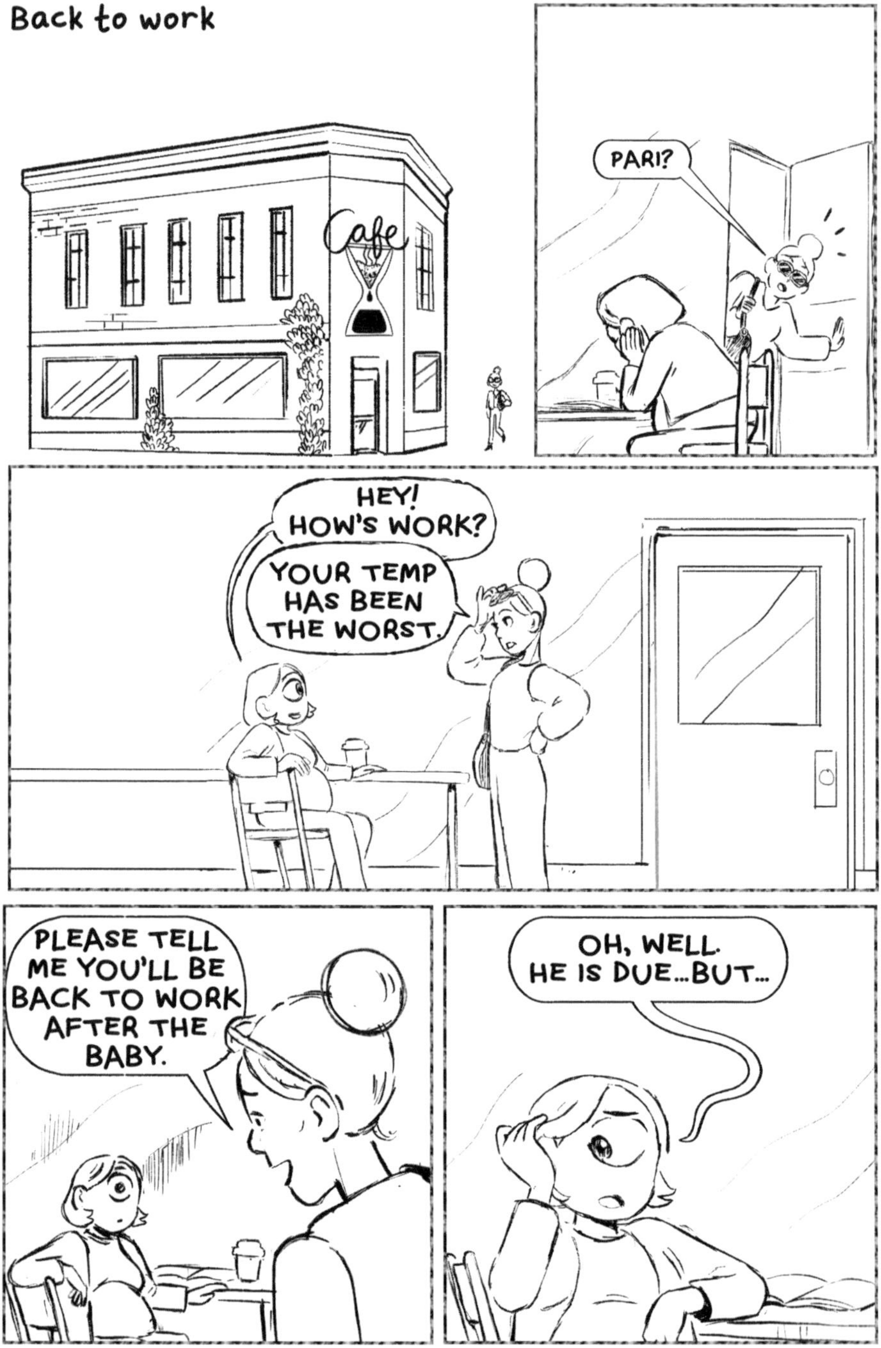
Cafe
PARI?
HEY! HOW'S WORK?
YOUR TEMP HAS BEEN THE WORST.
PLEASE TELL ME YOU'LL BE BACK TO WORK AFTER THE BABY.
OH, WELL. HE IS DUE...BUT...

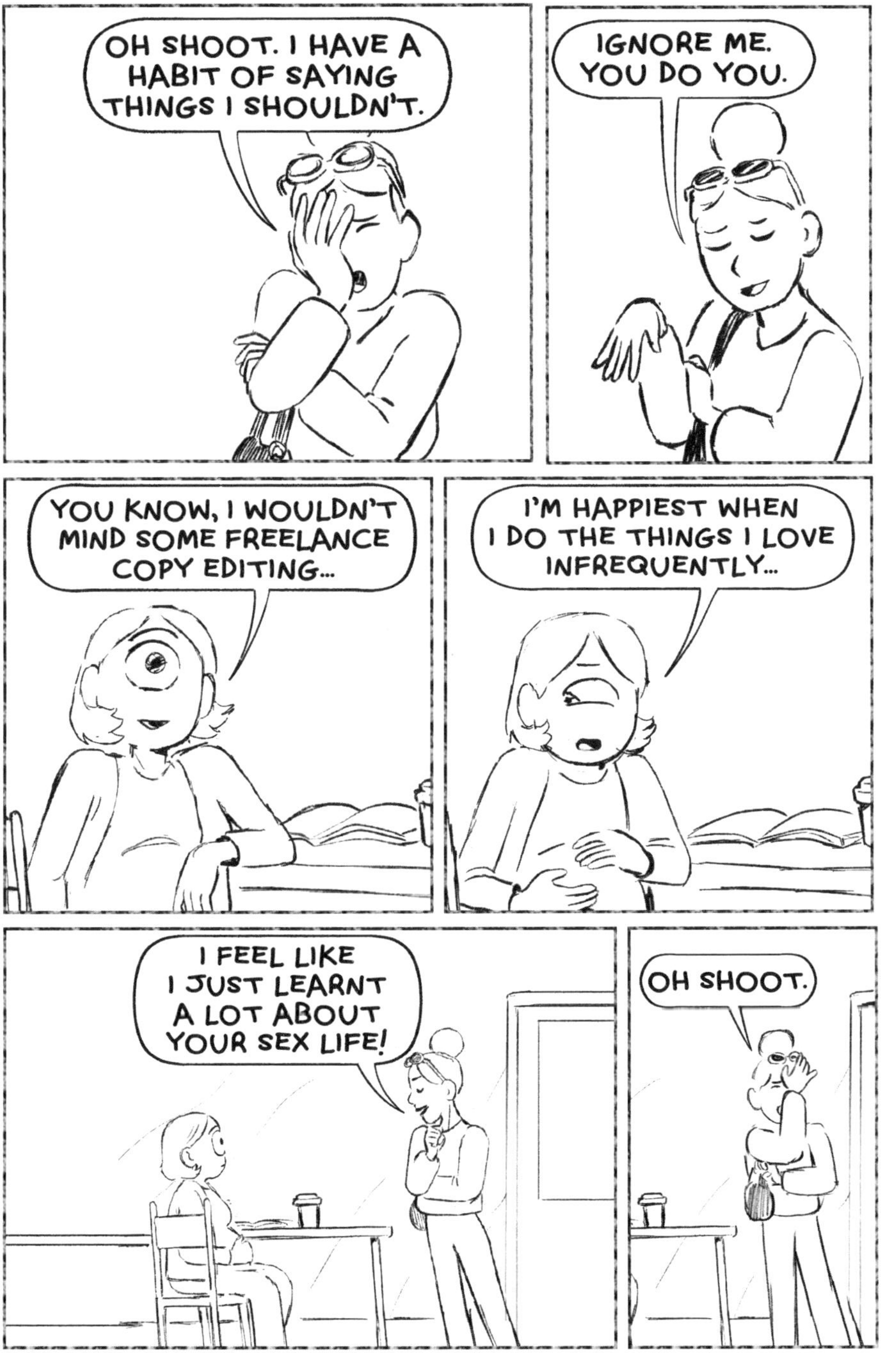
OH SHOOT. I HAVE A HABIT OF SAYING THINGS I SHOULDN'T.
IGNORE ME. YOU DO YOU.
YOU KNOW, I WOULDN'T MIND SOME FREELANCE COPY EDITING...
I'M HAPPIEST WHEN I DO THE THINGS I LOVE INFREQUENTLY...
I FEEL LIKE I JUST LEARNT A LOT ABOUT YOUR SEX LIFE!
OH SHOOT.

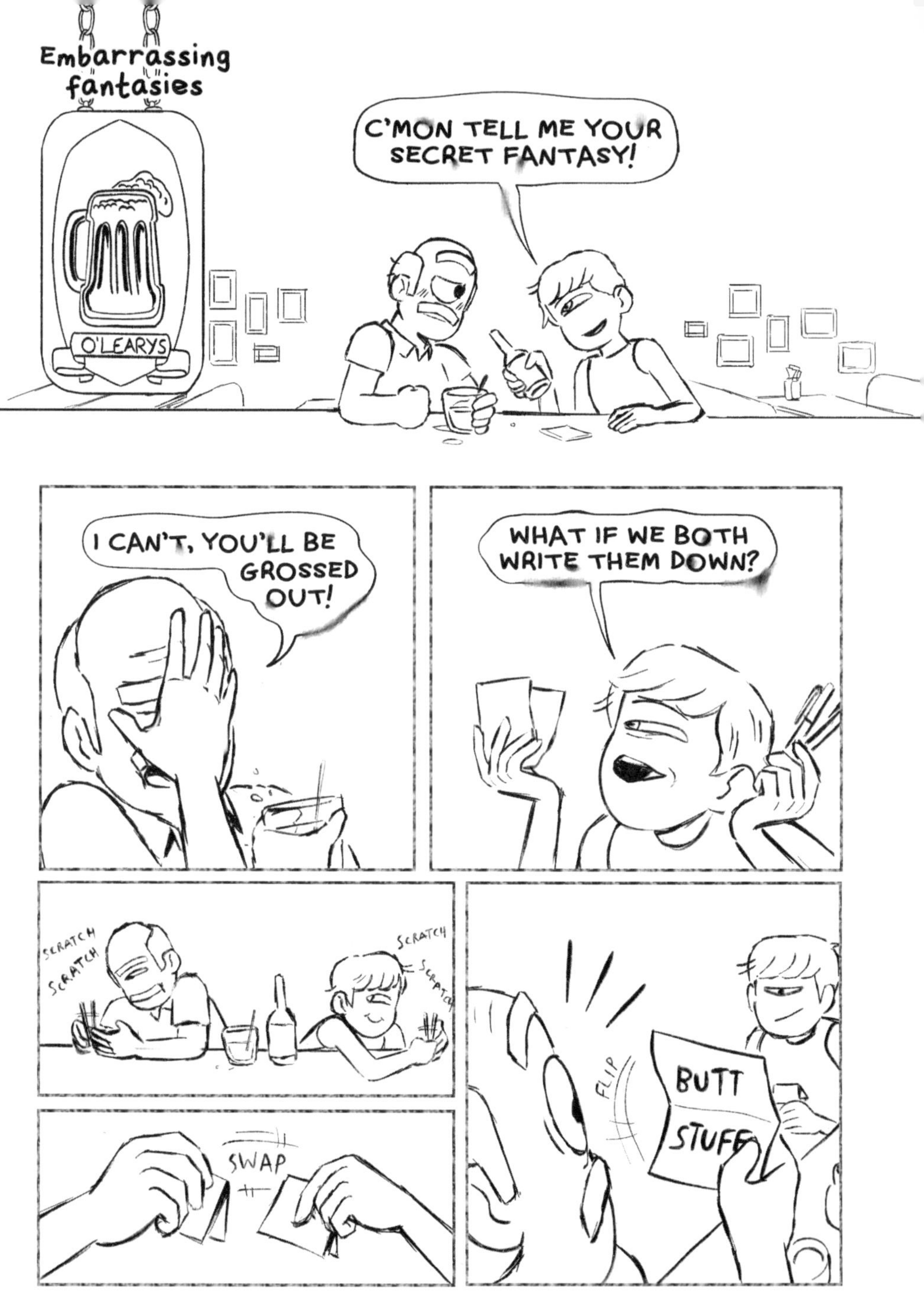
Embarrassing fantasies
O'LEARYS
C'MON TELL ME YOUR SECRET FANTASY!
I CAN'T, YOU'LL BE GROSSED OUT!
WHAT IF WE BOTH WRITE THEM DOWN?
SCRATCH SCRATCH
SCRATCH SCRATCH
SWAP
FLIP
BUTT STUFF

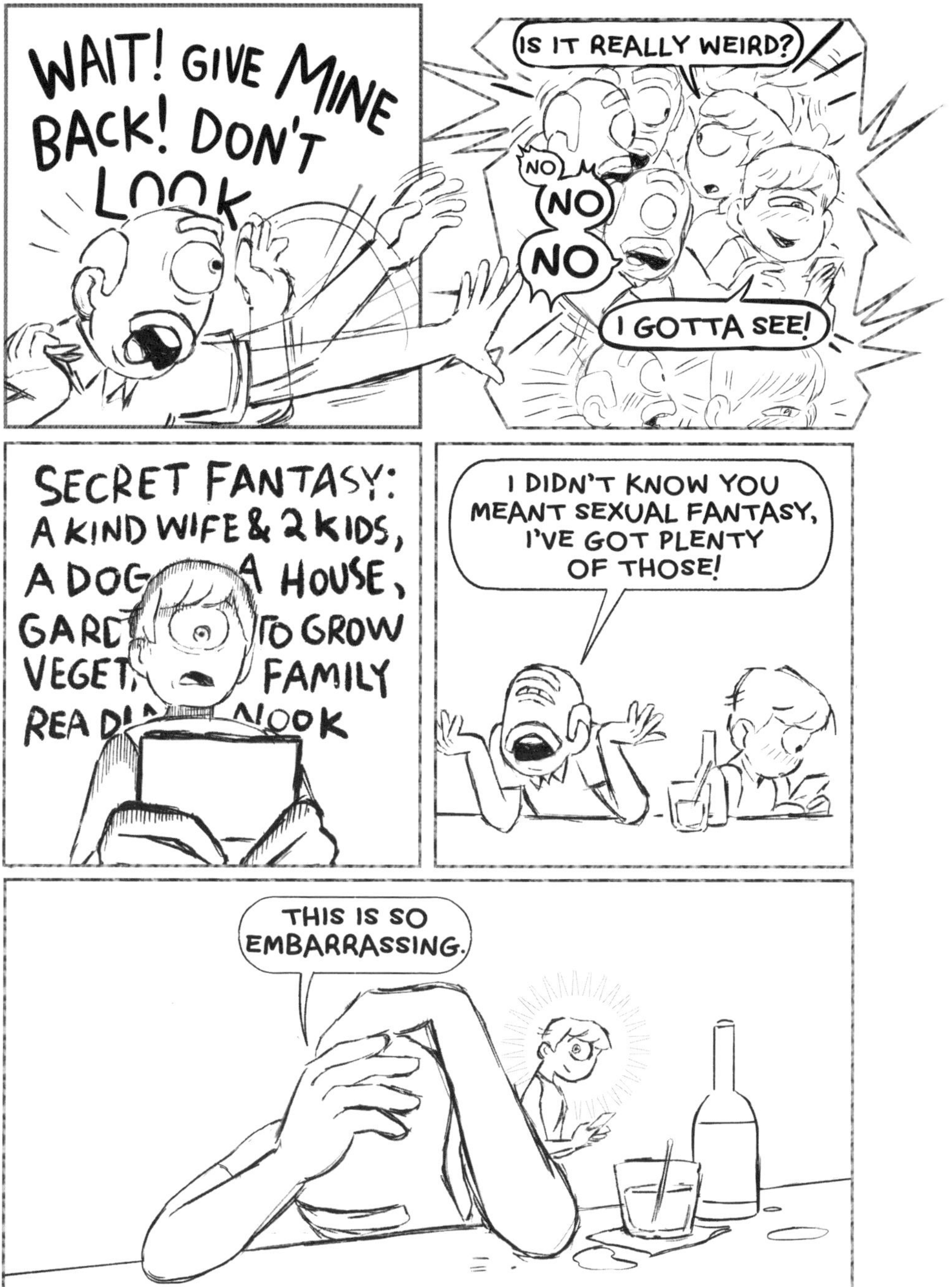
WAIT! GIVE MINE BACK! DON'T LOOK
IS IT REALLY WEIRD?
NO
NO
NO
I GOTTA SEE!
SECRET FANTASY:
A KIND WIFE & 2 KIDS,
A DOG A HOUSE,
GARD TO GROW
VEGET FAMILY
REA NOOK
I DIDN'T KNOW YOU MEANT SEXUAL FANTASY, I'VE GOT PLENTY OF THOSE!
THIS IS SO EMBARRASSING.

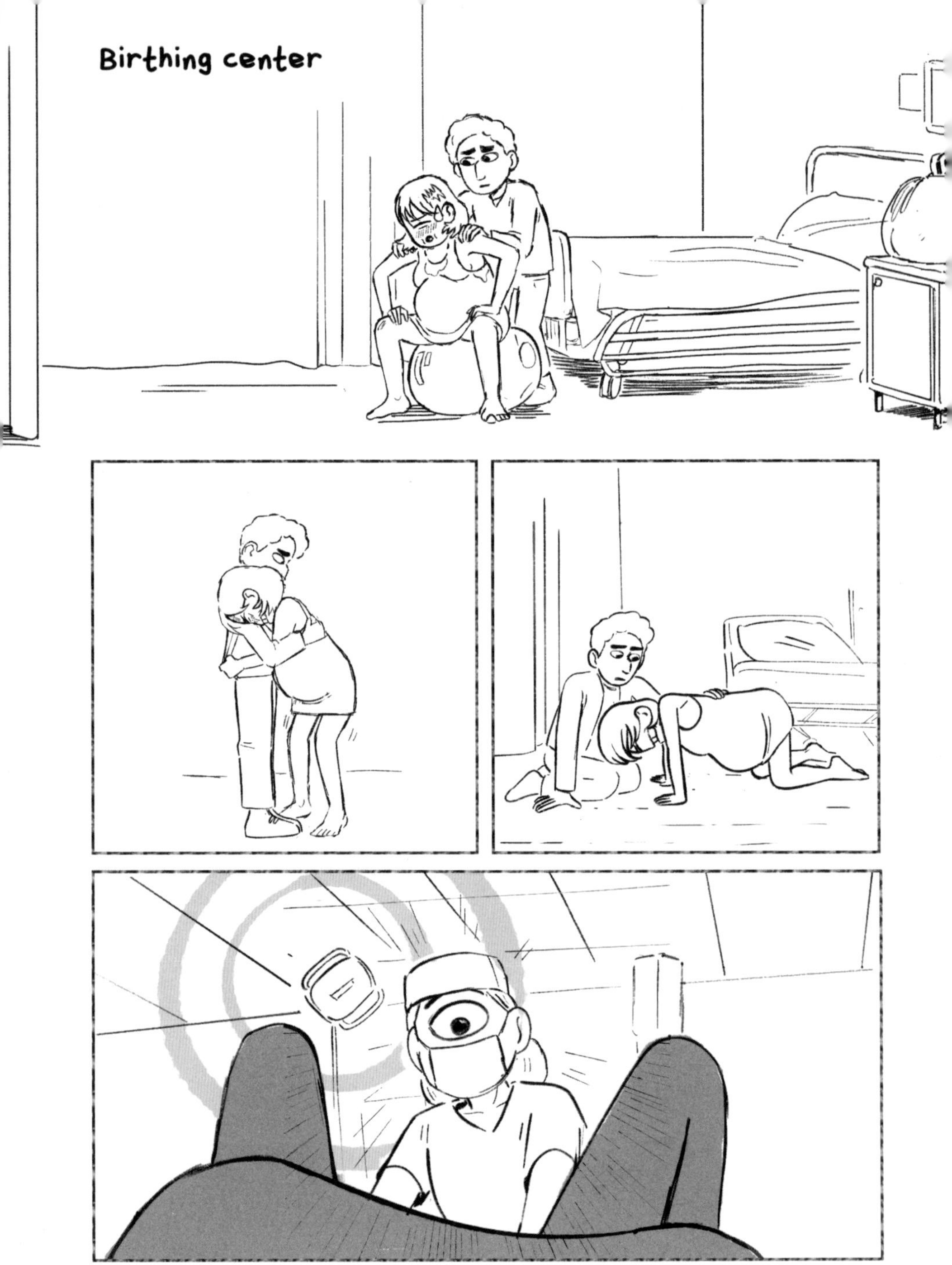
Birthing center

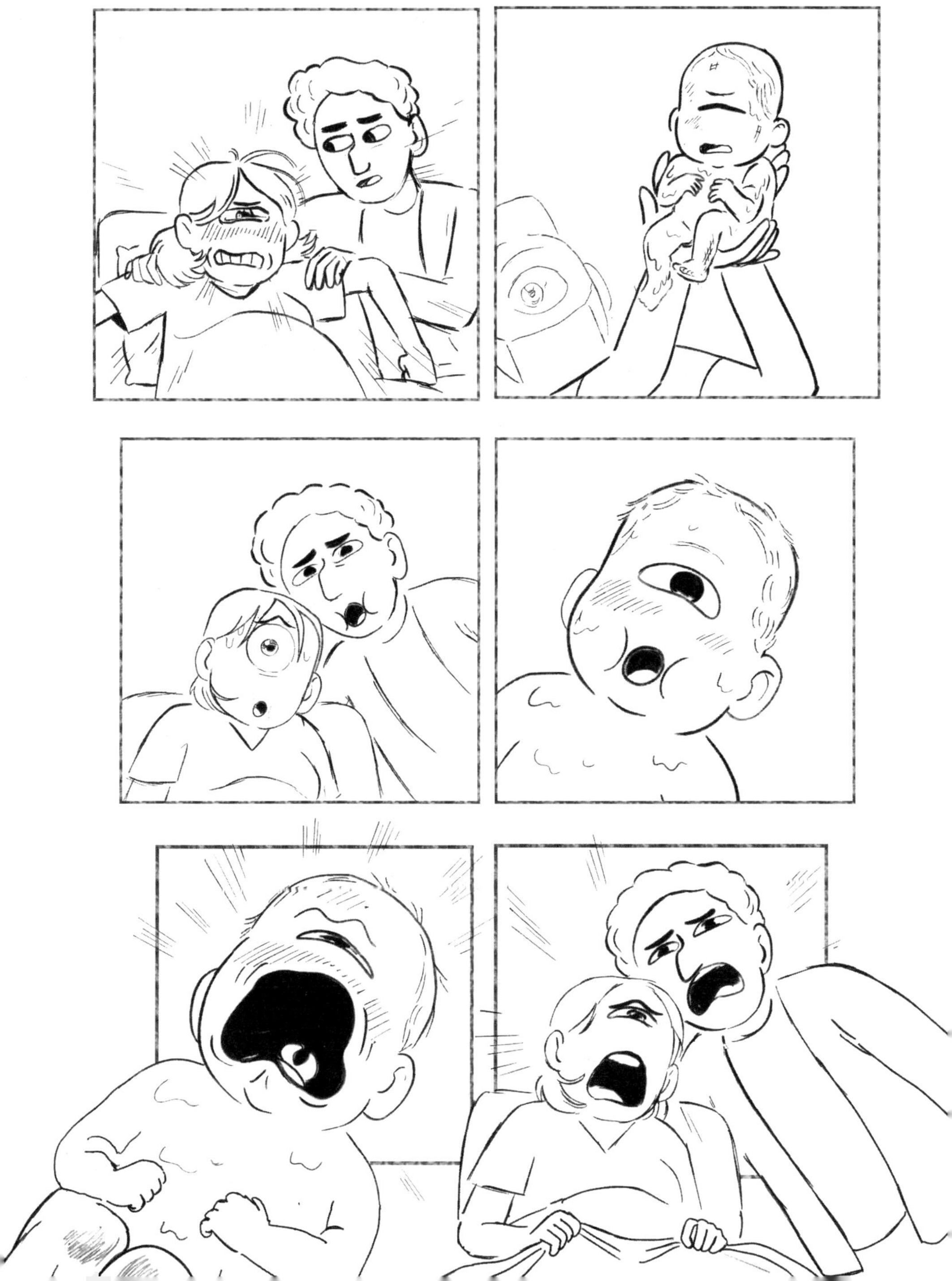

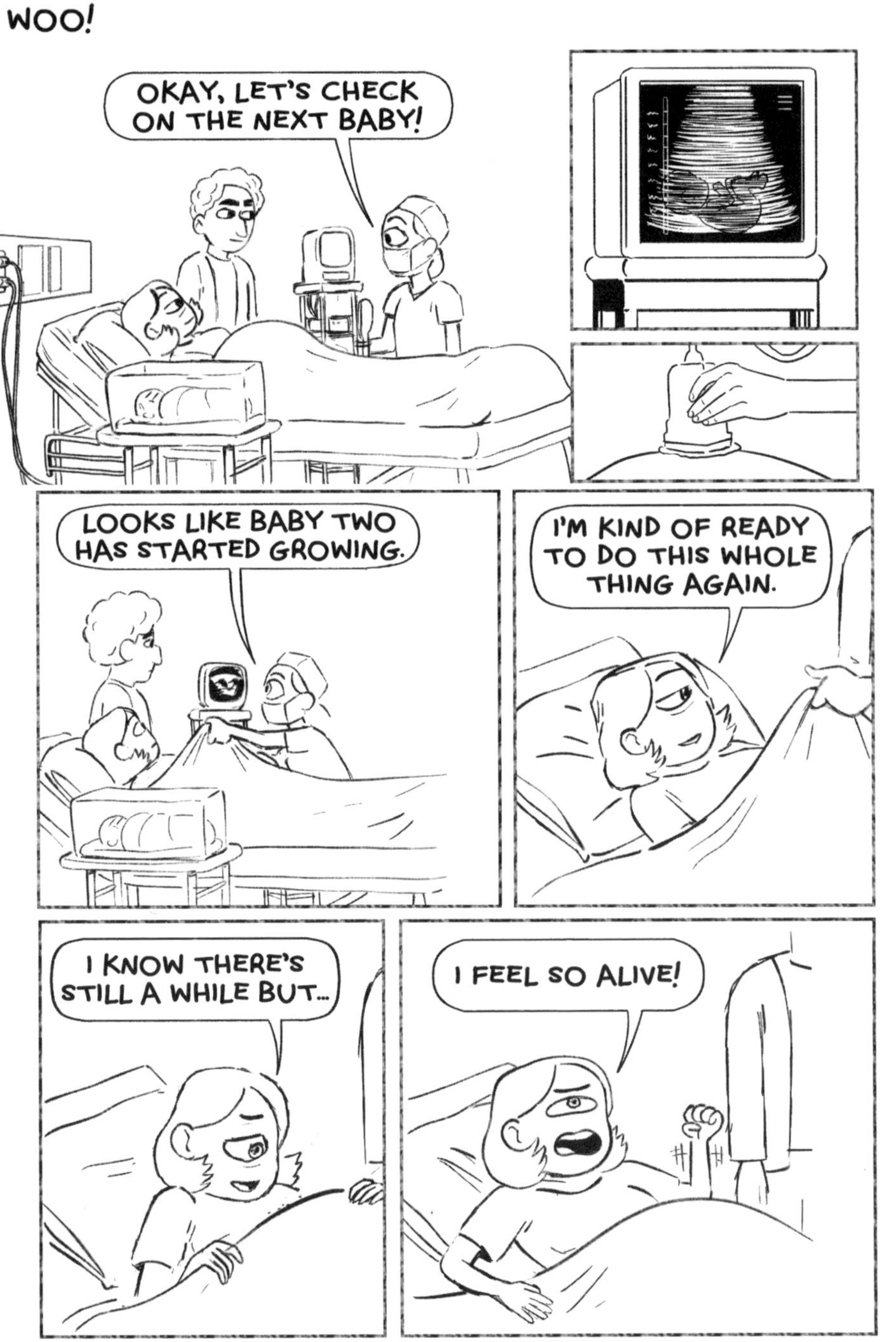
WOO!
OKAY, LET'S CHECK ON THE NEXT BABY!
LOOKS LIKE BABY TWO HAS STARTED GROWING.
I'M KIND OF READY TO DO THIS WHOLE THING AGAIN.
I KNOW THERE'S STILL A WHILE BUT...
I FEEL SO ALIVE!

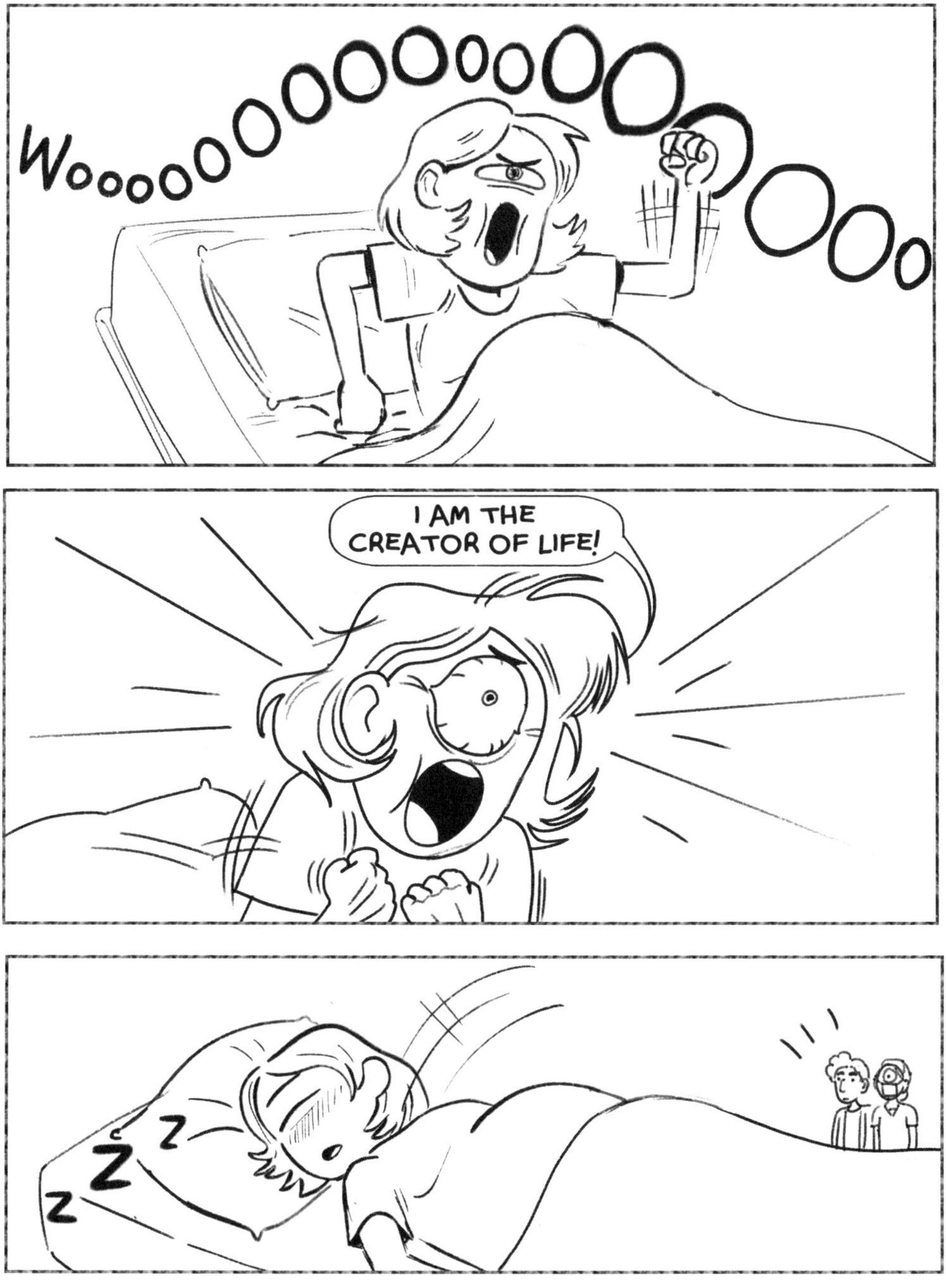
WoooooOOOOOOOooOOOOOOOOOo
I AM THE CREATOR OF LIFE!
zZz

say it without saying it

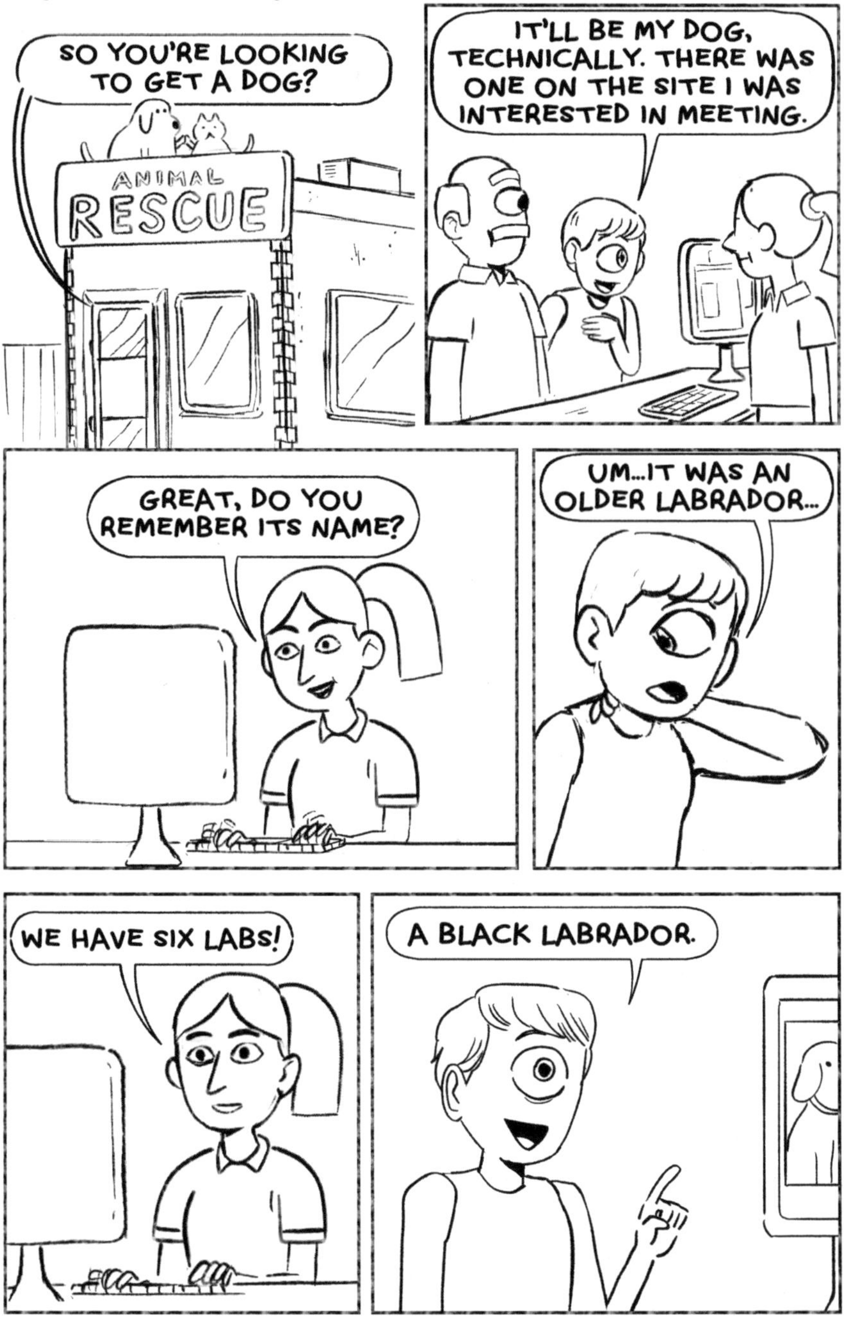
SO YOU'RE LOOKING TO GET A DOG?
ANIMAL RESCUE
IT'LL BE MY DOG, TECHNICALLY. THERE WAS ONE ON THE SITE I WAS INTERESTED IN MEETING.
GREAT, DO YOU REMEMBER ITS NAME?
UM...IT WAS AN OLDER LABRADOR...
WE HAVE SIX LABS!
A BLACK LABRADOR.

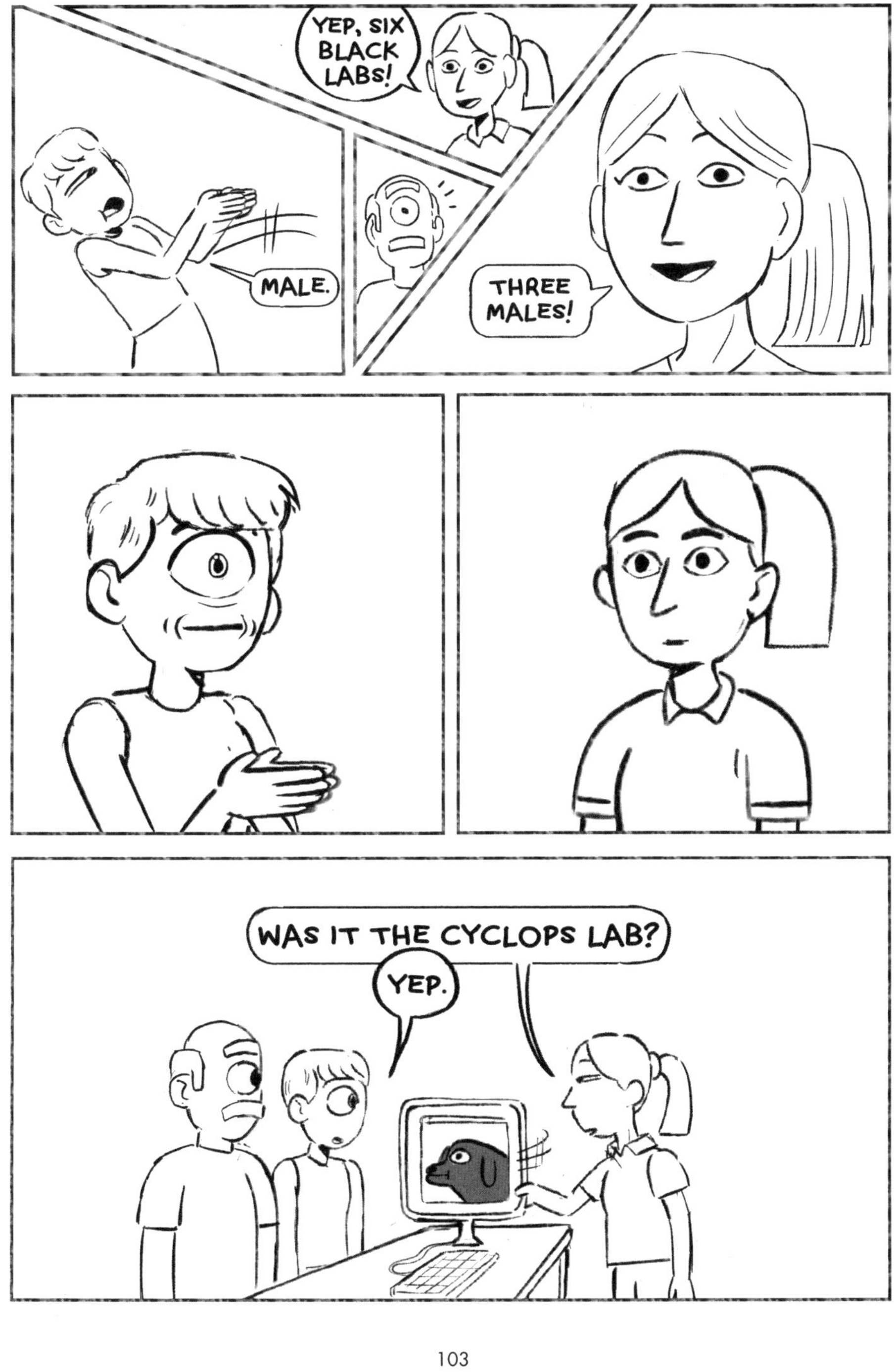

YEP, SIX BLACK LABS!
MALE.
THREE MALES!
WAS IT THE CYCLOPS LAB?
YEP.

Bully dogs

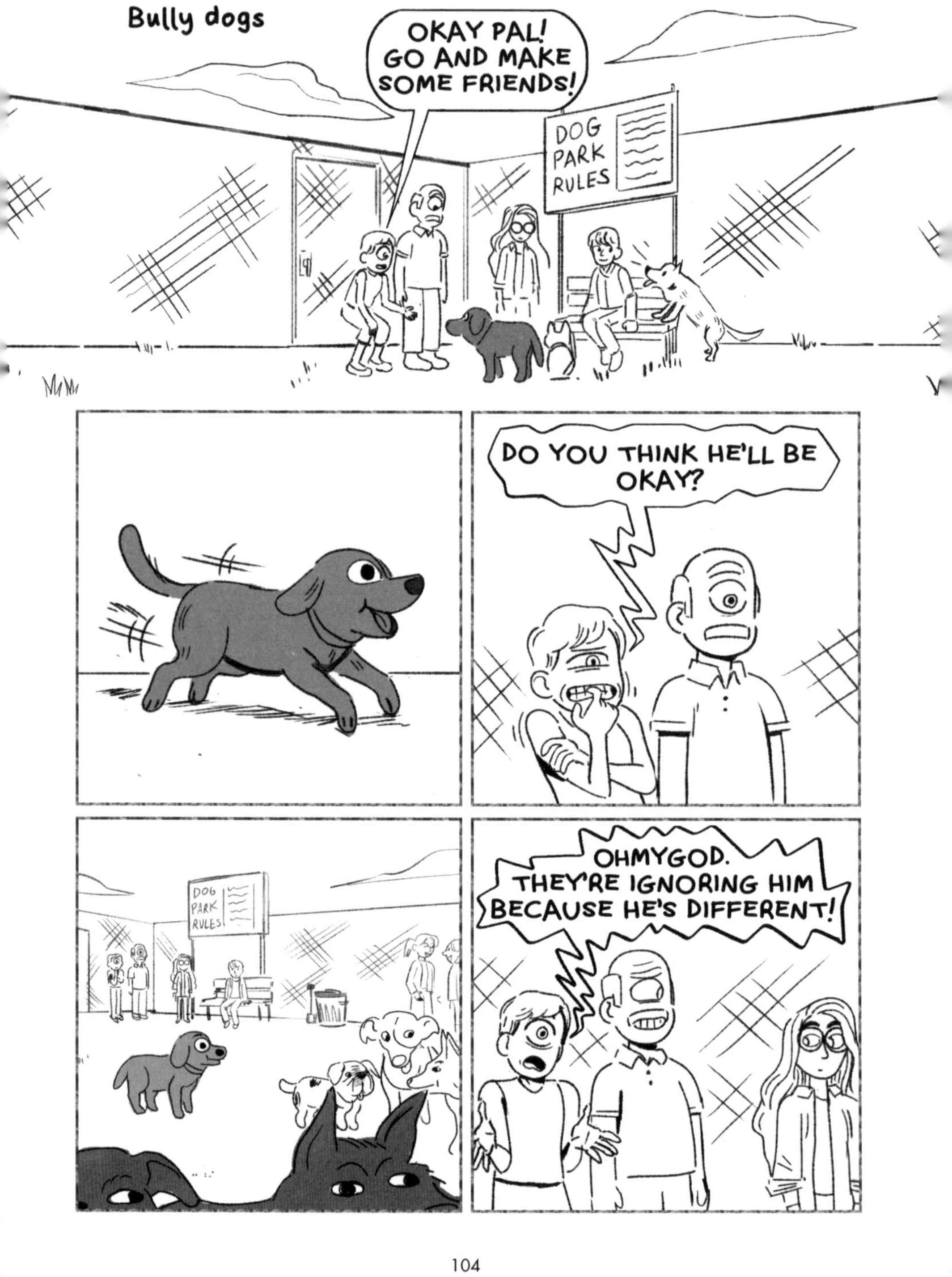
OKAY PAL! GO AND MAKE SOME FRIENDS!
DOG PARK RULES
DO YOU THINK HE'LL BE OKAY?
DOG PARK RULES
OHMYGOD. THEY'RE IGNORING HIM BECAUSE HE'S DIFFERENT!

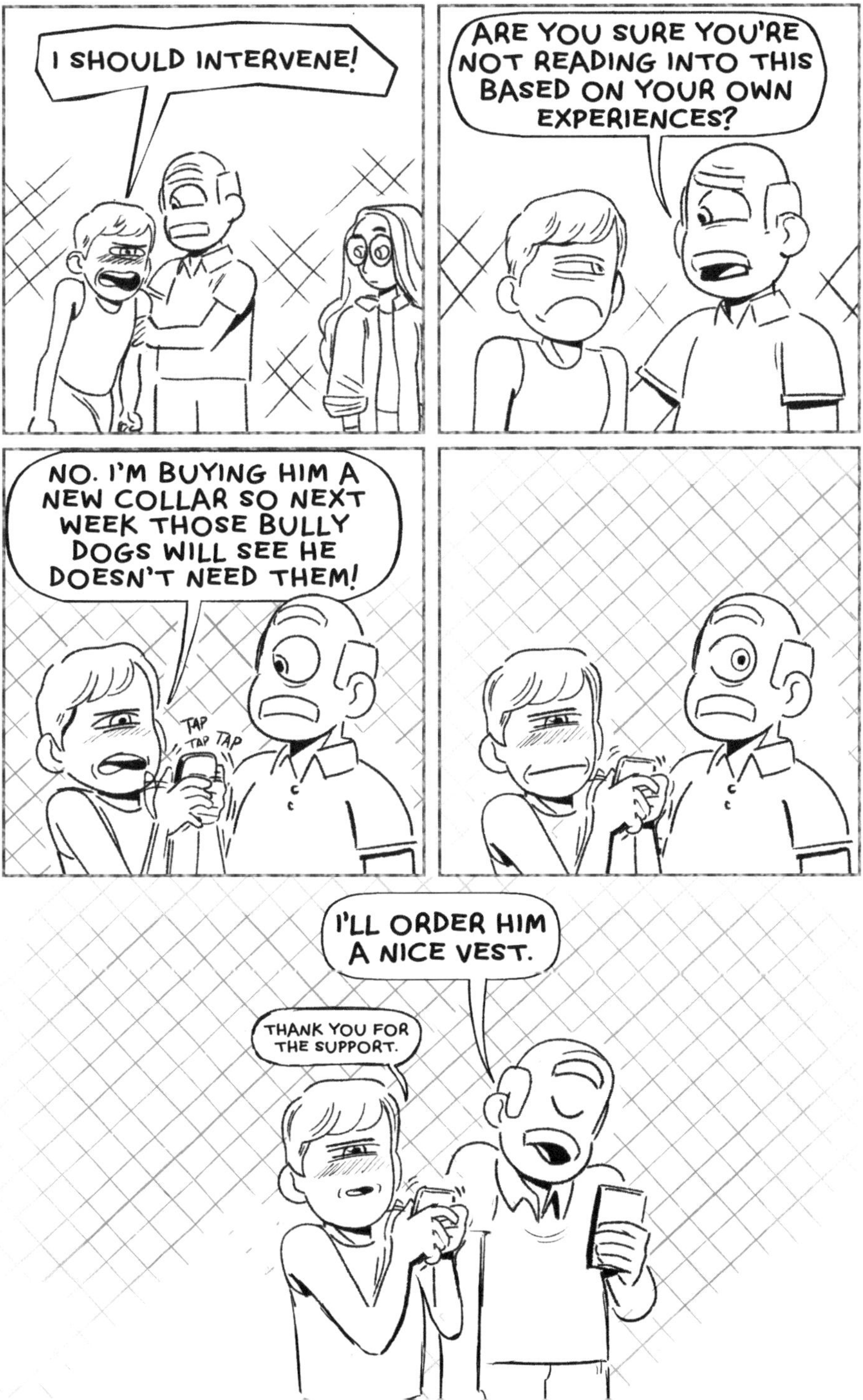
I SHOULD INTERVENE!
ARE YOU SURE YOU'RE NOT READING INTO THIS BASED ON YOUR OWN EXPERIENCES?
NO. I'M BUYING HIM A NEW COLLAR SO NEXT WEEK THOSE BULLY DOGS WILL SEE HE DOESN'T NEED THEM!
TAP TAP TAP
I'LL ORDER HIM A NICE VEST.
THANK YOU FOR THE SUPPORT.

Hidden messages

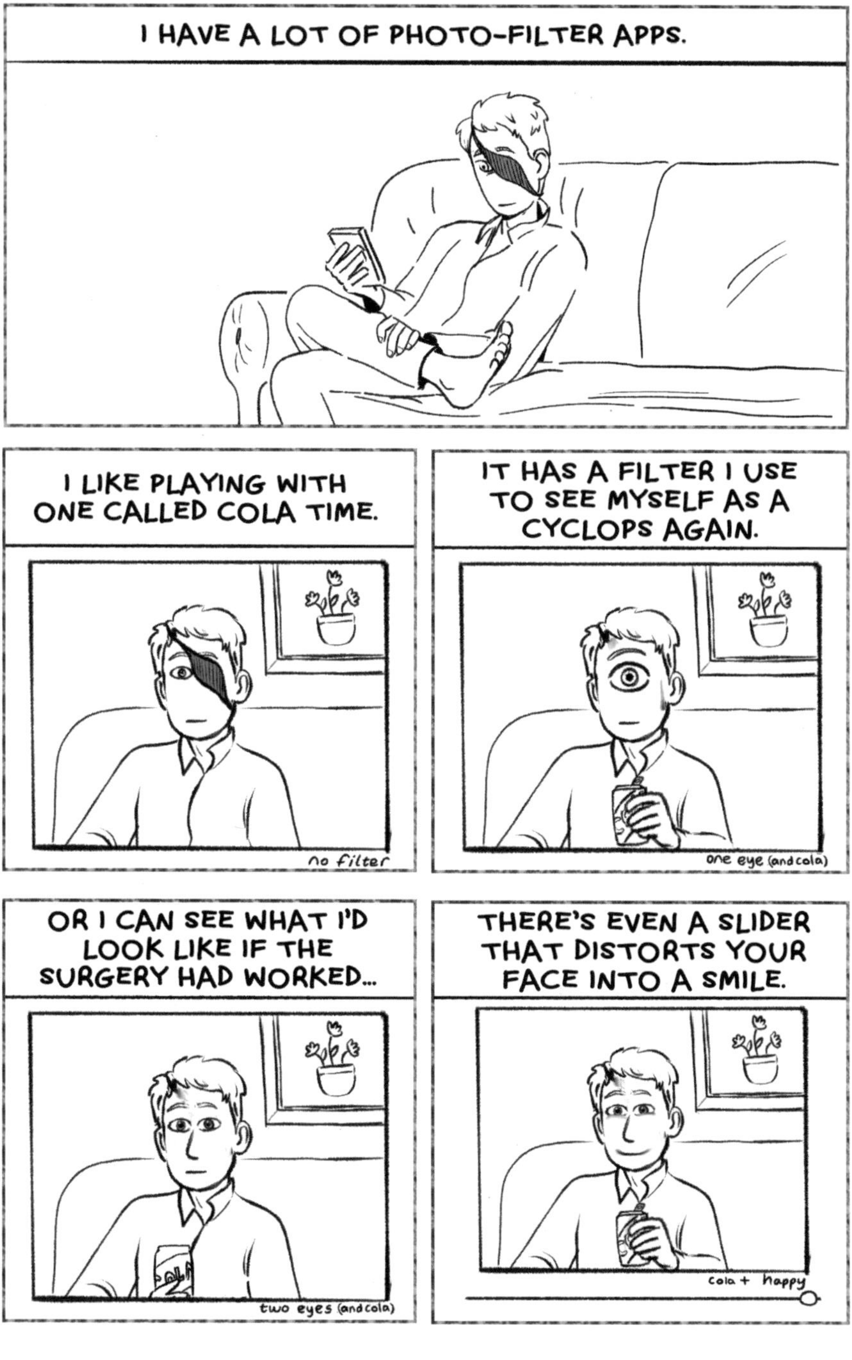
I HAVE A LOT OF PHOTO-FILTER APPS.
I LIKE PLAYING WITH ONE CALLED COLA TIME.
no filter
IT HAS A FILTER I USE TO SEE MYSELF AS A CYCLOPS AGAIN.
one eye (and cola)
OR I CAN SEE WHAT I'D LOOK LIKE IF THE SURGERY HAD WORKED...
two eyes (and cola)
THERE'S EVEN A SLIDER THAT DISTORTS YOUR FACE INTO A SMILE.
cola + happy

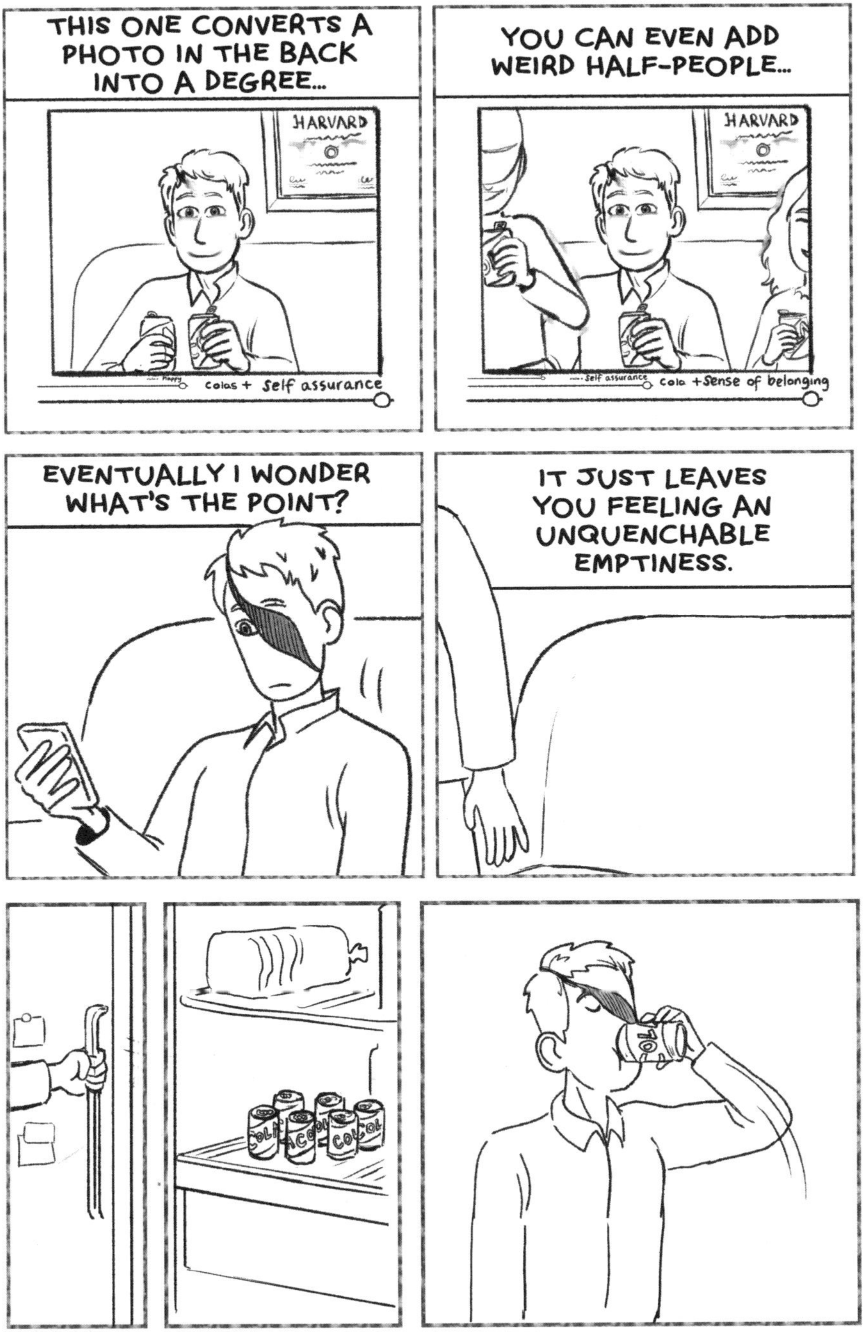
THIS ONE CONVERTS A PHOTO IN THE BACK INTO A DEGREE...
HARVARD
Colas + Self assurance
YOU CAN EVEN ADD WEIRD HALF-PEOPLE...
HARVARD
Self assurance
Cola + Sense of belonging
EVENTUALLY I WONDER WHAT'S THE POINT?
IT JUST LEAVES YOU FEELING AN UNQUENCHABLE EMPTINESS.

pari at the hospital

HI. HI PARI, I'M THE LACTATION SPECIALIST.

NICE TO MEET YOU!

BUT I CAN'T BREAST FEED BECAUSE OF A SURGERY I HAD WHEN I WAS YOUNGER.

THE SURGERY'S ILLEGAL NOW. I'M ONE OF THE FEW SURVIVORS...

A DIVIDING MAMMAPLASTY TO GET TWO BOOBS AND BE LESS CYCLOPSY!

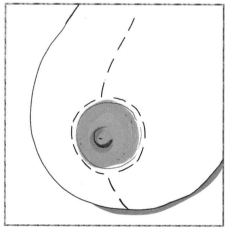

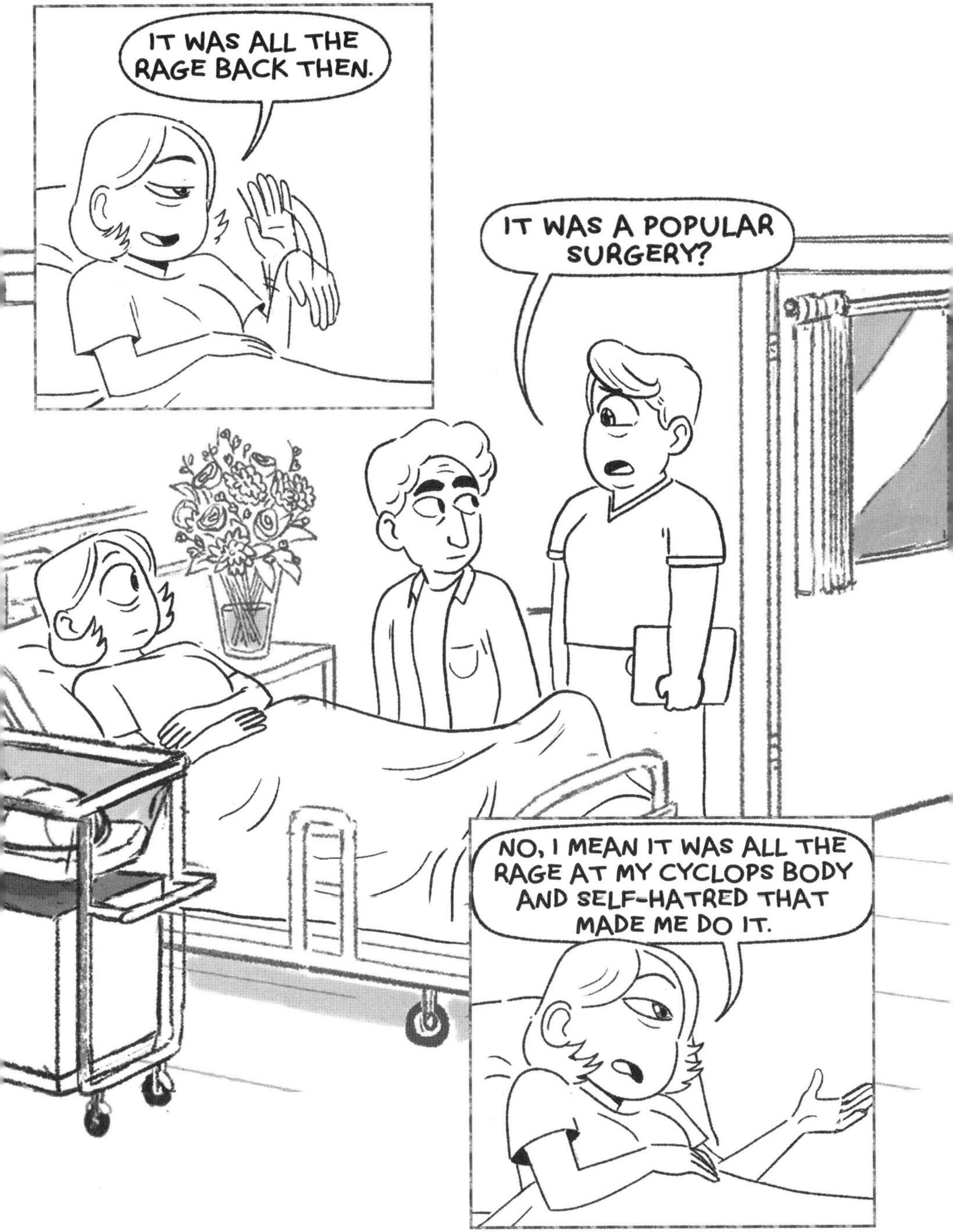
IT WAS ALL THE RAGE BACK THEN.
IT WAS A POPULAR SURGERY?
NO, I MEAN IT WAS ALL THE RAGE AT MY CYCLOPS BODY AND SELF-HATRED THAT MADE ME DO IT.

Only Arj

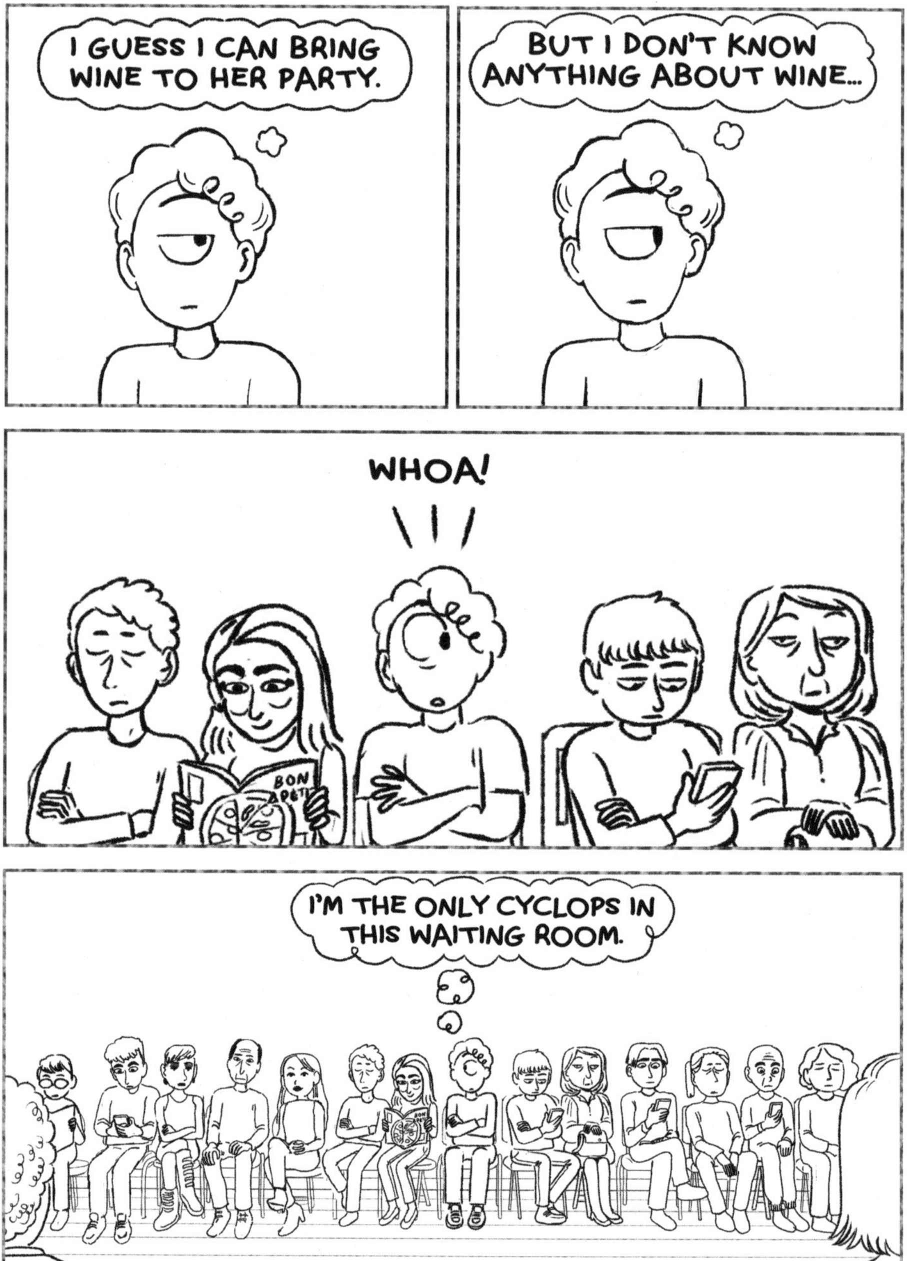
I GUESS I CAN BRING WINE TO HER PARTY.
BUT I DON'T KNOW ANYTHING ABOUT WINE...
WHOA!
BON APPETIT
I'M THE ONLY CYCLOPS IN THIS WAITING ROOM.

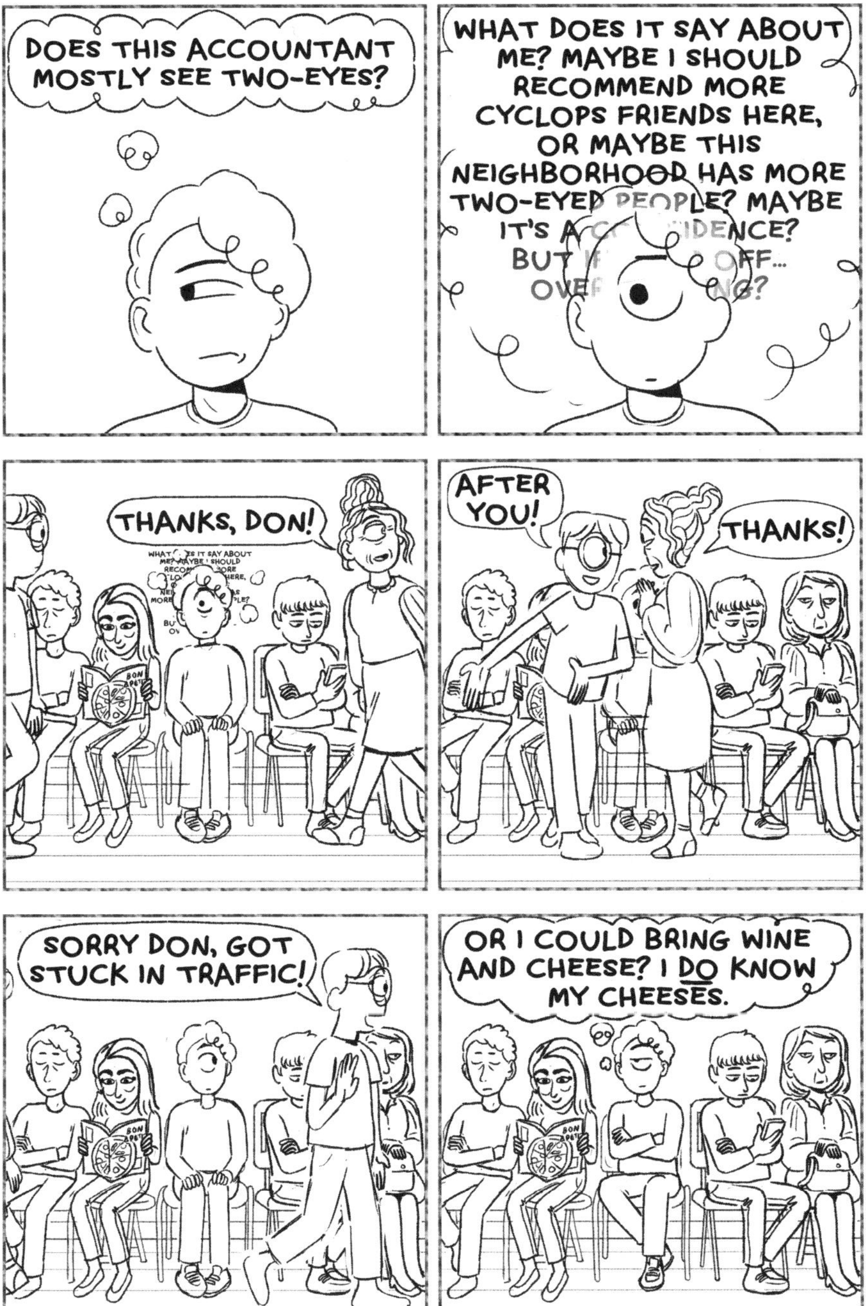
DOES THIS ACCOUNTANT MOSTLY SEE TWO-EYES?
WHAT DOES IT SAY ABOUT ME? MAYBE I SHOULD RECOMMEND MORE CYCLOPS FRIENDS HERE, OR MAYBE THIS NEIGHBORHOOD HAS MORE TWO-EYED PEOPLE? MAYBE
THANKS, DON!
AFTER YOU!
THANKS!
SORRY DON, GOT STUCK IN TRAFFIC!
OR I COULD BRING WINE AND CHEESE? I DO KNOW MY CHEESES.

Anti-Cyclops

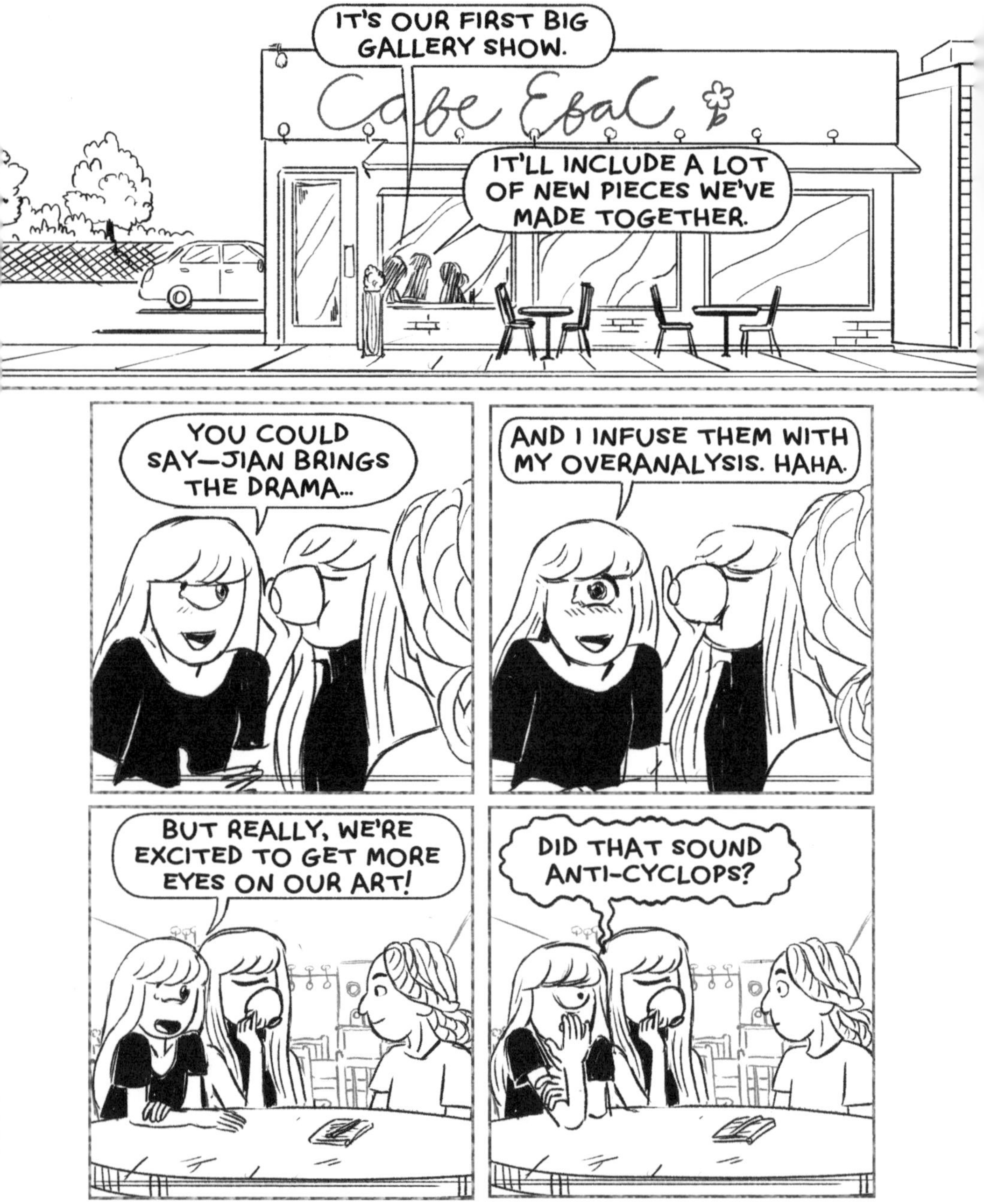

IT'S OUR FIRST BIG GALLERY SHOW.
Cafe Efac
IT'LL INCLUDE A LOT OF NEW PIECES WE'VE MADE TOGETHER.
YOU COULD SAY—JIAN BRINGS THE DRAMA...
AND I INFUSE THEM WITH MY OVERANALYSIS. HAHA.
BUT REALLY, WE'RE EXCITED TO GET MORE EYES ON OUR ART!
DID THAT SOUND ANTI-CYCLOPS?

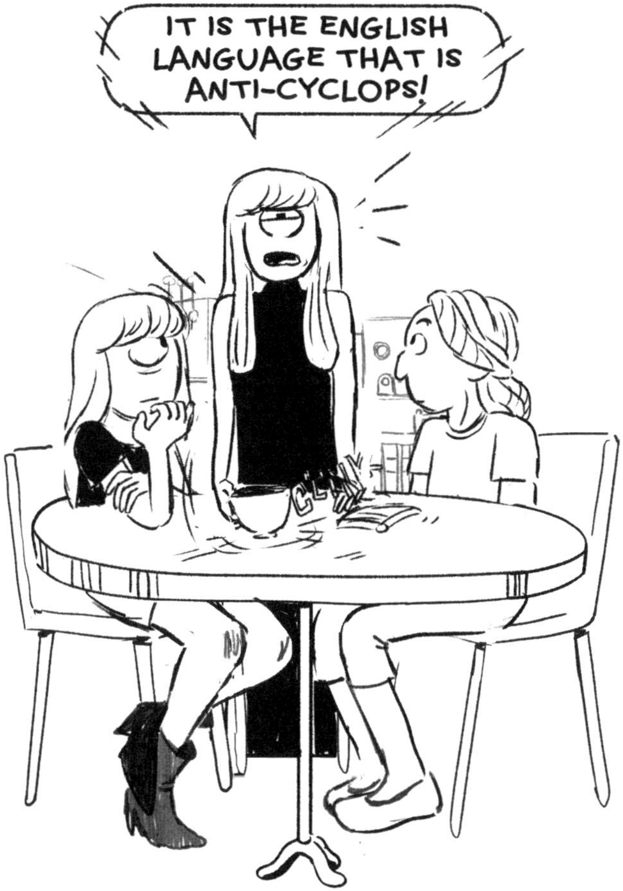
IT IS THE ENGLISH LANGUAGE THAT IS ANTI-CYCLOPS!

Real estate

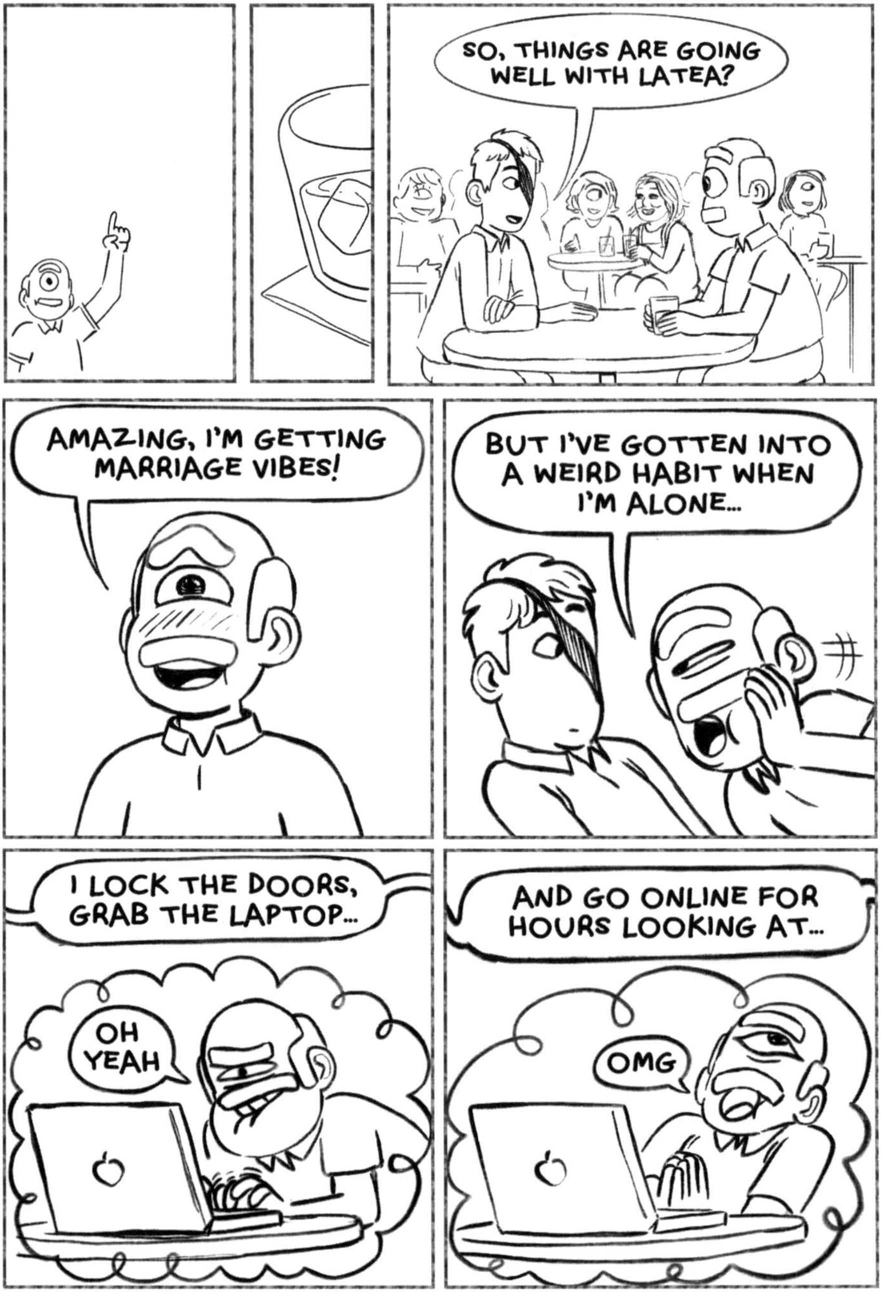
SO, THINGS ARE GOING WELL WITH LATEA?
AMAZING, I'M GETTING MARRIAGE VIBES!
BUT I'VE GOTTEN INTO A WEIRD HABIT WHEN I'M ALONE...
I LOCK THE DOORS, GRAB THE LAPTOP...
OH YEAH
AND GO ONLINE FOR HOURS LOOKING AT...
OMG

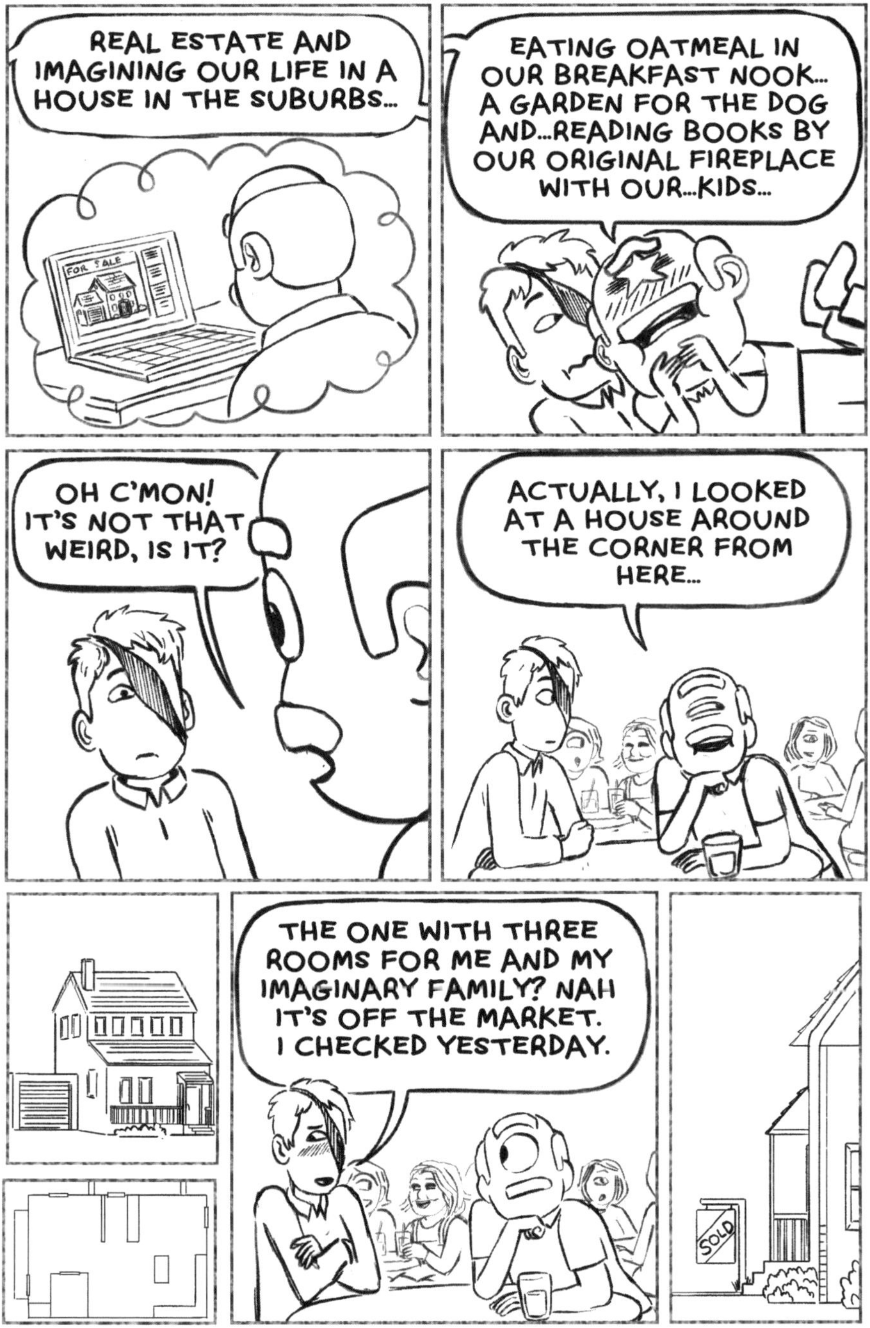
REAL ESTATE AND IMAGINING OUR LIFE IN A HOUSE IN THE SUBURBS...
FOR SALE
EATING OATMEAL IN OUR BREAKFAST NOOK... A GARDEN FOR THE DOG AND...READING BOOKS BY OUR ORIGINAL FIREPLACE WITH OUR...KIDS...
OH C'MON! IT'S NOT THAT WEIRD, IS IT?
ACTUALLY, I LOOKED AT A HOUSE AROUND THE CORNER FROM HERE...
THE ONE WITH THREE ROOMS FOR ME AND MY IMAGINARY FAMILY? NAH IT'S OFF THE MARKET. I CHECKED YESTERDAY.
SOLD

Feels

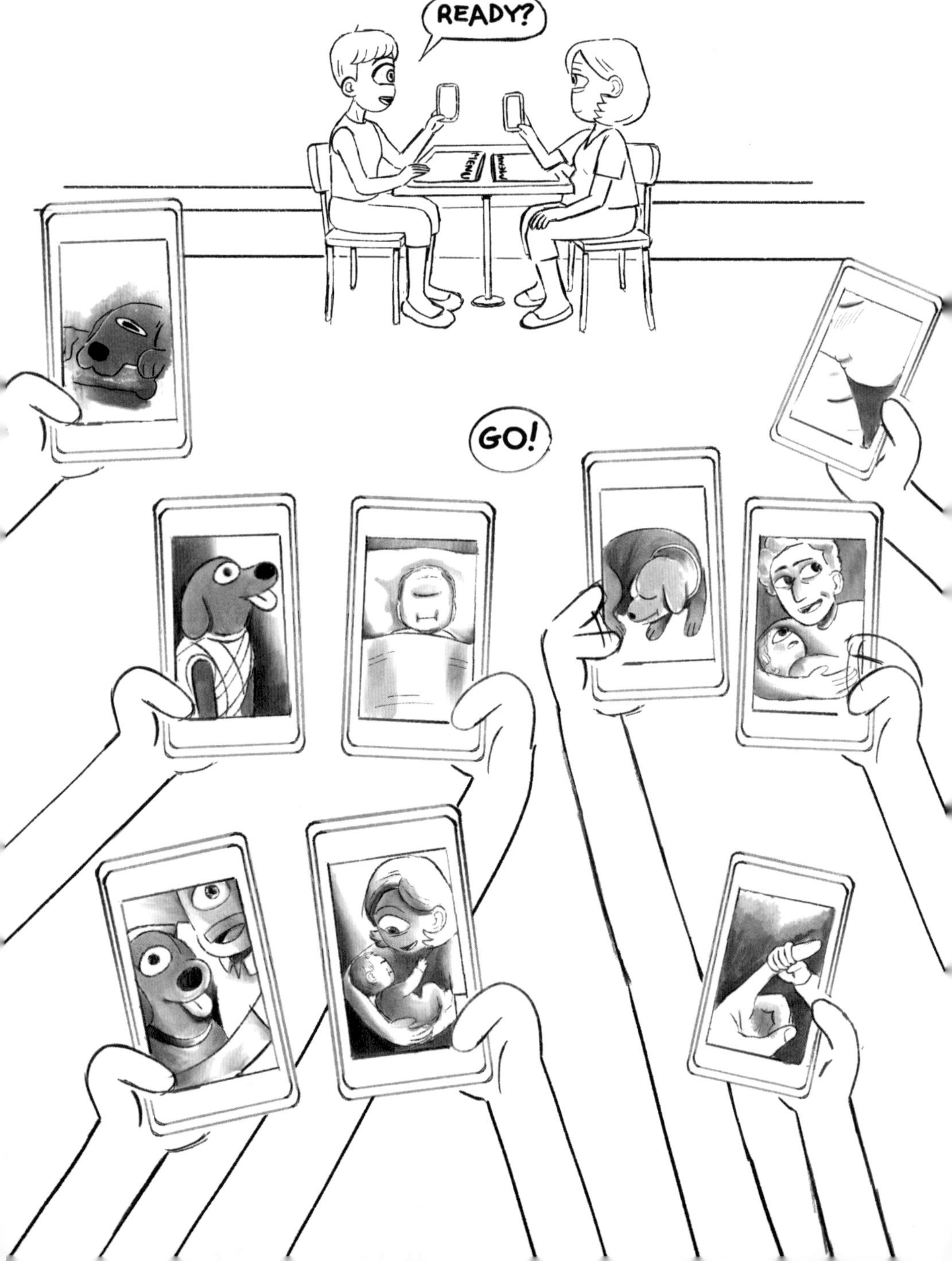
READY?
GO!

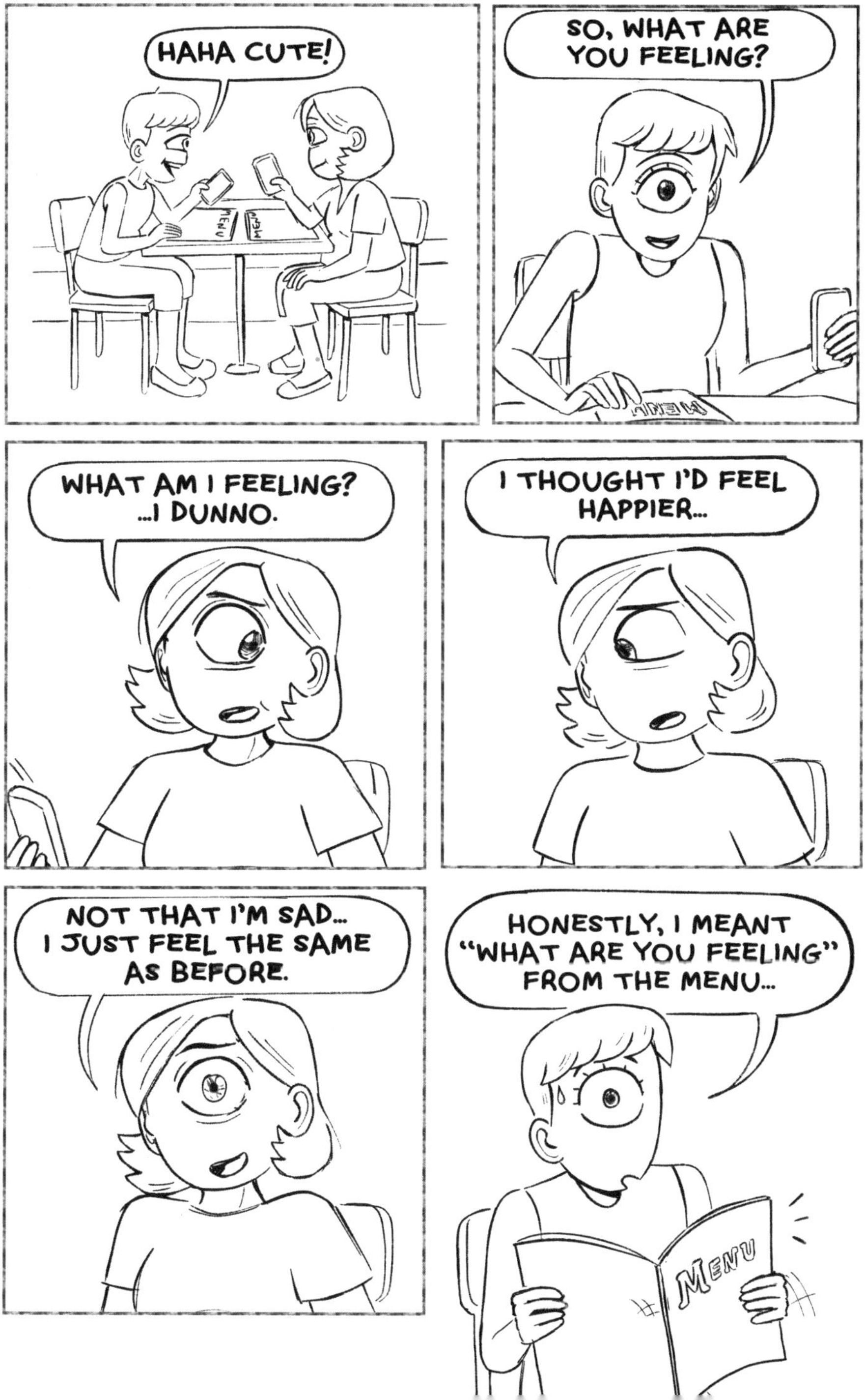
HAHA CUTE!
MENU
MENU
SO, WHAT ARE YOU FEELING?
MENU
WHAT AM I FEELING? ...I DUNNO.
I THOUGHT I'D FEEL HAPPIER...
NOT THAT I'M SAD... I JUST FEEL THE SAME AS BEFORE.
HONESTLY, I MEANT "WHAT ARE YOU FEELING" FROM THE MENU...
MENU

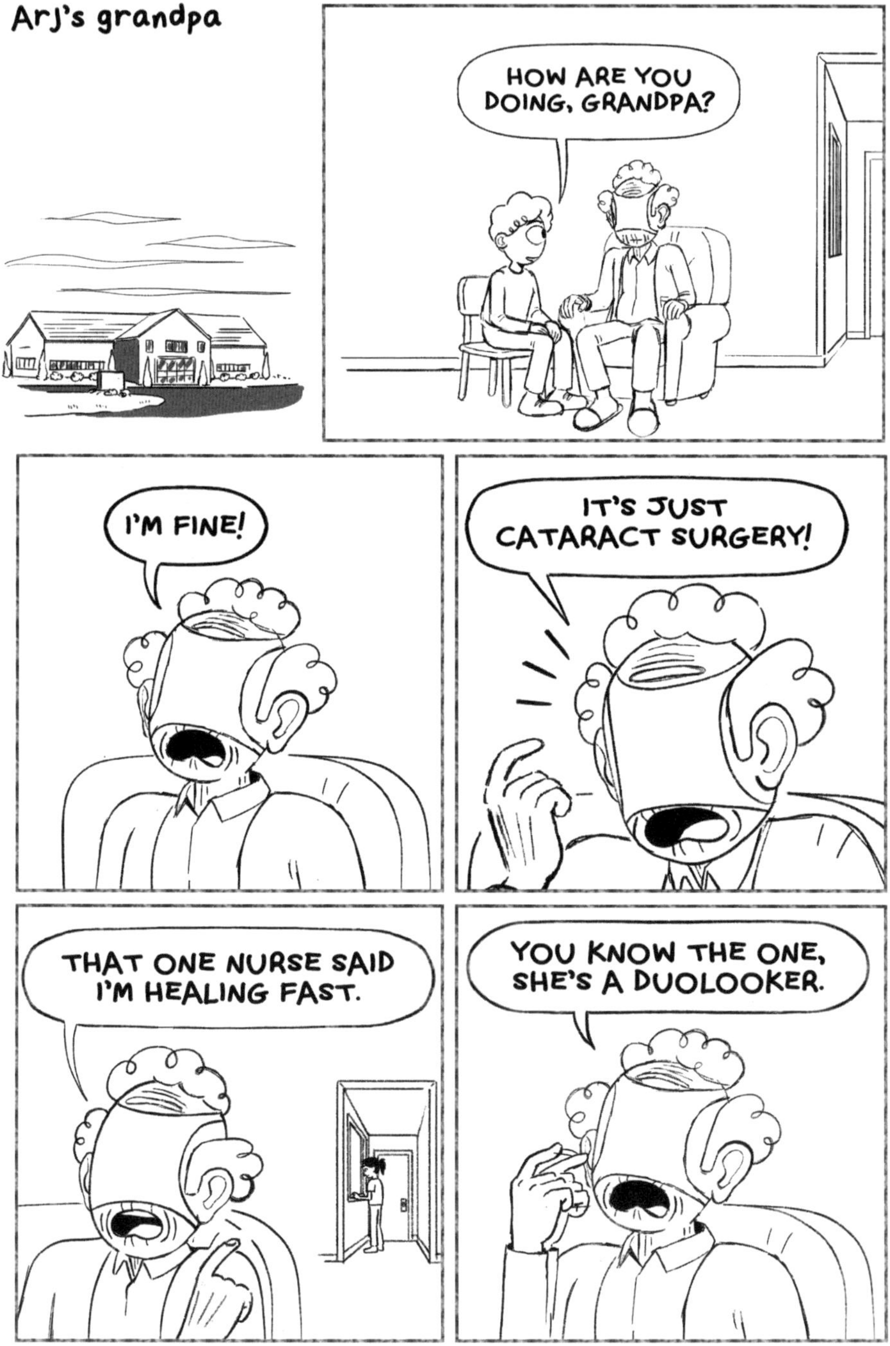
Arj's grandpa
HOW ARE YOU DOING, GRANDPA?
I'M FINE!
IT'S JUST CATARACT SURGERY!
THAT ONE NURSE SAID I'M HEALING FAST.
YOU KNOW THE ONE, SHE'S A DUOLOOKER.

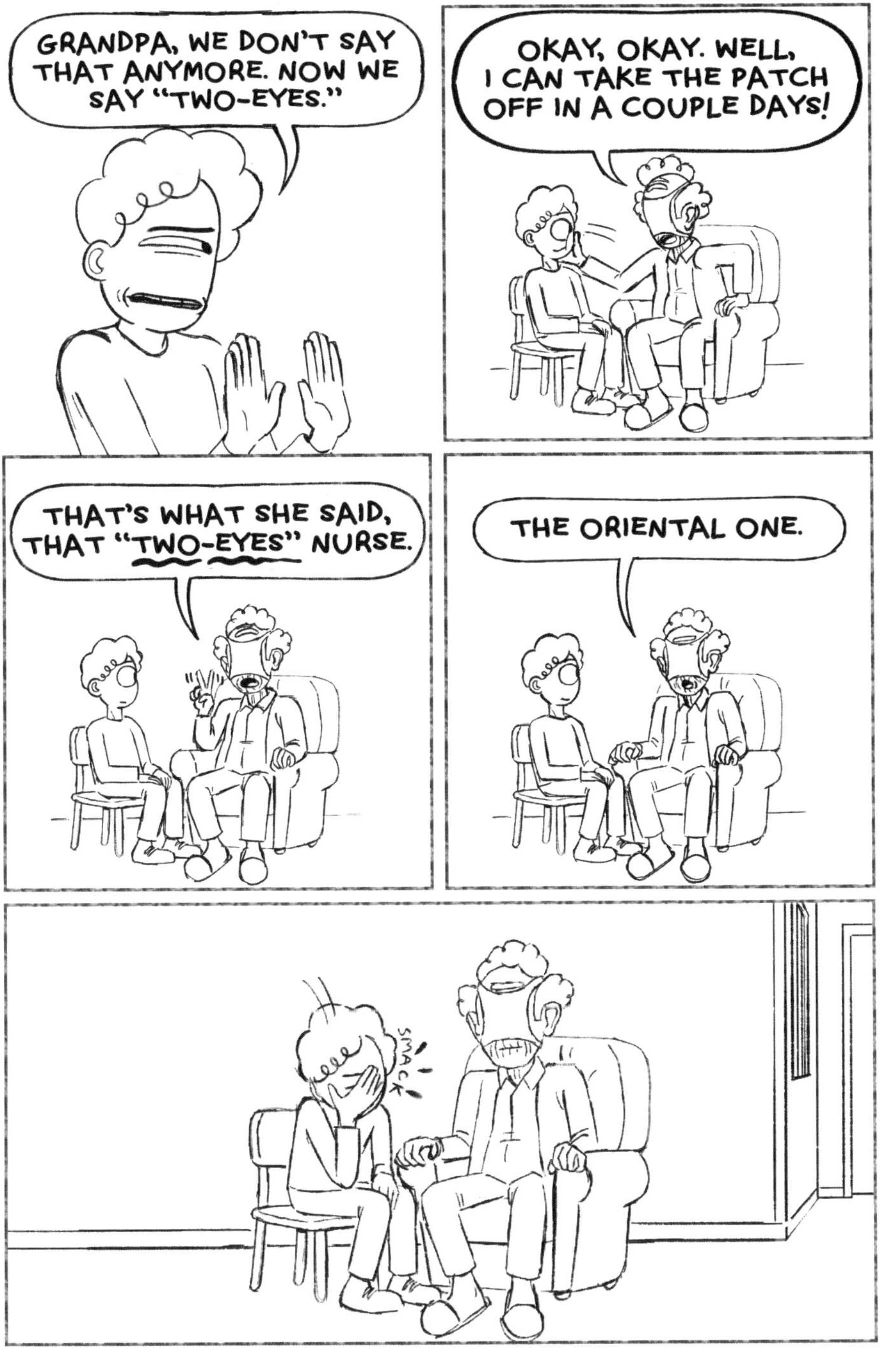
GRANDPA, WE DON'T SAY THAT ANYMORE. NOW WE SAY "TWO-EYES."
OKAY, OKAY. WELL, I CAN TAKE THE PATCH OFF IN A COUPLE DAYS!
THAT'S WHAT SHE SAID, THAT "TWO-EYES" NURSE.
THE ORIENTAL ONE.
SMACK

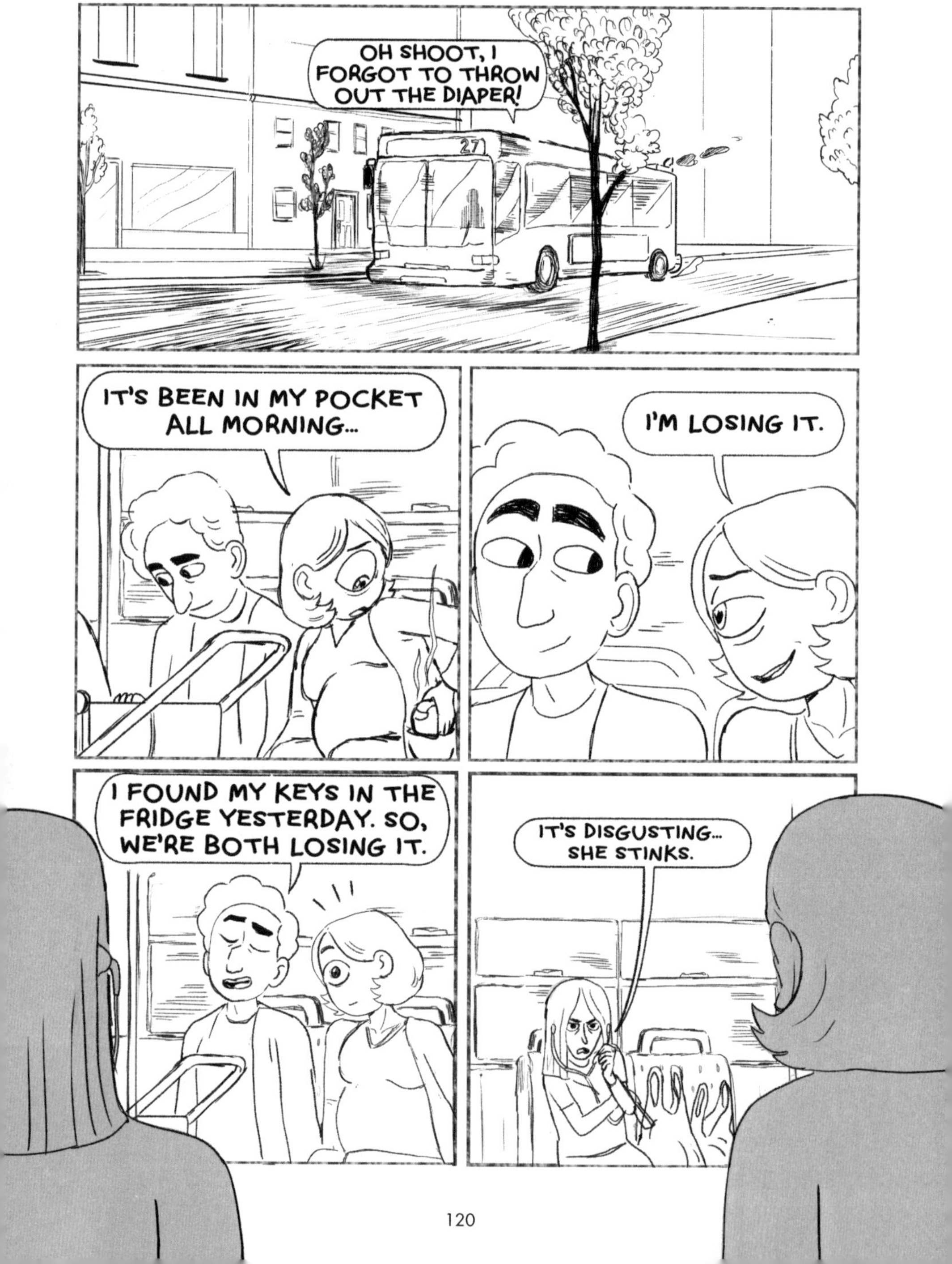
OH SHOOT, I FORGOT TO THROW OUT THE DIAPER!
27
IT'S BEEN IN MY POCKET ALL MORNING...
I'M LOSING IT.
I FOUND MY KEYS IN THE FRIDGE YESTERDAY. SO, WE'RE BOTH LOSING IT.
IT'S DISGUSTING... SHE STINKS.

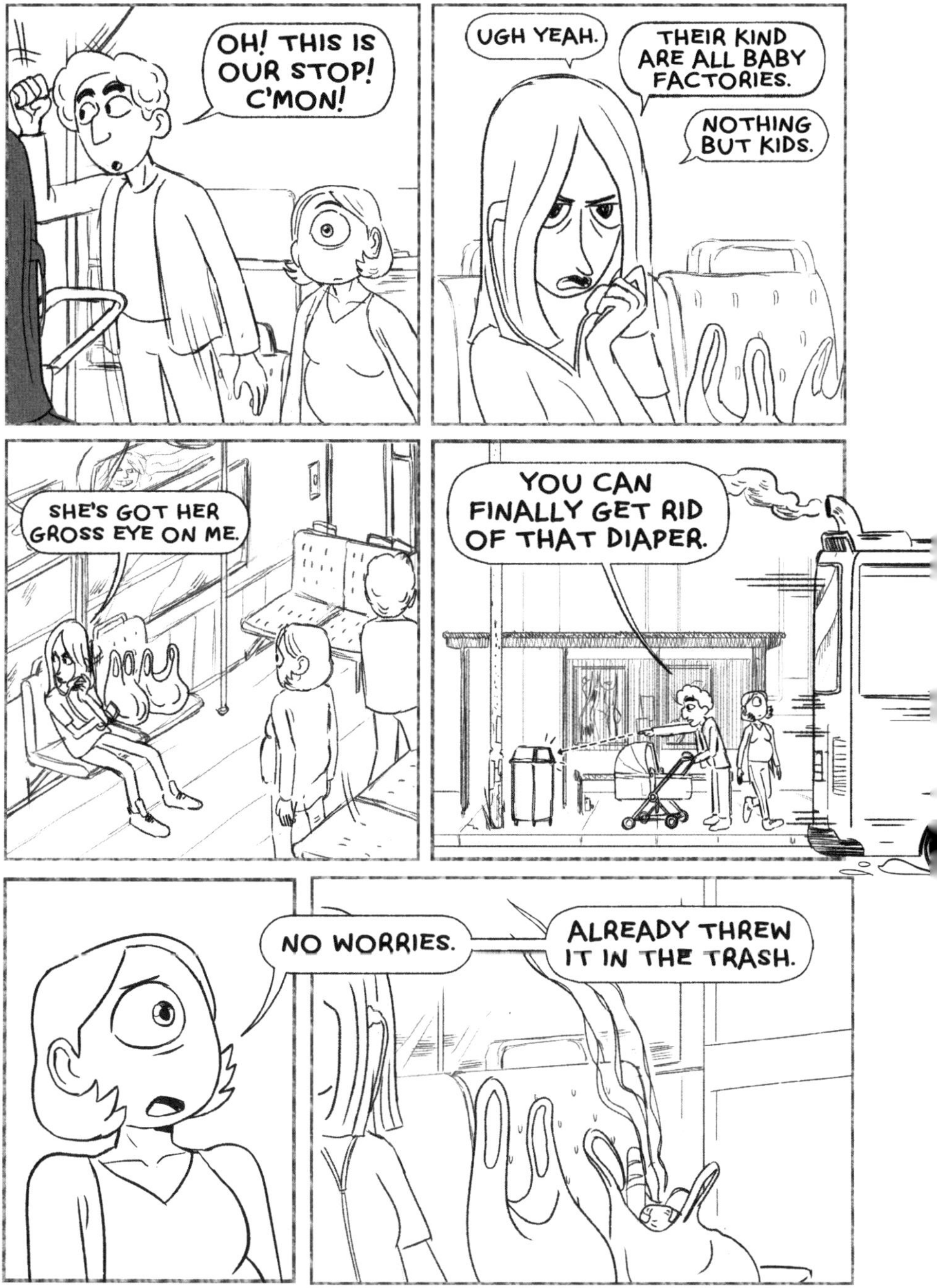
OH! THIS IS OUR STOP! C'MON!
UGH YEAH.
THEIR KIND ARE ALL BABY FACTORIES.
NOTHING BUT KIDS.
SHE'S GOT HER GROSS EYE ON ME.
YOU CAN FINALLY GET RID OF THAT DIAPER.
NO WORRIES.
ALREADY THREW IT IN THE TRASH.

I know art

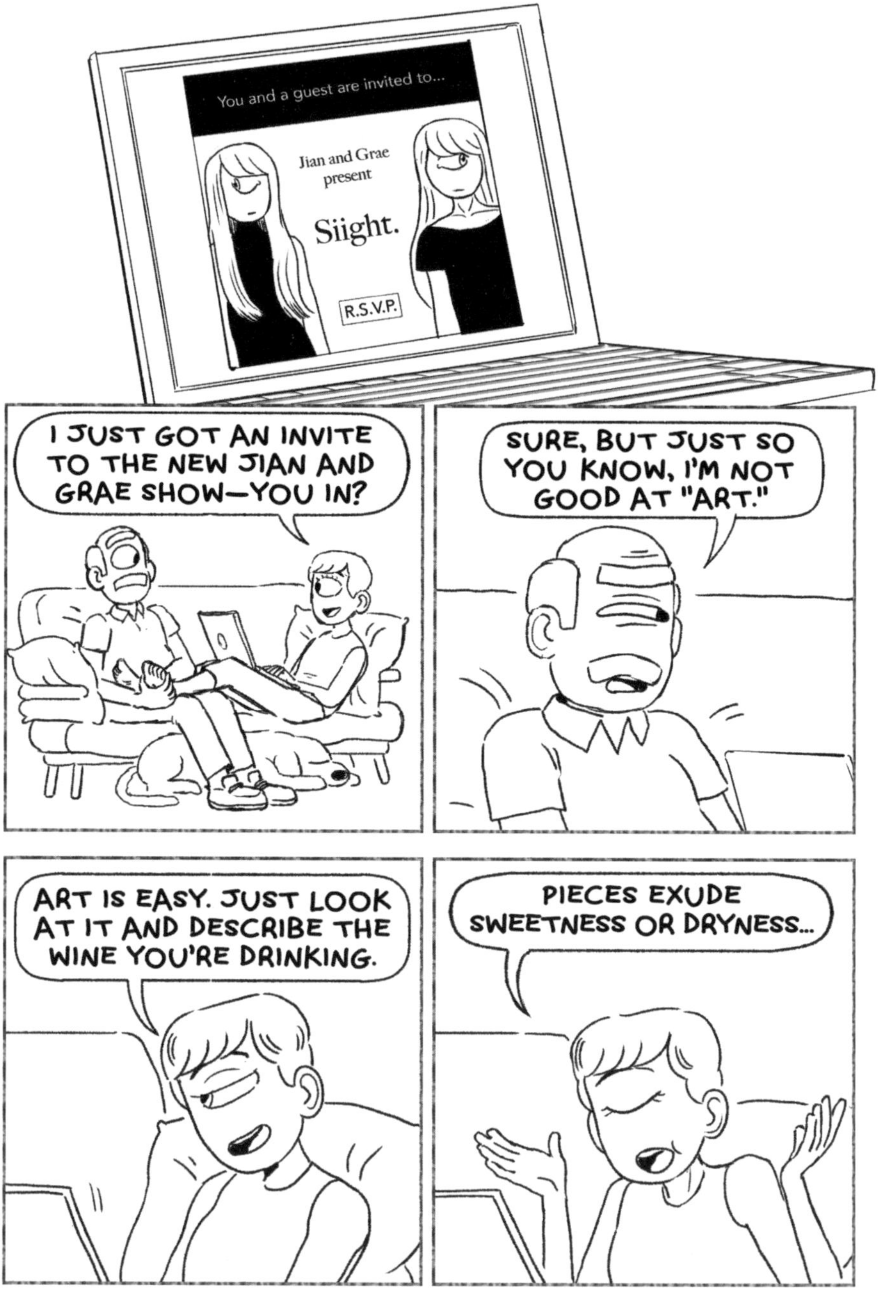
You and a guest are invited to...
Jian and Grae present
Siight.
R.S.V.P.
I JUST GOT AN INVITE TO THE NEW JIAN AND GRAE SHOW—YOU IN?
SURE, BUT JUST SO YOU KNOW, I'M NOT GOOD AT "ART."
ART IS EASY. JUST LOOK AT IT AND DESCRIBE THE WINE YOU'RE DRINKING.
PIECES EXUDE SWEETNESS OR DRYNESS...

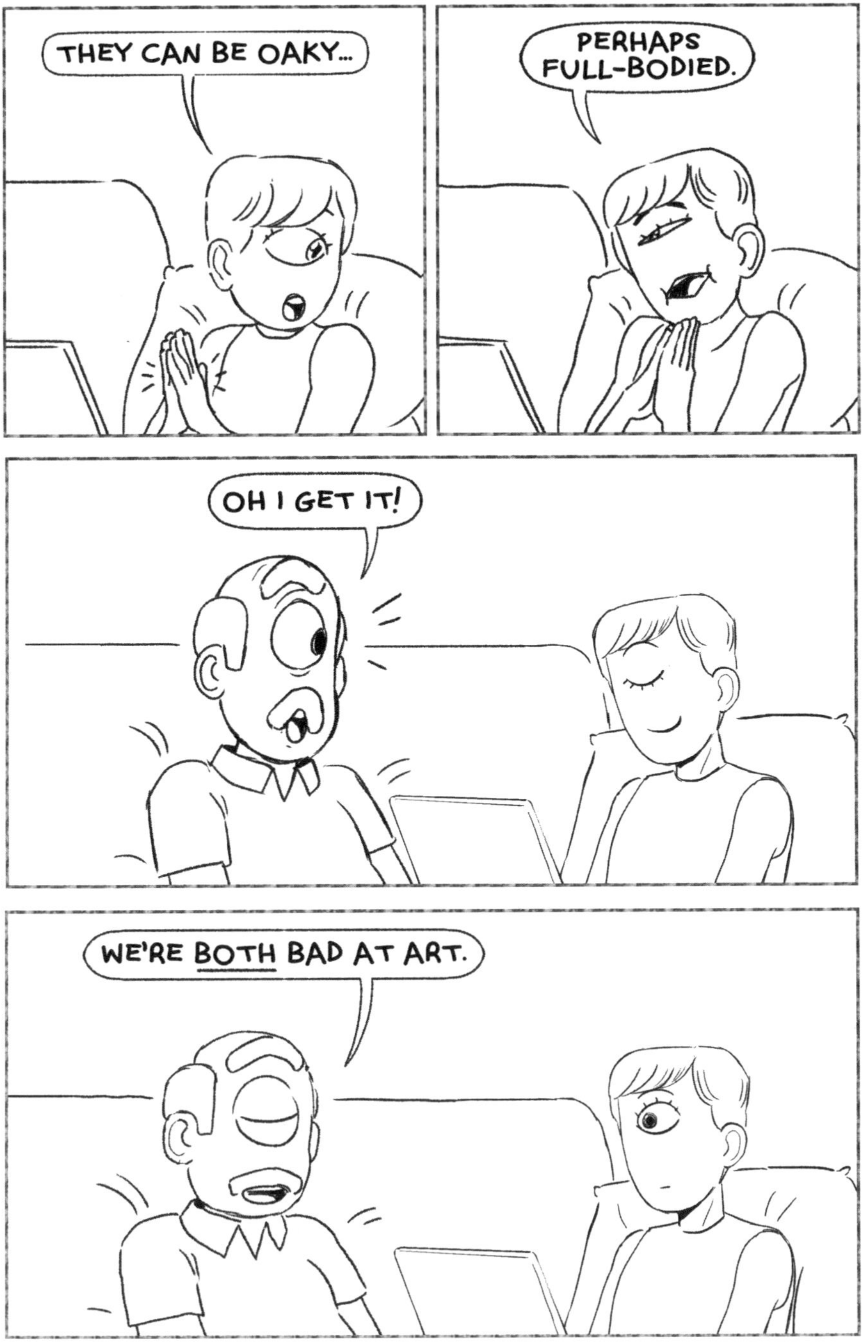
THEY CAN BE OAKY...
PERHAPS FULL-BODIED.
OH I GET IT!
WE'RE BOTH BAD AT ART.

Editors

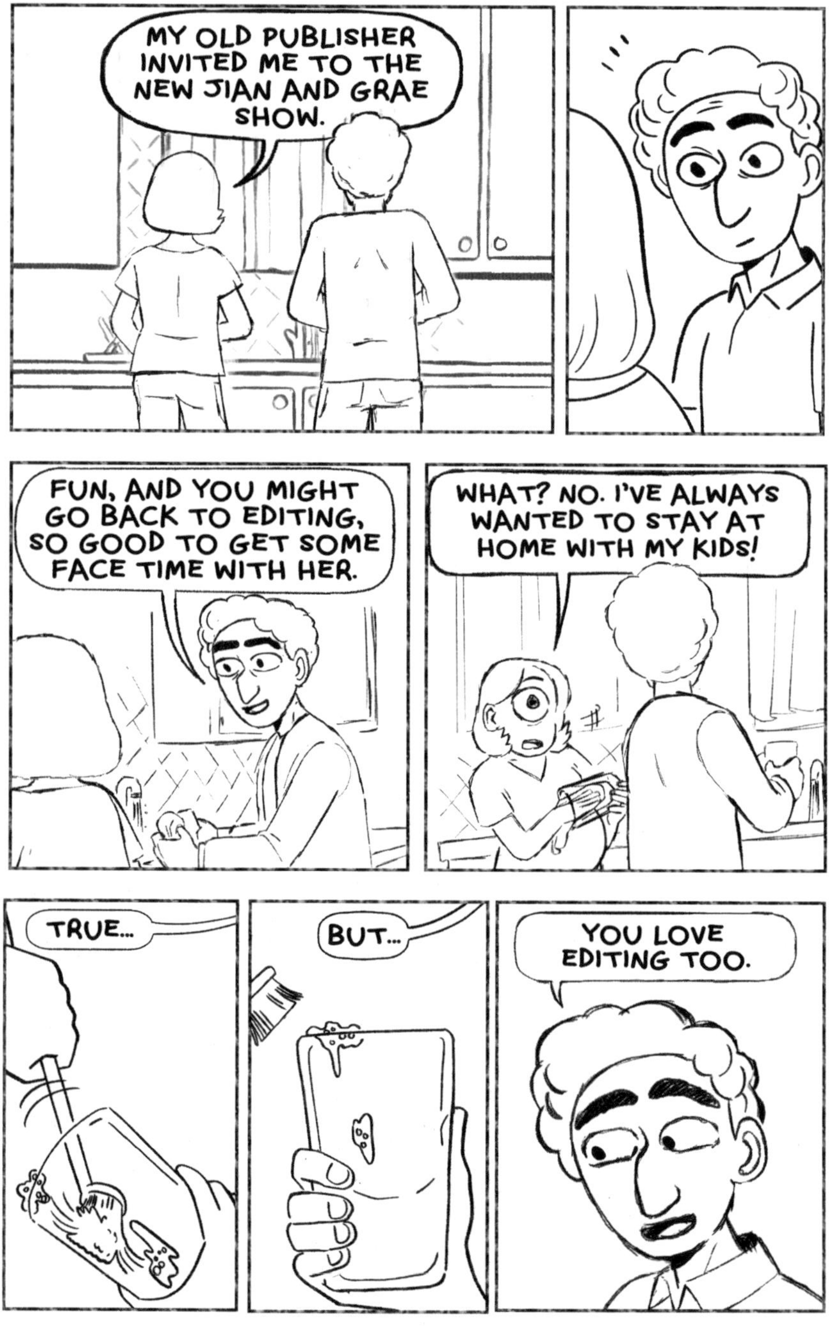
MY OLD PUBLISHER INVITED ME TO THE NEW JIAN AND GRAE SHOW.
FUN, AND YOU MIGHT GO BACK TO EDITING, SO GOOD TO GET SOME FACE TIME WITH HER.
WHAT? NO. I'VE ALWAYS WANTED TO STAY AT HOME WITH MY KIDS!
TRUE...
BUT...
YOU LOVE EDITING TOO.

YOU'RE ONE OF THOSE WEIRDOS WHOM LOVE GRAMMAR.
DON'T SAY THAT!
YOU'RE RIGHT. BACK TO WORK OR STAY AT HOME, YOUR DECISION.
NO, IT'S "YOU'RE ONE OF THOSE WEIRDOS WHO LOVE GRAMMAR."

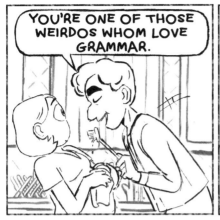

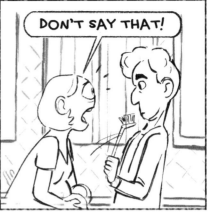

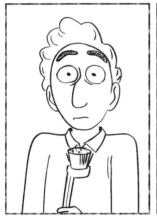

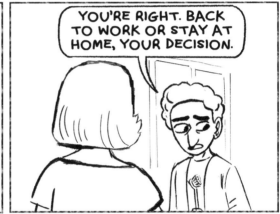

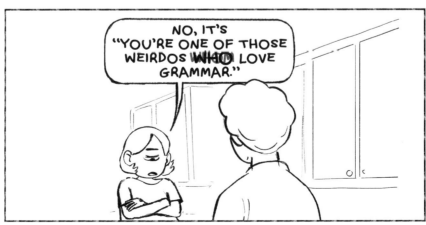

The elite

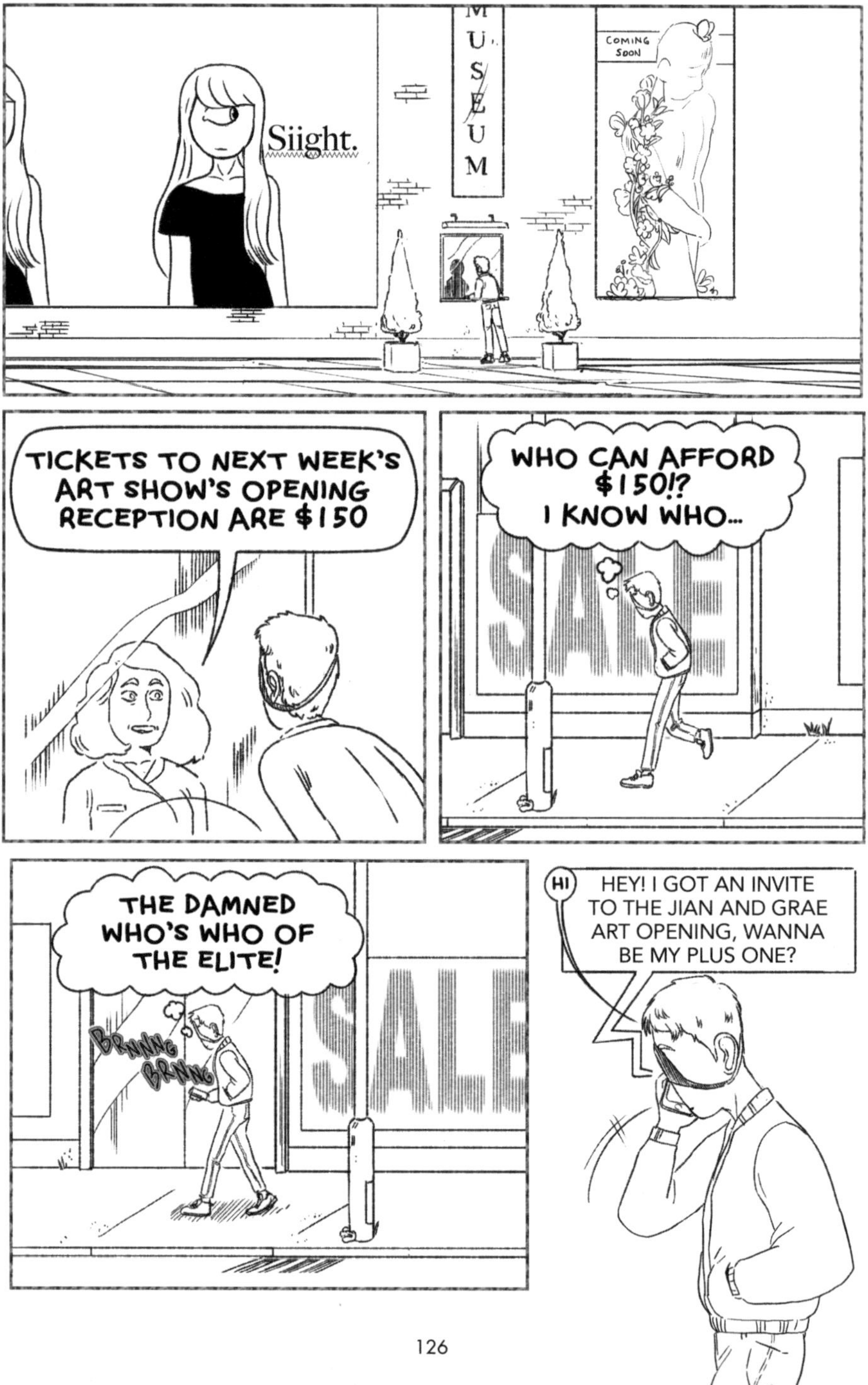

COMING SOON
MUSEUM
Siight.
TICKETS TO NEXT WEEK'S ART SHOW'S OPENING RECEPTION ARE $150
WHO CAN AFFORD $150!? I KNOW WHO...
SALE
THE DAMNED WHO'S WHO OF THE ELITE!
BRNNNG BRNNG
SALE
HI
HEY! I GOT AN INVITE TO THE JIAN AND GRAE ART OPENING, WANNA BE MY PLUS ONE?

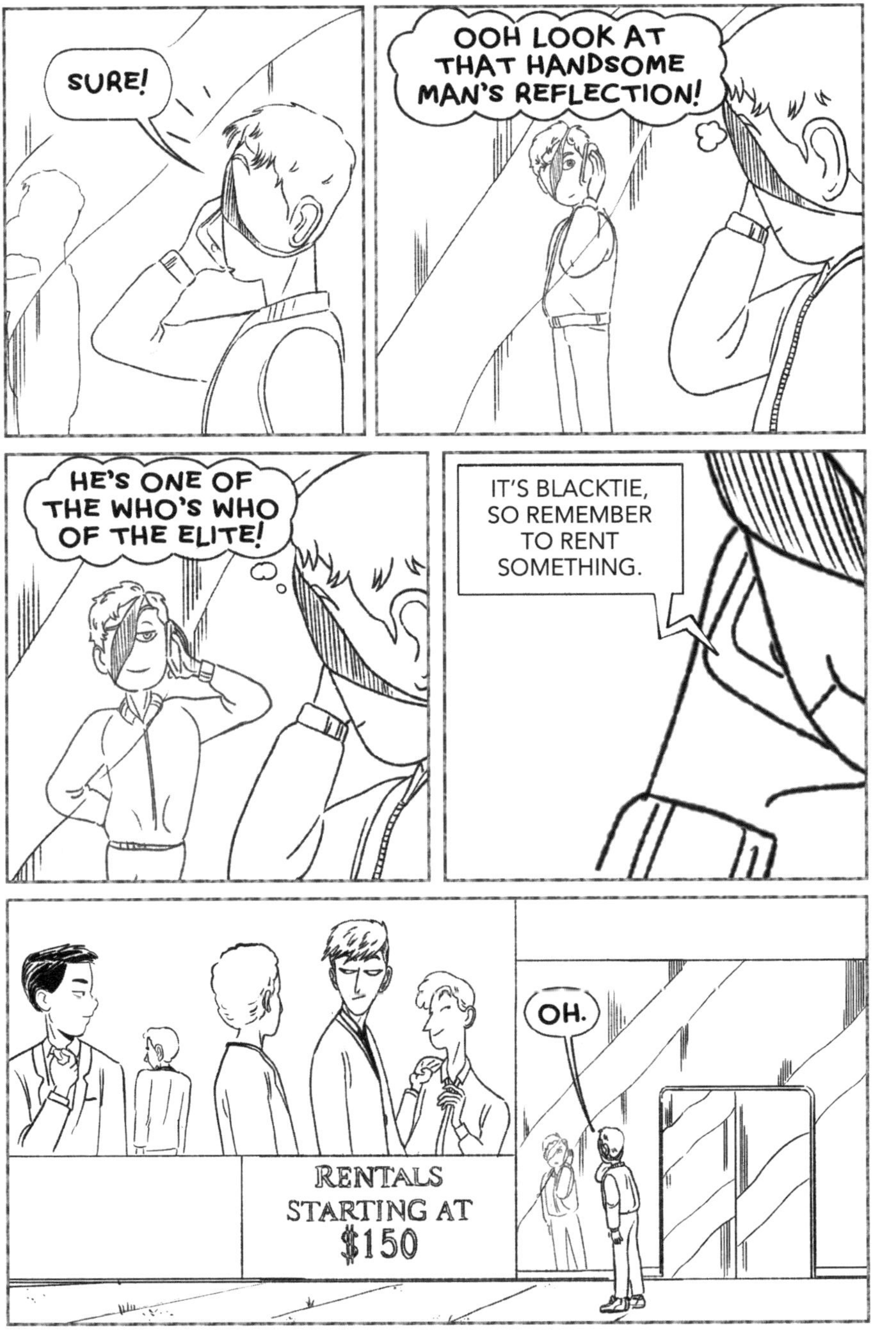
SURE!
OOH LOOK AT THAT HANDSOME MAN'S REFLECTION!
HE'S ONE OF THE WHO'S WHO OF THE ELITE!
IT'S BLACKTIE, SO REMEMBER TO RENT SOMETHING.
RENTALS STARTING AT $150
OH.

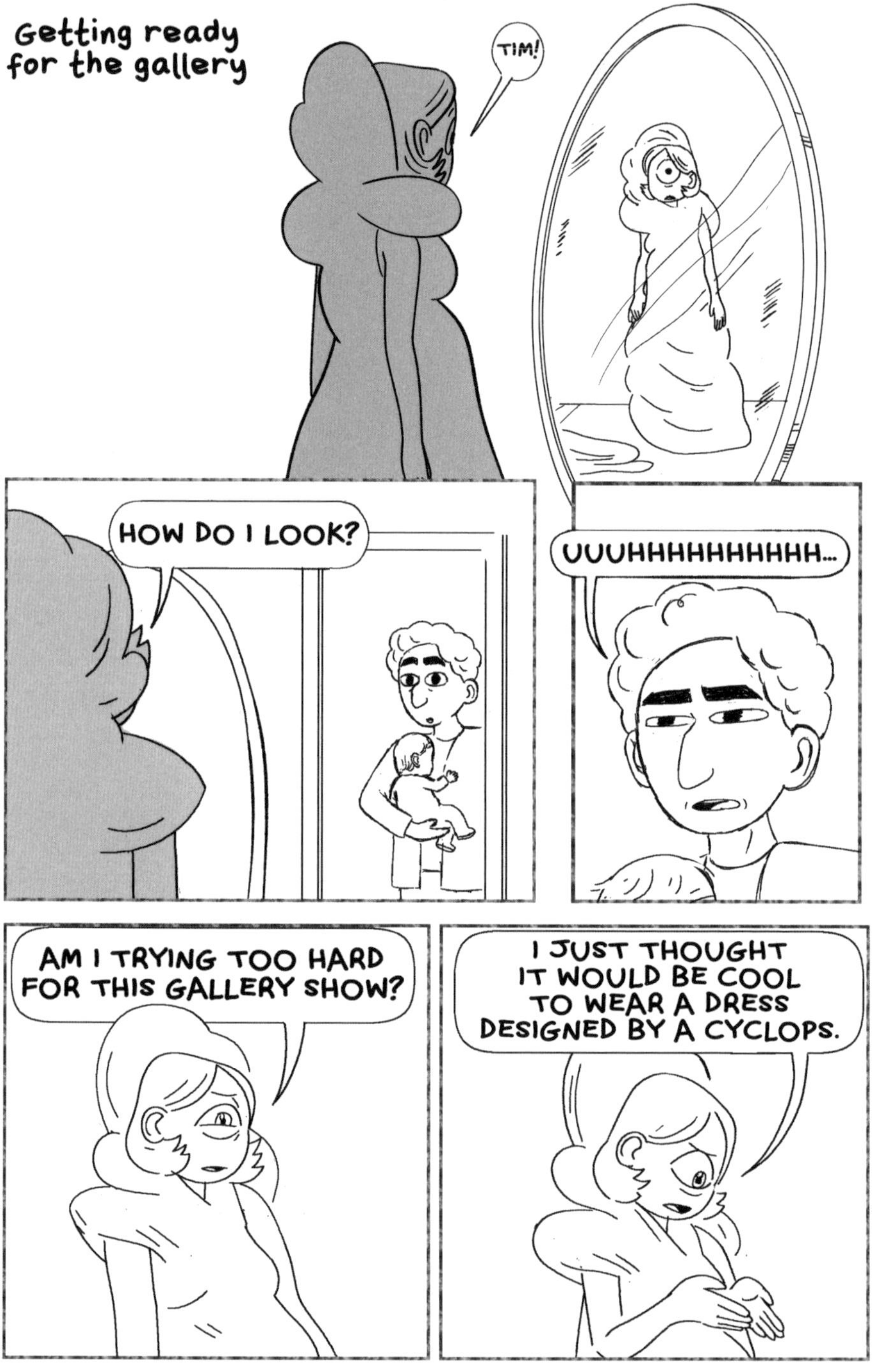
Getting ready for the gallery
TIM!
HOW DO I LOOK?
UUUHHHHHHHHHH...
AM I TRYING TOO HARD FOR THIS GALLERY SHOW?
I JUST THOUGHT IT WOULD BE COOL TO WEAR A DRESS DESIGNED BY A CYCLOPS.

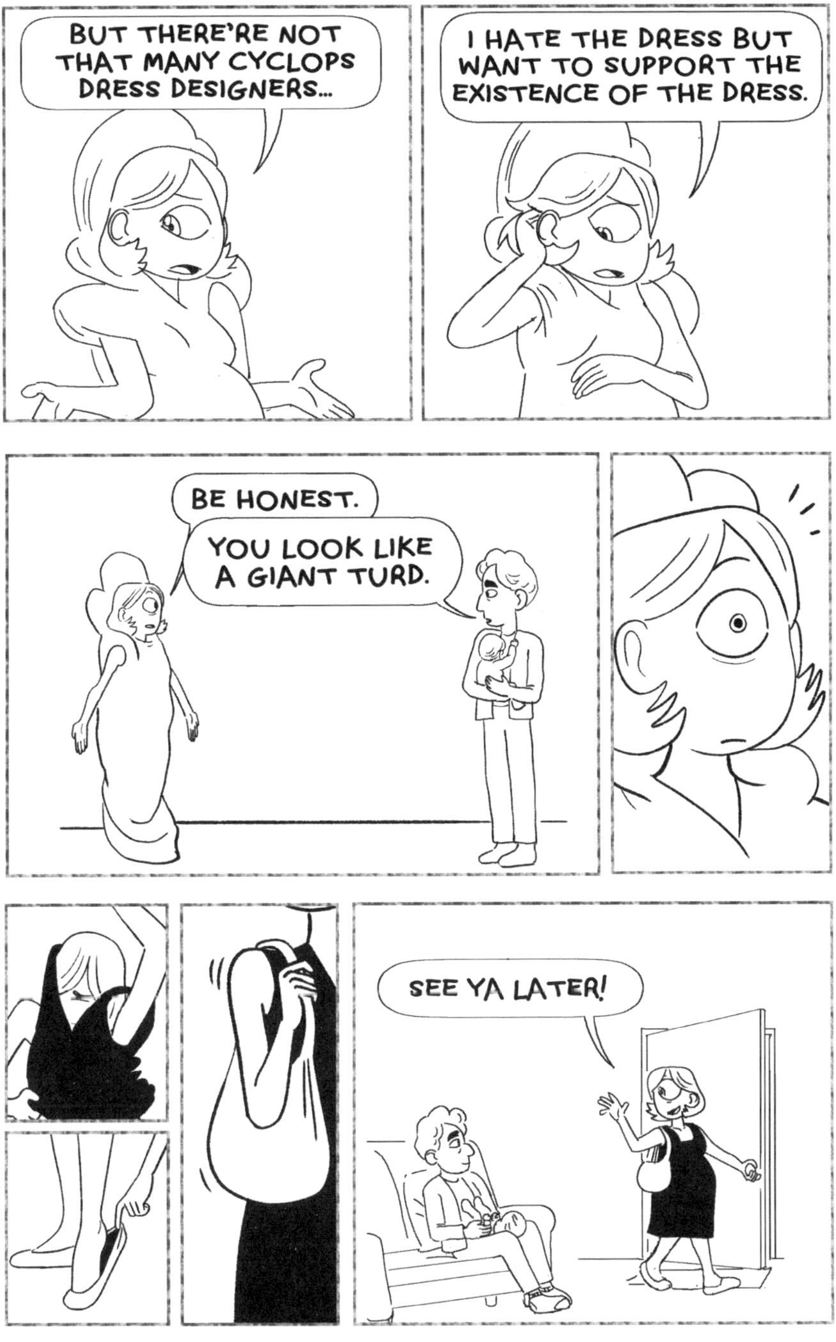

BUT THERE'RE NOT THAT MANY CYCLOPS DRESS DESIGNERS...
I HATE THE DRESS BUT WANT TO SUPPORT THE EXISTENCE OF THE DRESS.
BE HONEST.
YOU LOOK LIKE A GIANT TURD.
SEE YA LATER!

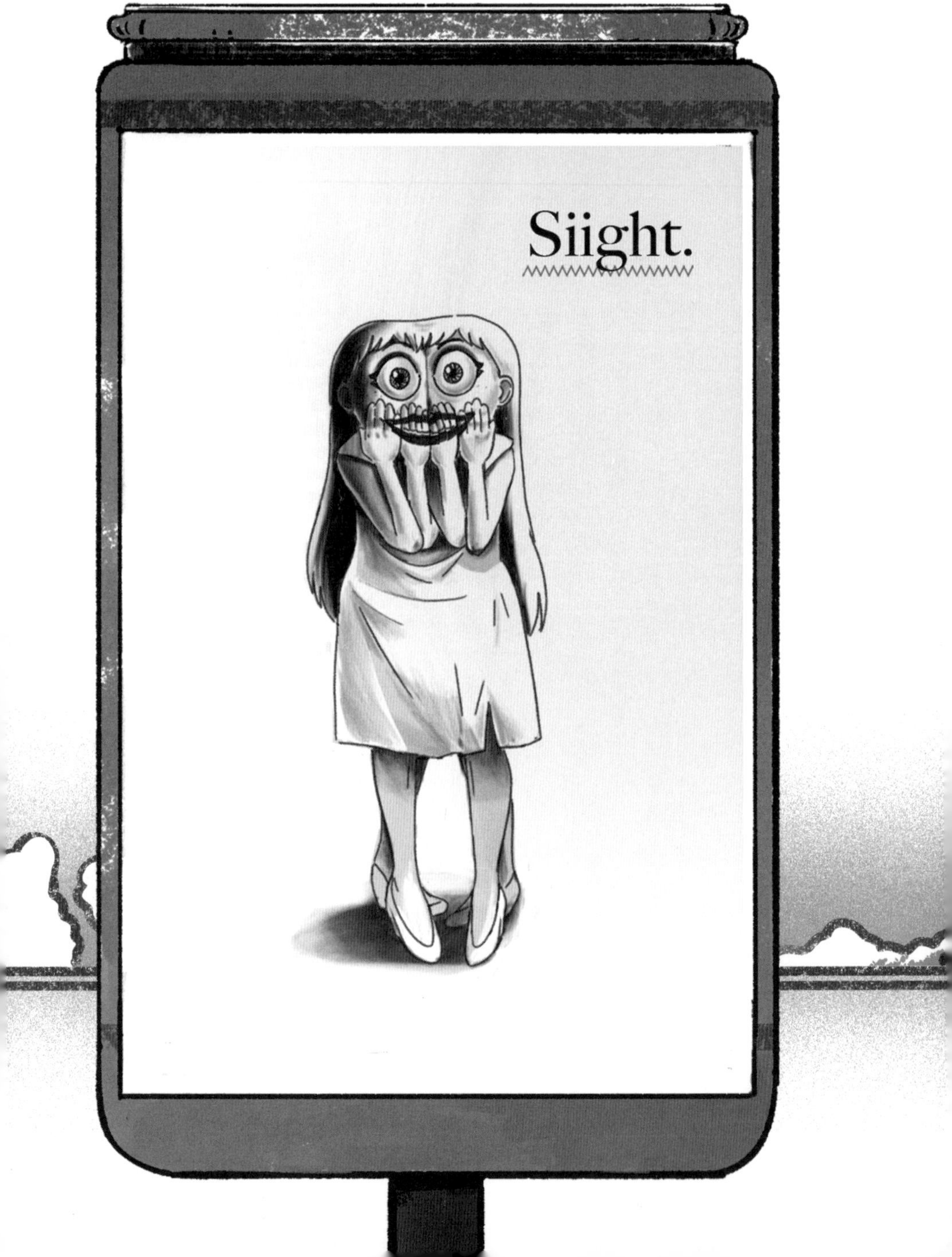
Siight.

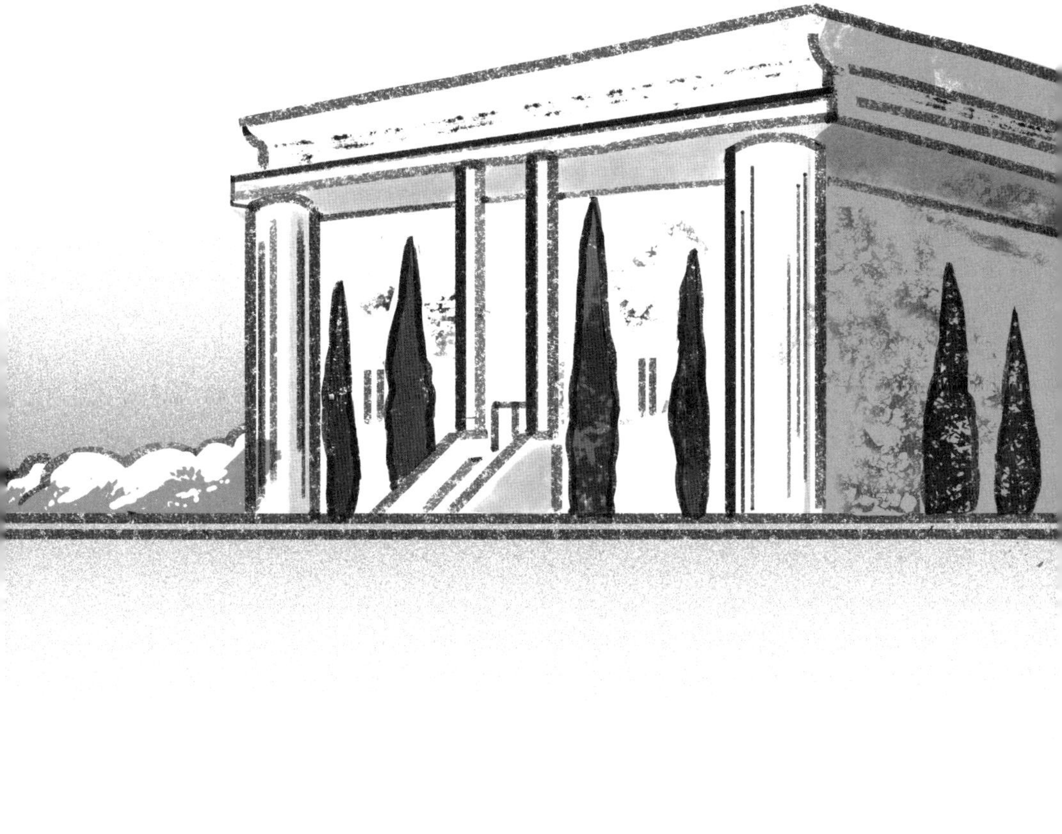

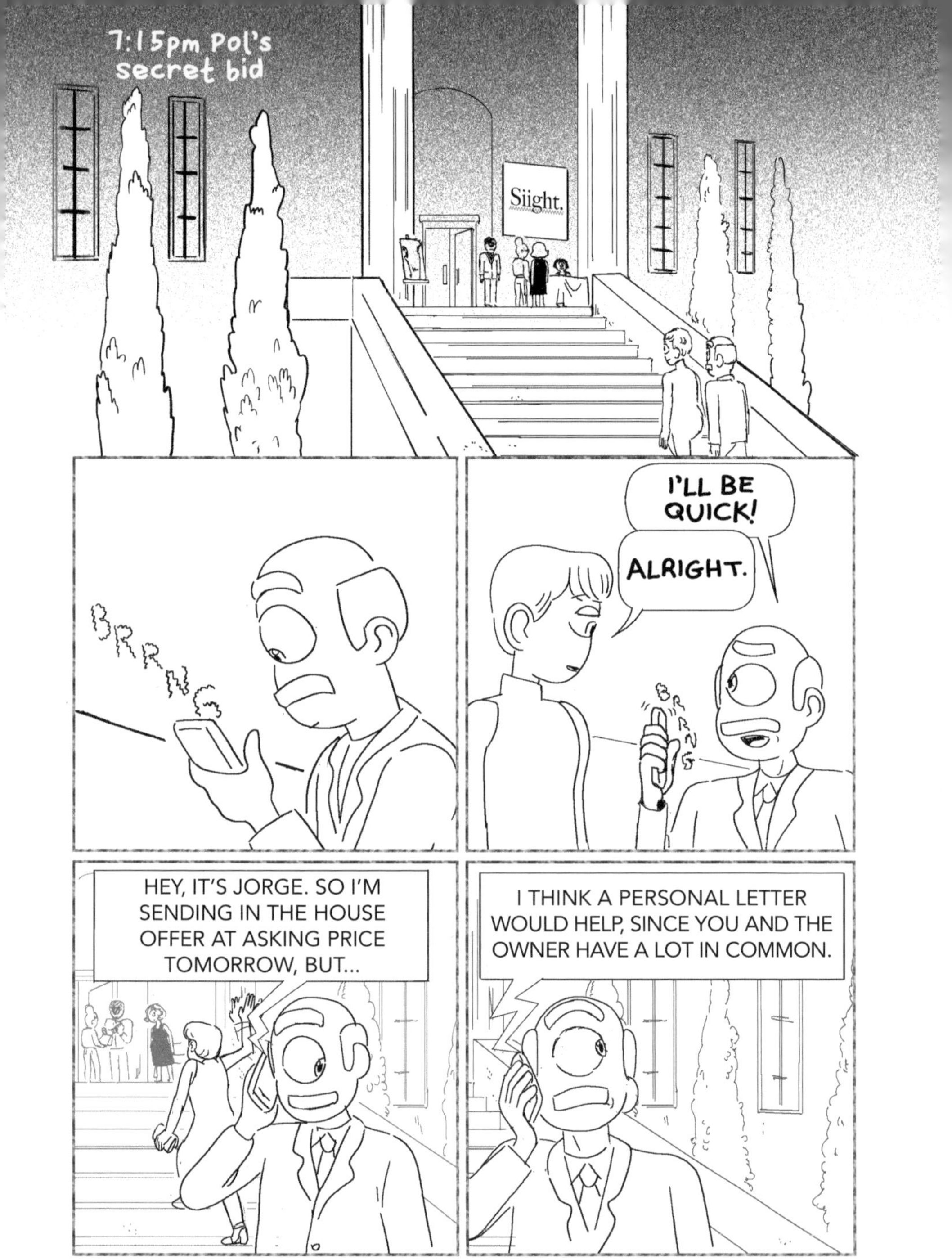
7:15pm Pol's secret bid
Siight.
BRRNG
I'LL BE QUICK!
ALRIGHT.
BRRNG
HEY, IT'S JORGE. SO I'M SENDING IN THE HOUSE OFFER AT ASKING PRICE TOMORROW, BUT...
I THINK A PERSONAL LETTER WOULD HELP, SINCE YOU AND THE OWNER HAVE A LOT IN COMMON.

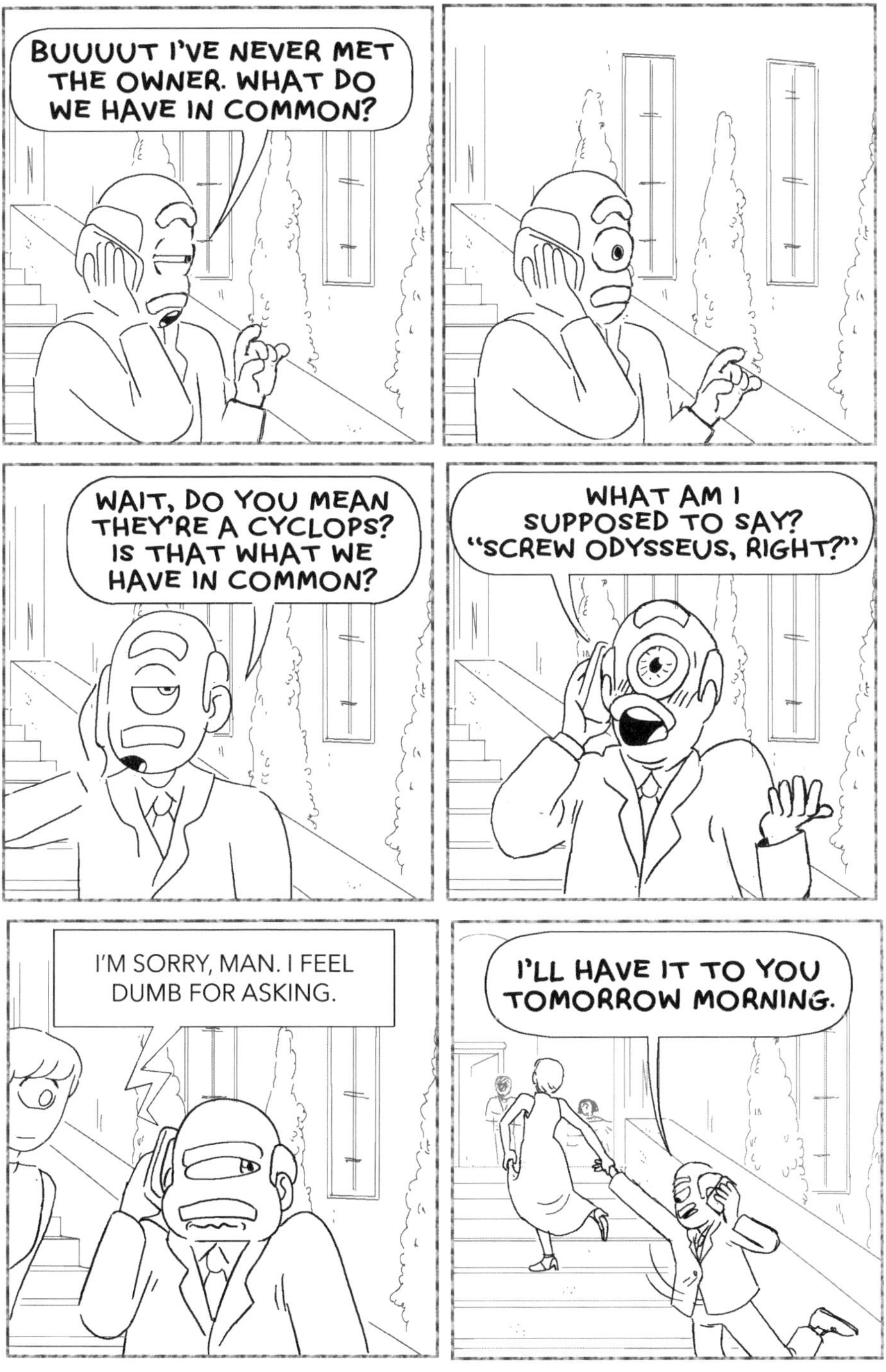
BUUUUT I'VE NEVER MET THE OWNER. WHAT DO WE HAVE IN COMMON?
WAIT, DO YOU MEAN THEY'RE A CYCLOPS? IS THAT WHAT WE HAVE IN COMMON?
WHAT AM I SUPPOSED TO SAY? "SCREW ODYSSEUS, RIGHT?"
I'M SORRY, MAN. I FEEL DUMB FOR ASKING.
I'LL HAVE IT TO YOU TOMORROW MORNING.

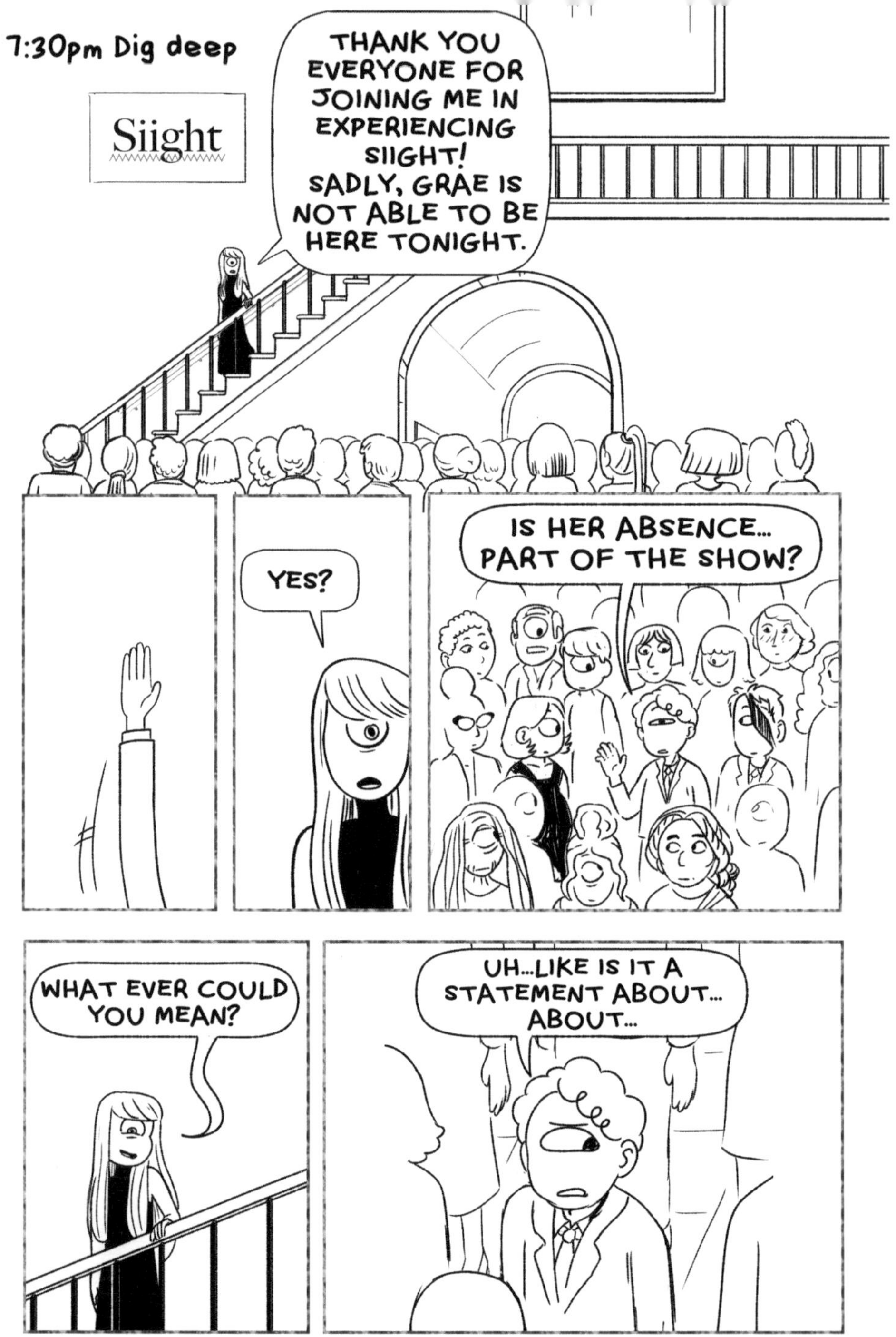
7:30pm Dig deep
Siight
THANK YOU EVERYONE FOR JOINING ME IN EXPERIENCING SIIGHT! SADLY, GRAE IS NOT ABLE TO BE HERE TONIGHT.
YES?
IS HER ABSENCE... PART OF THE SHOW?
WHAT EVER COULD YOU MEAN?
UH...LIKE IS IT A STATEMENT ABOUT... ABOUT...

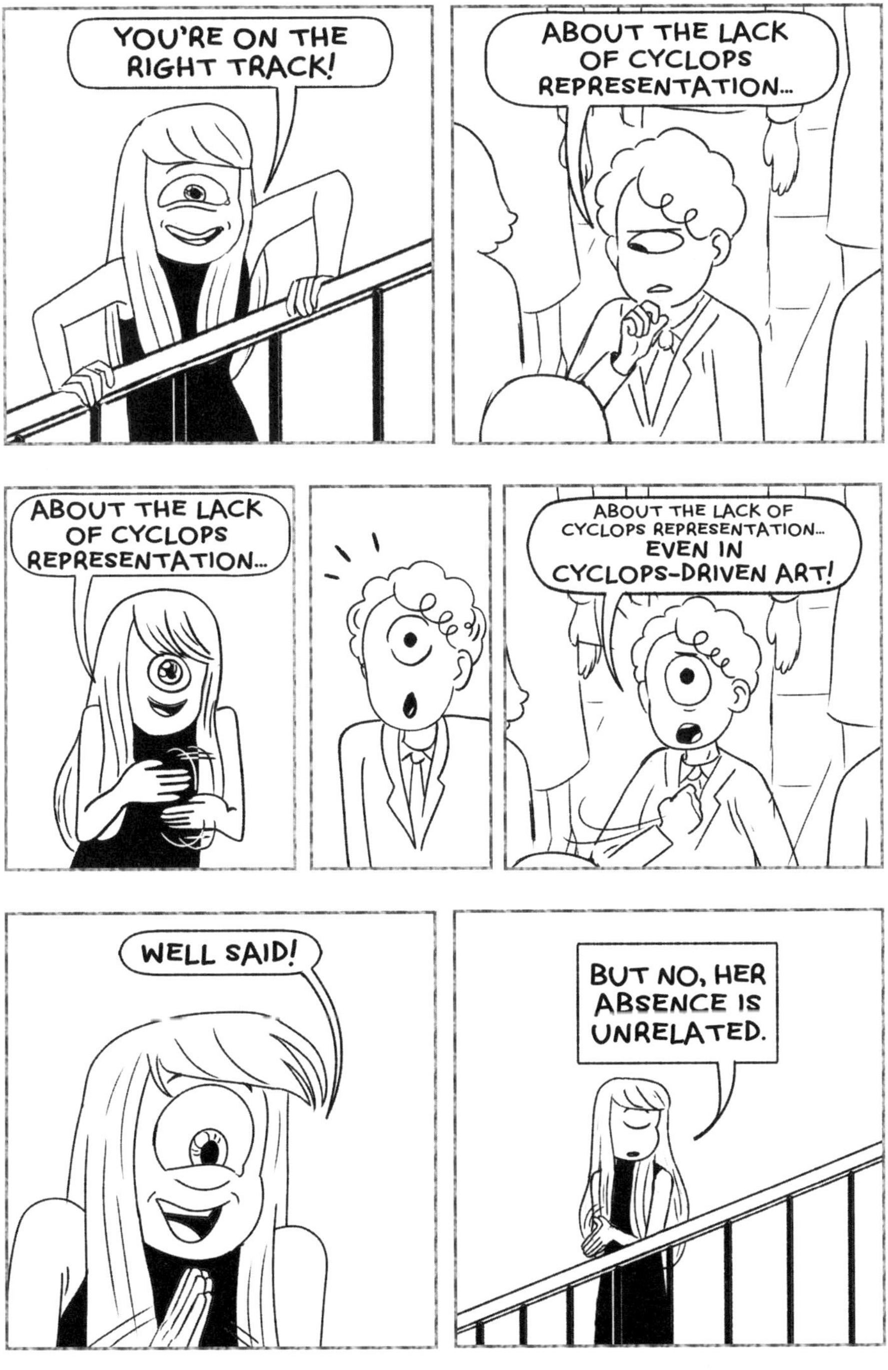
YOU'RE ON THE RIGHT TRACK!
ABOUT THE LACK OF CYCLOPS REPRESENTATION...
ABOUT THE LACK OF CYCLOPS REPRESENTATION...
ABOUT THE LACK OF CYCLOPS REPRESENTATION... EVEN IN CYCLOPS-DRIVEN ART!
WELL SAID!
BUT NO, HER ABSENCE IS UNRELATED.

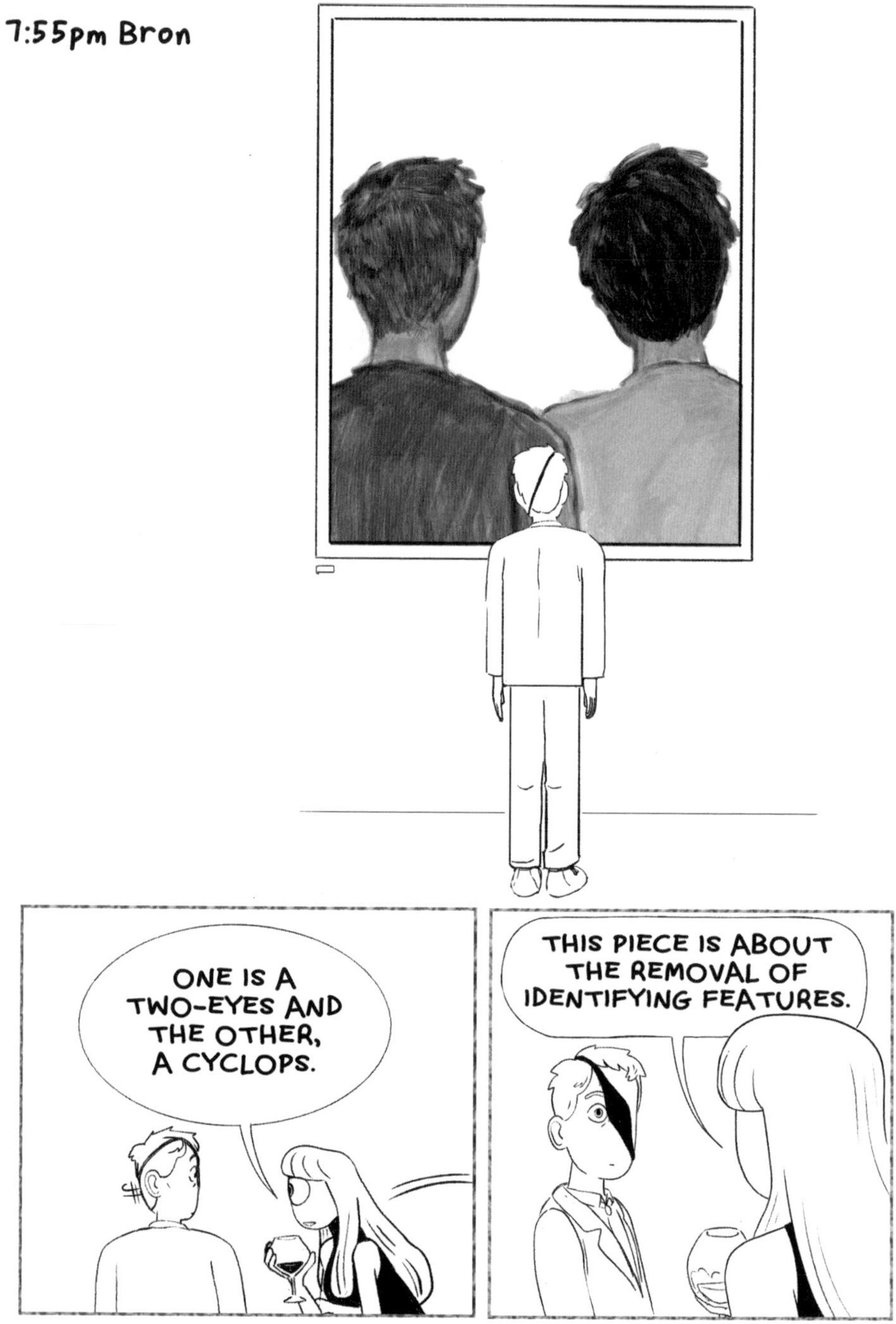
7:55pm Bron
ONE IS A TWO-EYES AND THE OTHER, A CYCLOPS.
THIS PIECE IS ABOUT THE REMOVAL OF IDENTIFYING FEATURES.

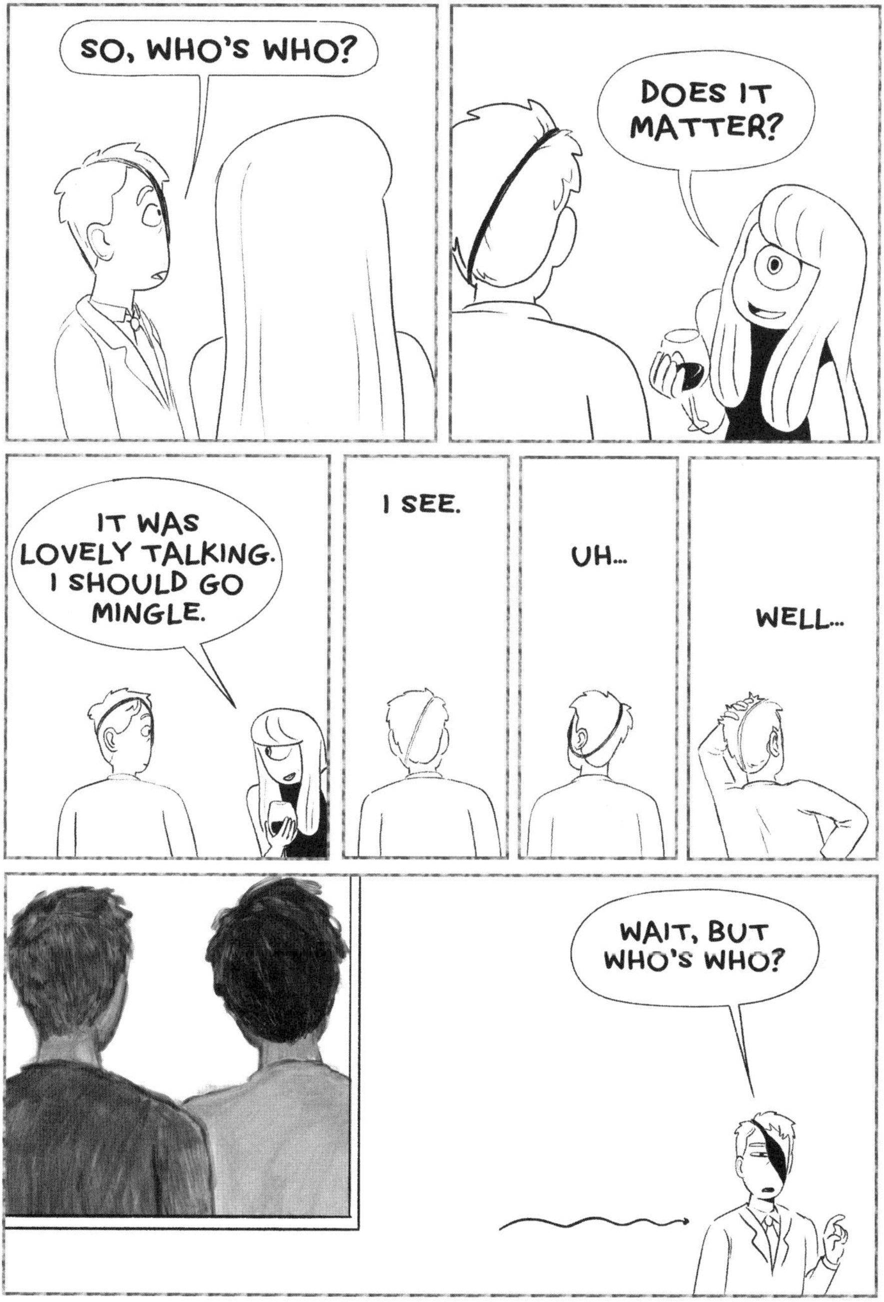
SO, WHO'S WHO?
DOES IT MATTER?
IT WAS LOVELY TALKING. I SHOULD GO MINGLE.
I SEE.
UH...
WELL...
WAIT, BUT WHO'S WHO?

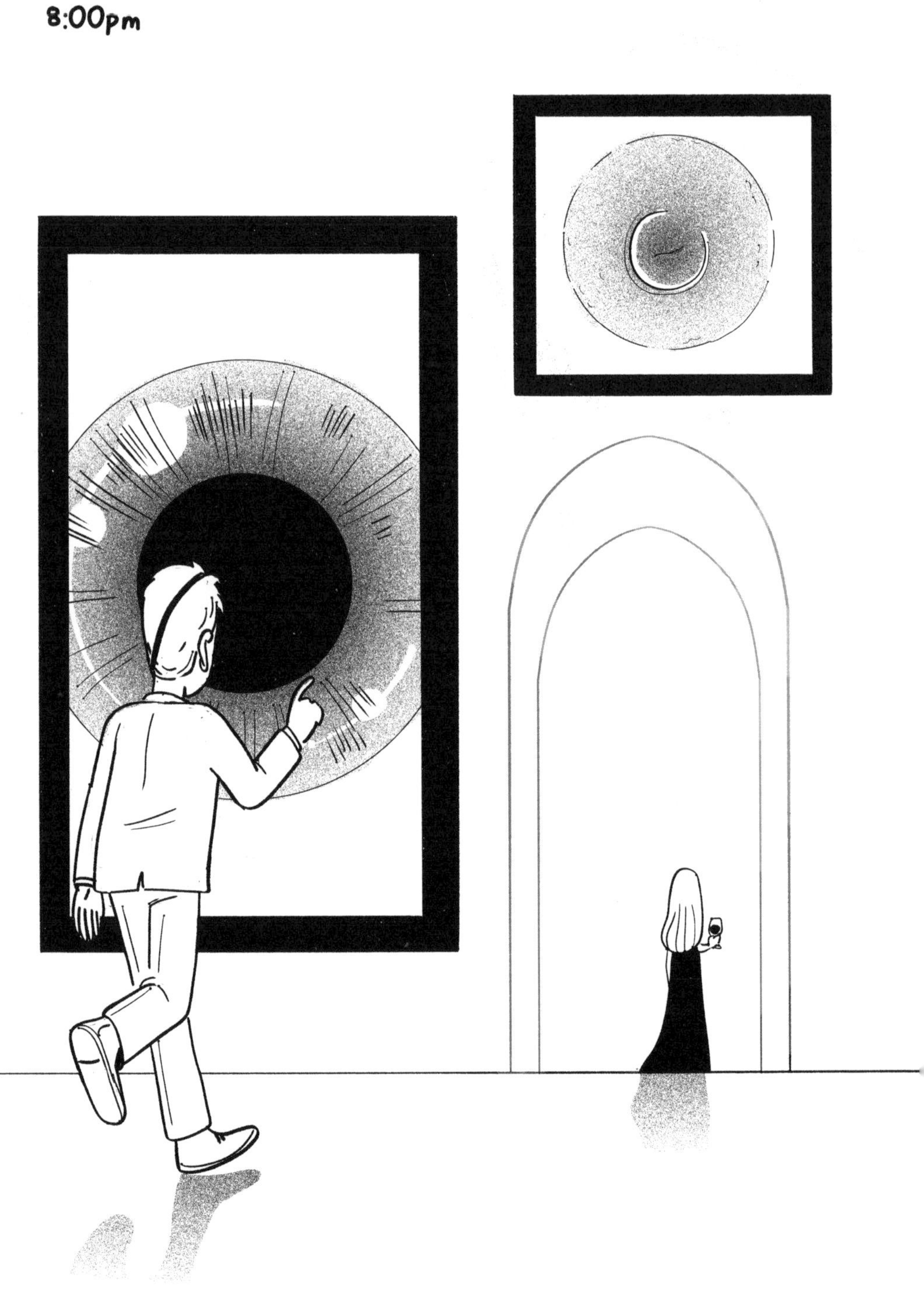
8:00pm

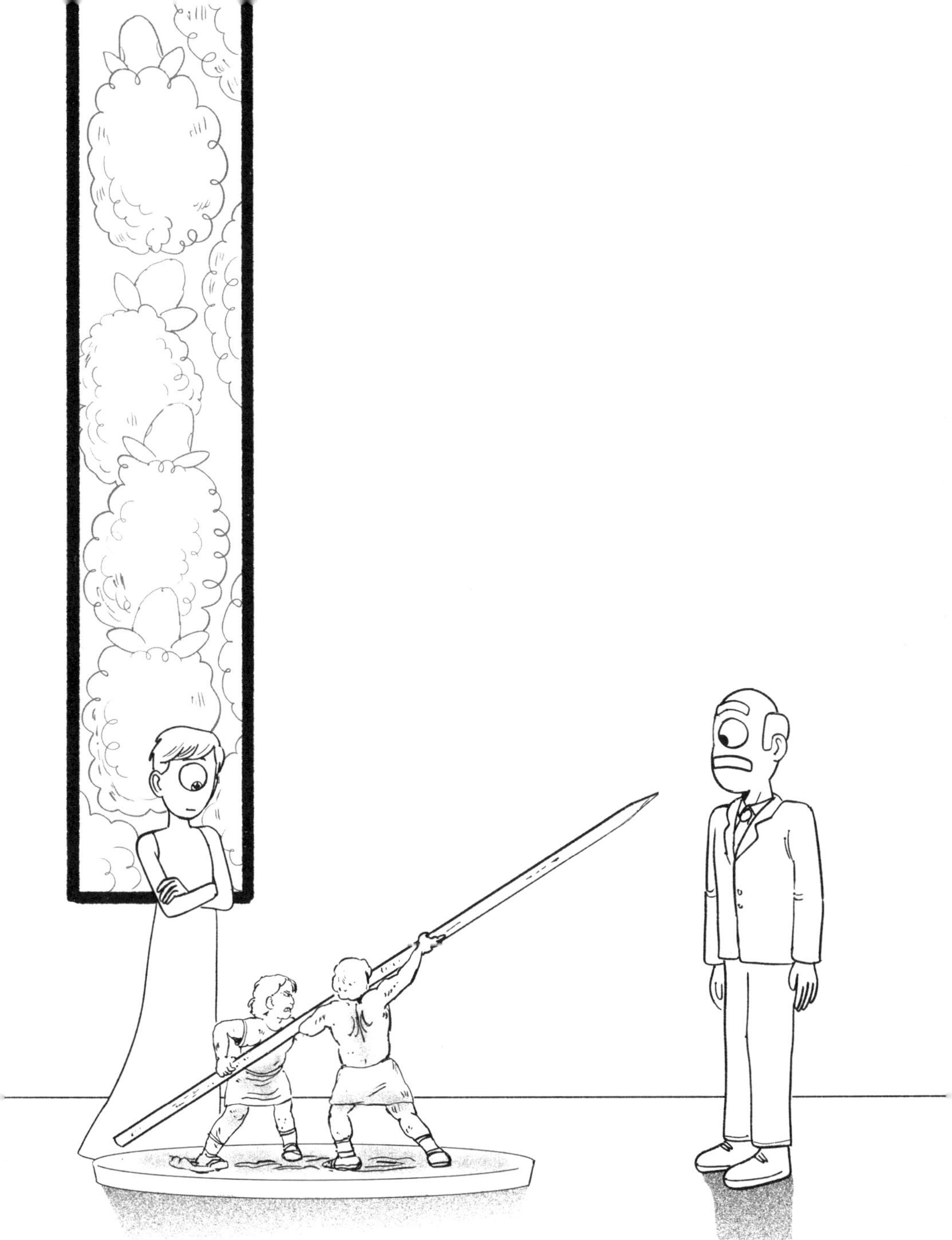

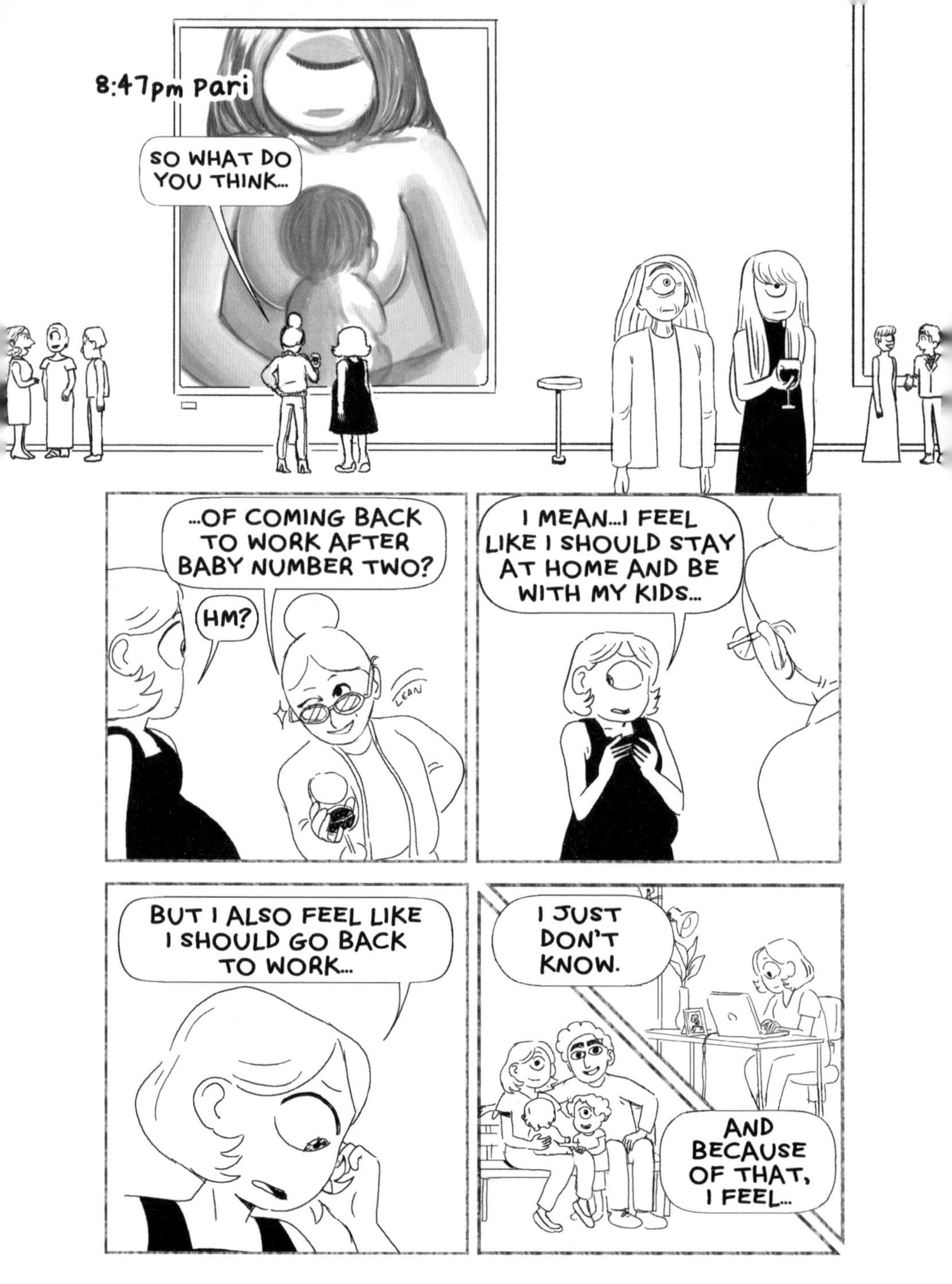
8:47pm Pari
SO WHAT DO YOU THINK...
...OF COMING BACK TO WORK AFTER BABY NUMBER TWO?
HM?
LEAN
I MEAN...I FEEL LIKE I SHOULD STAY AT HOME AND BE WITH MY KIDS...
BUT I ALSO FEEL LIKE I SHOULD GO BACK TO WORK...
I JUST DON'T KNOW.
AND BECAUSE OF THAT, I FEEL...

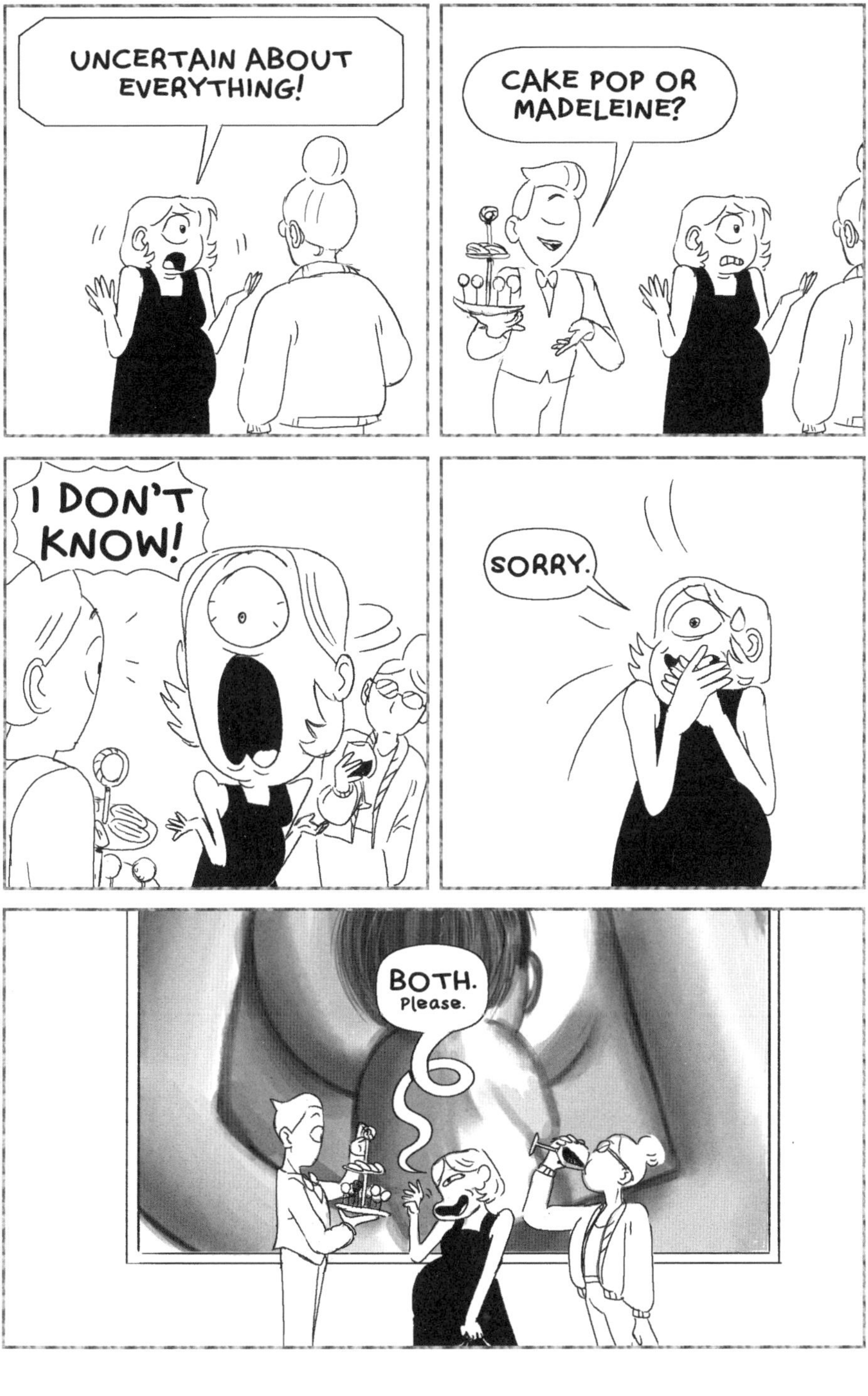
UNCERTAIN ABOUT EVERYTHING!
CAKE POP OR MADELEINE?
I DON'T KNOW!
SORRY.
BOTH. Please.

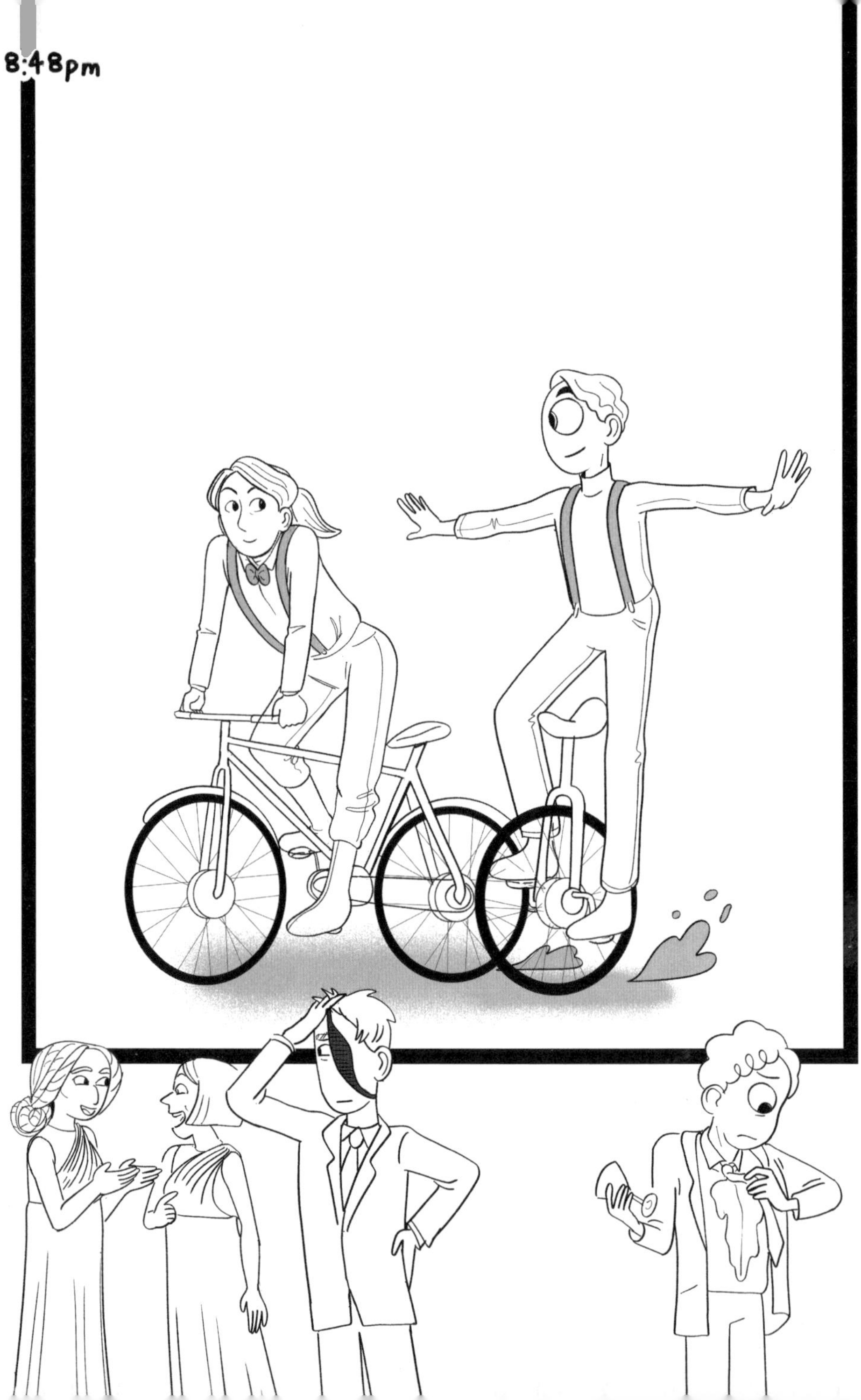
8:48pm

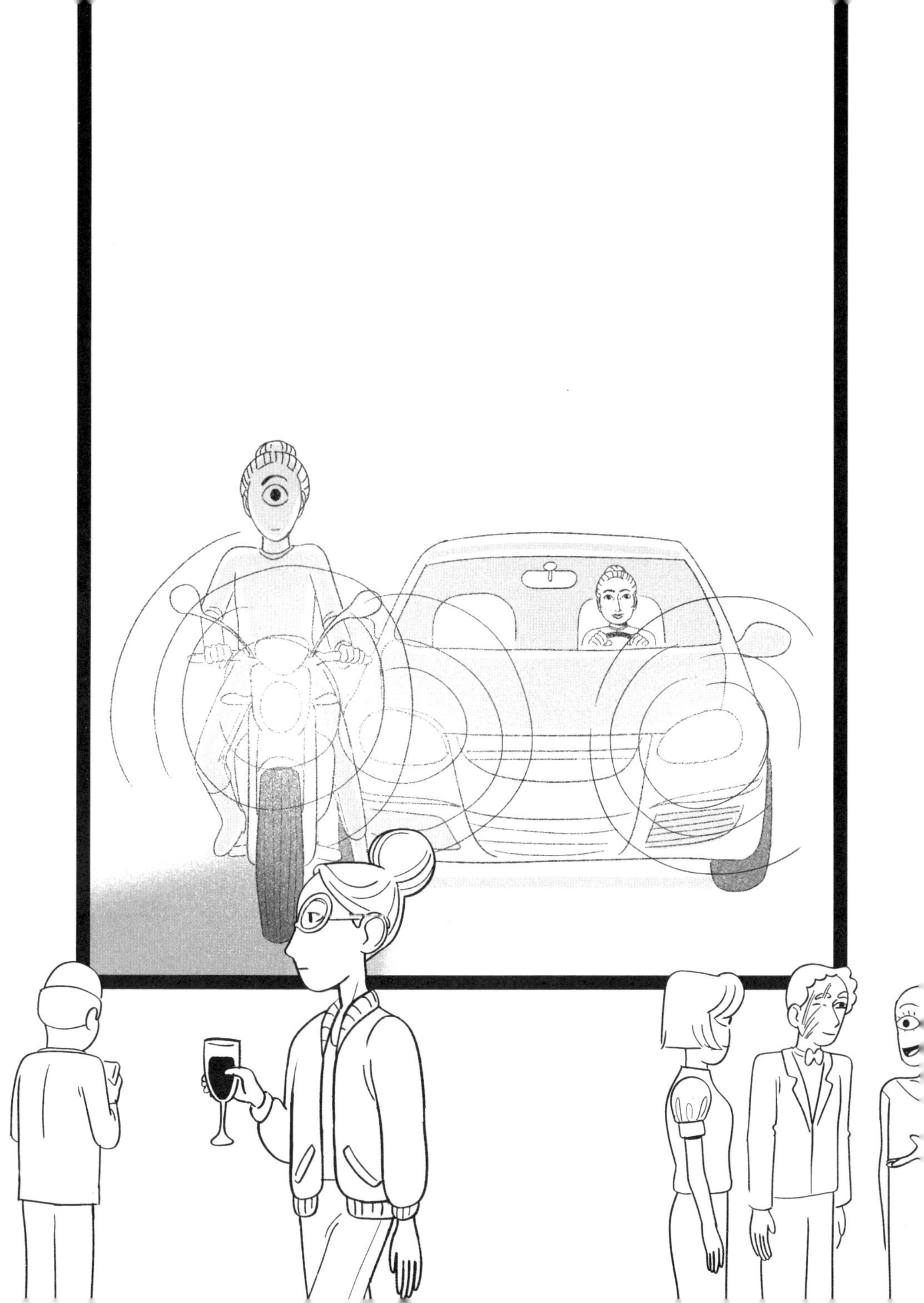

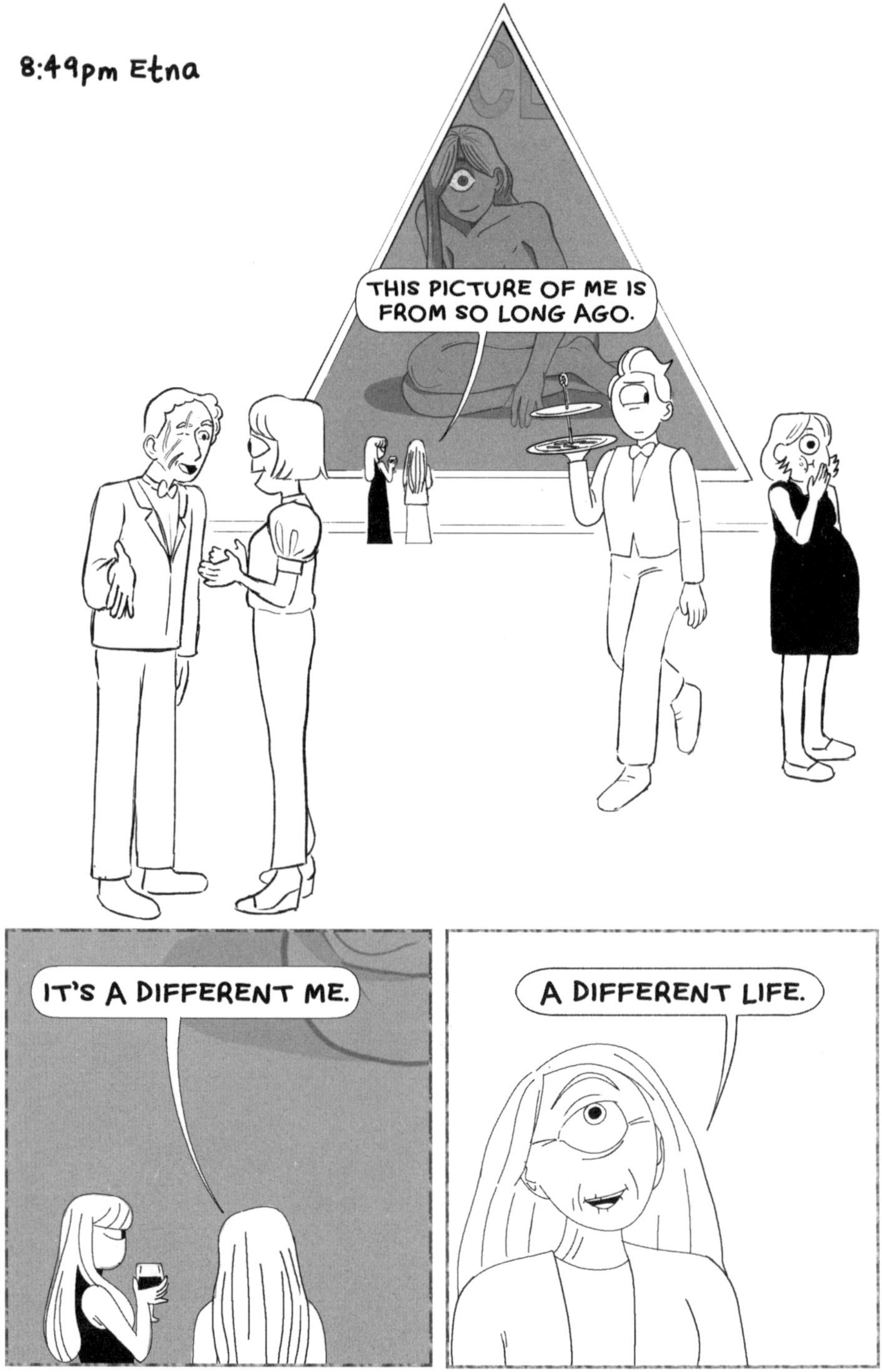
8:49pm Etna
THIS PICTURE OF ME IS FROM SO LONG AGO.
IT'S A DIFFERENT ME.
A DIFFERENT LIFE.

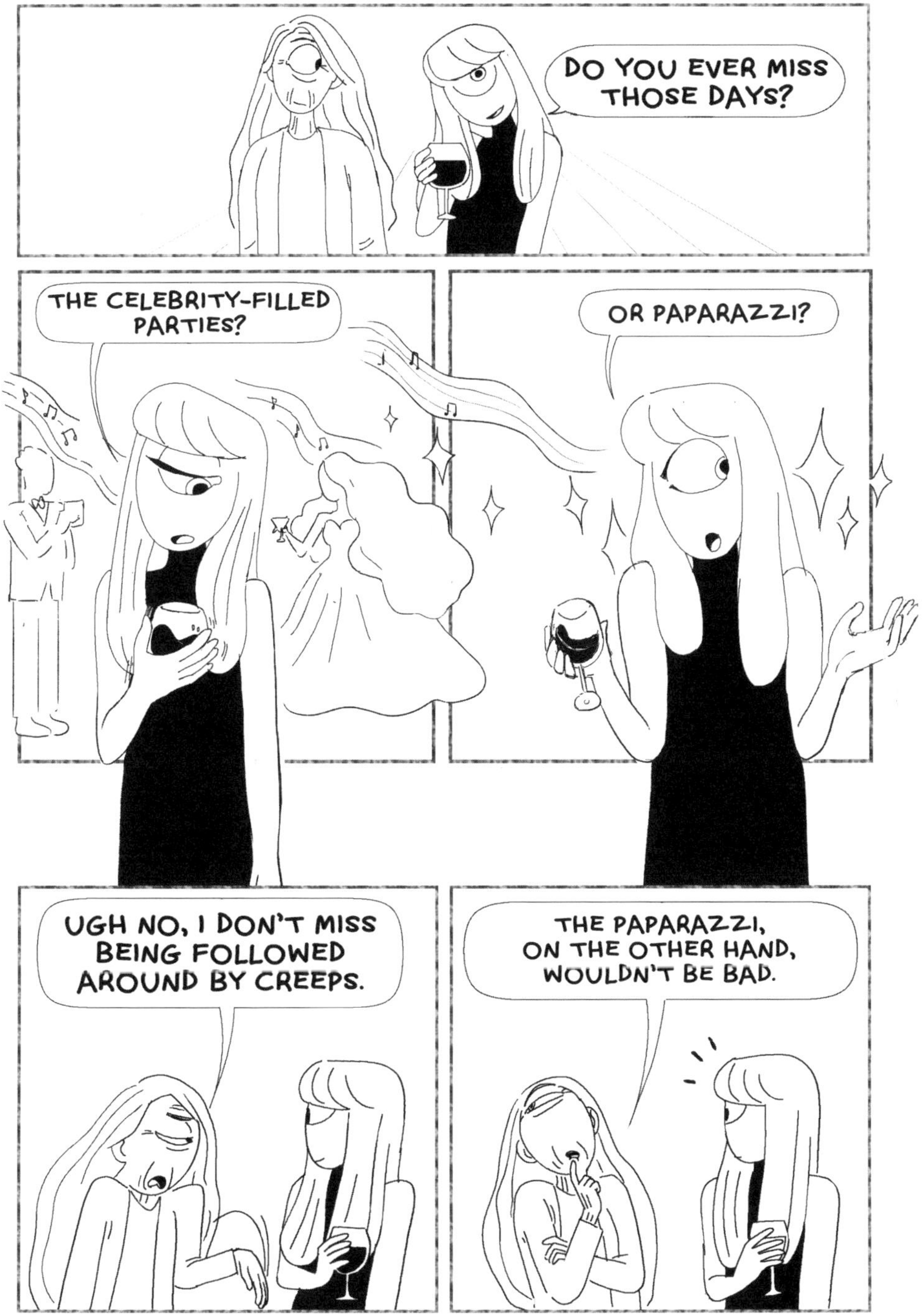
DO YOU EVER MISS THOSE DAYS?
THE CELEBRITY-FILLED PARTIES?
OR PAPARAZZI?
UGH NO, I DON'T MISS BEING FOLLOWED AROUND BY CREEPS.
THE PAPARAZZI, ON THE OTHER HAND, WOULDN'T BE BAD.

8:50pm Pol & Latea

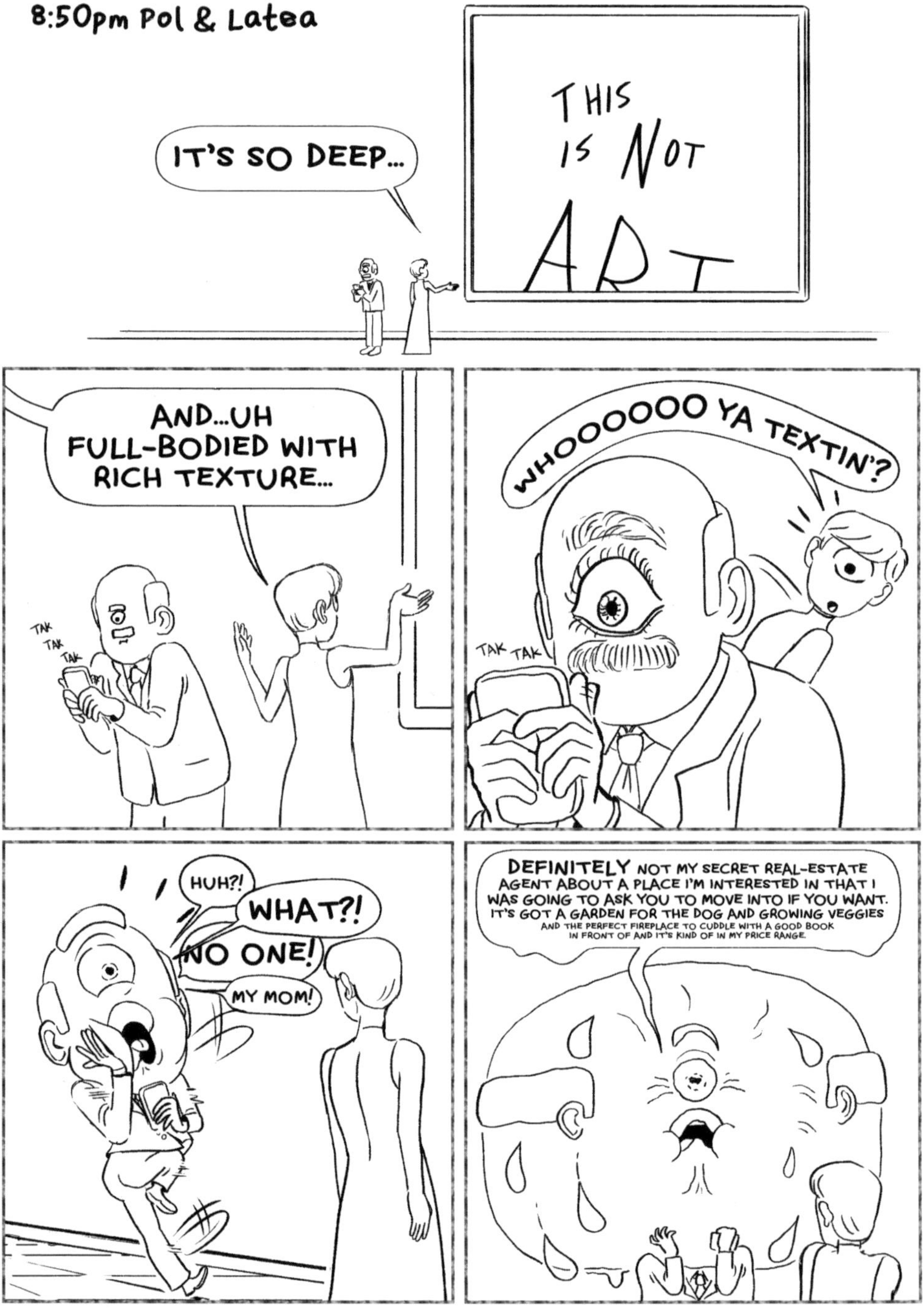
THIS IS NOT ART
IT'S SO DEEP...
AND...UH FULL-BODIED WITH RICH TEXTURE...
TAK TAK TAK
WHOOOOOO YA TEXTIN'?
TAK TAK
HUH?!
WHAT?!
NO ONE!
MY MOM!
DEFINITELY NOT MY SECRET REAL-ESTATE AGENT ABOUT A PLACE I'M INTERESTED IN THAT I WAS GOING TO ASK YOU TO MOVE INTO IF YOU WANT. IT'S GOT A GARDEN FOR THE DOG AND GROWING VEGGIES AND THE PERFECT FIREPLACE TO CUDDLE WITH A GOOD BOOK IN FRONT OF AND IT'S KIND OF IN MY PRICE RANGE.

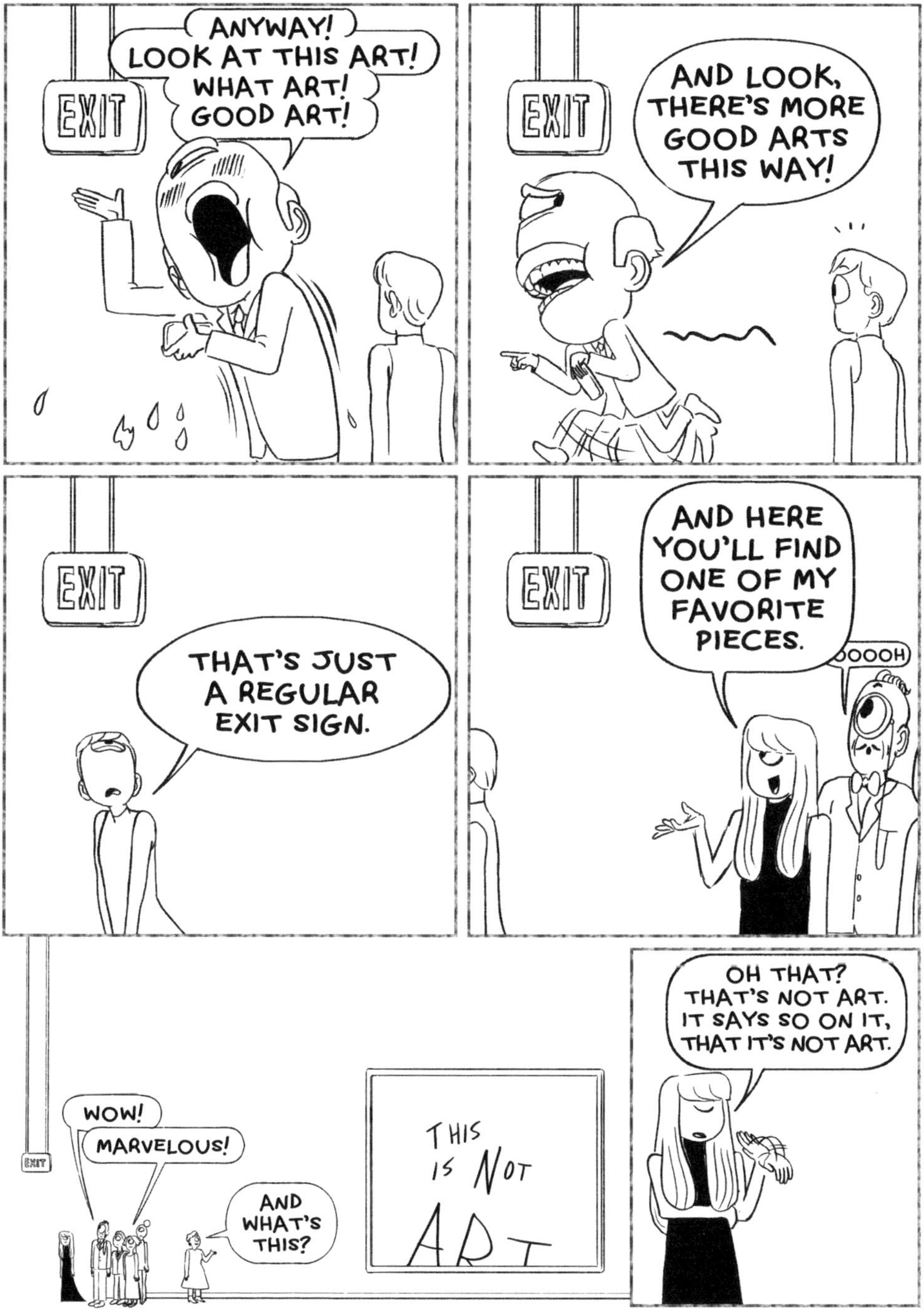
EXIT
ANYWAY!
LOOK AT THIS ART!
WHAT ART!
GOOD ART!
EXIT
AND LOOK, THERE'S MORE GOOD ARTS THIS WAY!
EXIT
THAT'S JUST A REGULAR EXIT SIGN.
EXIT
AND HERE YOU'LL FIND ONE OF MY FAVORITE PIECES.
OOOOH
EXIT
WOW!
MARVELOUS!
AND WHAT'S THIS?
THIS IS NOT ART
OH THAT? THAT'S NOT ART. IT SAYS SO ON IT, THAT IT'S NOT ART.

9:04pm Pari & Latea

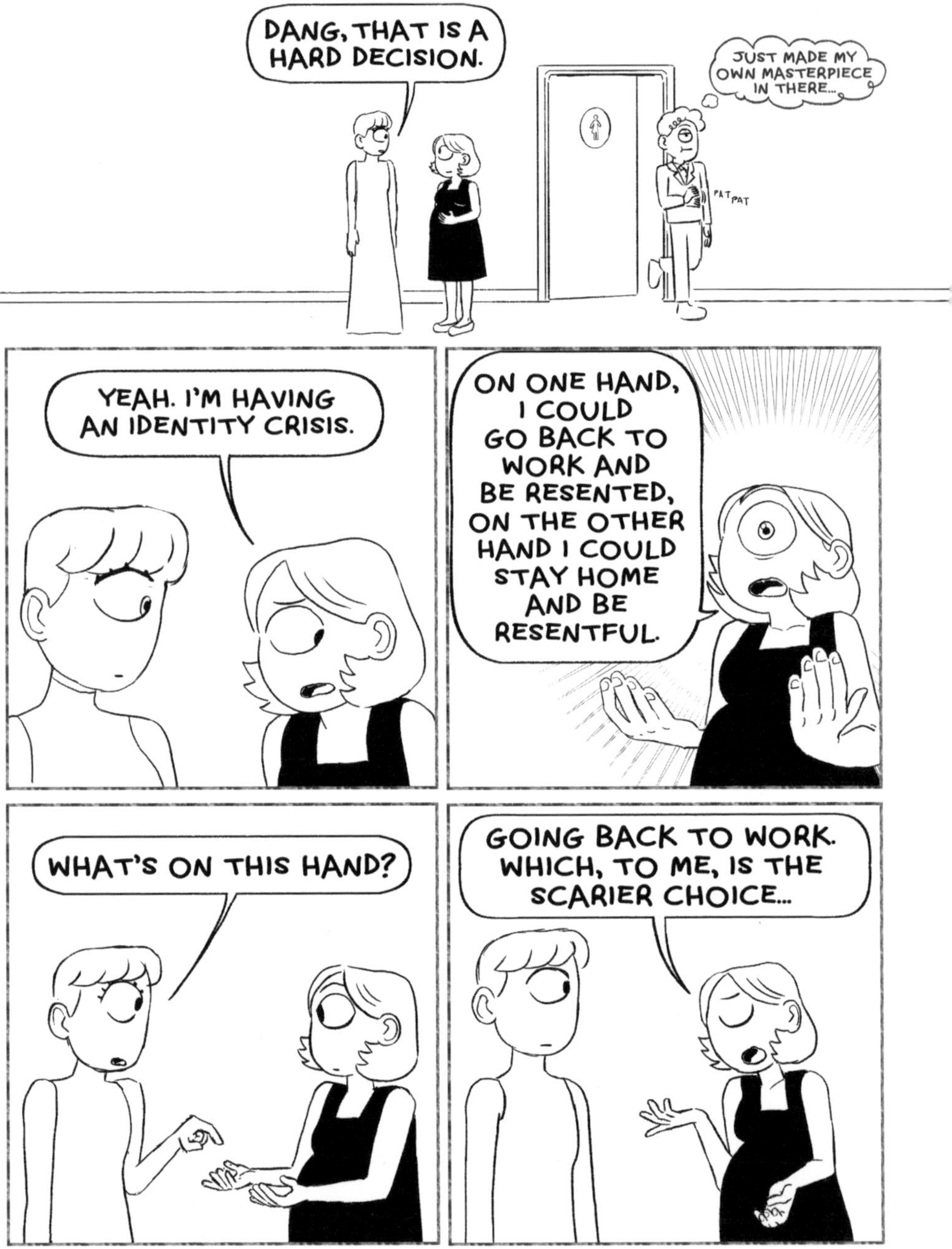

DANG, THAT IS A HARD DECISION.
JUST MADE MY OWN MASTERPIECE IN THERE...
PAT PAT
YEAH. I'M HAVING AN IDENTITY CRISIS.
ON ONE HAND, I COULD GO BACK TO WORK AND BE RESENTED, ON THE OTHER HAND I COULD STAY HOME AND BE RESENTFUL.
WHAT'S ON THIS HAND?
GOING BACK TO WORK. WHICH, TO ME, IS THE SCARIER CHOICE...

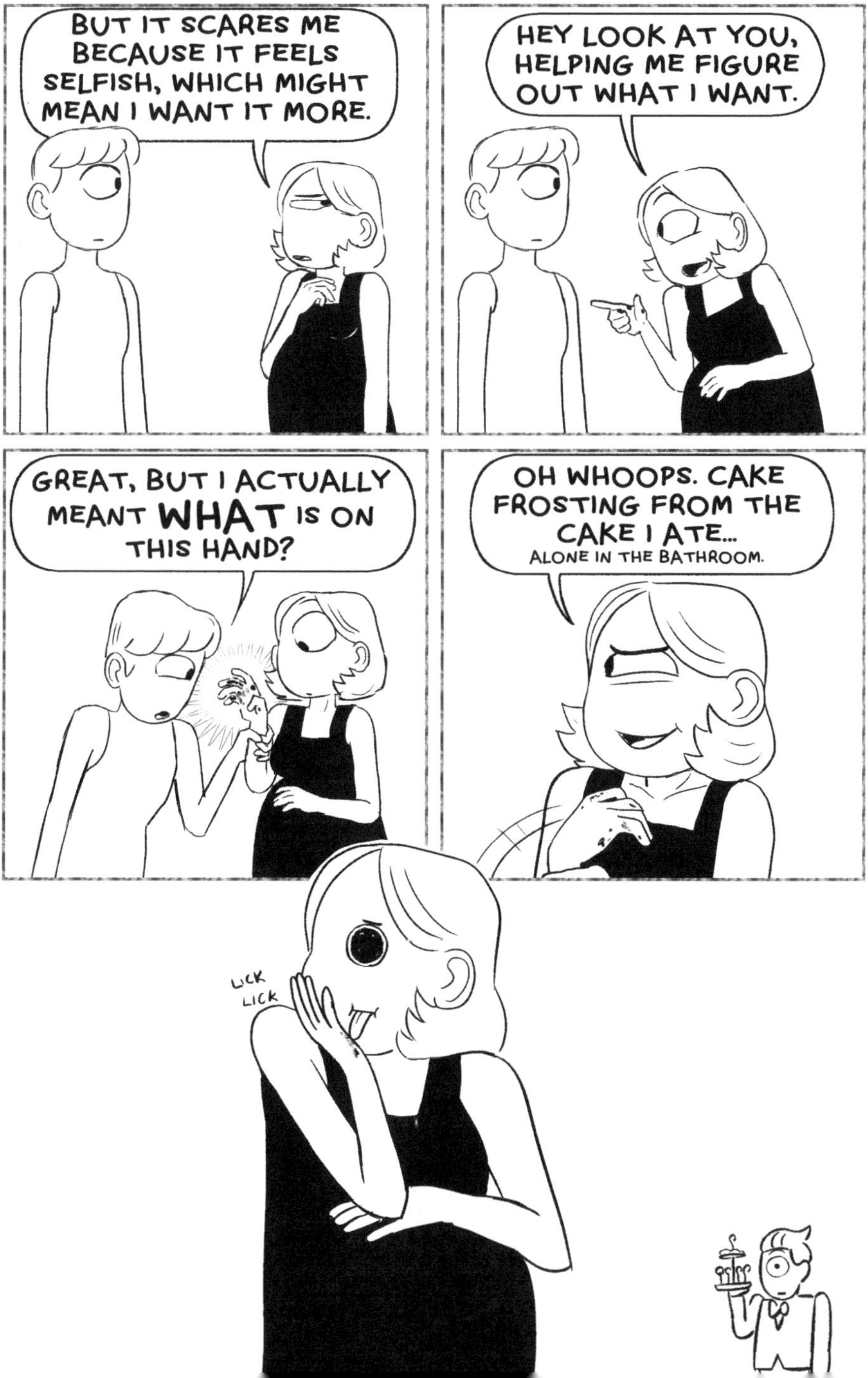
BUT IT SCARES ME BECAUSE IT FEELS SELFISH, WHICH MIGHT MEAN I WANT IT MORE.
HEY LOOK AT YOU, HELPING ME FIGURE OUT WHAT I WANT.
GREAT, BUT I ACTUALLY MEANT WHAT IS ON THIS HAND?
OH WHOOPS. CAKE FROSTING FROM THE CAKE I ATE... ALONE IN THE BATHROOM.
LICK LICK

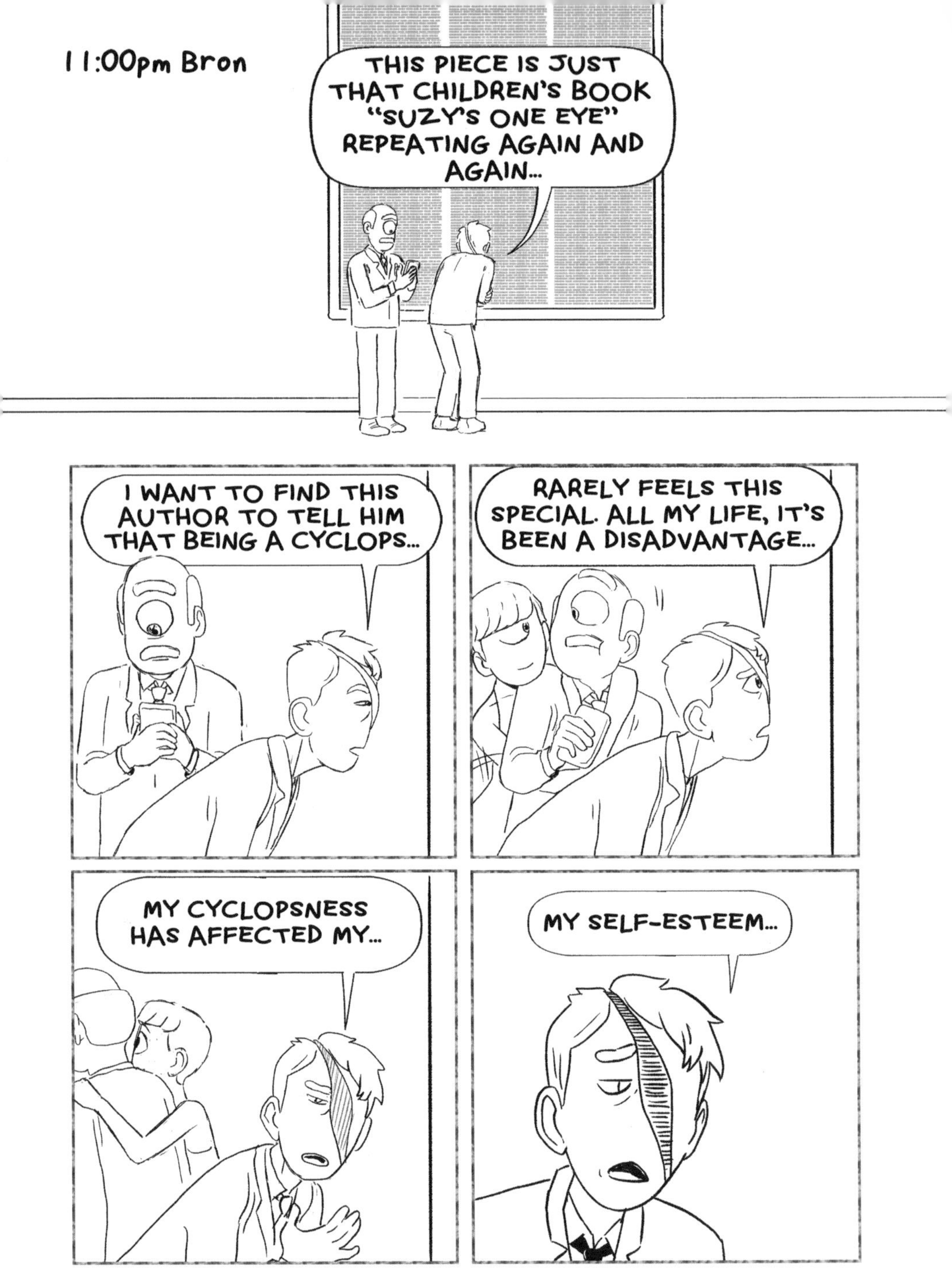
11:00pm Bron
THIS PIECE IS JUST THAT CHILDREN'S BOOK "SUZY'S ONE EYE" REPEATING AGAIN AND AGAIN...
I WANT TO FIND THIS AUTHOR TO TELL HIM THAT BEING A CYCLOPS...
RARELY FEELS THIS SPECIAL. ALL MY LIFE, IT'S BEEN A DISADVANTAGE...
MY CYCLOPSNESS HAS AFFECTED MY...
MY SELF-ESTEEM...

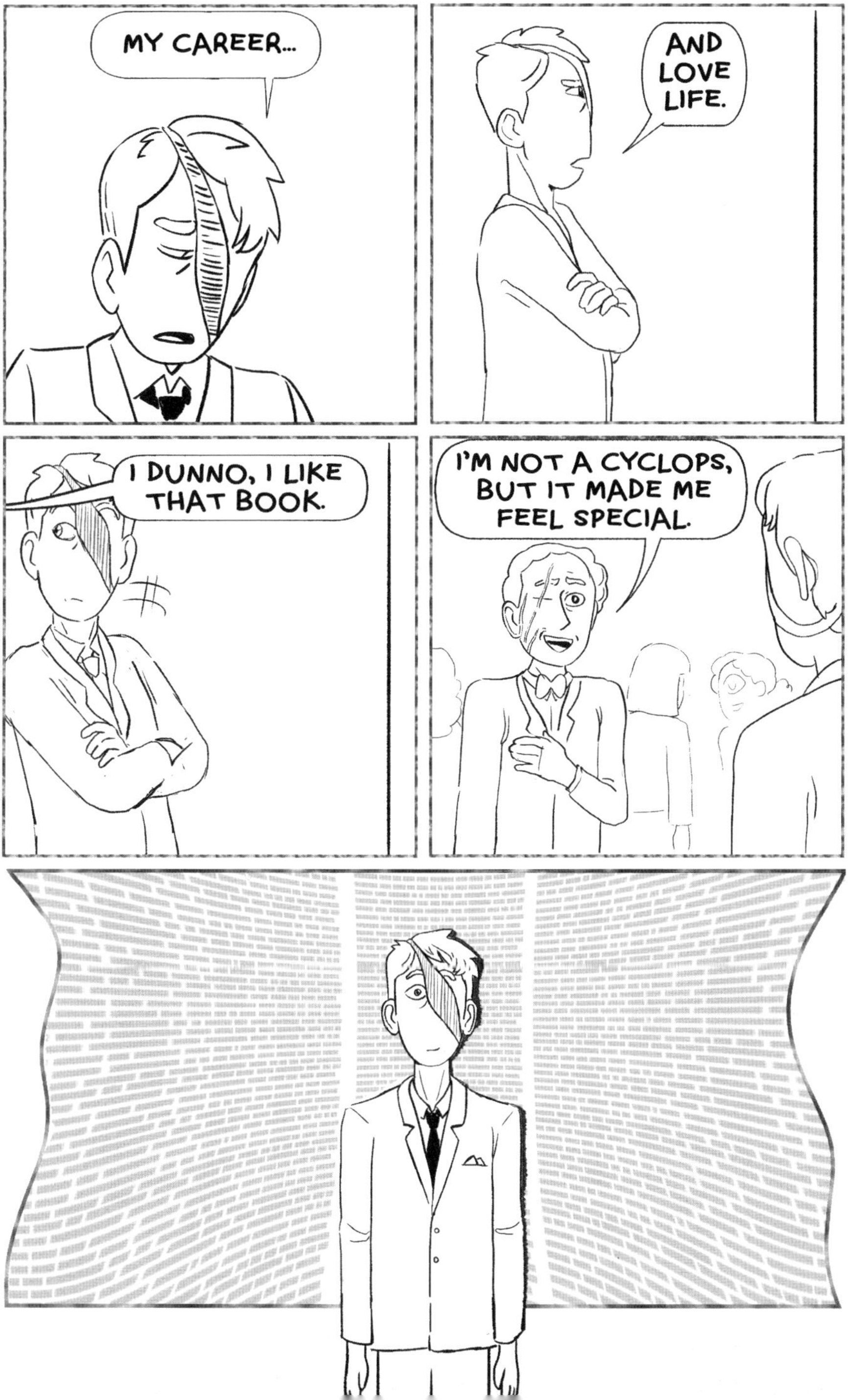
MY CAREER...
AND LOVE LIFE.
I DUNNO, I LIKE THAT BOOK.
I'M NOT A CYCLOPS, BUT IT MADE ME FEEL SPECIAL.

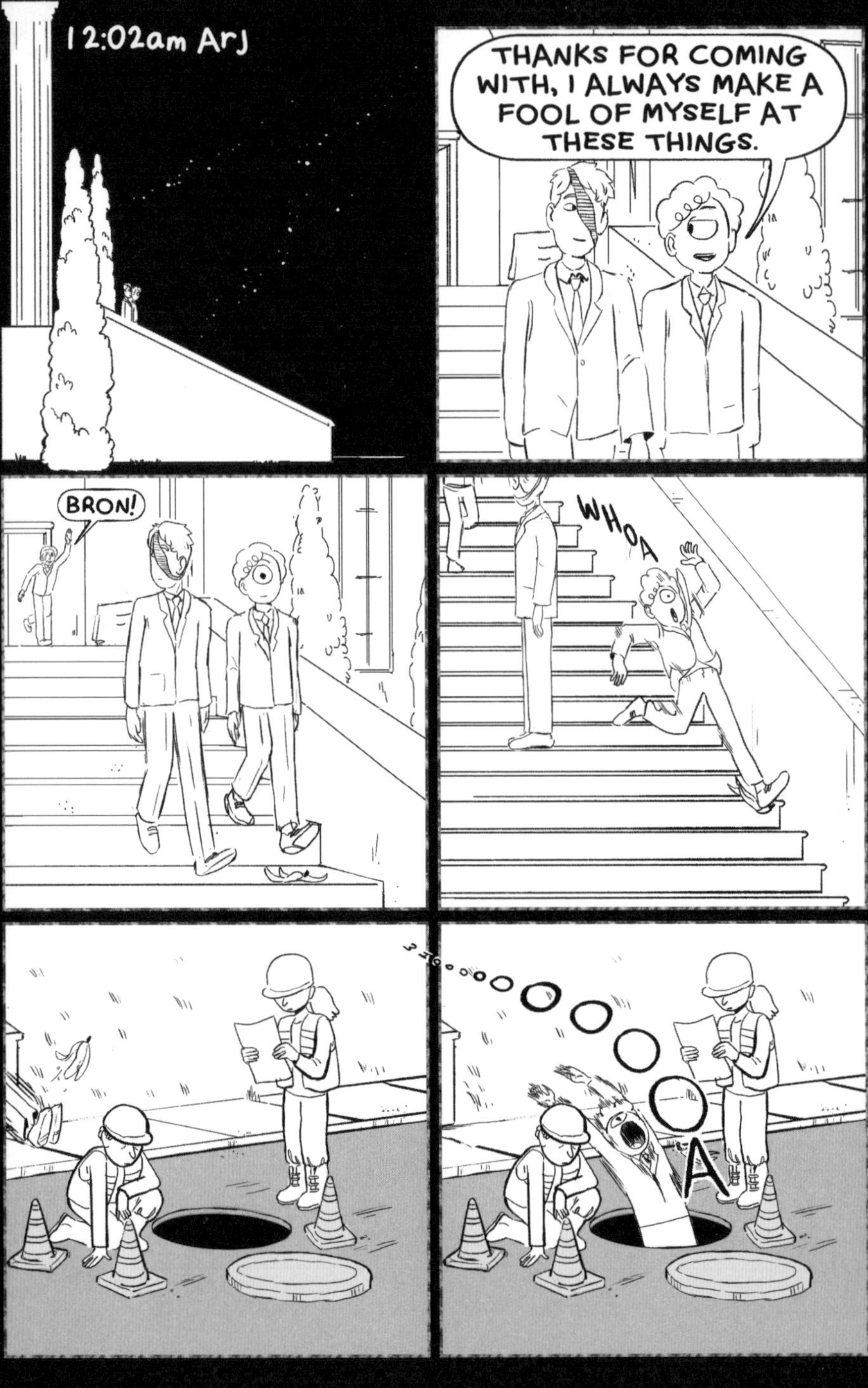
12:02am Arj
THANKS FOR COMING WITH, I ALWAYS MAKE A FOOL OF MYSELF AT THESE THINGS.
BRON!
WHOA

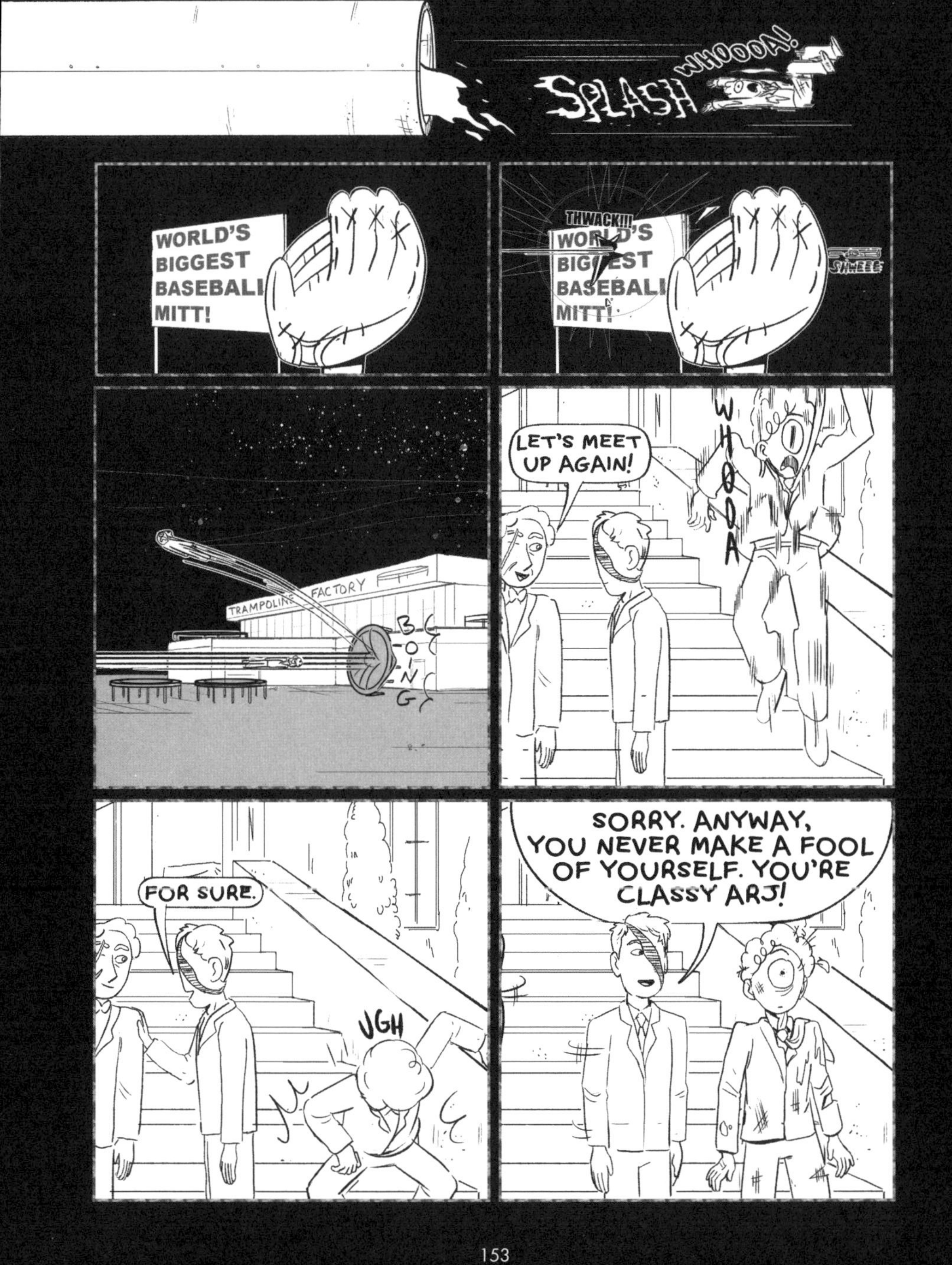
SPLASH
WHOOOA!
THWACK!!!
WORLD'S BIGGEST BASEBALL MITT!
SHWEEE
TRAMPOLINE FACTORY
BOING
LET'S MEET UP AGAIN!
WHOOA
FOR SURE.
UGH
SORRY. ANYWAY, YOU NEVER MAKE A FOOL OF YOURSELF. YOU'RE CLASSY ARJ!

12:18am
Pari

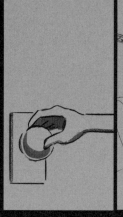

CREEEAK

HEY STRANGER, GOOD NIGHT?

GREAT NIGHT, I FIGURED OUT SOME LIFE STUFF.

SO YOU'RE GOING BACK TO WORK?

HOW'D YOU KNOW?

GIMME SOME CREDIT. I MAKE A LOT OF DAD-PUNS, BUT I KNOW MY WIFE.

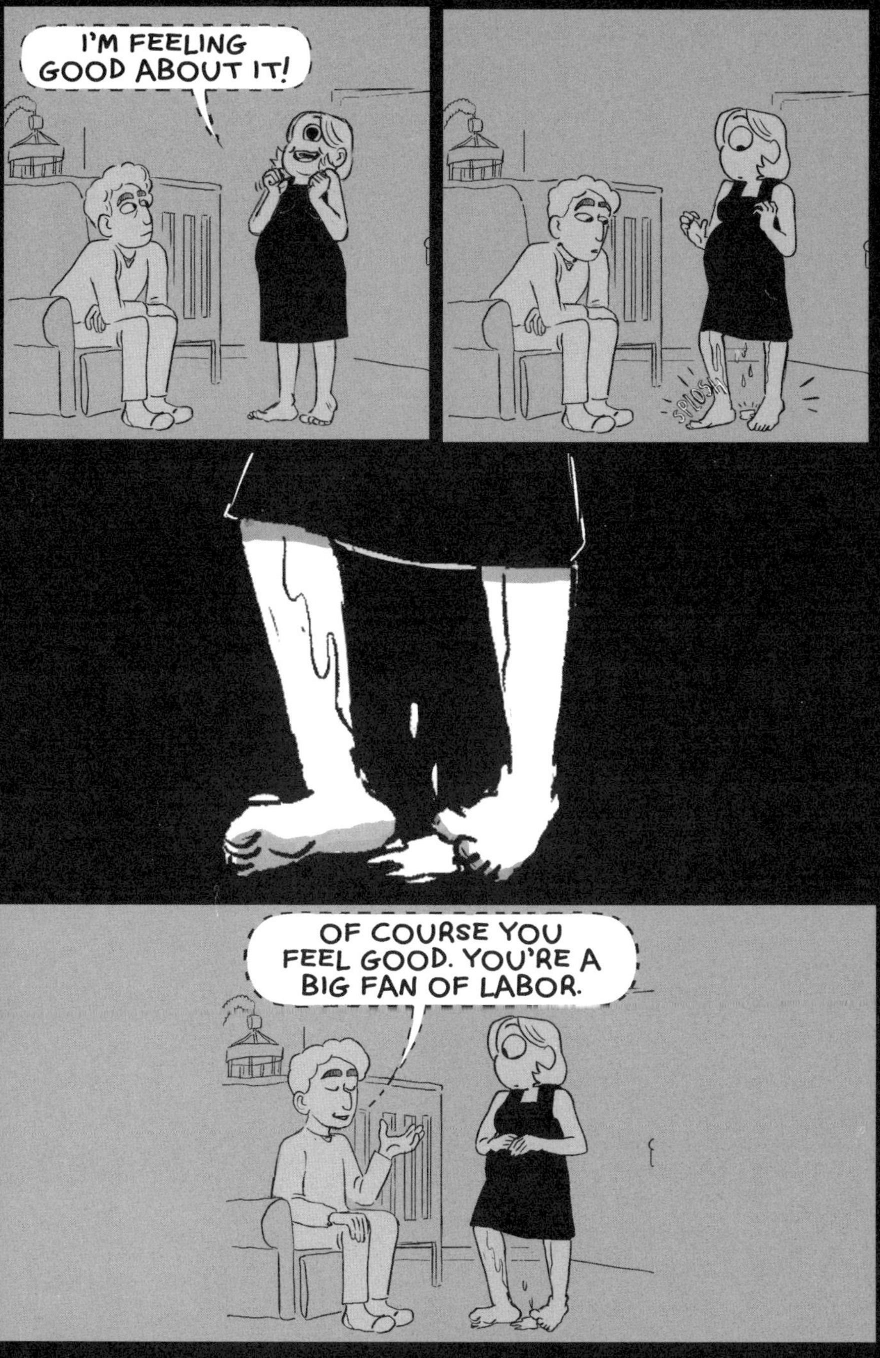
I'M FEELING GOOD ABOUT IT!
SPLOSH
OF COURSE YOU FEEL GOOD. YOU'RE A BIG FAN OF LABOR.

3:00am Pol

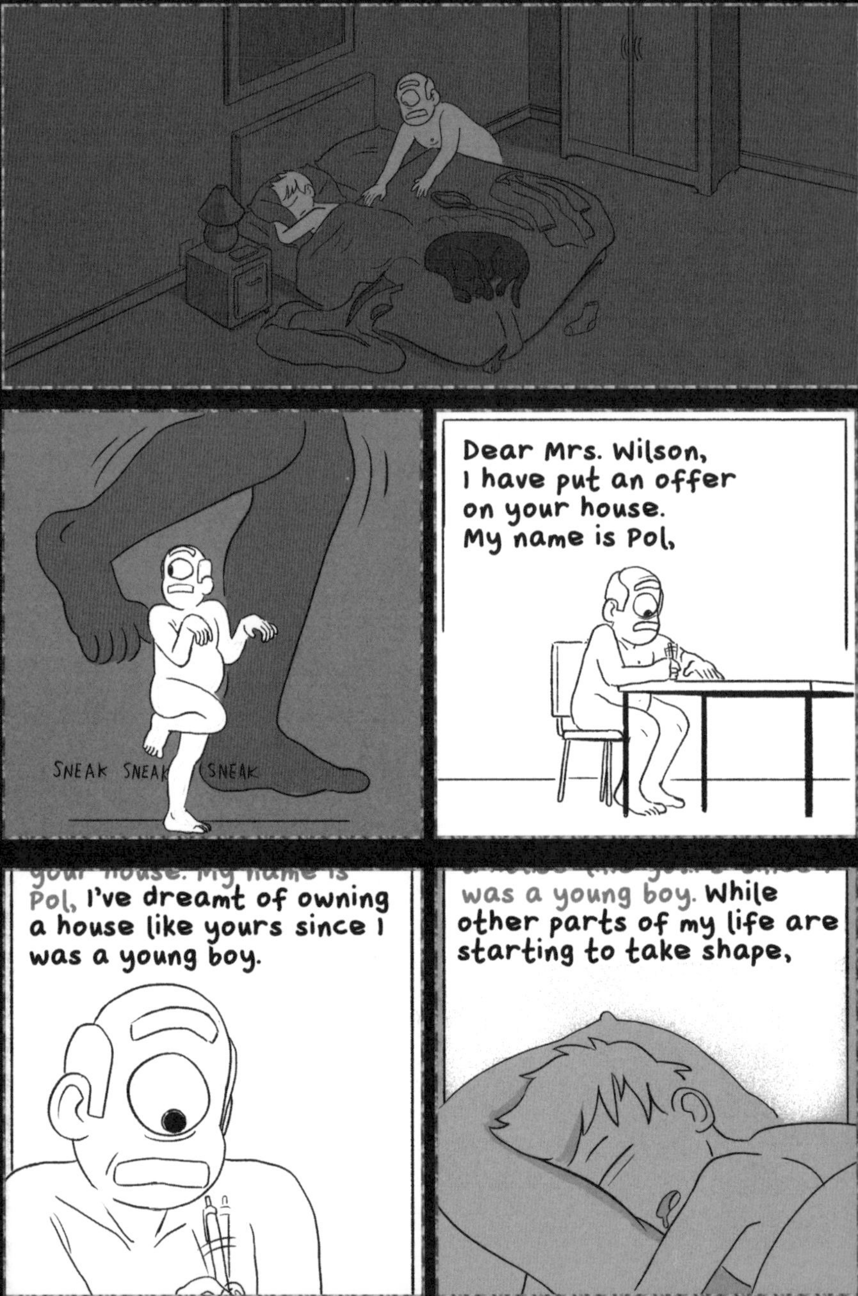

SNEAK SNEAK SNEAK
Dear Mrs. Wilson,
I have put an offer
on your house.
My name is Pol,
Pol, I've dreamt of owning a house like yours since I was a young boy.
was a young boy. While other parts of my life are starting to take shape,

starting to take shape,
the only thing that is
missing are the four walls
to surround my beautiful
life.

life. Like many minorities,
I had a complicated
childhood. I come from a
single-parent immigrant
household.

household.
I was taught to work hard
and keep my guard up.
Thankfully the hard work
has led me to this offer.

has led me to this offer.
A perfect house, like
yours, dominates my
fantasy life. It
represents stability,
safety, and is a
life-milestone I've been
chasing for years,

life-milestone I've been
chasing for years,
regardless of the weird
street name.   Thank you for
                      your time,
                      PL

BUTTFART St

Bron's best self

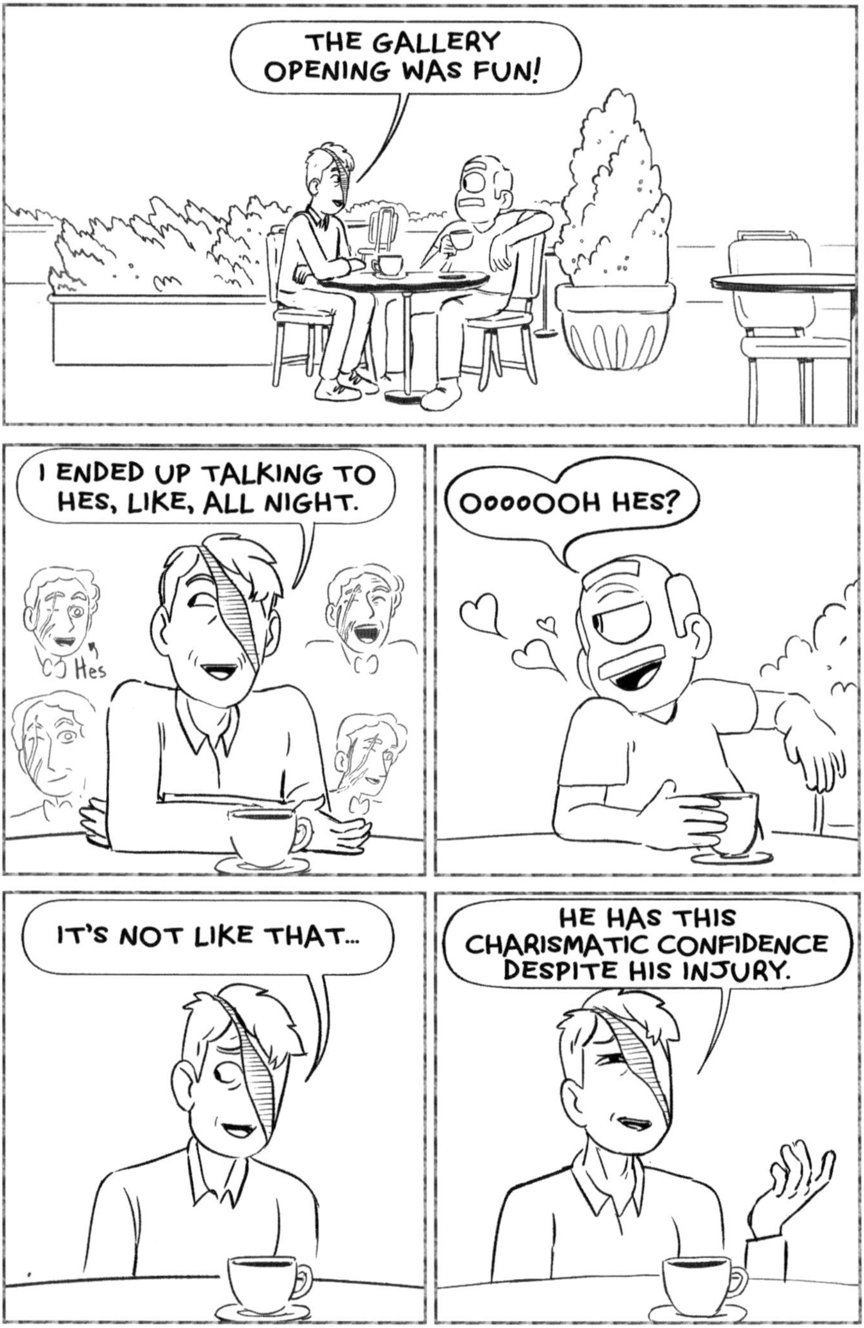
THE GALLERY OPENING WAS FUN!
I ENDED UP TALKING TO HES, LIKE, ALL NIGHT.
Hes
OooOOOH HES?
IT'S NOT LIKE THAT...
HE HAS THIS CHARISMATIC CONFIDENCE DESPITE HIS INJURY.

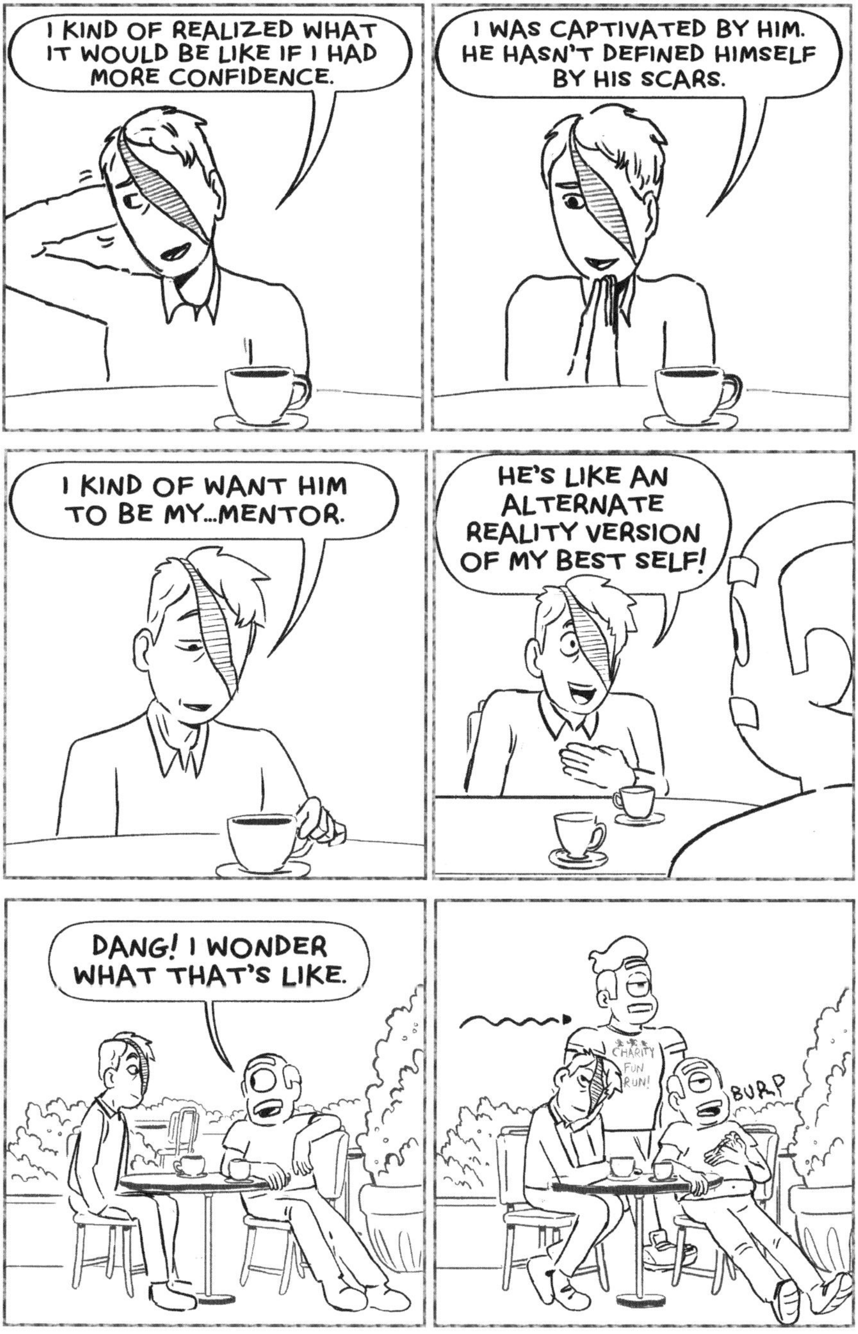
I KIND OF REALIZED WHAT IT WOULD BE LIKE IF I HAD MORE CONFIDENCE.
I WAS CAPTIVATED BY HIM. HE HASN'T DEFINED HIMSELF BY HIS SCARS.
I KIND OF WANT HIM TO BE MY...MENTOR.
HE'S LIKE AN ALTERNATE REALITY VERSION OF MY BEST SELF!
DANG! I WONDER WHAT THAT'S LIKE.
CHARITY FUN RUN!
BURP

Morning after gallery opening, Jian's apartment

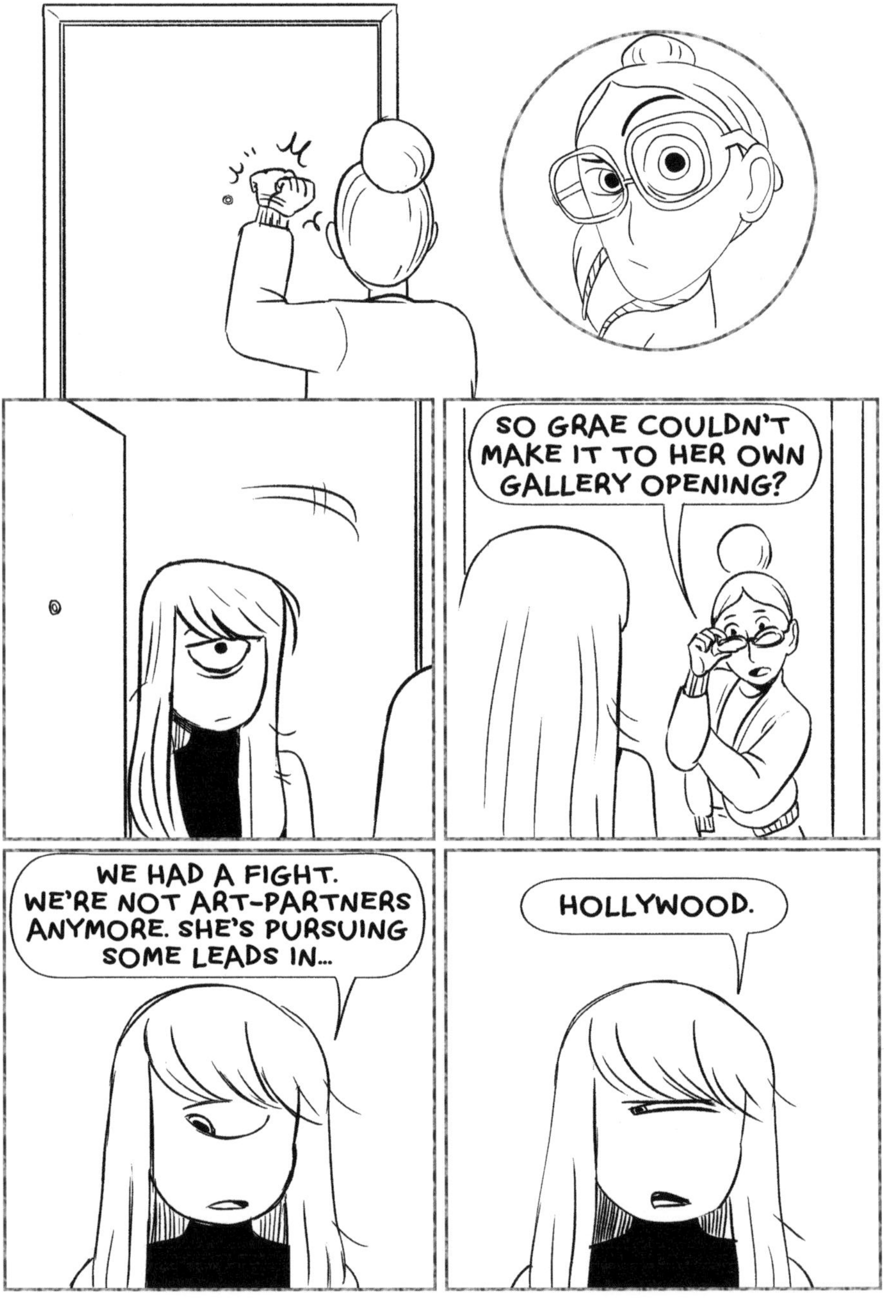
SO GRAE COULDN'T MAKE IT TO HER OWN GALLERY OPENING?
WE HAD A FIGHT. WE'RE NOT ART-PARTNERS ANYMORE. SHE'S PURSUING SOME LEADS IN...
HOLLYWOOD.

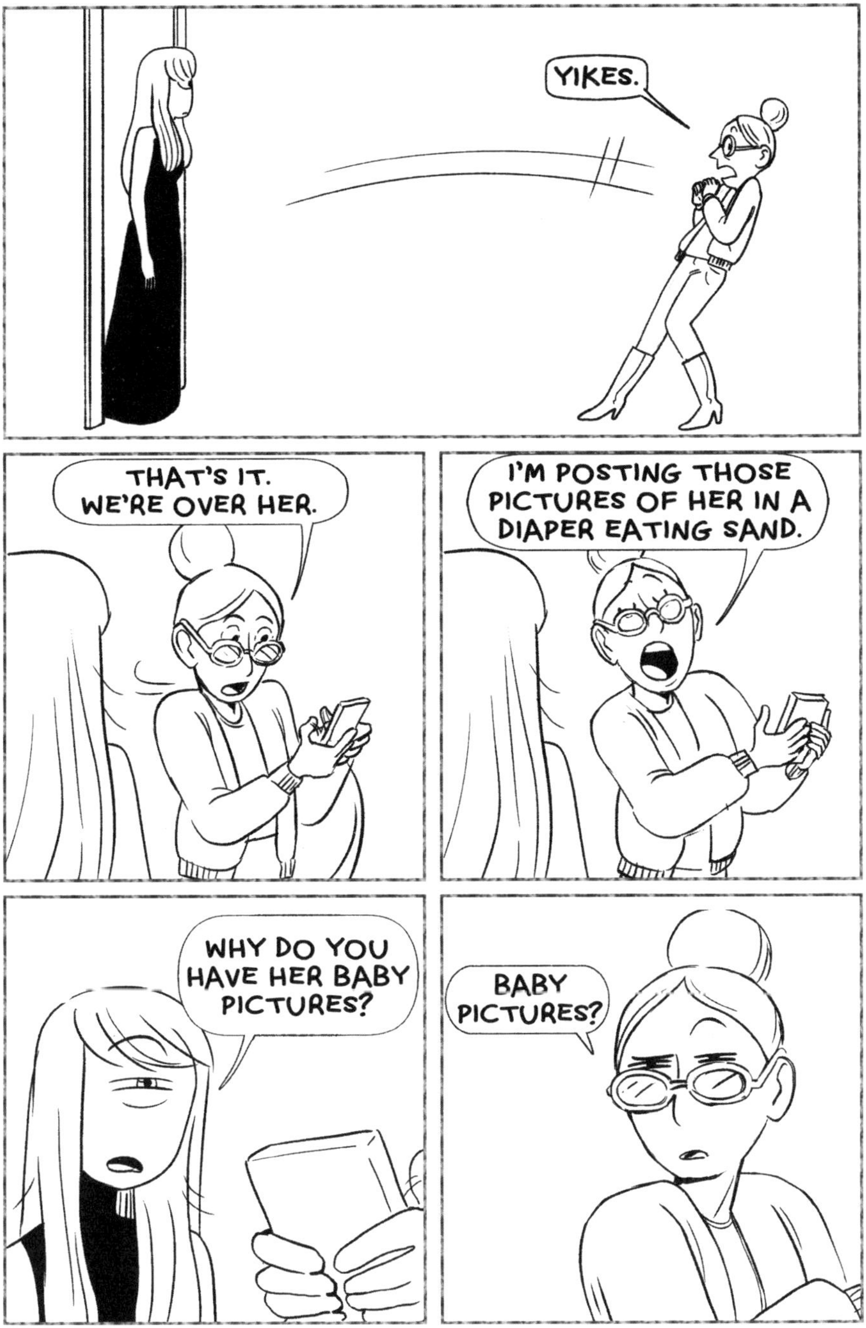
YIKES.
THAT'S IT. WE'RE OVER HER.
I'M POSTING THOSE PICTURES OF HER IN A DIAPER EATING SAND.
WHY DO YOU HAVE HER BABY PICTURES?
BABY PICTURES?

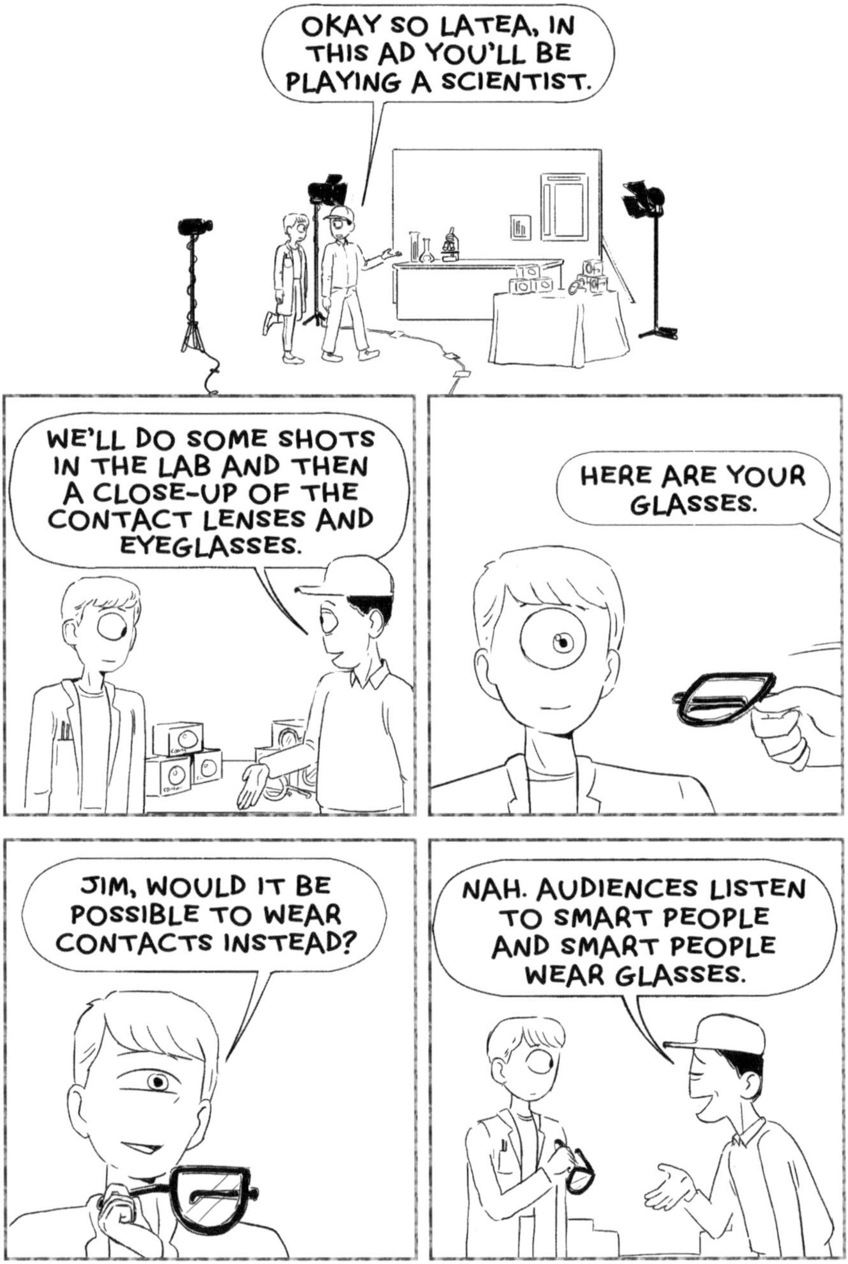
OKAY SO LATEA, IN THIS AD YOU'LL BE PLAYING A SCIENTIST.
WE'LL DO SOME SHOTS IN THE LAB AND THEN A CLOSE-UP OF THE CONTACT LENSES AND EYEGLASSES.
HERE ARE YOUR GLASSES.
JIM, WOULD IT BE POSSIBLE TO WEAR CONTACTS INSTEAD?
NAH. AUDIENCES LISTEN TO SMART PEOPLE AND SMART PEOPLE WEAR GLASSES.

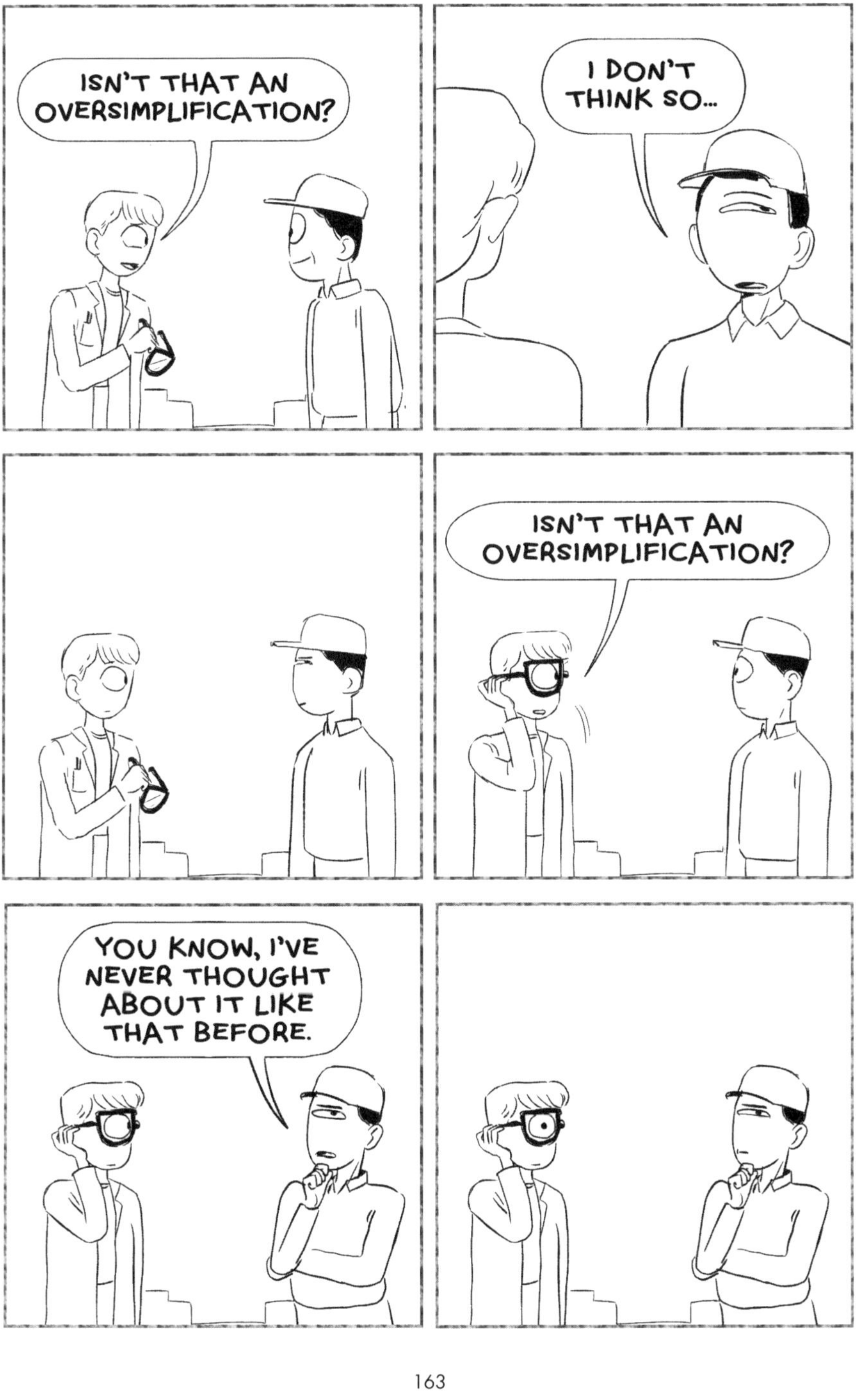
ISN'T THAT AN OVERSIMPLIFICATION?
I DON'T THINK SO...
ISN'T THAT AN OVERSIMPLIFICATION?
YOU KNOW, I'VE NEVER THOUGHT ABOUT IT LIKE THAT BEFORE.

The overly enthusiastic

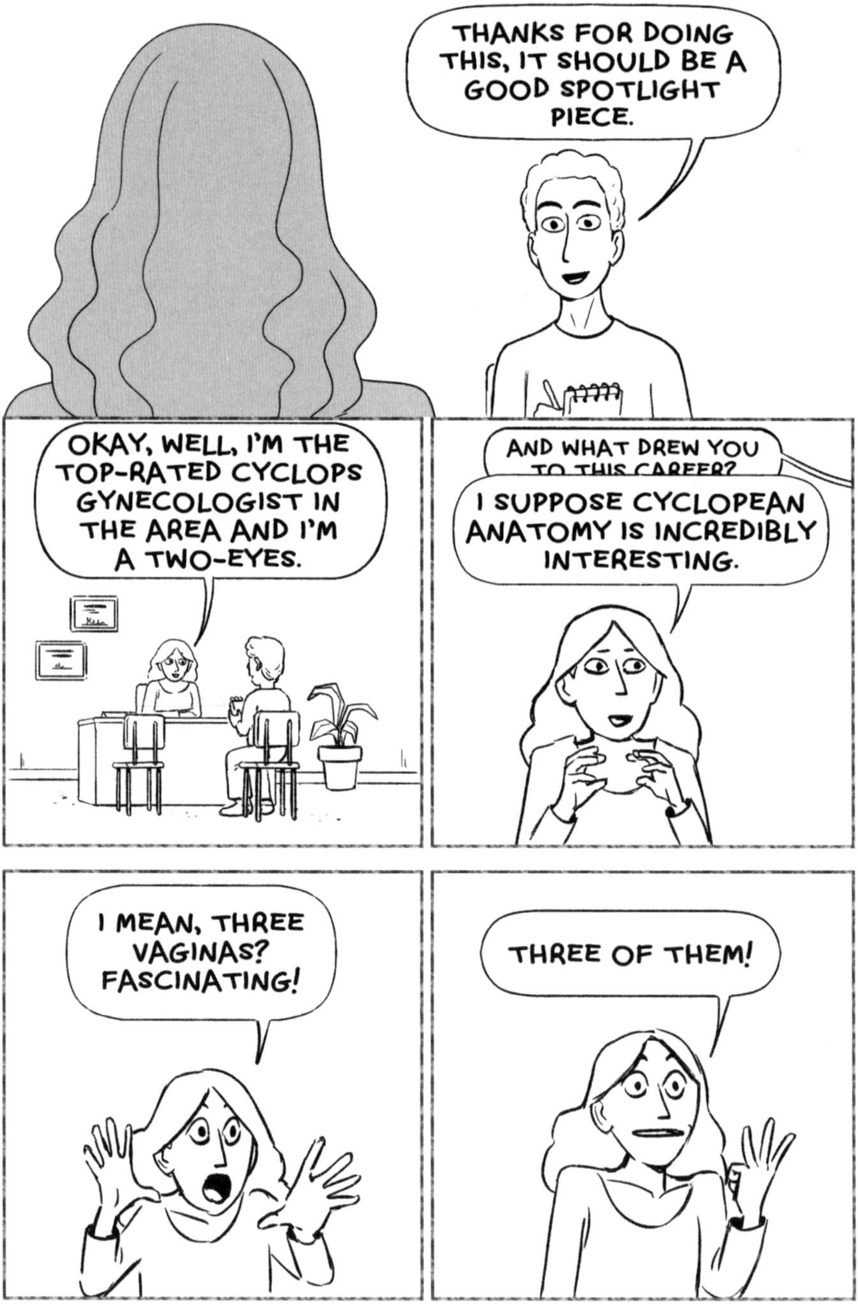
THANKS FOR DOING THIS, IT SHOULD BE A GOOD SPOTLIGHT PIECE.
OKAY, WELL, I'M THE TOP-RATED CYCLOPS GYNECOLOGIST IN THE AREA AND I'M A TWO-EYES.
AND WHAT DREW YOU
I SUPPOSE CYCLOPEAN ANATOMY IS INCREDIBLY INTERESTING.
I MEAN, THREE VAGINAS? FASCINATING!
THREE OF THEM!

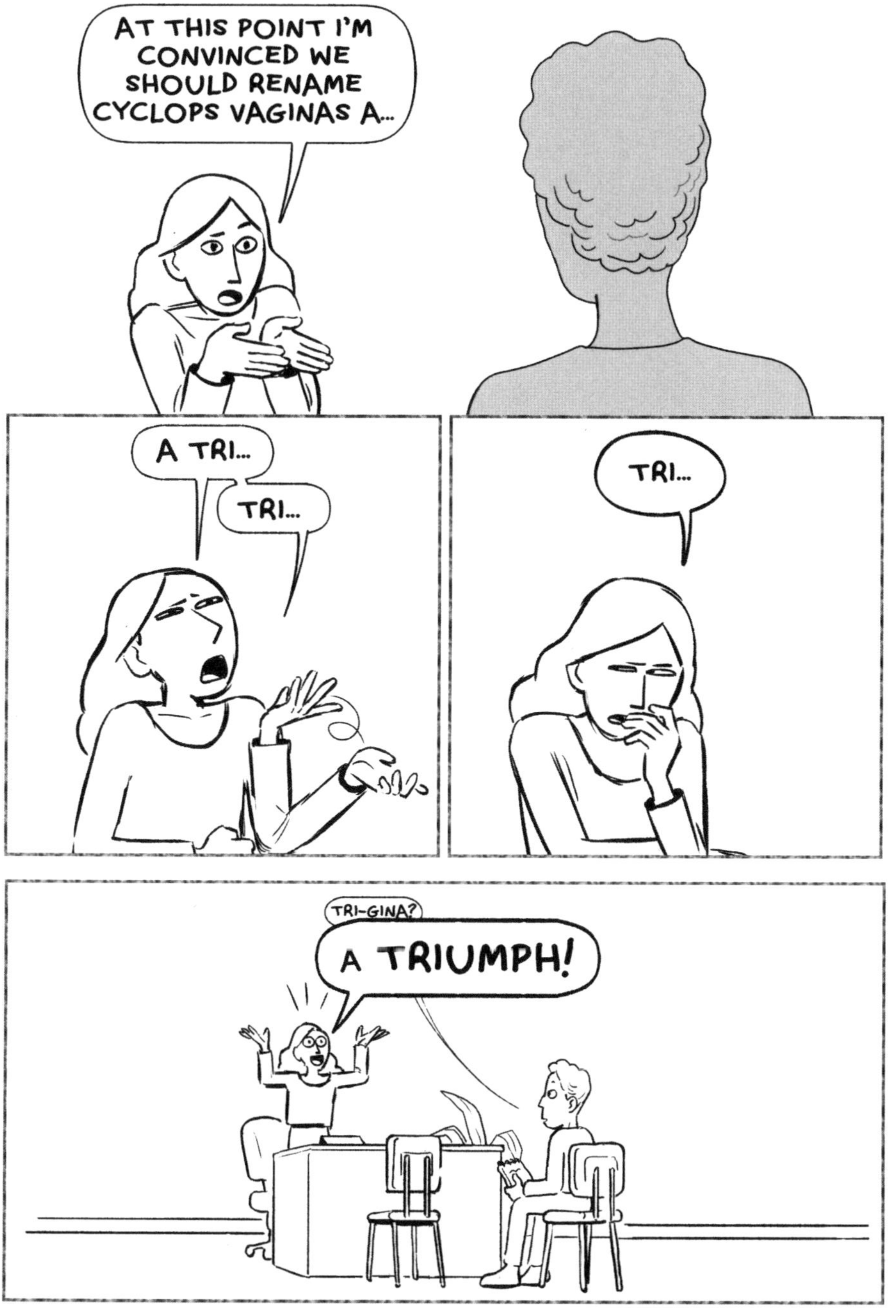
AT THIS POINT I'M CONVINCED WE SHOULD RENAME CYCLOPS VAGINAS A...
A TRI...
TRI...
TRI...
TRI-GINA?
A TRIUMPH!

Family

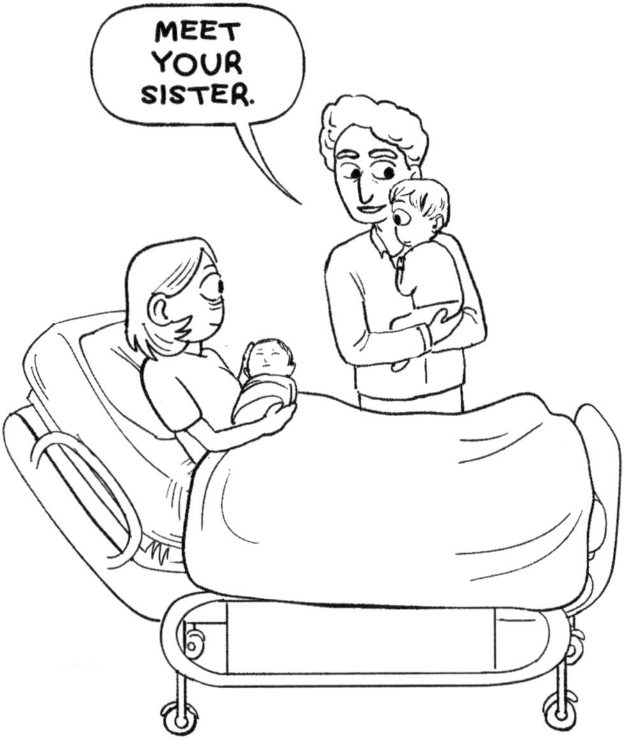
MEET YOUR SISTER.

Called out

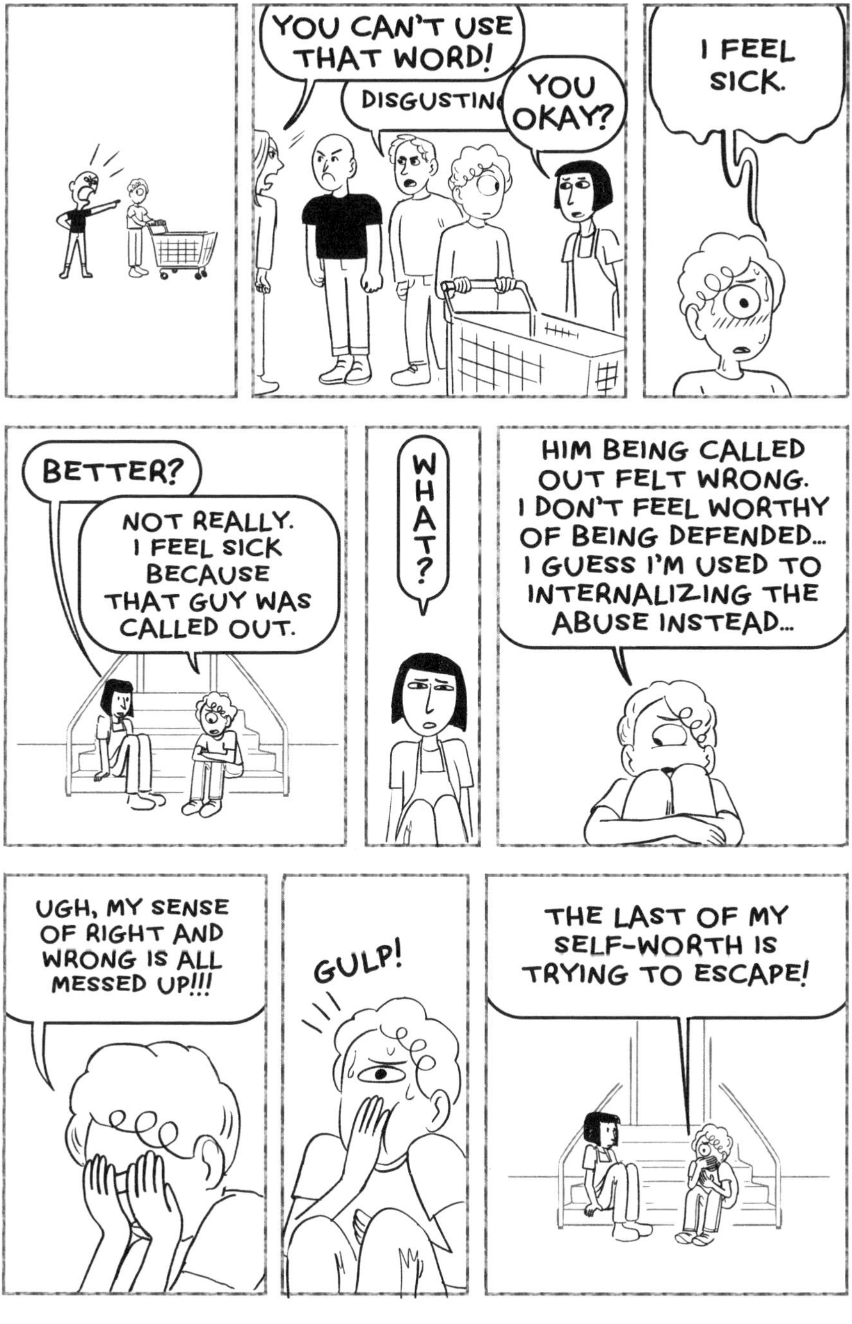
YOU CAN'T USE THAT WORD!
DISGUSTIN
YOU OKAY?
I FEEL SICK.
BETTER?
NOT REALLY. I FEEL SICK BECAUSE THAT GUY WAS CALLED OUT.
WHAT?
HIM BEING CALLED OUT FELT WRONG. I DON'T FEEL WORTHY OF BEING DEFENDED... I GUESS I'M USED TO INTERNALIZING THE ABUSE INSTEAD...
UGH, MY SENSE OF RIGHT AND WRONG IS ALL MESSED UP!!!
GULP!
THE LAST OF MY SELF-WORTH IS TRYING TO ESCAPE!

Grae lands in Hollywood

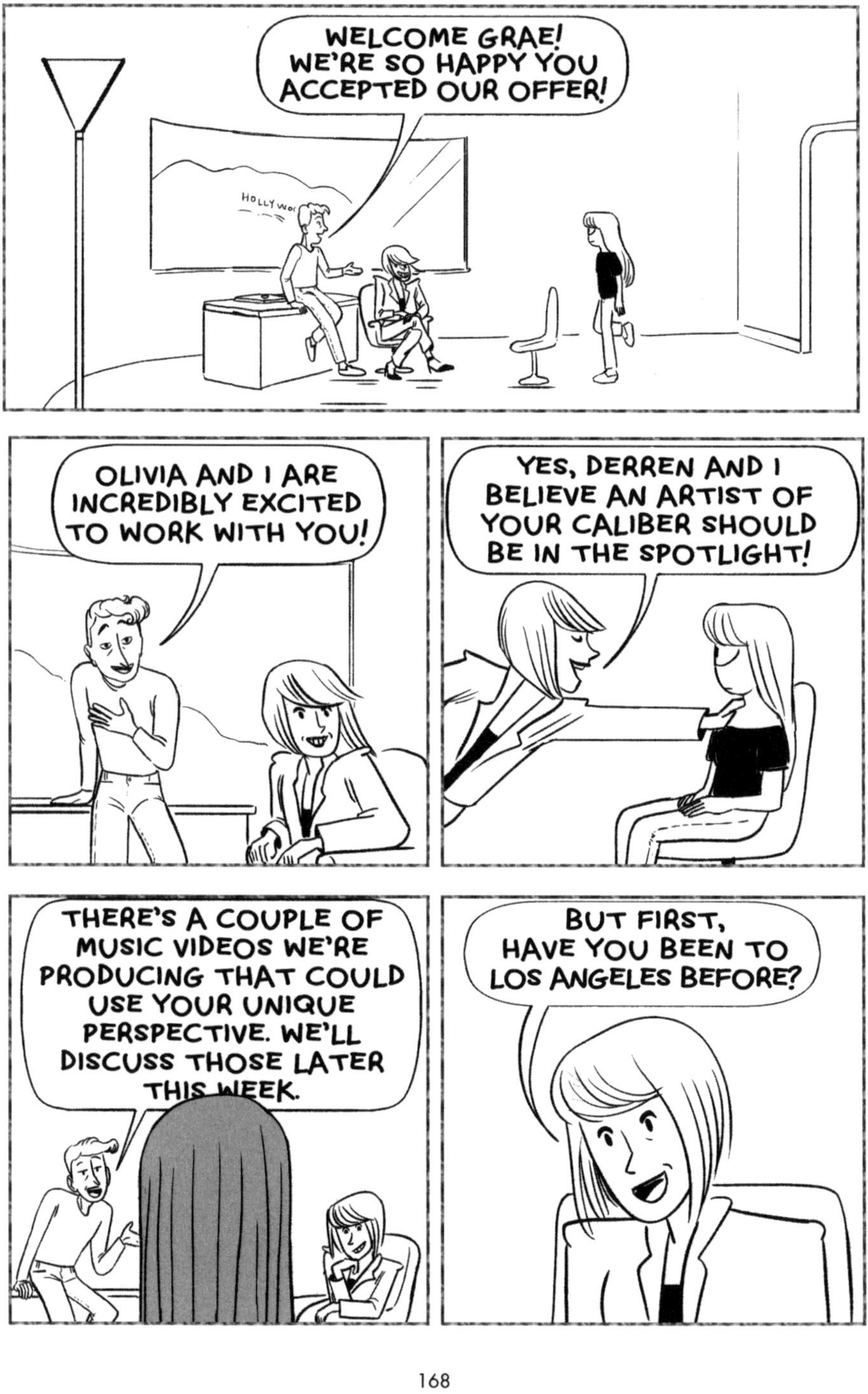
WELCOME GRAE! WE'RE SO HAPPY YOU ACCEPTED OUR OFFER!
OLIVIA AND I ARE INCREDIBLY EXCITED TO WORK WITH YOU!
YES, DERREN AND I BELIEVE AN ARTIST OF YOUR CALIBER SHOULD BE IN THE SPOTLIGHT!
THERE'S A COUPLE OF MUSIC VIDEOS WE'RE PRODUCING THAT COULD USE YOUR UNIQUE PERSPECTIVE. WE'LL DISCUSS THOSE LATER THIS WEEK.
BUT FIRST, HAVE YOU BEEN TO LOS ANGELES BEFORE?

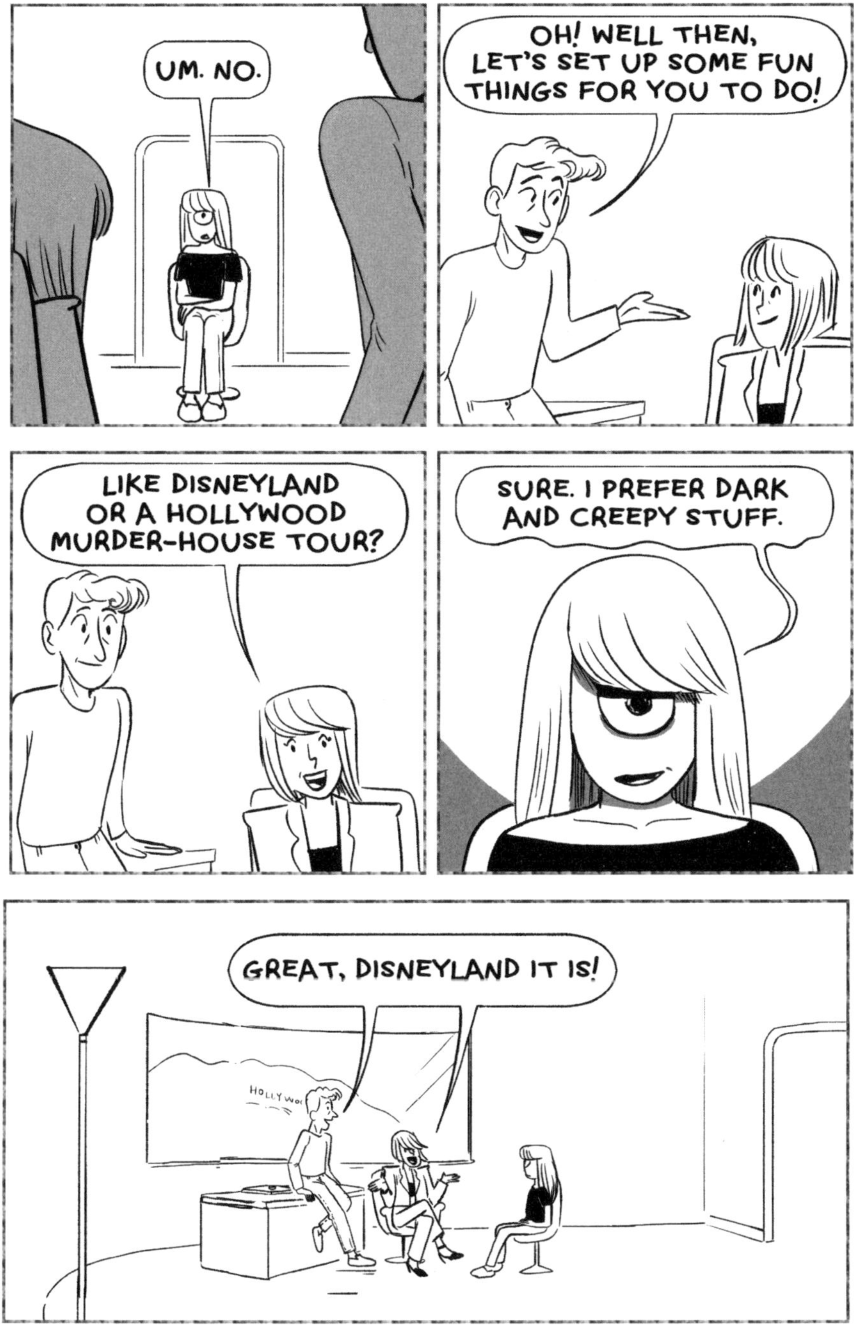
UM. NO.
OH! WELL THEN, LET'S SET UP SOME FUN THINGS FOR YOU TO DO!
LIKE DISNEYLAND OR A HOLLYWOOD MURDER-HOUSE TOUR?
SURE. I PREFER DARK AND CREEPY STUFF.
GREAT, DISNEYLAND IT IS!

Tired

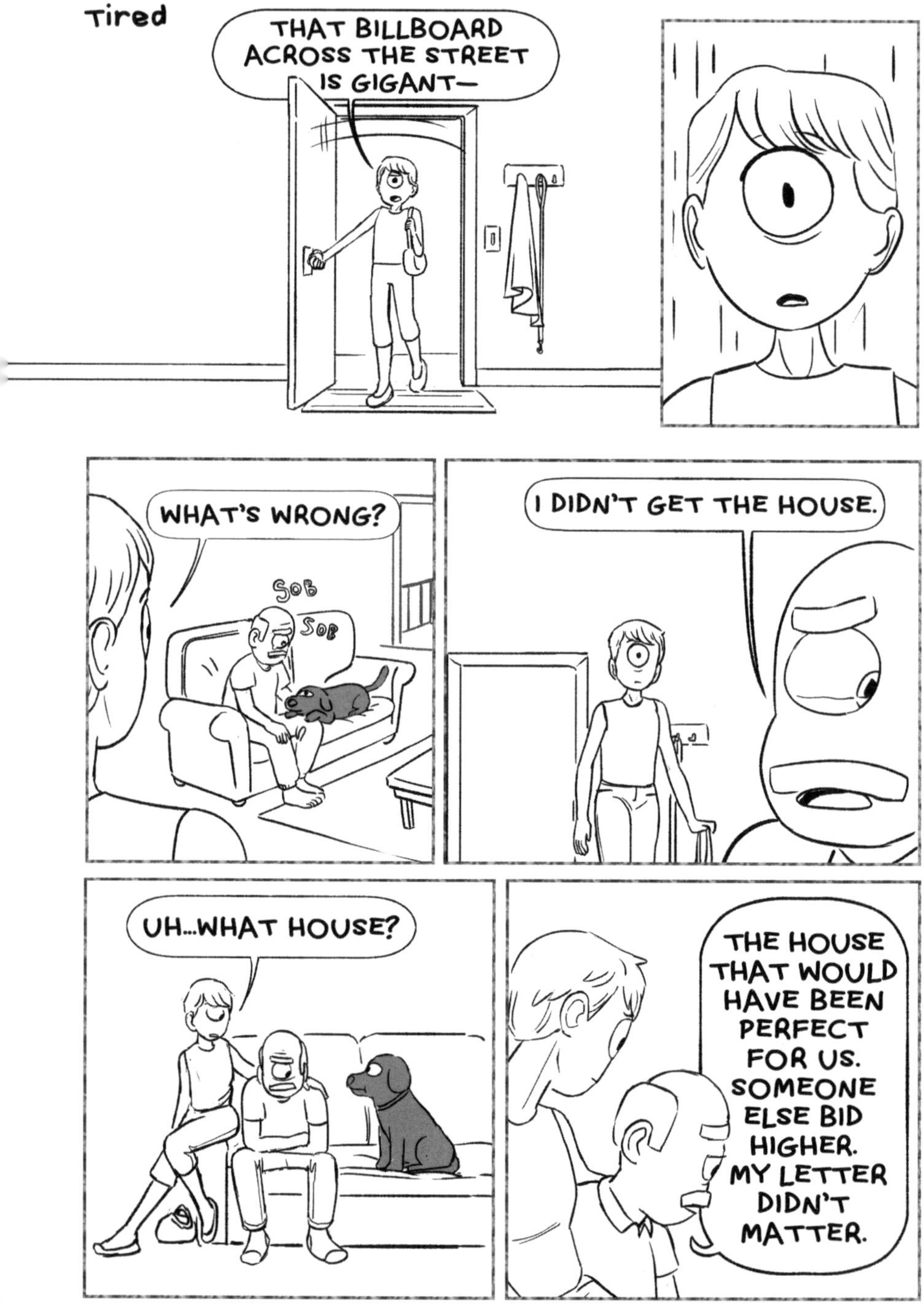
THAT BILLBOARD ACROSS THE STREET IS GIGANT—
WHAT'S WRONG?
SOB
SOB
I DIDN'T GET THE HOUSE.
UH...WHAT HOUSE?
THE HOUSE THAT WOULD HAVE BEEN PERFECT FOR US. SOMEONE ELSE BID HIGHER. MY LETTER DIDN'T MATTER.

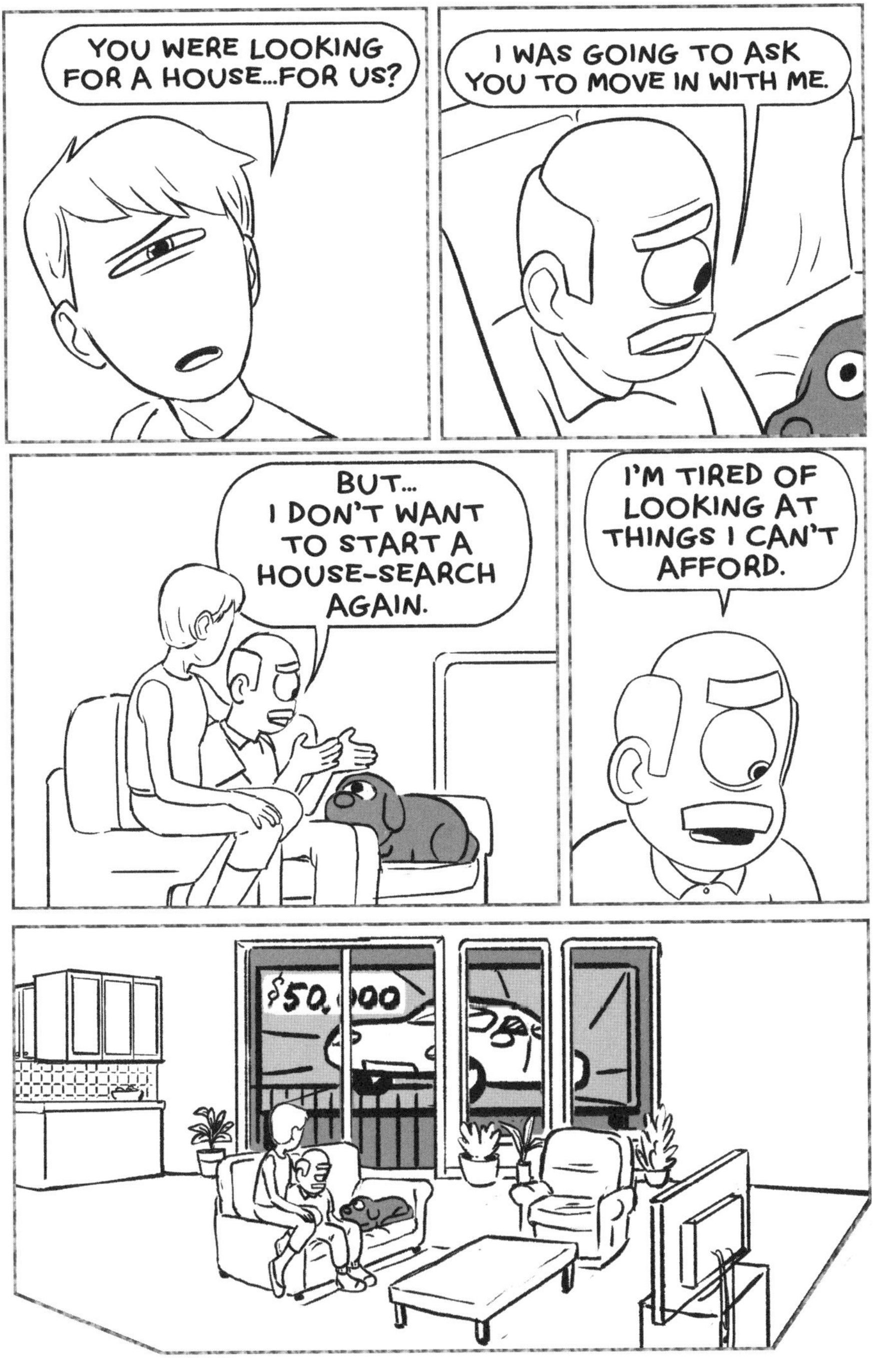
YOU WERE LOOKING FOR A HOUSE...FOR US?
I WAS GOING TO ASK YOU TO MOVE IN WITH ME.
BUT... I DON'T WANT TO START A HOUSE-SEARCH AGAIN.
I'M TIRED OF LOOKING AT THINGS I CAN'T AFFORD.

Facing your past at the mall

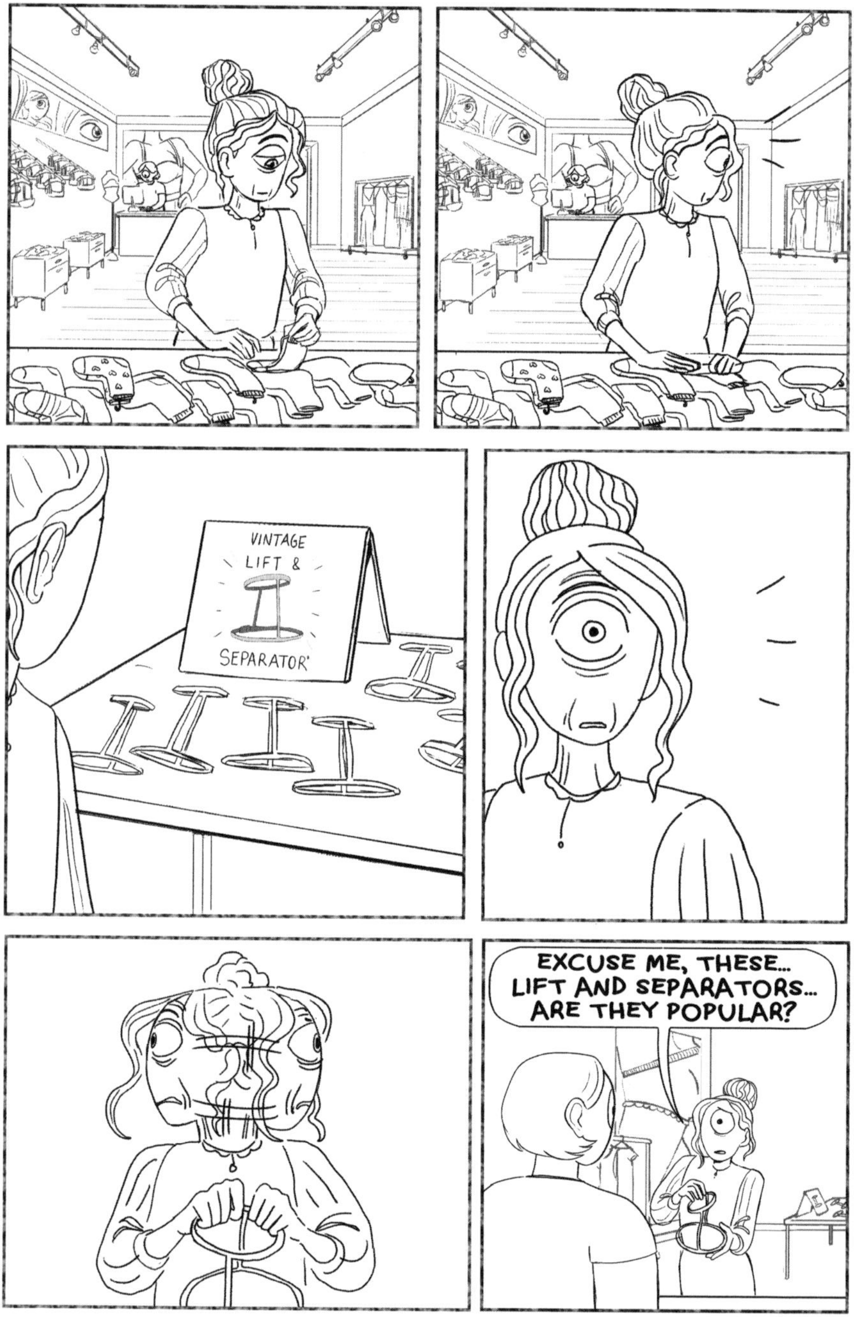
VINTAGE LIFT & SEPARATOR
EXCUSE ME, THESE... LIFT AND SEPARATORS... ARE THEY POPULAR?

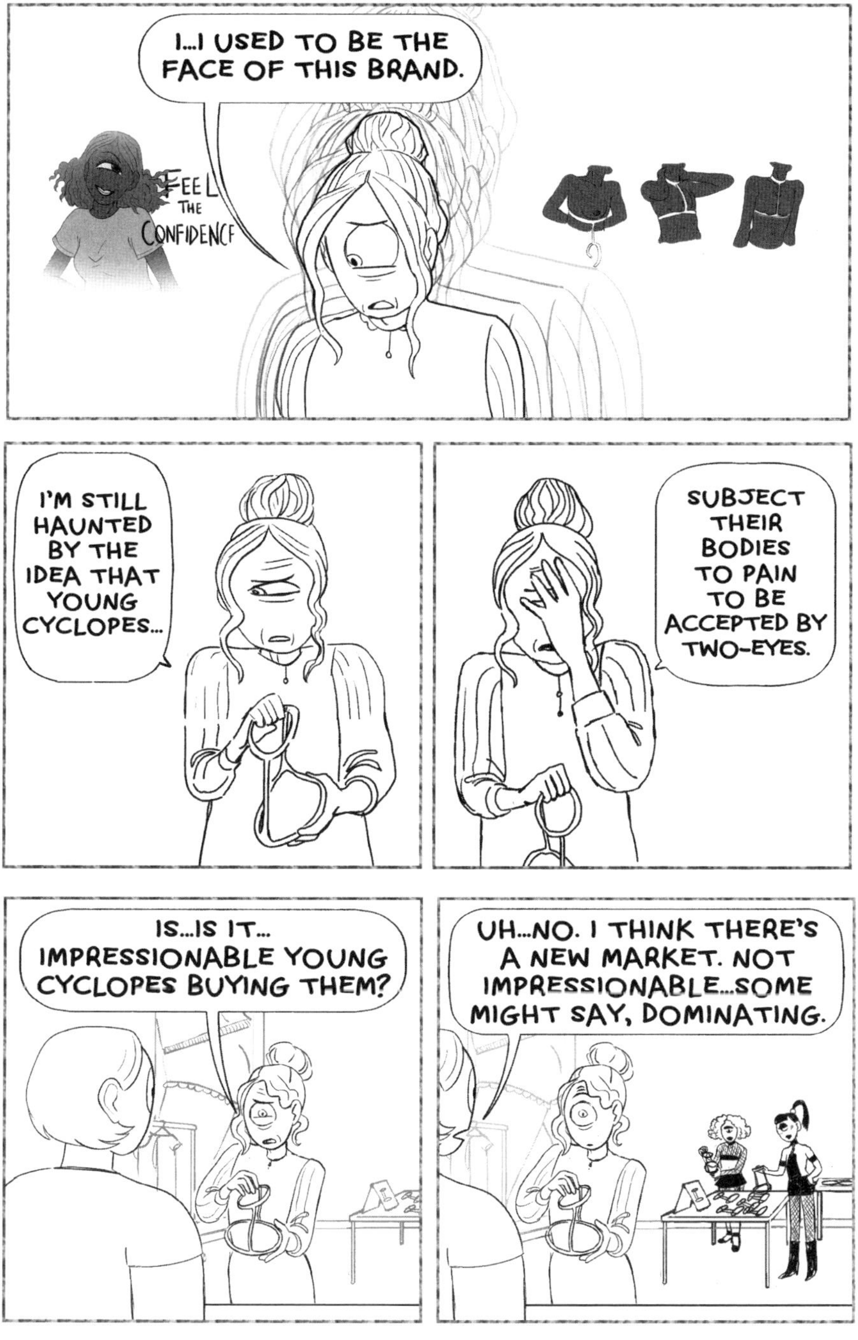
I...I USED TO BE THE FACE OF THIS BRAND.
FEEL THE CONFIDENCE
I'M STILL HAUNTED BY THE IDEA THAT YOUNG CYCLOPES...
SUBJECT THEIR BODIES TO PAIN TO BE ACCEPTED BY TWO-EYES.
IS...IS IT... IMPRESSIONABLE YOUNG CYCLOPES BUYING THEM?
UH...NO. I THINK THERE'S A NEW MARKET. NOT IMPRESSIONABLE...SOME MIGHT SAY, DOMINATING.

Titles

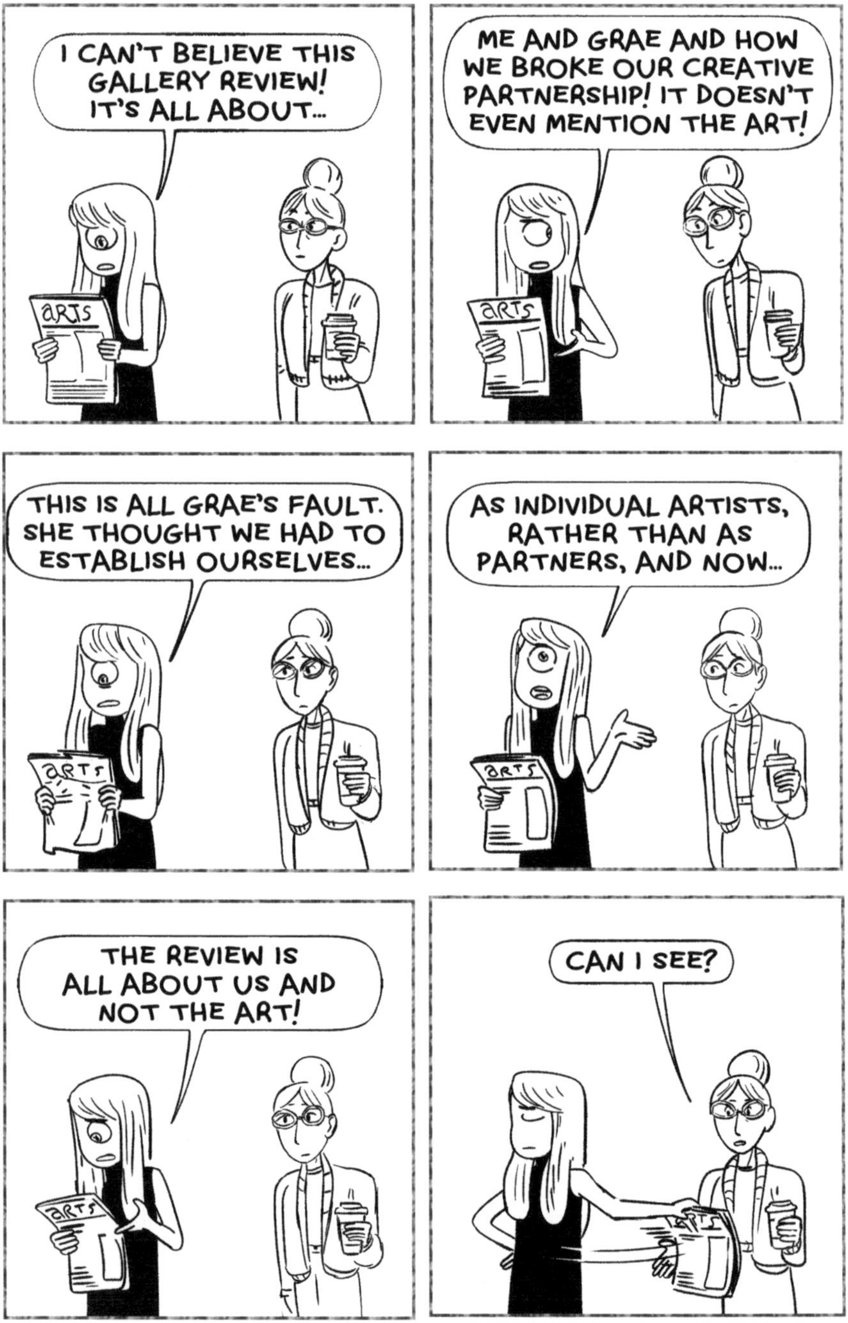
I CAN'T BELIEVE THIS GALLERY REVIEW! IT'S ALL ABOUT...
ARTS
ME AND GRAE AND HOW WE BROKE OUR CREATIVE PARTNERSHIP! IT DOESN'T EVEN MENTION THE ART!
ARTS
THIS IS ALL GRAE'S FAULT. SHE THOUGHT WE HAD TO ESTABLISH OURSELVES...
ARTS
AS INDIVIDUAL ARTISTS, RATHER THAN AS PARTNERS, AND NOW...
ARTS
THE REVIEW IS ALL ABOUT US AND NOT THE ART!
ARTS
CAN I SEE?

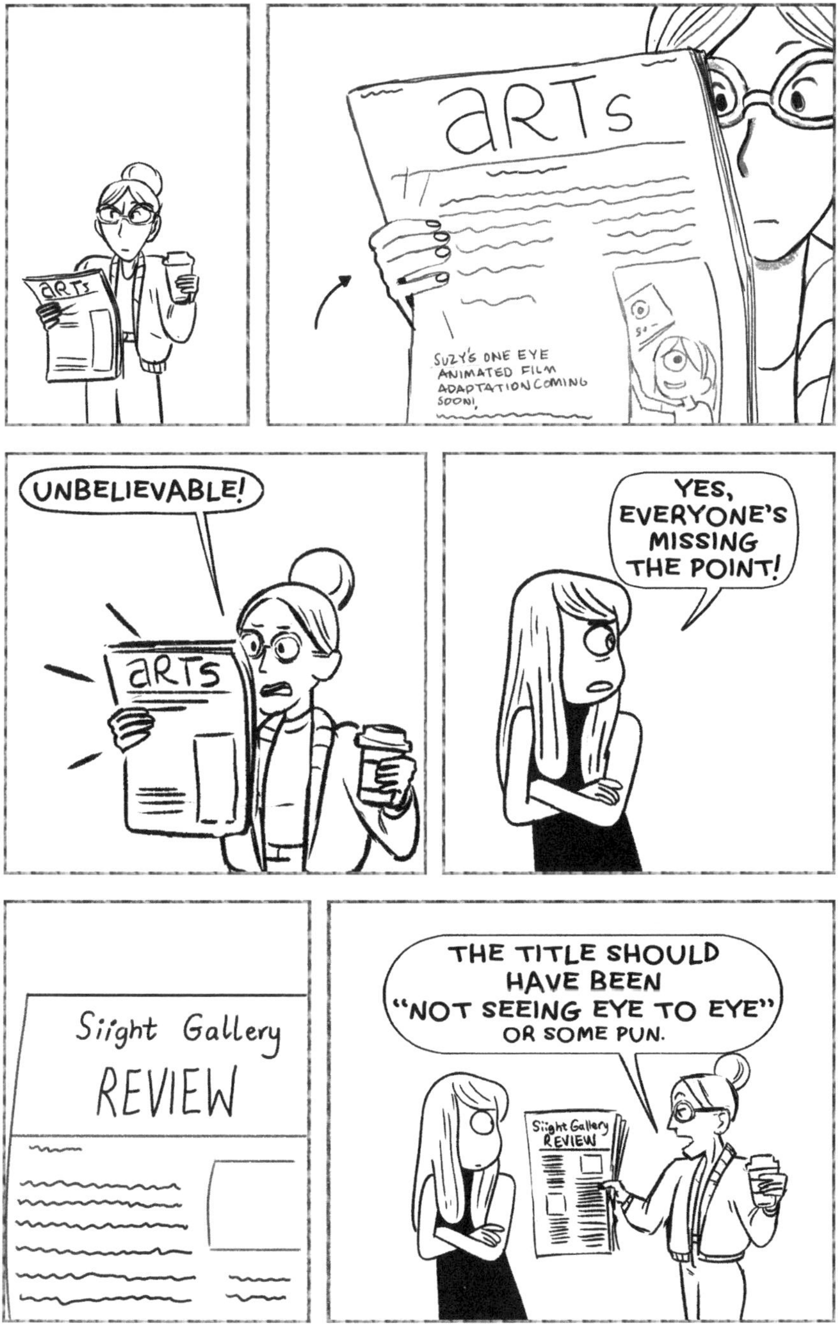
aRTs
aRTs
SUZY'S ONE EYE ANIMATED FILM ADAPTATION COMING SOON!
UNBELIEVABLE!
aRTs
YES, EVERYONE'S MISSING THE POINT!
Siight Gallery
REVIEW
THE TITLE SHOULD HAVE BEEN "NOT SEEING EYE TO EYE" OR SOME PUN.
Siight Gallery REVIEW

scopophilia

ALRIGHT, IN THIS CLASS WE'LL BE TALKING ABOUT SCOPOPHILIA AND CINEMA, WHICH WE'LL CALL THE VOYEUR'S MEDIUM.

WE'LL LOOK AT CYCLOPS REPRESENTATION...

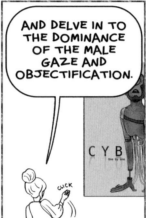

AND DELVE IN TO THE DOMINANCE OF THE MALE GAZE AND OBJECTIFICATION.

CLICK

CYB

one by one

ANYWAY, ALL YOU NEED TO KNOW FOR TODAY IS SCOPOPHILIA IS THE PLEASURE OF LOOKING WITHOUT BEING SEEN.

CREEEEEAK

OH SORRY! I JUST WANT TO SIT IN AND AUDIT THE CLASS TO SEE IF I SHOULD TAKE IT, PRETEND I'M NOT HERE.

PLEASE TAKE A SEAT. YOU'VE REALLY ARRIVED AT THE PERFECT MOMENT.

Mistakes were made

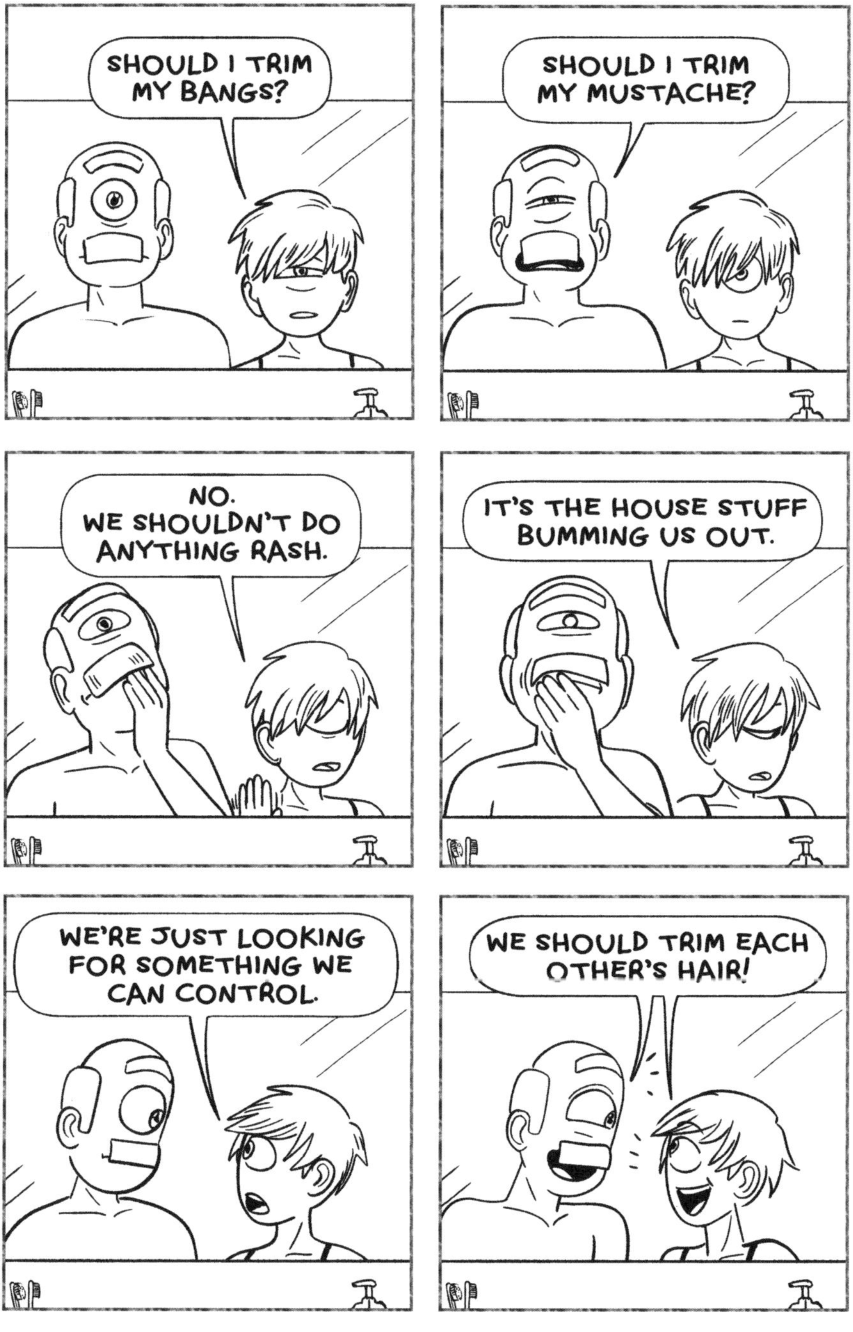
SHOULD I TRIM MY BANGS?
SHOULD I TRIM MY MUSTACHE?
NO. WE SHOULDN'T DO ANYTHING RASH.
IT'S THE HOUSE STUFF BUMMING US OUT.
WE'RE JUST LOOKING FOR SOMETHING WE CAN CONTROL.
WE SHOULD TRIM EACH OTHER'S HAIR!

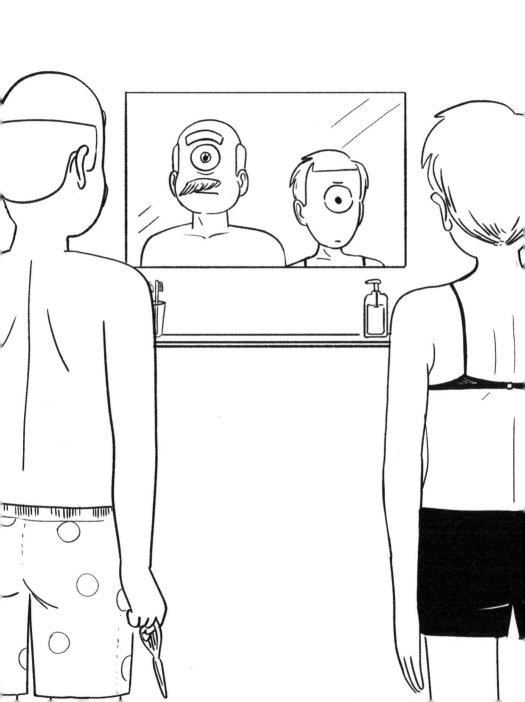

screwing up

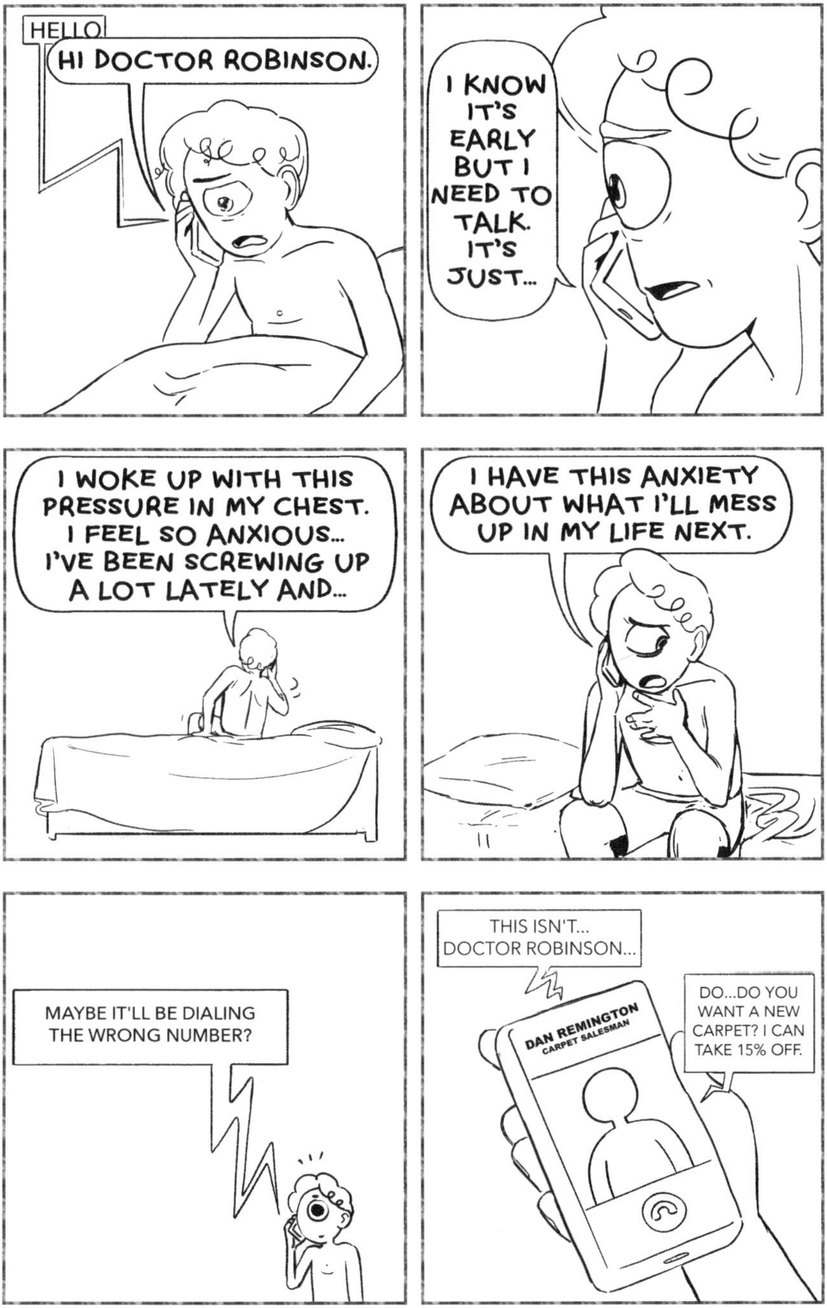
HELLO
HI DOCTOR ROBINSON.
I KNOW IT'S EARLY BUT I NEED TO TALK. IT'S JUST...
I WOKE UP WITH THIS PRESSURE IN MY CHEST. I FEEL SO ANXIOUS... I'VE BEEN SCREWING UP A LOT LATELY AND...
I HAVE THIS ANXIETY ABOUT WHAT I'LL MESS UP IN MY LIFE NEXT.
MAYBE IT'LL BE DIALING THE WRONG NUMBER?
THIS ISN'T... DOCTOR ROBINSON...
DAN REMINGTON
CARPET SALESMAN
DO...DO YOU WANT A NEW CARPET? I CAN TAKE 15% OFF.

Your body is public

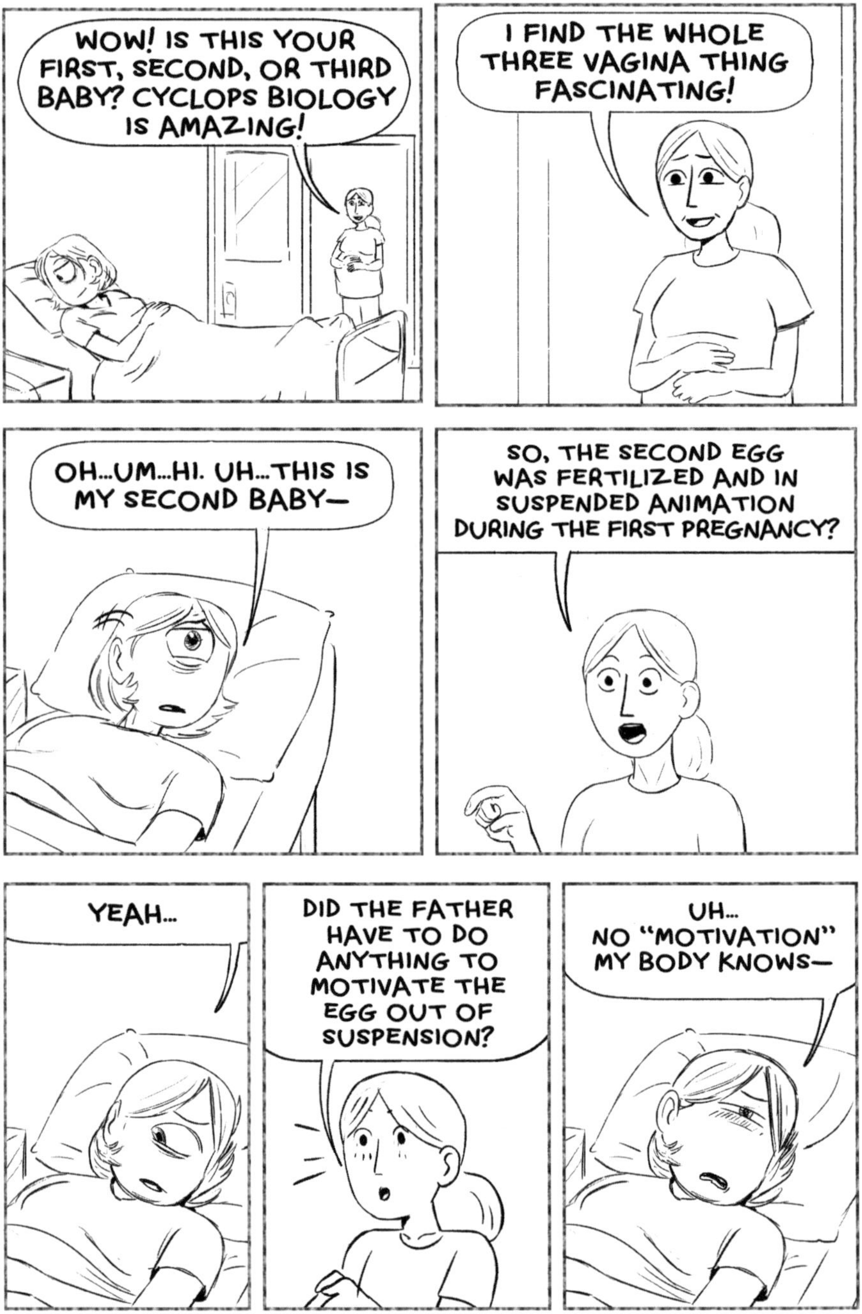
WOW! IS THIS YOUR FIRST, SECOND, OR THIRD BABY? CYCLOPS BIOLOGY IS AMAZING!
I FIND THE WHOLE THREE VAGINA THING FASCINATING!
OH...UM...HI. UH...THIS IS MY SECOND BABY—
SO, THE SECOND EGG WAS FERTILIZED AND IN SUSPENDED ANIMATION DURING THE FIRST PREGNANCY?
YEAH...
DID THE FATHER HAVE TO DO ANYTHING TO MOTIVATE THE EGG OUT OF SUSPENSION?
UH... NO "MOTIVATION" MY BODY KNOWS—

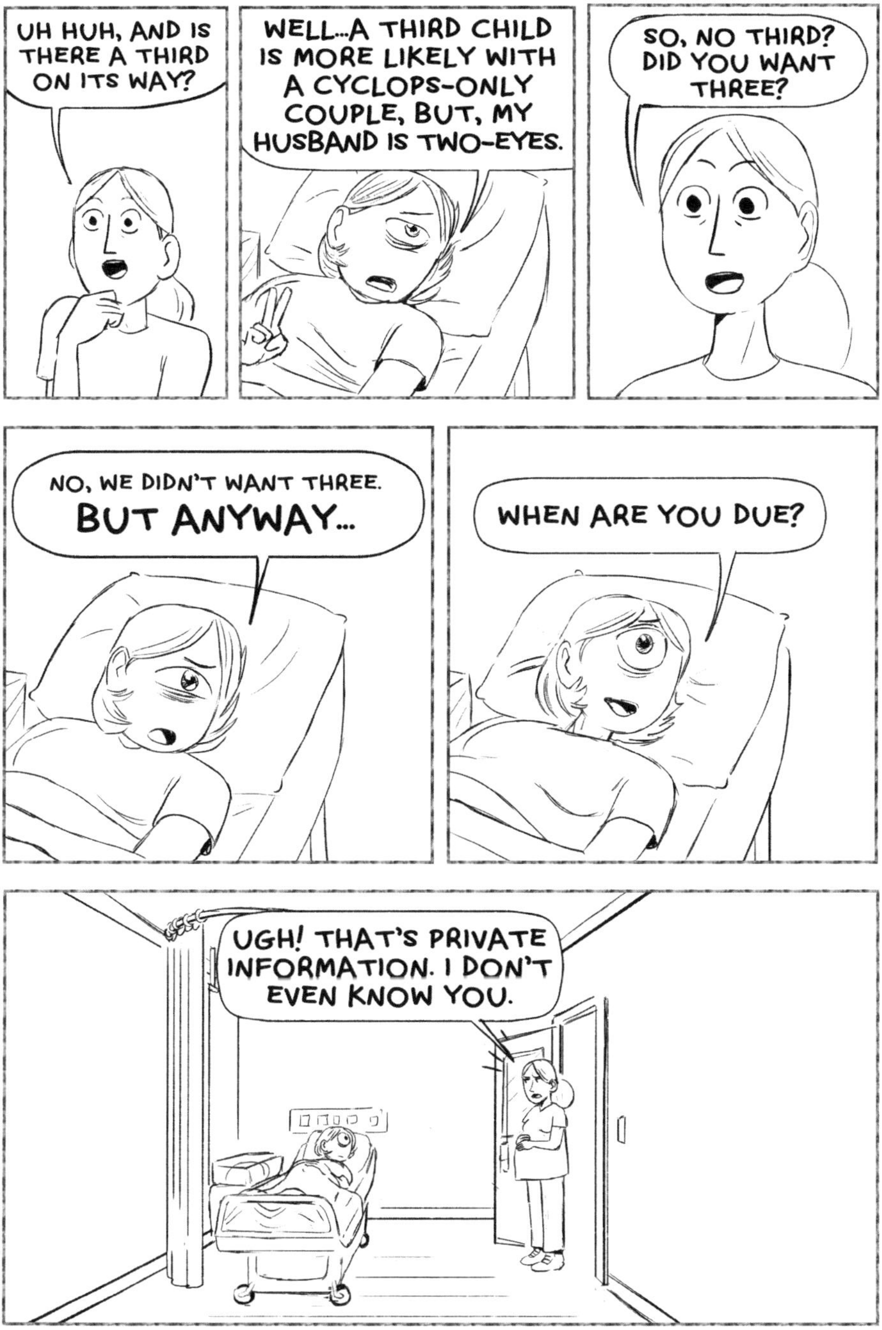
UH HUH, AND IS THERE A THIRD ON ITS WAY?
WELL...A THIRD CHILD IS MORE LIKELY WITH A CYCLOPS-ONLY COUPLE, BUT, MY HUSBAND IS TWO-EYES.
SO, NO THIRD? DID YOU WANT THREE?
NO, WE DIDN'T WANT THREE. BUT ANYWAY...
WHEN ARE YOU DUE?
UGH! THAT'S PRIVATE INFORMATION. I DON'T EVEN KNOW YOU.

Mentor

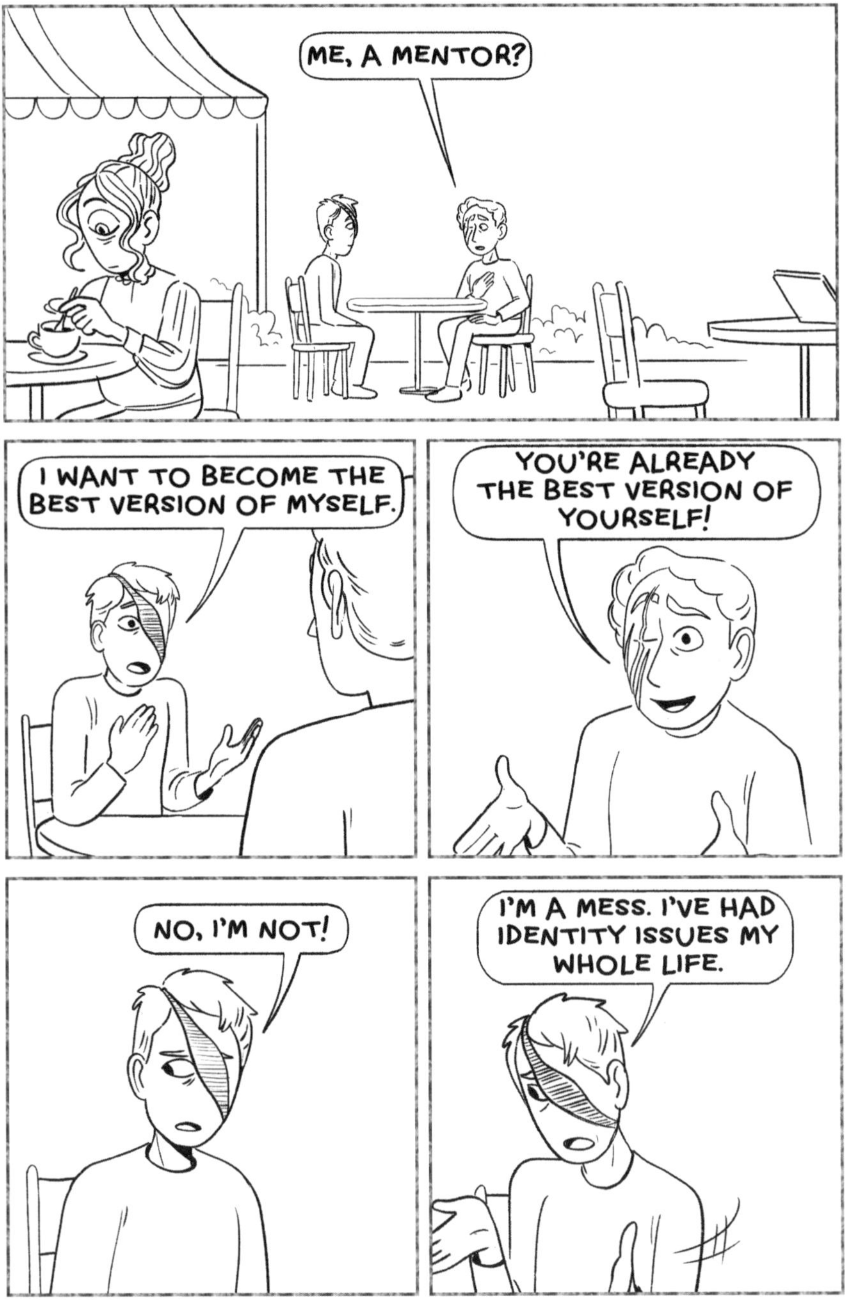
ME, A MENTOR?
I WANT TO BECOME THE BEST VERSION OF MYSELF.
YOU'RE ALREADY THE BEST VERSION OF YOURSELF!
NO, I'M NOT!
I'M A MESS. I'VE HAD IDENTITY ISSUES MY WHOLE LIFE.

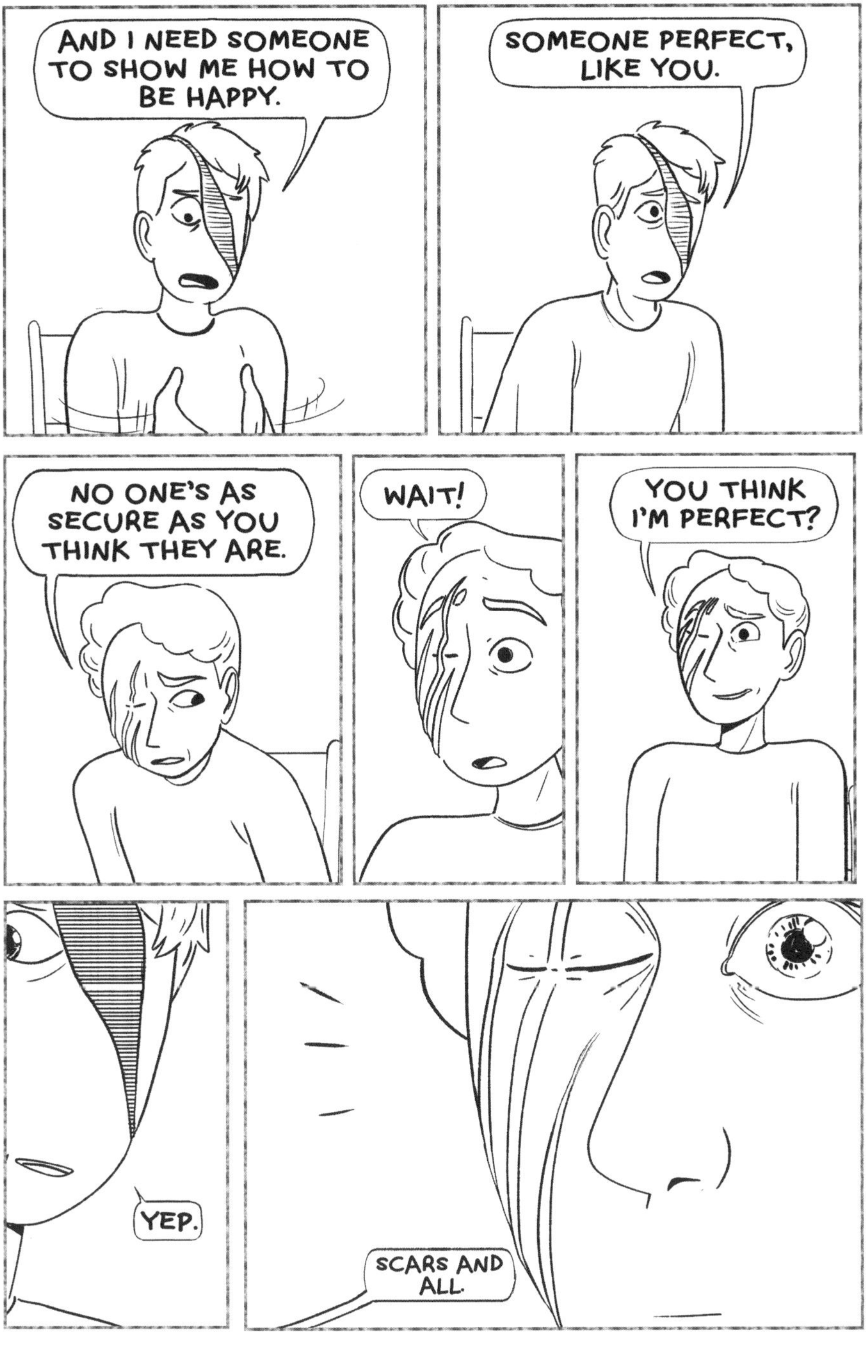
AND I NEED SOMEONE TO SHOW ME HOW TO BE HAPPY.
SOMEONE PERFECT, LIKE YOU.
NO ONE'S AS SECURE AS YOU THINK THEY ARE.
WAIT!
YOU THINK I'M PERFECT?
YEP.
SCARS AND ALL.

Differences

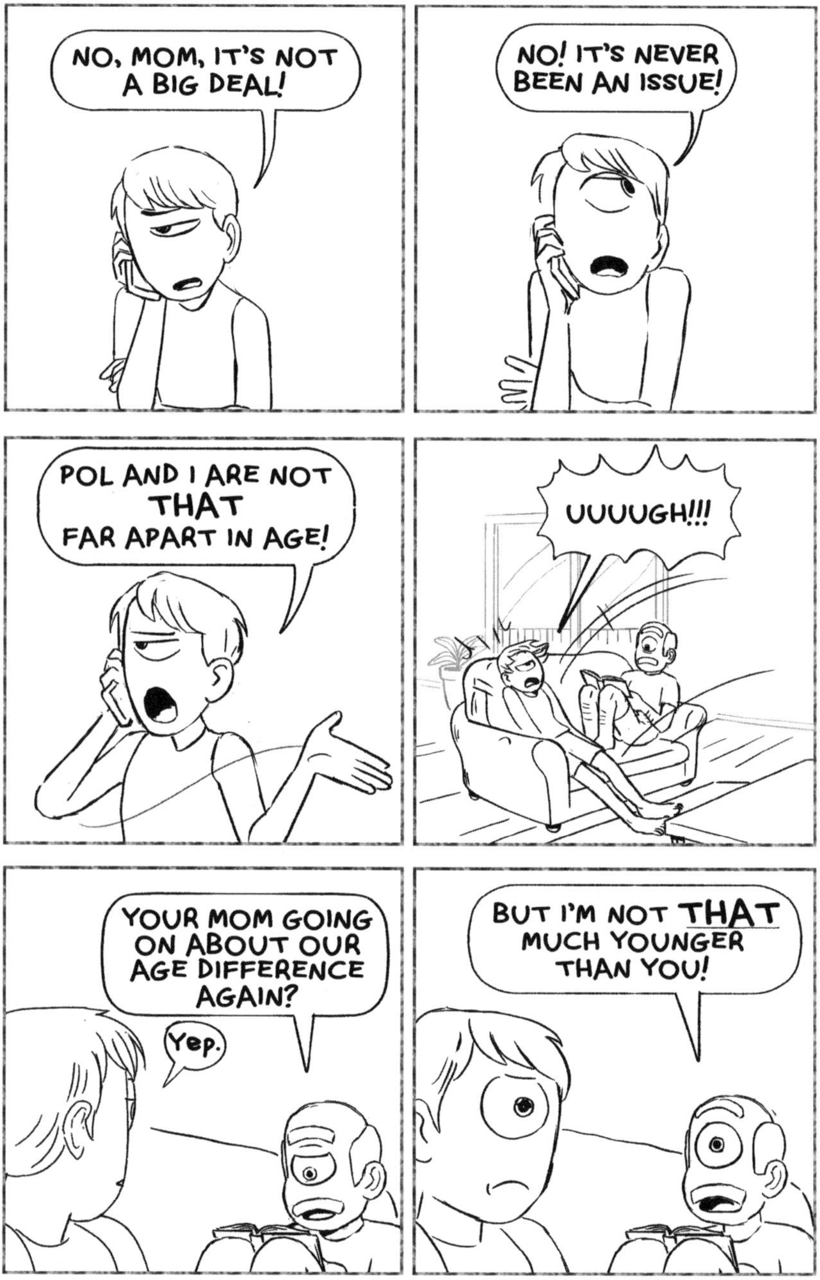

NO, MOM, IT'S NOT A BIG DEAL!
NO! IT'S NEVER BEEN AN ISSUE!
POL AND I ARE NOT THAT FAR APART IN AGE!
UUUUGH!!!
YOUR MOM GOING ON ABOUT OUR AGE DIFFERENCE AGAIN?
Yep.
BUT I'M NOT THAT MUCH YOUNGER THAN YOU!

stereograms

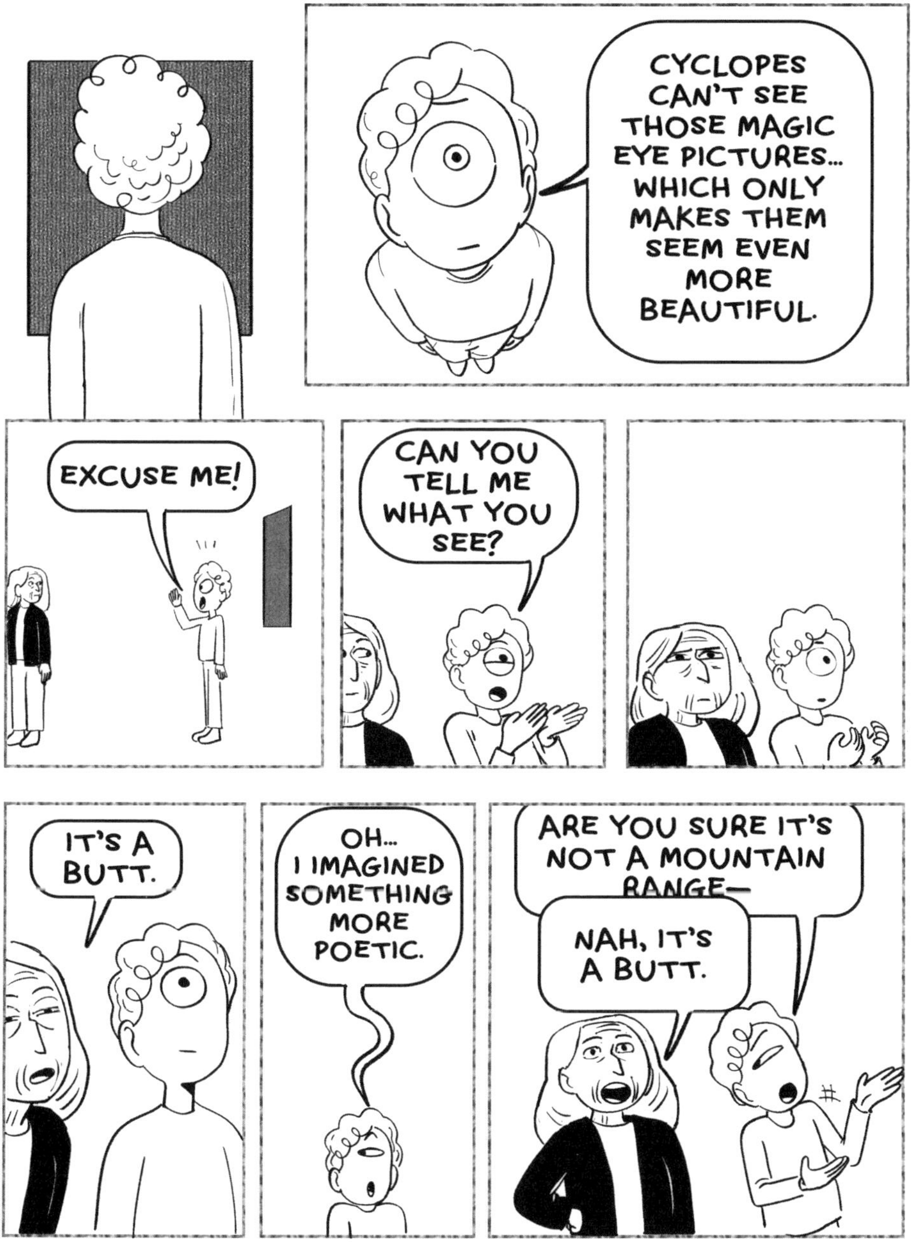
CYCLOPES CAN'T SEE THOSE MAGIC EYE PICTURES... WHICH ONLY MAKES THEM SEEM EVEN MORE BEAUTIFUL.
EXCUSE ME!
CAN YOU TELL ME WHAT YOU SEE?
IT'S A BUTT.
OH... I IMAGINED SOMETHING MORE POETIC.
ARE YOU SURE IT'S NOT A MOUNTAIN RANGE—
NAH, IT'S A BUTT.

The Cyclops experience

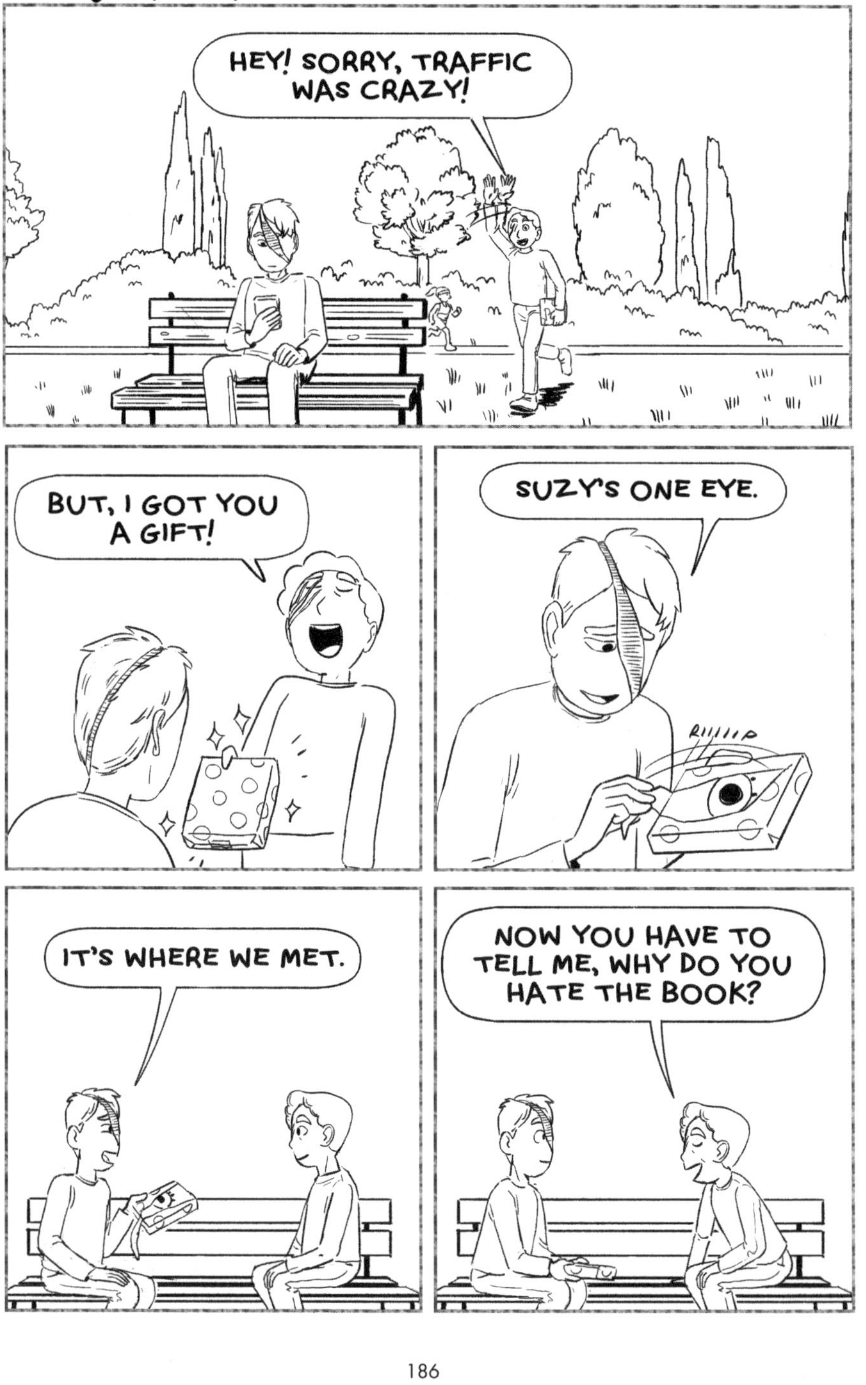
HEY! SORRY, TRAFFIC WAS CRAZY!
BUT, I GOT YOU A GIFT!
SUZY'S ONE EYE.
RIIIIIP
IT'S WHERE WE MET.
NOW YOU HAVE TO TELL ME, WHY DO YOU HATE THE BOOK?

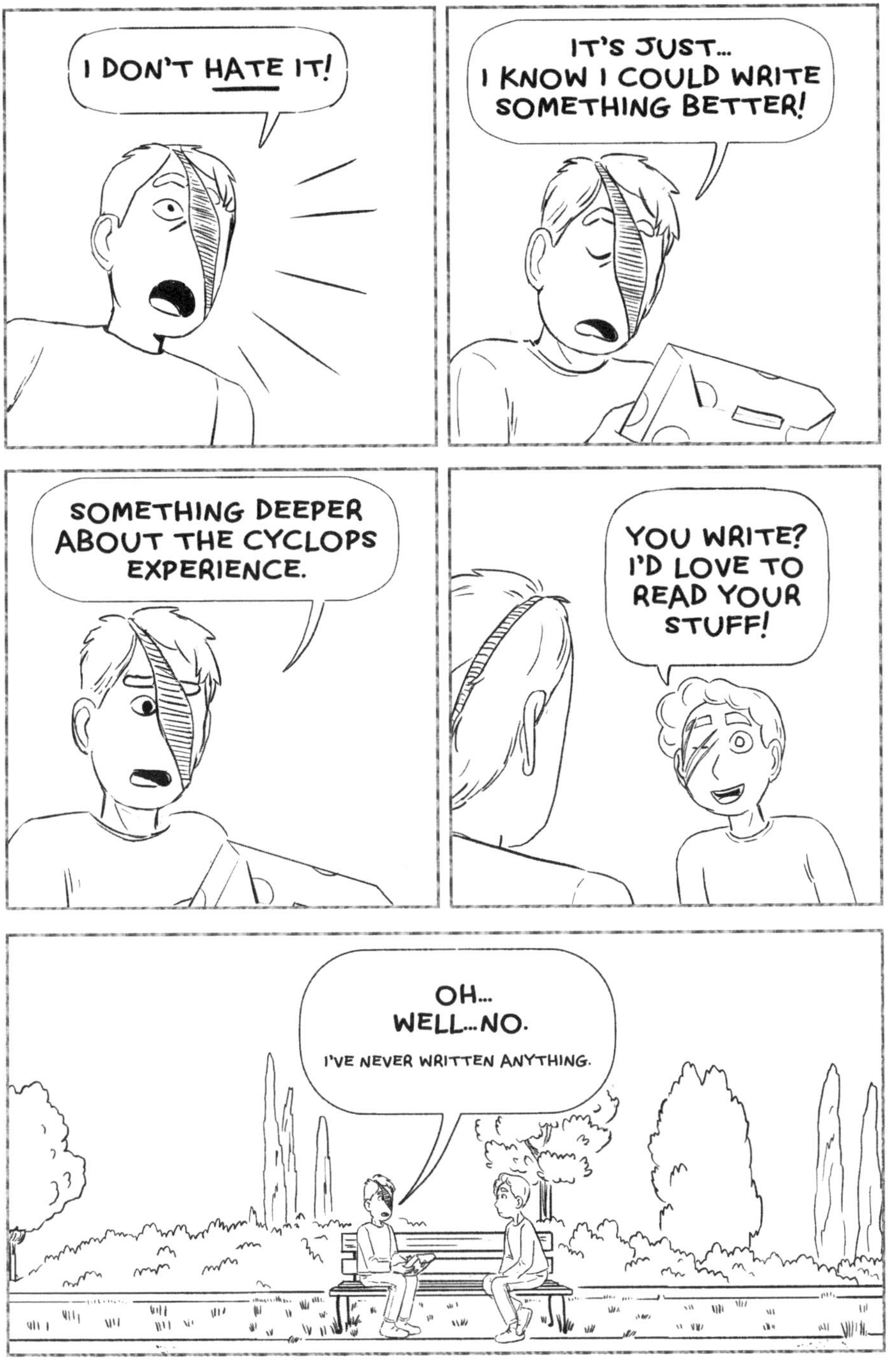
I DON'T HATE IT!
IT'S JUST... I KNOW I COULD WRITE SOMETHING BETTER!
SOMETHING DEEPER ABOUT THE CYCLOPS EXPERIENCE.
YOU WRITE? I'D LOVE TO READ YOUR STUFF!
OH... WELL...NO.
I'VE NEVER WRITTEN ANYTHING.

Followed

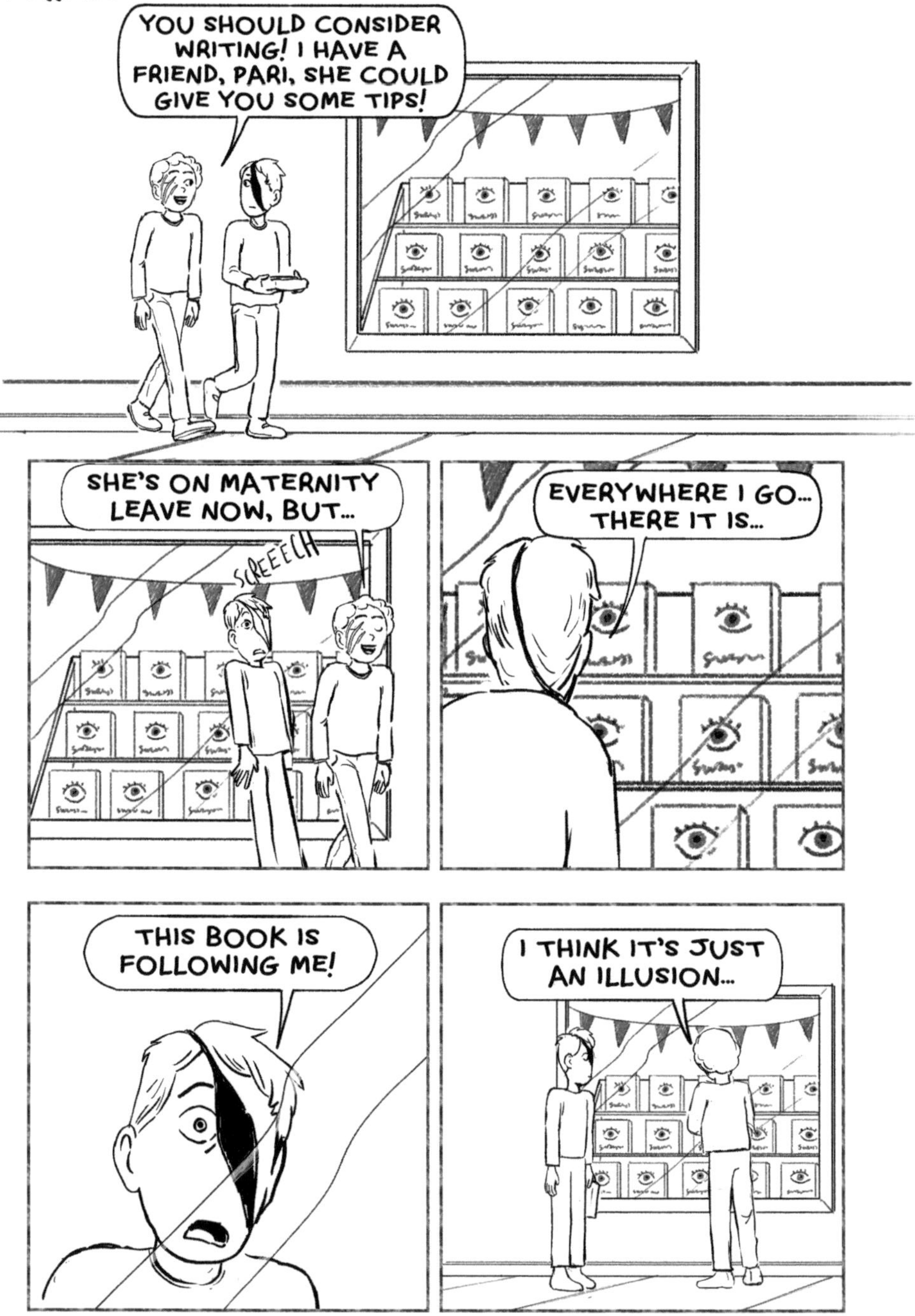
YOU SHOULD CONSIDER WRITING! I HAVE A FRIEND, PARI, SHE COULD GIVE YOU SOME TIPS!
SHE'S ON MATERNITY LEAVE NOW, BUT...
SCREEECH
EVERYWHERE I GO... THERE IT IS...
THIS BOOK IS FOLLOWING ME!
I THINK IT'S JUST AN ILLUSION...

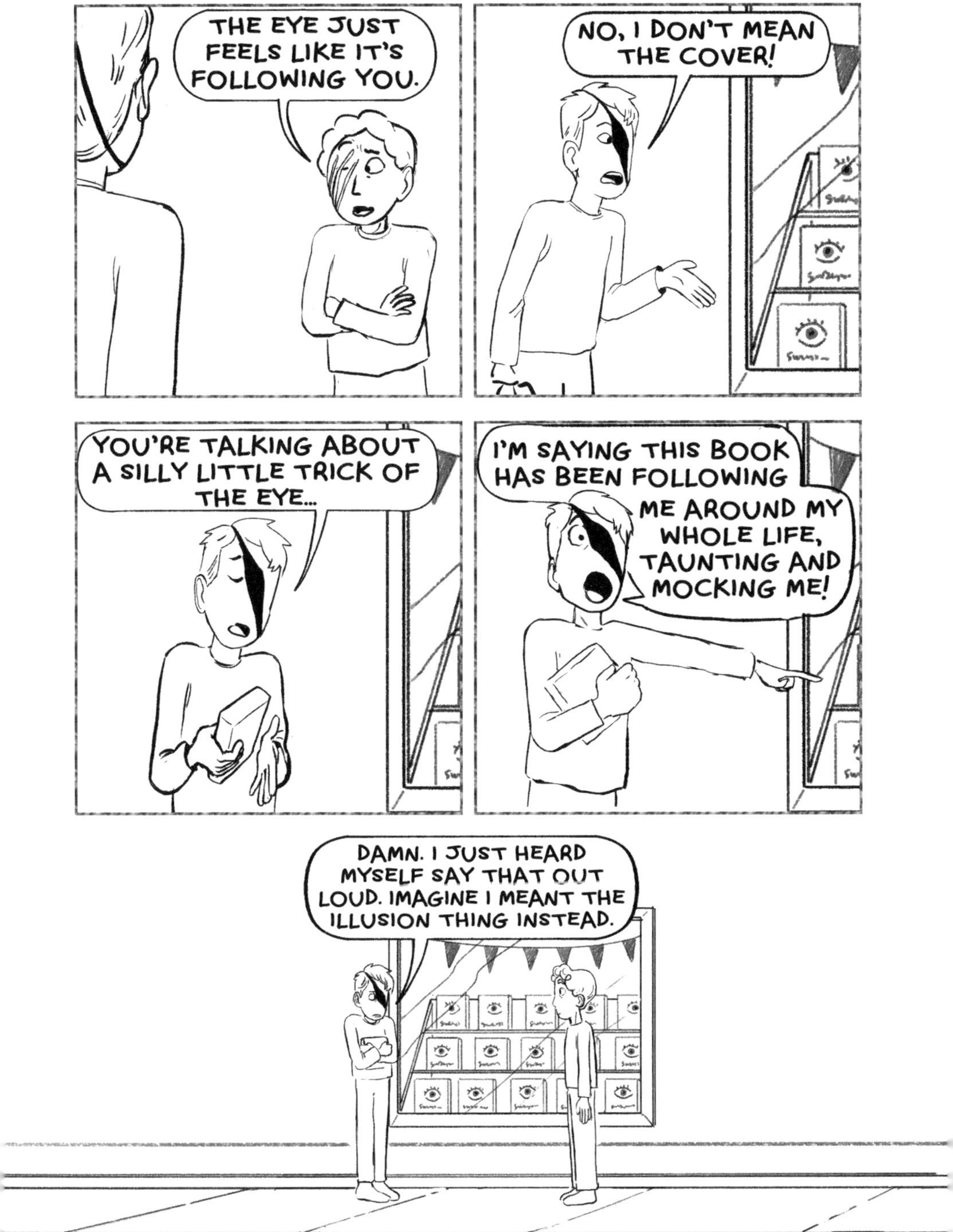
THE EYE JUST FEELS LIKE IT'S FOLLOWING YOU.
NO, I DON'T MEAN THE COVER!
YOU'RE TALKING ABOUT A SILLY LITTLE TRICK OF THE EYE...
I'M SAYING THIS BOOK HAS BEEN FOLLOWING
ME AROUND MY WHOLE LIFE, TAUNTING AND MOCKING ME!
DAMN. I JUST HEARD MYSELF SAY THAT OUT LOUD. IMAGINE I MEANT THE ILLUSION THING INSTEAD.

Canceled galleries

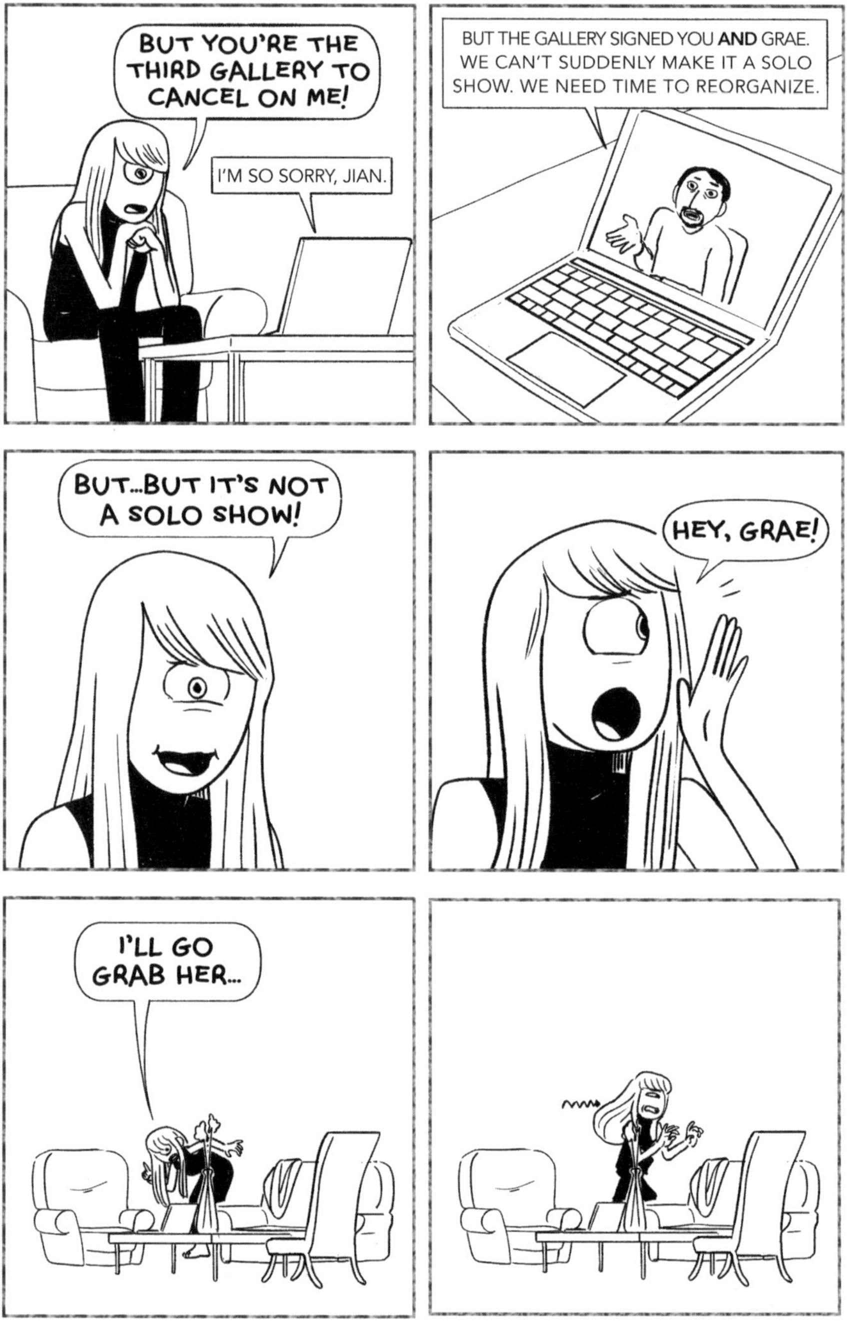
BUT YOU'RE THE THIRD GALLERY TO CANCEL ON ME!
I'M SO SORRY, JIAN.
BUT THE GALLERY SIGNED YOU **AND** GRAE. WE CAN'T SUDDENLY MAKE IT A SOLO SHOW. WE NEED TIME TO REORGANIZE.
BUT...BUT IT'S NOT A SOLO SHOW!
HEY, GRAE!
I'LL GO GRAB HER...

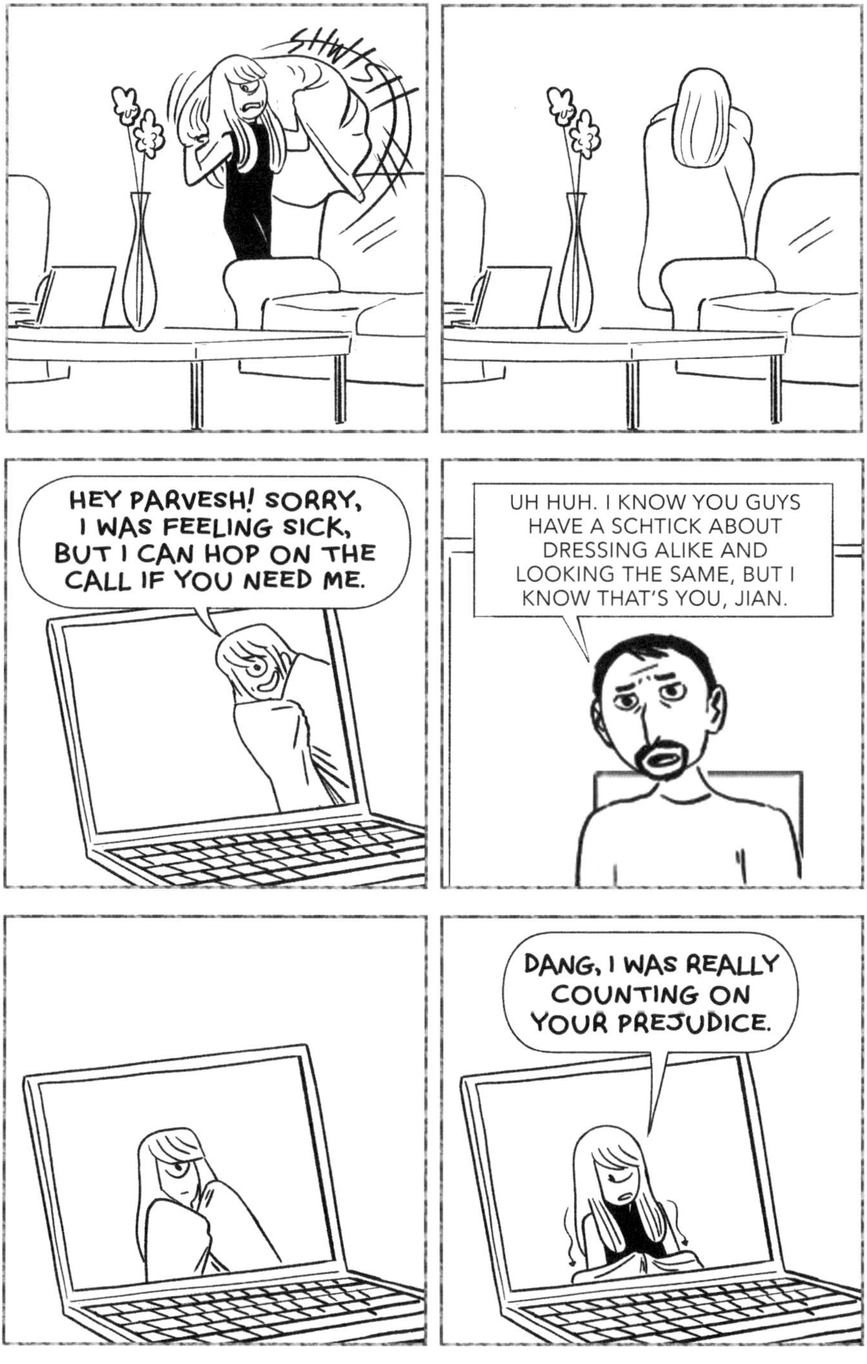
SHWISH
HEY PARVESH! SORRY, I WAS FEELING SICK, BUT I CAN HOP ON THE CALL IF YOU NEED ME.
UH HUH. I KNOW YOU GUYS HAVE A SCHTICK ABOUT DRESSING ALIKE AND LOOKING THE SAME, BUT I KNOW THAT'S YOU, JIAN.
DANG, I WAS REALLY COUNTING ON YOUR PREJUDICE.

Grae in Hollywood

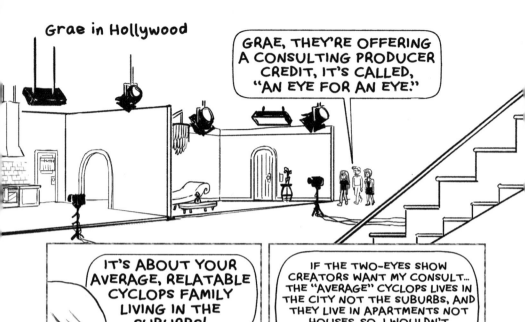

GRAE, THEY'RE OFFERING A CONSULTING PRODUCER CREDIT, IT'S CALLED, "AN EYE FOR AN EYE."

IT'S ABOUT YOUR AVERAGE, RELATABLE CYCLOPS FAMILY LIVING IN THE SUBURBS!

IF THE TWO-EYES SHOW CREATORS WANT MY CONSULT... THE "AVERAGE" CYCLOPS LIVES IN THE CITY NOT THE SUBURBS, AND THEY LIVE IN APARTMENTS NOT HOUSES. SO, I WOULDN'T ADVERTISE A SHOW LIKE THIS AS "AVERAGE" OR "RELATABLE."

IT LOOKS BIG, BECAUSE IT'S A SET! THE CAMERA SHRINKS EVERYTHING!

BUT THE CAMERA WON'T MAKE A HOUSE LOOK LIKE AN APARTMENT.

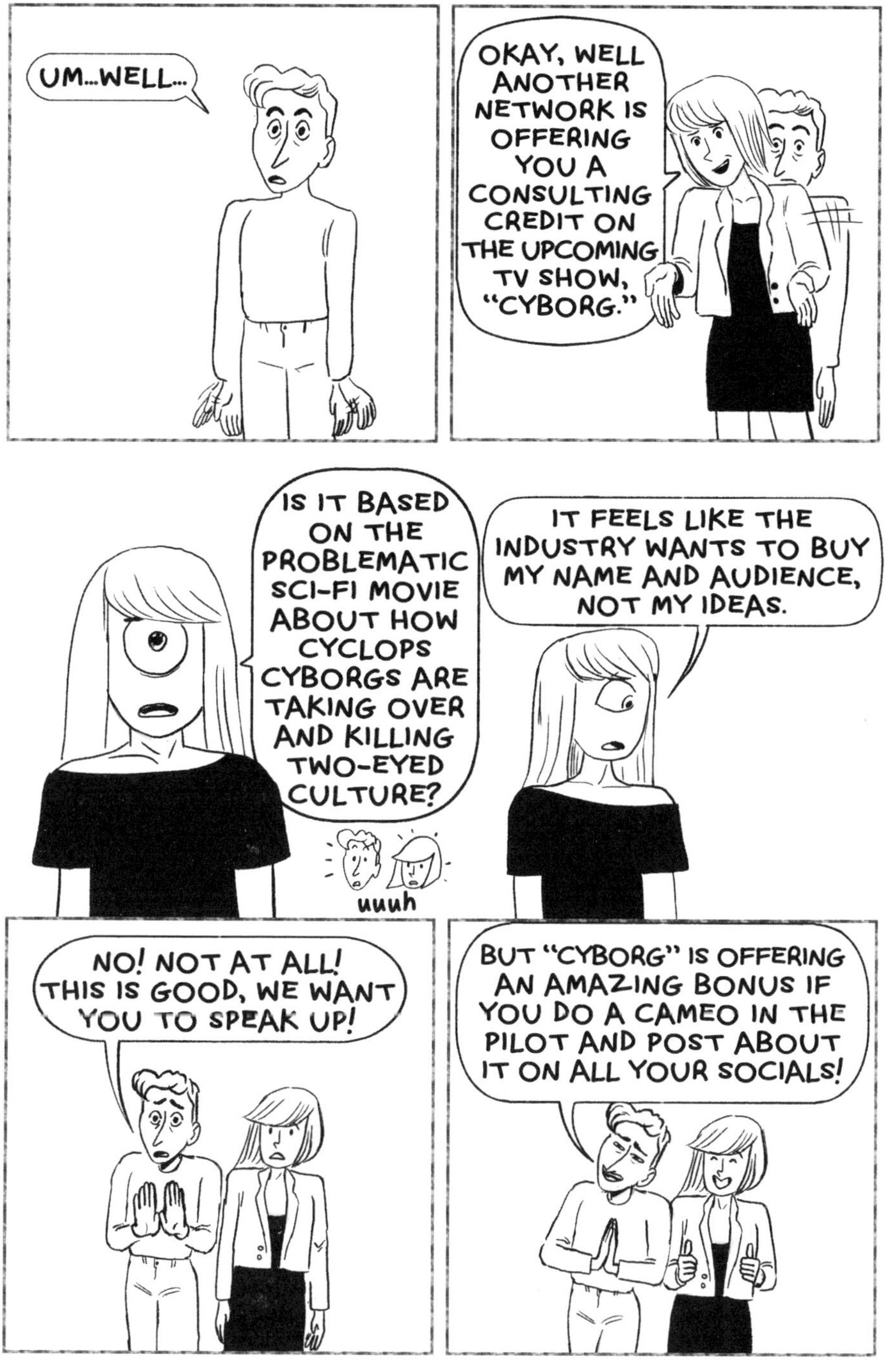
UM...WELL...
OKAY, WELL ANOTHER NETWORK IS OFFERING YOU A CONSULTING CREDIT ON THE UPCOMING TV SHOW, "CYBORG."
IS IT BASED ON THE PROBLEMATIC SCI-FI MOVIE ABOUT HOW CYCLOPS CYBORGS ARE TAKING OVER AND KILLING TWO-EYED CULTURE?
IT FEELS LIKE THE INDUSTRY WANTS TO BUY MY NAME AND AUDIENCE, NOT MY IDEAS.
uuuh
NO! NOT AT ALL! THIS IS GOOD, WE WANT YOU TO SPEAK UP!
BUT "CYBORG" IS OFFERING AN AMAZING BONUS IF YOU DO A CAMEO IN THE PILOT AND POST ABOUT IT ON ALL YOUR SOCIALS!

Etna gives back to the community

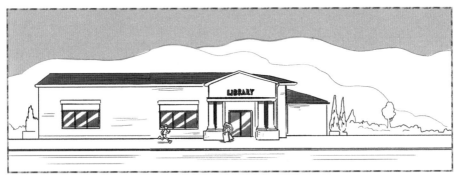

THE ETNA PROJECT! TODAY @ 4PM

WOW! I HEARD ABOUT THIS ON THE NEWS! GOOD ON YOU TO HELP YOUNG, AT-RISK CYCLOPES!

THANK YOU. I FEEL THE BIGGEST ISSUE CYCLOPES FACE IS...

THE UNDER-FUNDED SCHOOL SYSTEMS, THE BIAS IN HEALTHCARE, ESPECIALLY IN THE TREATMENT OF PREGNANCIES, AND...

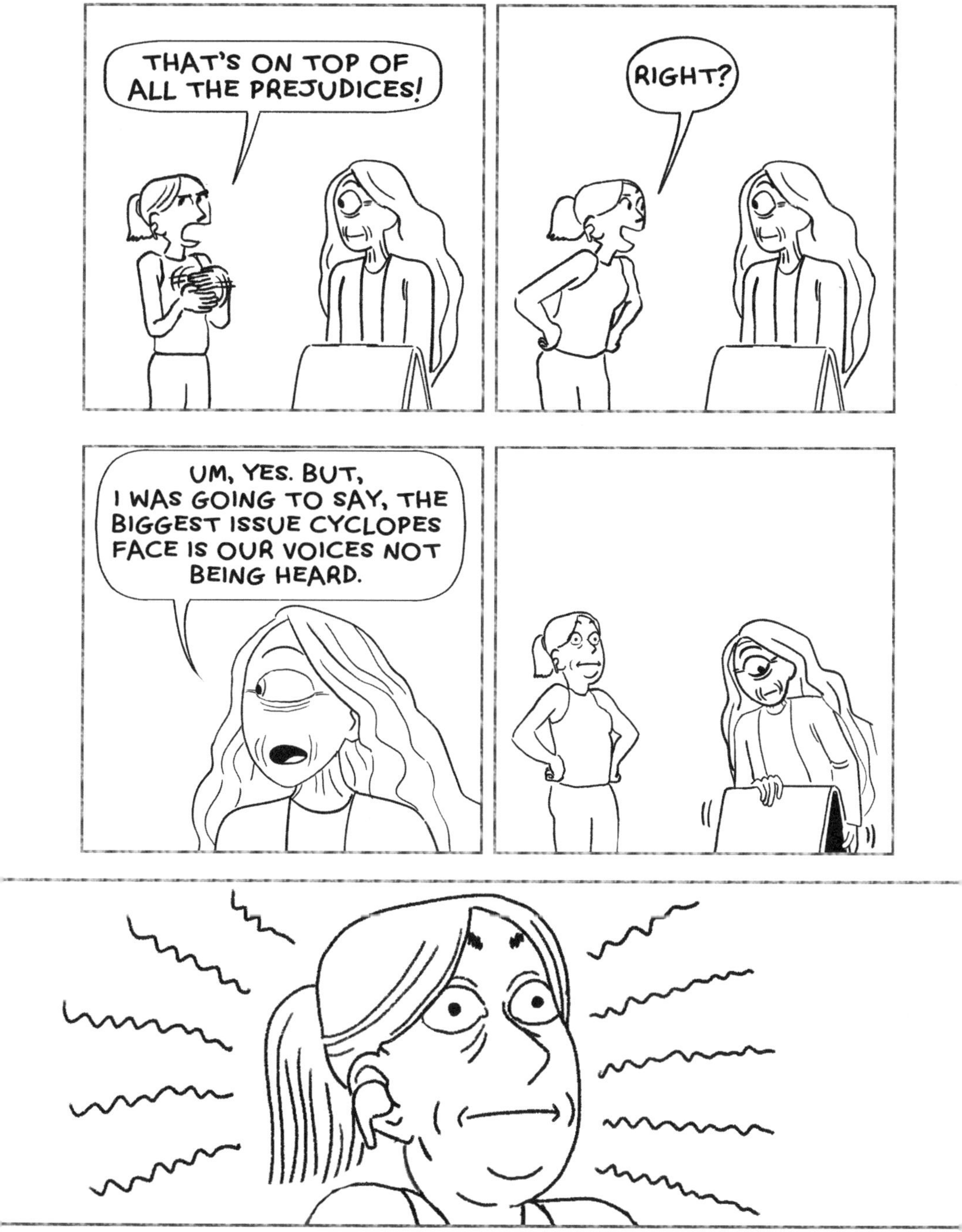
THAT'S ON TOP OF ALL THE PREJUDICES!
RIGHT?
UM, YES. BUT, I WAS GOING TO SAY, THE BIGGEST ISSUE CYCLOPES FACE IS OUR VOICES NOT BEING HEARD.

Tim and Pari leave the hospital

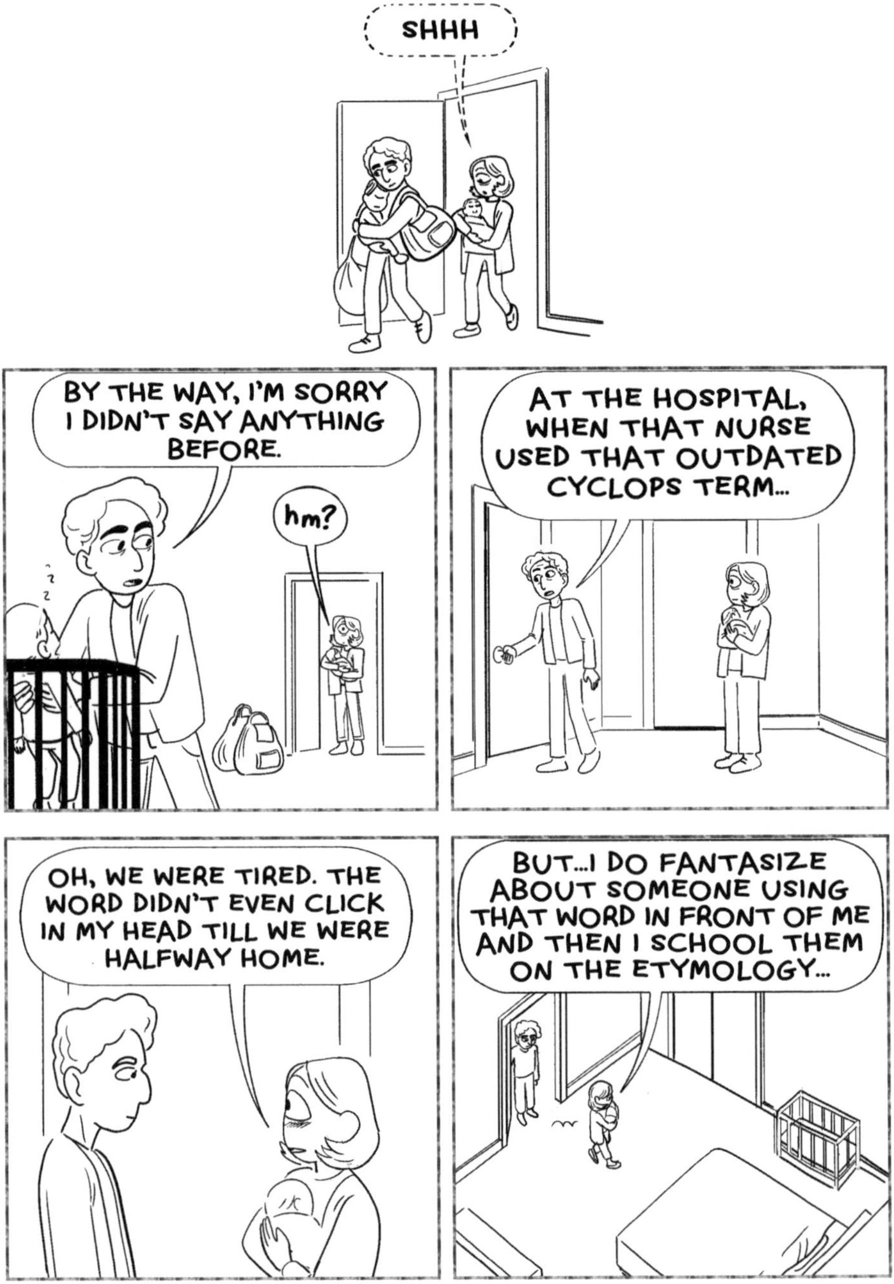
SHHH
BY THE WAY, I'M SORRY I DIDN'T SAY ANYTHING BEFORE.
hm?
AT THE HOSPITAL, WHEN THAT NURSE USED THAT OUTDATED CYCLOPS TERM...
OH, WE WERE TIRED. THE WORD DIDN'T EVEN CLICK IN MY HEAD TILL WE WERE HALFWAY HOME.
BUT...I DO FANTASIZE ABOUT SOMEONE USING THAT WORD IN FRONT OF ME AND THEN I SCHOOL THEM ON THE ETYMOLOGY...

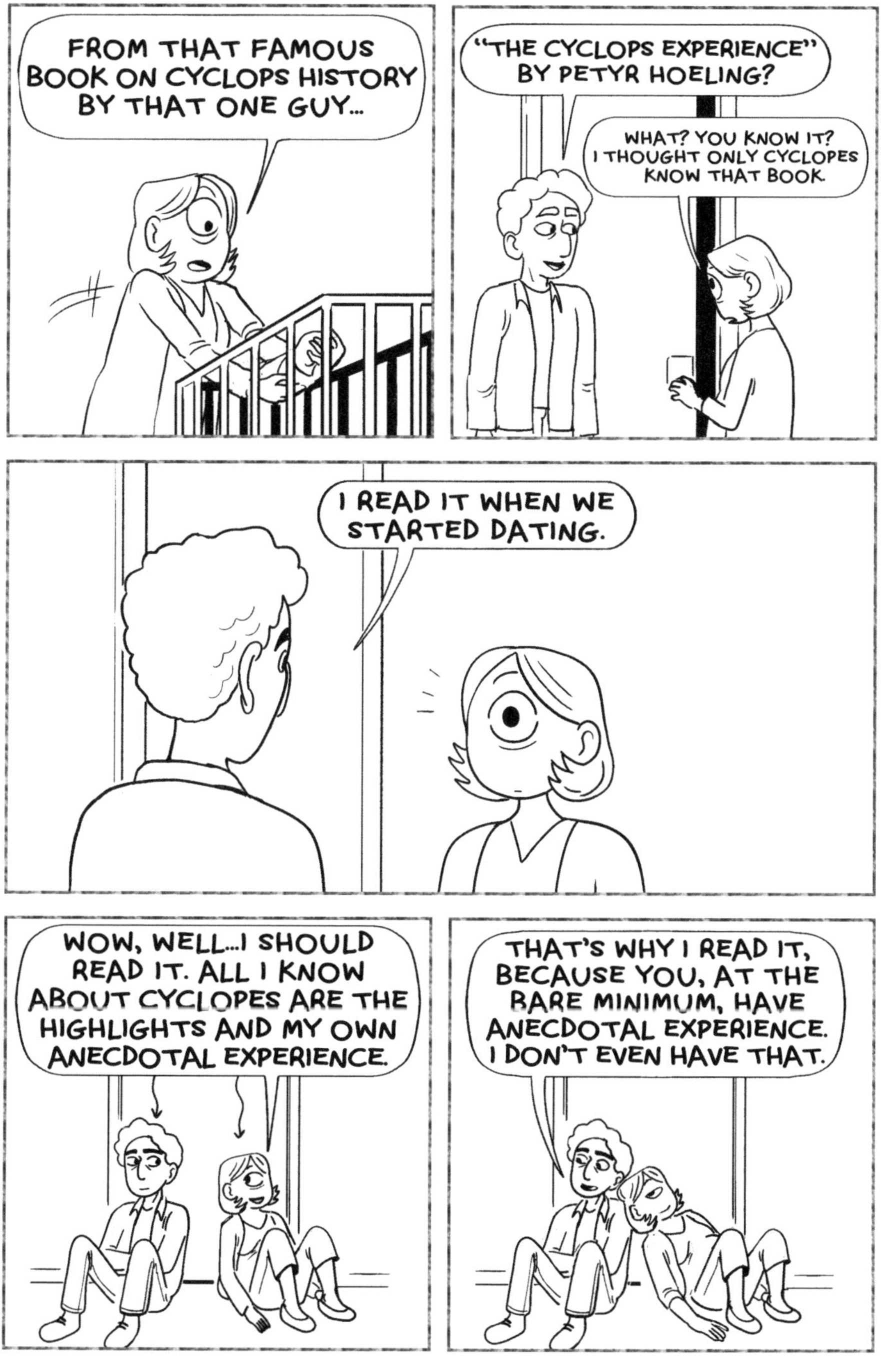
FROM THAT FAMOUS BOOK ON CYCLOPS HISTORY BY THAT ONE GUY...
"THE CYCLOPS EXPERIENCE" BY PETYR HOELING?
WHAT? YOU KNOW IT? I THOUGHT ONLY CYCLOPES KNOW THAT BOOK.
I READ IT WHEN WE STARTED DATING.
WOW, WELL...I SHOULD READ IT. ALL I KNOW ABOUT CYCLOPES ARE THE HIGHLIGHTS AND MY OWN ANECDOTAL EXPERIENCE.
THAT'S WHY I READ IT, BECAUSE YOU, AT THE BARE MINIMUM, HAVE ANECDOTAL EXPERIENCE. I DON'T EVEN HAVE THAT.

Reflecting

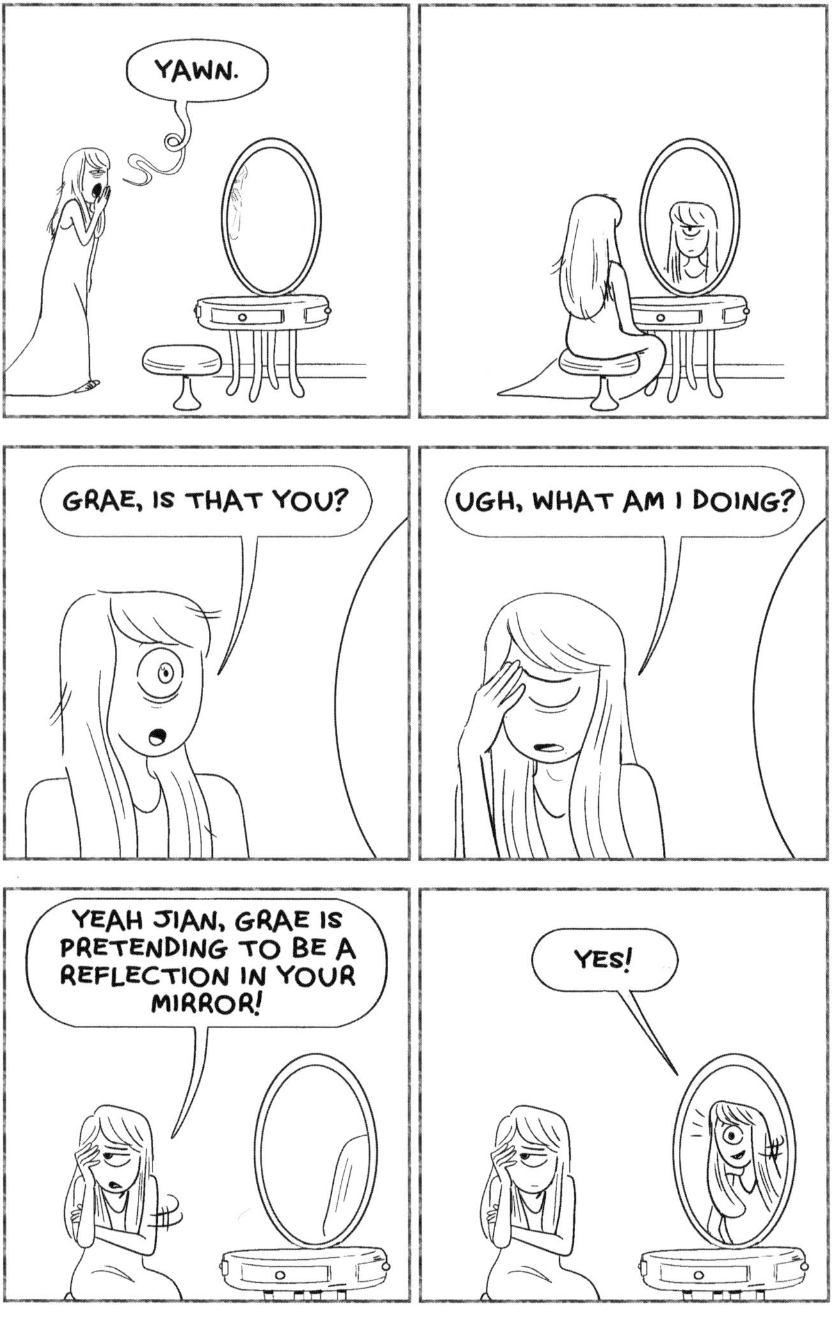
YAWN.
GRAE, IS THAT YOU?
UGH, WHAT AM I DOING?
YEAH JIAN, GRAE IS PRETENDING TO BE A REFLECTION IN YOUR MIRROR!
YES!

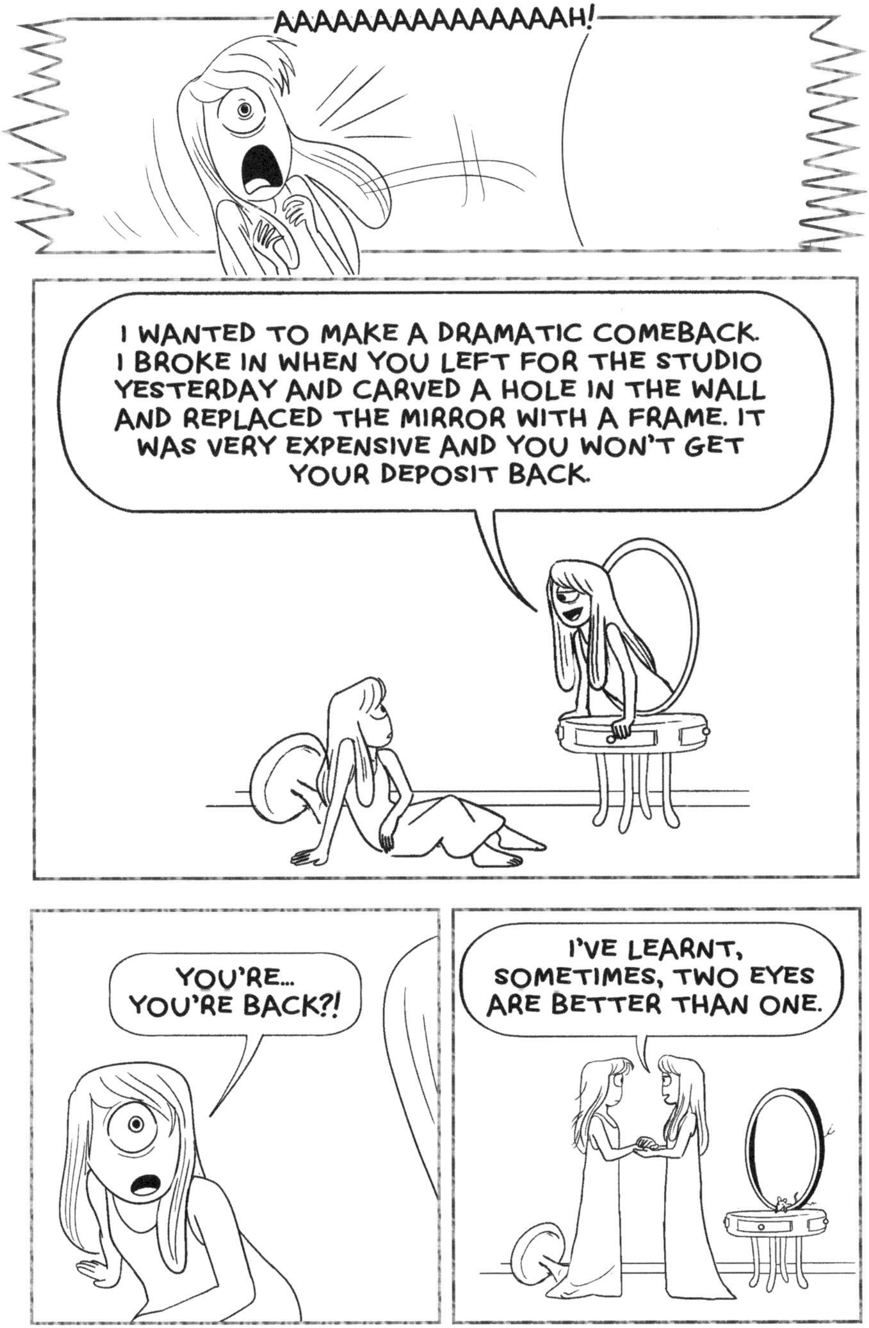
AAAAAAAAAAAAAAAH!
I WANTED TO MAKE A DRAMATIC COMEBACK. I BROKE IN WHEN YOU LEFT FOR THE STUDIO YESTERDAY AND CARVED A HOLE IN THE WALL AND REPLACED THE MIRROR WITH A FRAME. IT WAS VERY EXPENSIVE AND YOU WON'T GET YOUR DEPOSIT BACK.
YOU'RE... YOU'RE BACK?!
I'VE LEARNT, SOMETIMES, TWO EYES ARE BETTER THAN ONE.

Eric Wood

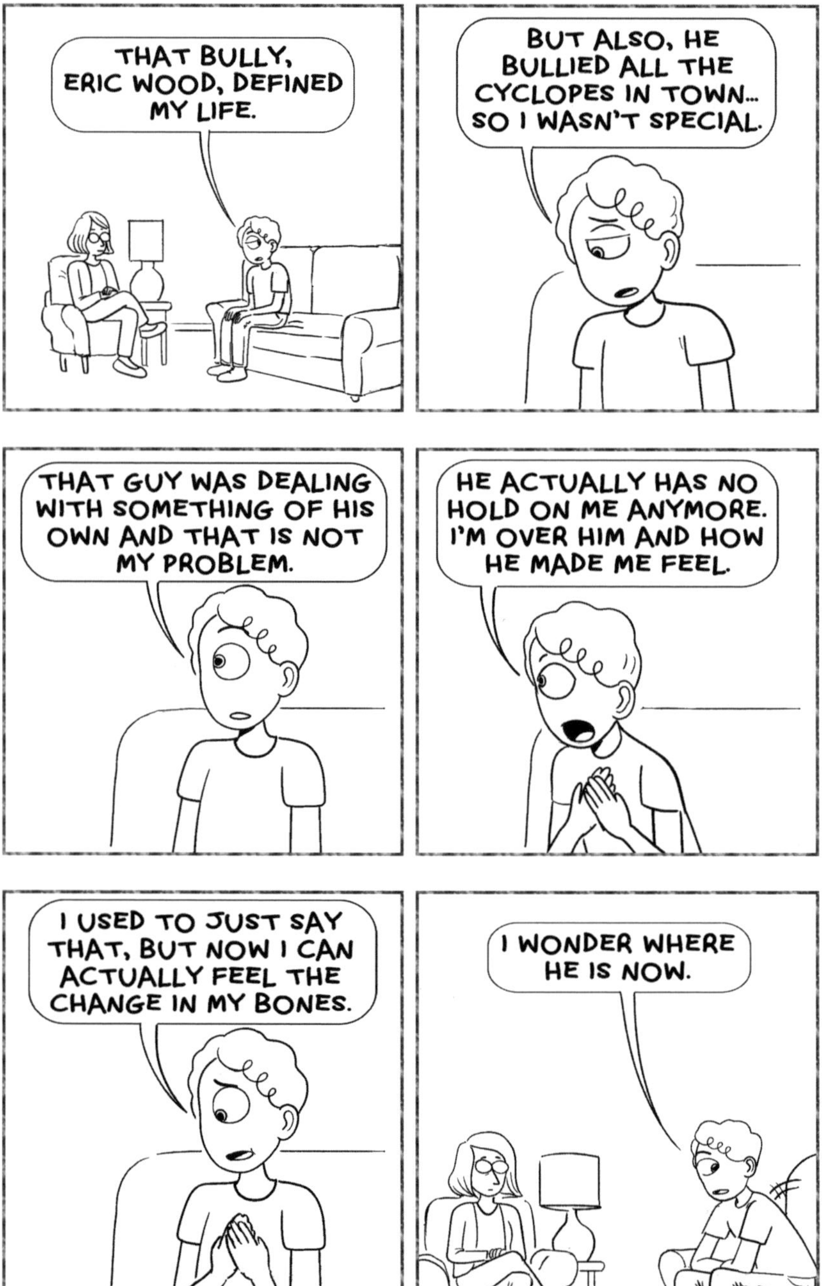
THAT BULLY, ERIC WOOD, DEFINED MY LIFE.
BUT ALSO, HE BULLIED ALL THE CYCLOPES IN TOWN... SO I WASN'T SPECIAL.
THAT GUY WAS DEALING WITH SOMETHING OF HIS OWN AND THAT IS NOT MY PROBLEM.
HE ACTUALLY HAS NO HOLD ON ME ANYMORE. I'M OVER HIM AND HOW HE MADE ME FEEL.
I USED TO JUST SAY THAT, BUT NOW I CAN ACTUALLY FEEL THE CHANGE IN MY BONES.
I WONDER WHERE HE IS NOW.

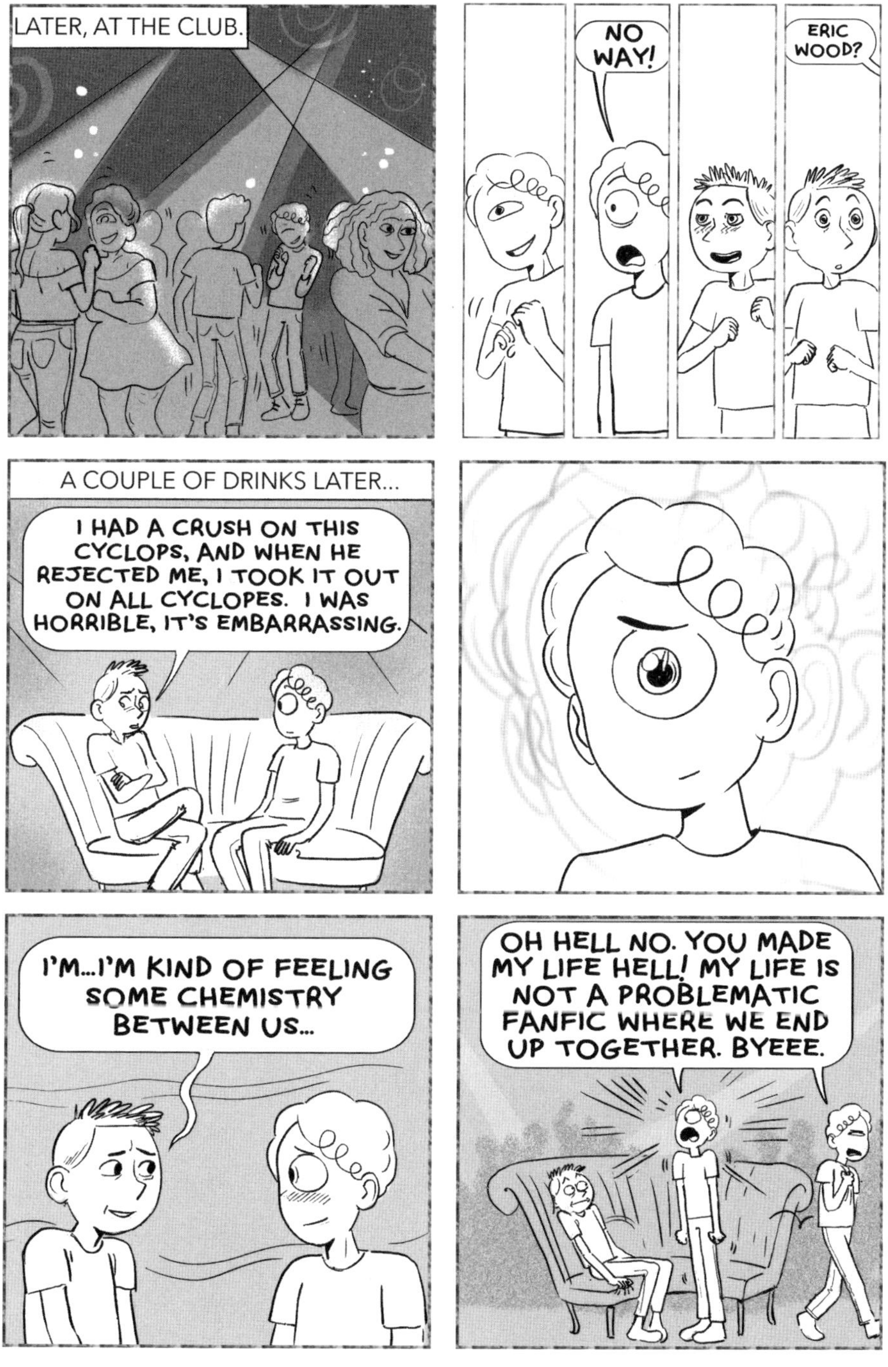
LATER, AT THE CLUB.
NO WAY!
ERIC WOOD?
A COUPLE OF DRINKS LATER...
I HAD A CRUSH ON THIS CYCLOPS, AND WHEN HE REJECTED ME, I TOOK IT OUT ON ALL CYCLOPES. I WAS HORRIBLE, IT'S EMBARRASSING.
I'M...I'M KIND OF FEELING SOME CHEMISTRY BETWEEN US...
OH HELL NO. YOU MADE MY LIFE HELL! MY LIFE IS NOT A PROBLEMATIC FANFIC WHERE WE END UP TOGETHER. BYEEE.

Rethink things

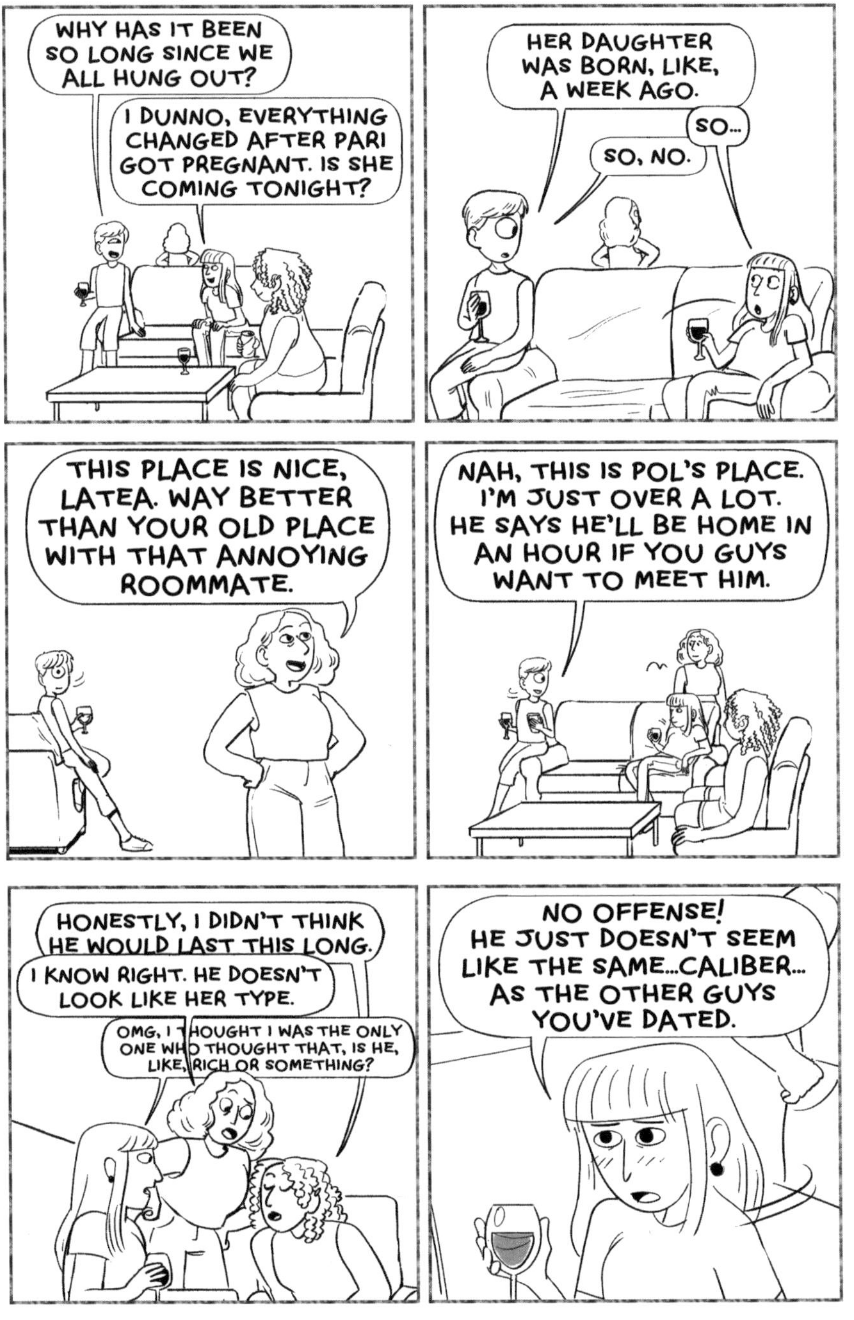

WHY HAS IT BEEN SO LONG SINCE WE ALL HUNG OUT?
I DUNNO, EVERYTHING CHANGED AFTER PARI GOT PREGNANT. IS SHE COMING TONIGHT?
HER DAUGHTER WAS BORN, LIKE, A WEEK AGO.
SO, NO.
SO...
THIS PLACE IS NICE, LATEA. WAY BETTER THAN YOUR OLD PLACE WITH THAT ANNOYING ROOMMATE.
NAH, THIS IS POL'S PLACE. I'M JUST OVER A LOT. HE SAYS HE'LL BE HOME IN AN HOUR IF YOU GUYS WANT TO MEET HIM.
HONESTLY, I DIDN'T THINK HE WOULD LAST THIS LONG.
I KNOW RIGHT. HE DOESN'T LOOK LIKE HER TYPE.
OMG, I THOUGHT I WAS THE ONLY ONE WHO THOUGHT THAT, IS HE, LIKE, RICH OR SOMETHING?
NO OFFENSE! HE JUST DOESN'T SEEM LIKE THE SAME...CALIBER... AS THE OTHER GUYS YOU'VE DATED.

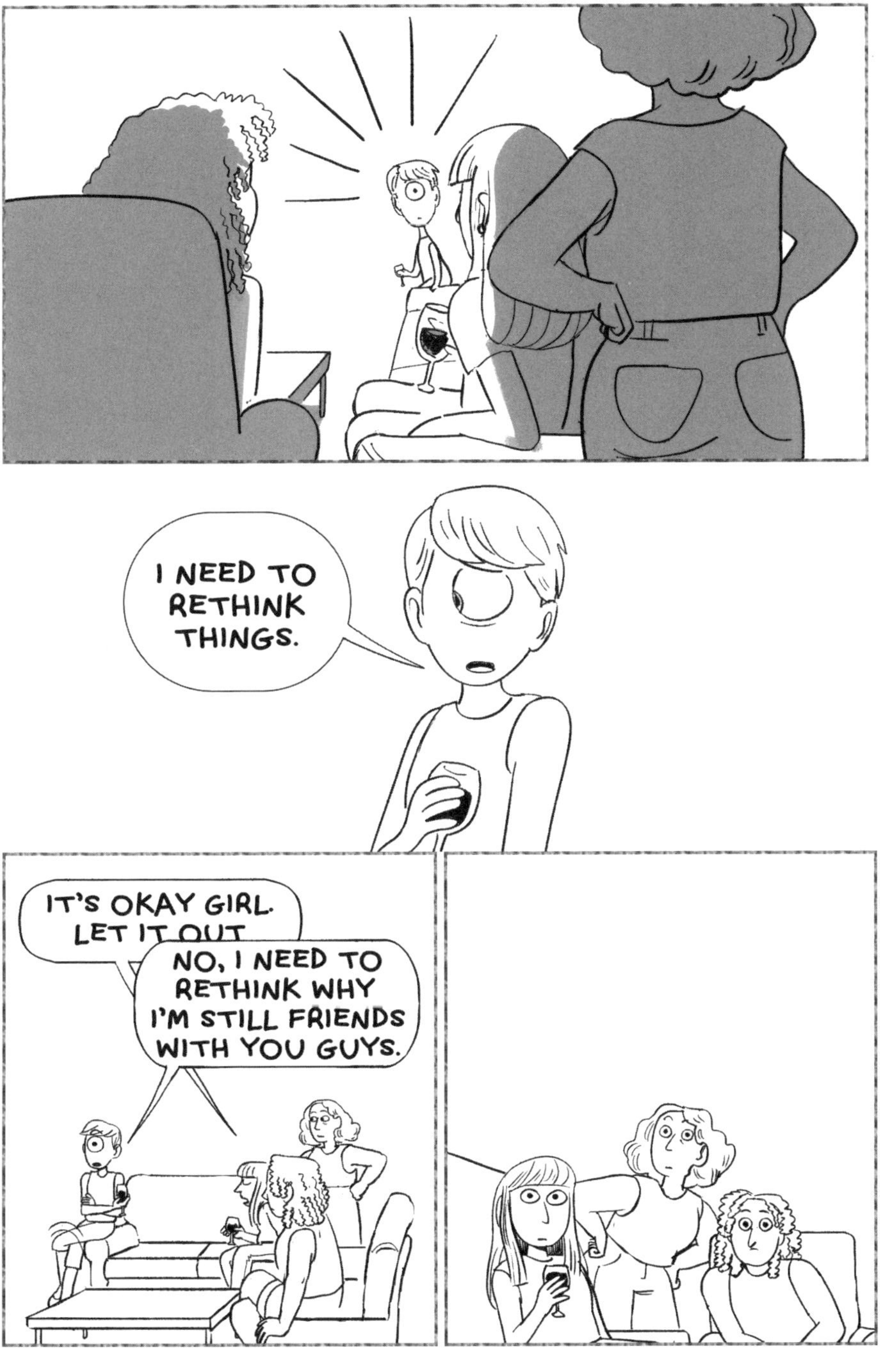
I NEED TO RETHINK THINGS.
IT'S OKAY GIRL. LET IT OUT
NO, I NEED TO RETHINK WHY I'M STILL FRIENDS WITH YOU GUYS.

Always right

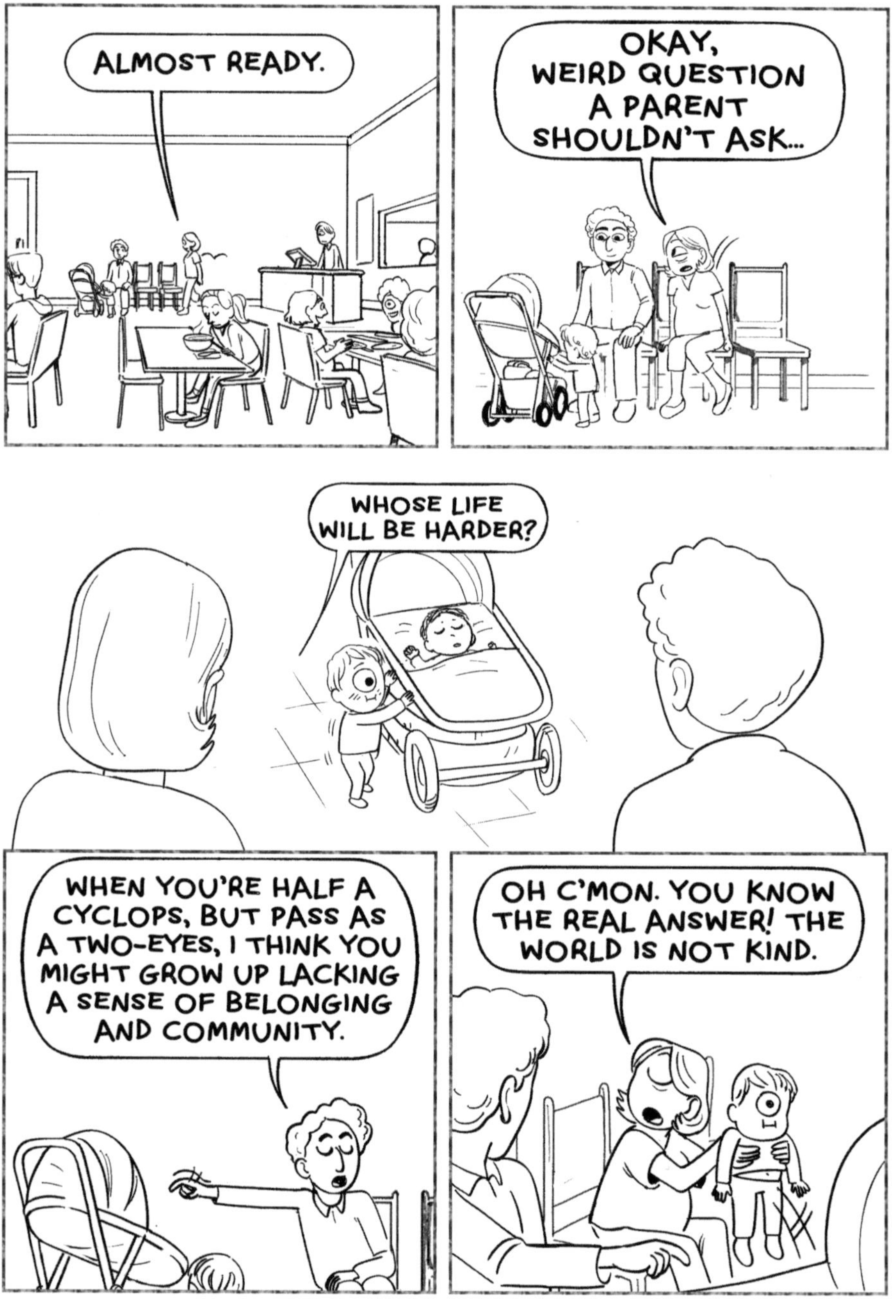
ALMOST READY.
OKAY, WEIRD QUESTION A PARENT SHOULDN'T ASK...
WHOSE LIFE WILL BE HARDER?
WHEN YOU'RE HALF A CYCLOPS, BUT PASS AS A TWO-EYES, I THINK YOU MIGHT GROW UP LACKING A SENSE OF BELONGING AND COMMUNITY.
OH C'MON. YOU KNOW THE REAL ANSWER! THE WORLD IS NOT KIND.

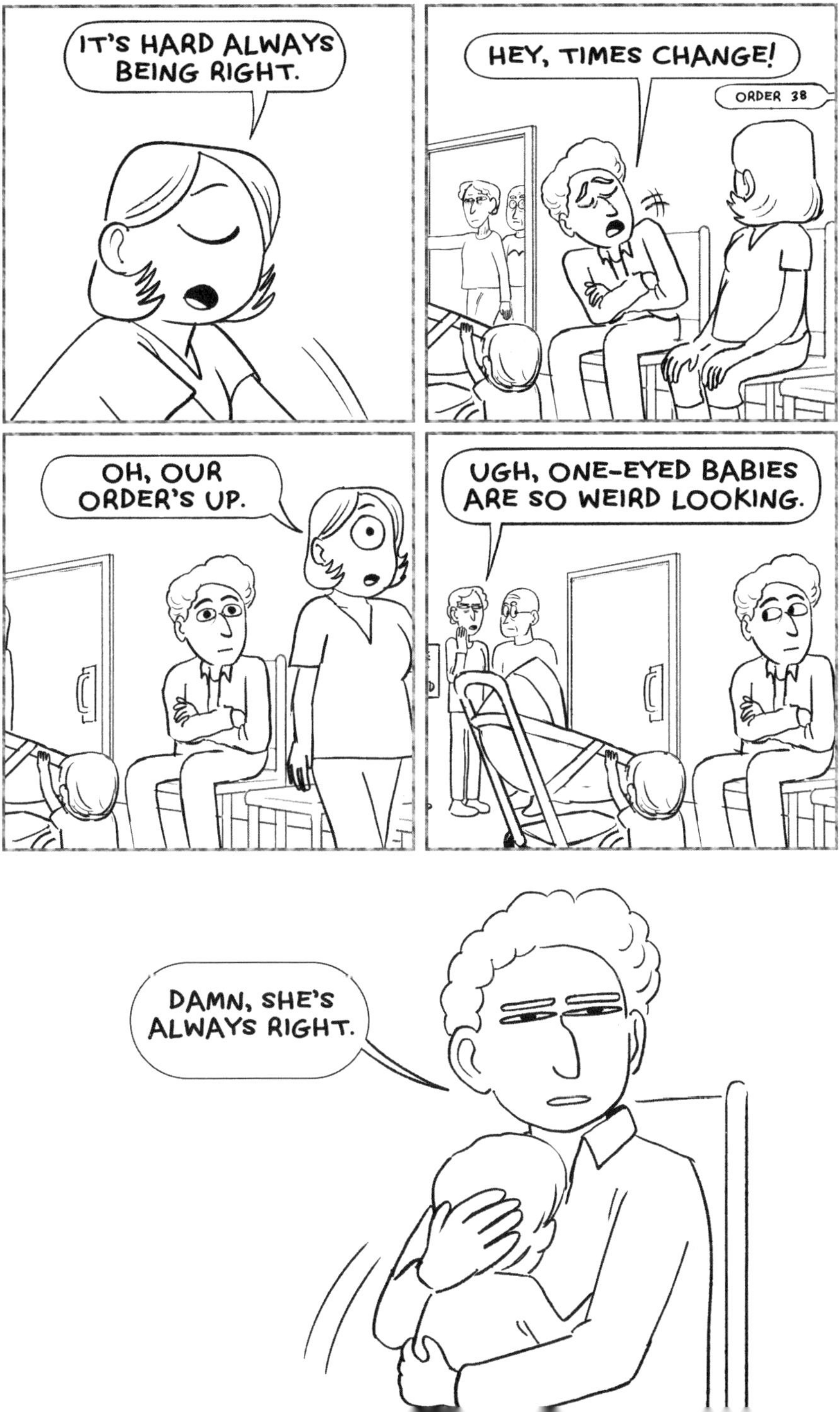
IT'S HARD ALWAYS BEING RIGHT.
HEY, TIMES CHANGE!
ORDER 38
OH, OUR ORDER'S UP.
UGH, ONE-EYED BABIES ARE SO WEIRD LOOKING.
DAMN, SHE'S ALWAYS RIGHT.

Fundraiser

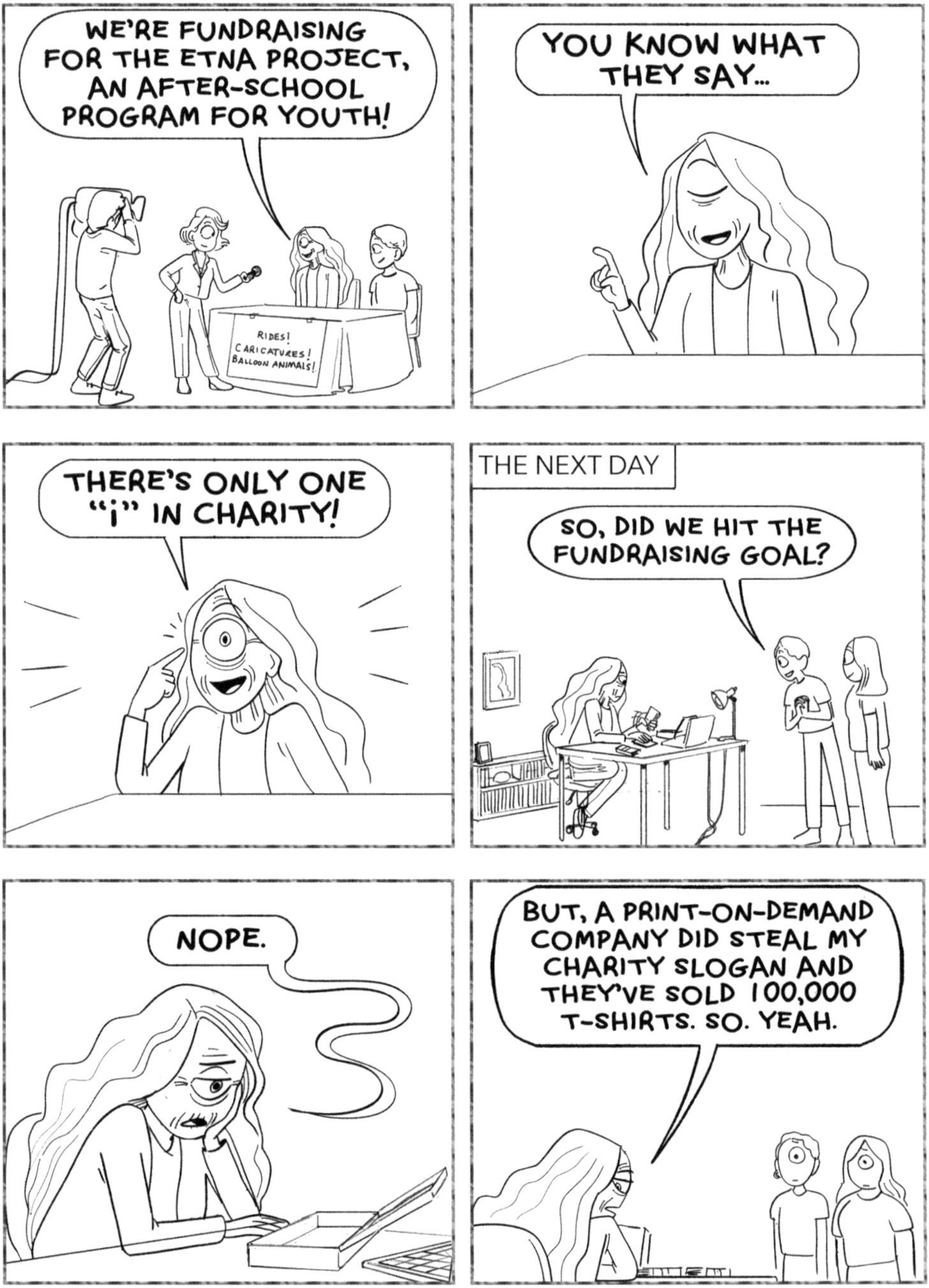
WE'RE FUNDRAISING FOR THE ETNA PROJECT, AN AFTER-SCHOOL PROGRAM FOR YOUTH!
RIDES! CARICATURES! BALLOON ANIMALS!
YOU KNOW WHAT THEY SAY...
THERE'S ONLY ONE "i" IN CHARITY!
THE NEXT DAY
SO, DID WE HIT THE FUNDRAISING GOAL?
NOPE.
BUT, A PRINT-ON-DEMAND COMPANY DID STEAL MY CHARITY SLOGAN AND THEY'VE SOLD 100,000 T-SHIRTS. SO. YEAH.

Arj gets a new job

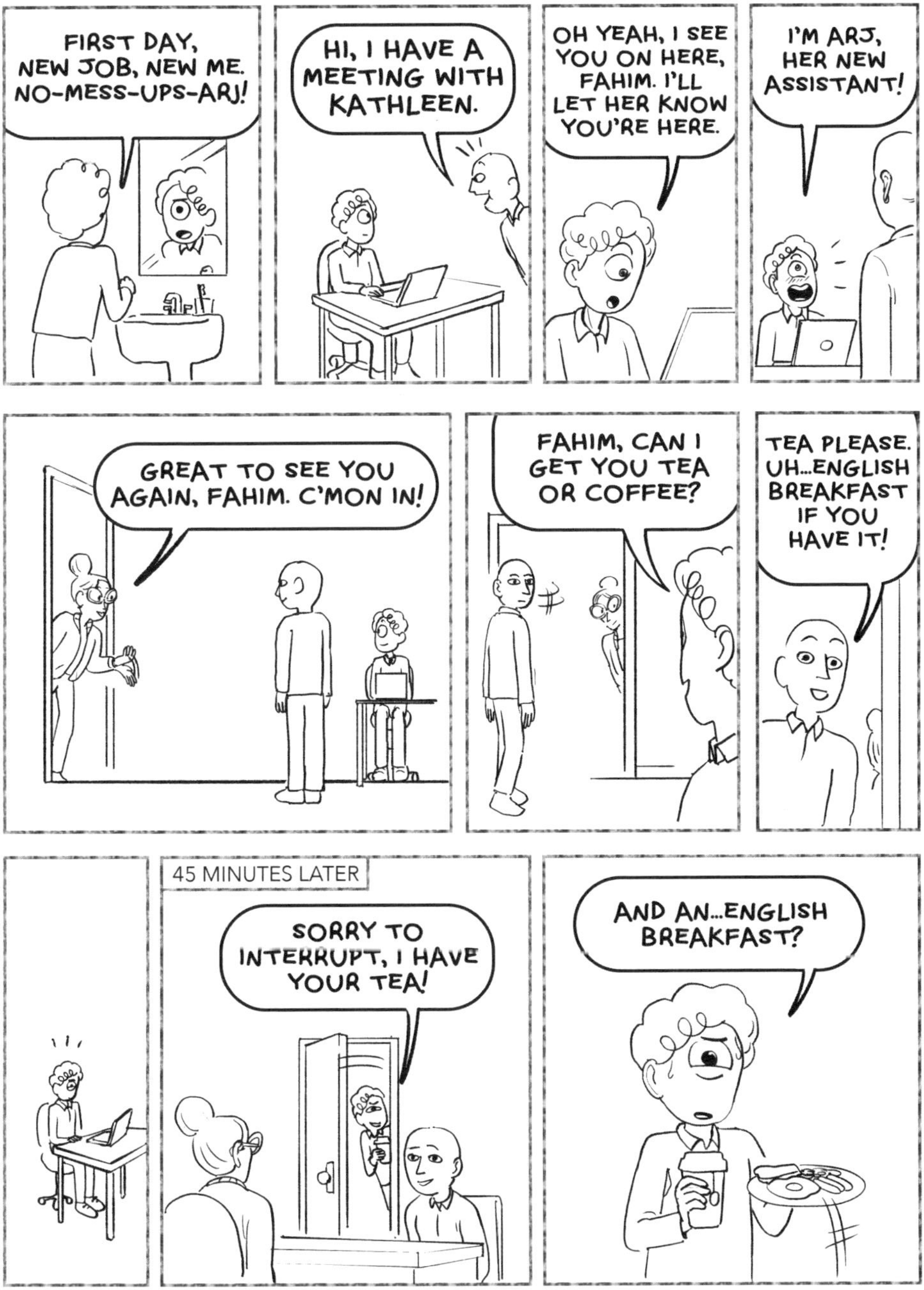
FIRST DAY, NEW JOB, NEW ME. NO-MESS-UPS-ARJ!
HI, I HAVE A MEETING WITH KATHLEEN.
OH YEAH, I SEE YOU ON HERE, FAHIM. I'LL LET HER KNOW YOU'RE HERE.
I'M ARJ, HER NEW ASSISTANT!
GREAT TO SEE YOU AGAIN, FAHIM. C'MON IN!
FAHIM, CAN I GET YOU TEA OR COFFEE?
TEA PLEASE. UH...ENGLISH BREAKFAST IF YOU HAVE IT!
45 MINUTES LATER
SORRY TO INTERRUPT, I HAVE YOUR TEA!
AND AN...ENGLISH BREAKFAST?

Pol and Latea

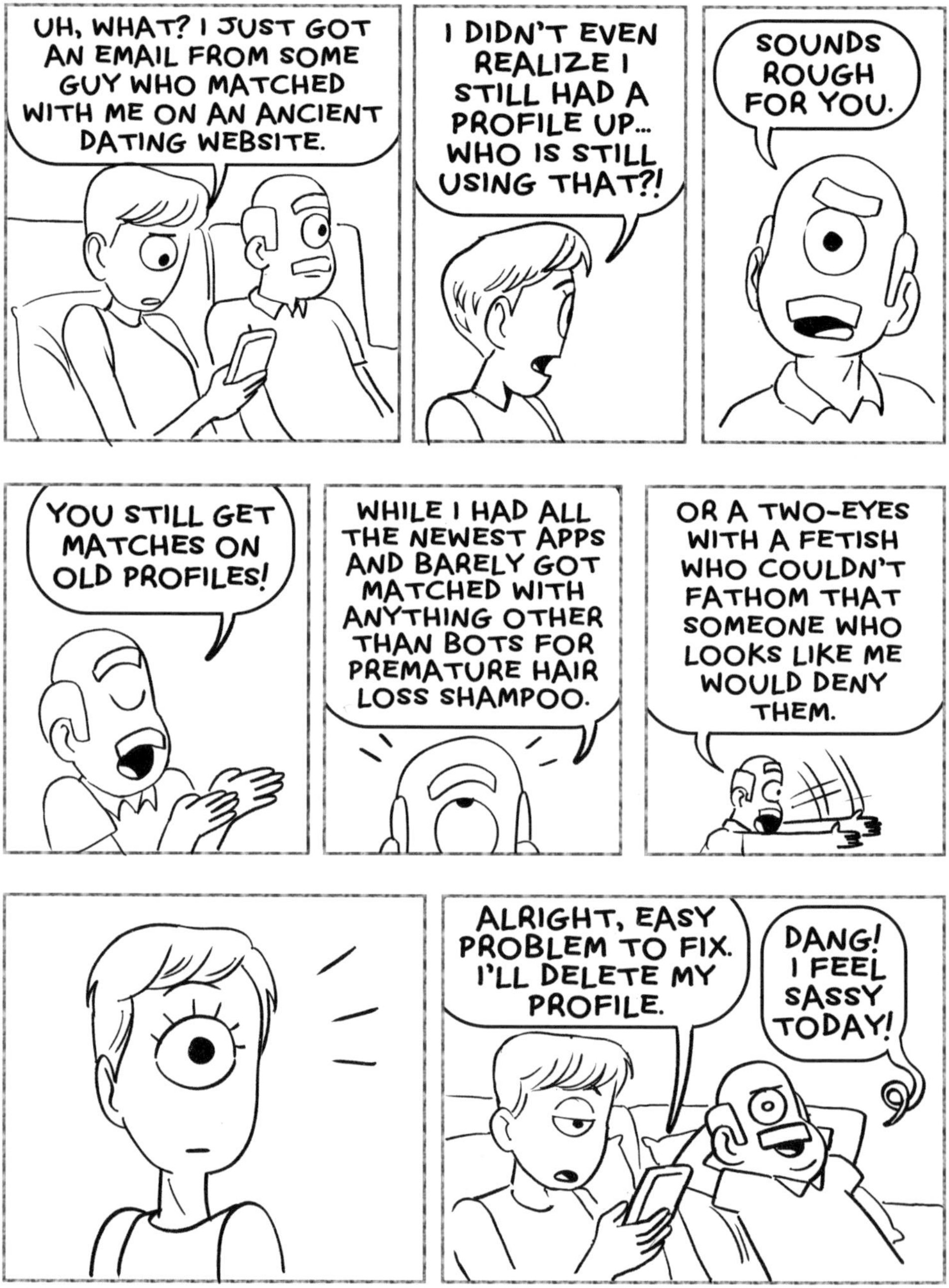
UH, WHAT? I JUST GOT AN EMAIL FROM SOME GUY WHO MATCHED WITH ME ON AN ANCIENT DATING WEBSITE.
I DIDN'T EVEN REALIZE I STILL HAD A PROFILE UP... WHO IS STILL USING THAT?!
SOUNDS ROUGH FOR YOU.
YOU STILL GET MATCHES ON OLD PROFILES!
WHILE I HAD ALL THE NEWEST APPS AND BARELY GOT MATCHED WITH ANYTHING OTHER THAN BOTS FOR PREMATURE HAIR LOSS SHAMPOO.
OR A TWO-EYES WITH A FETISH WHO COULDN'T FATHOM THAT SOMEONE WHO LOOKS LIKE ME WOULD DENY THEM.
ALRIGHT, EASY PROBLEM TO FIX. I'LL DELETE MY PROFILE.
DANG! I FEEL SASSY TODAY!

A new Arj

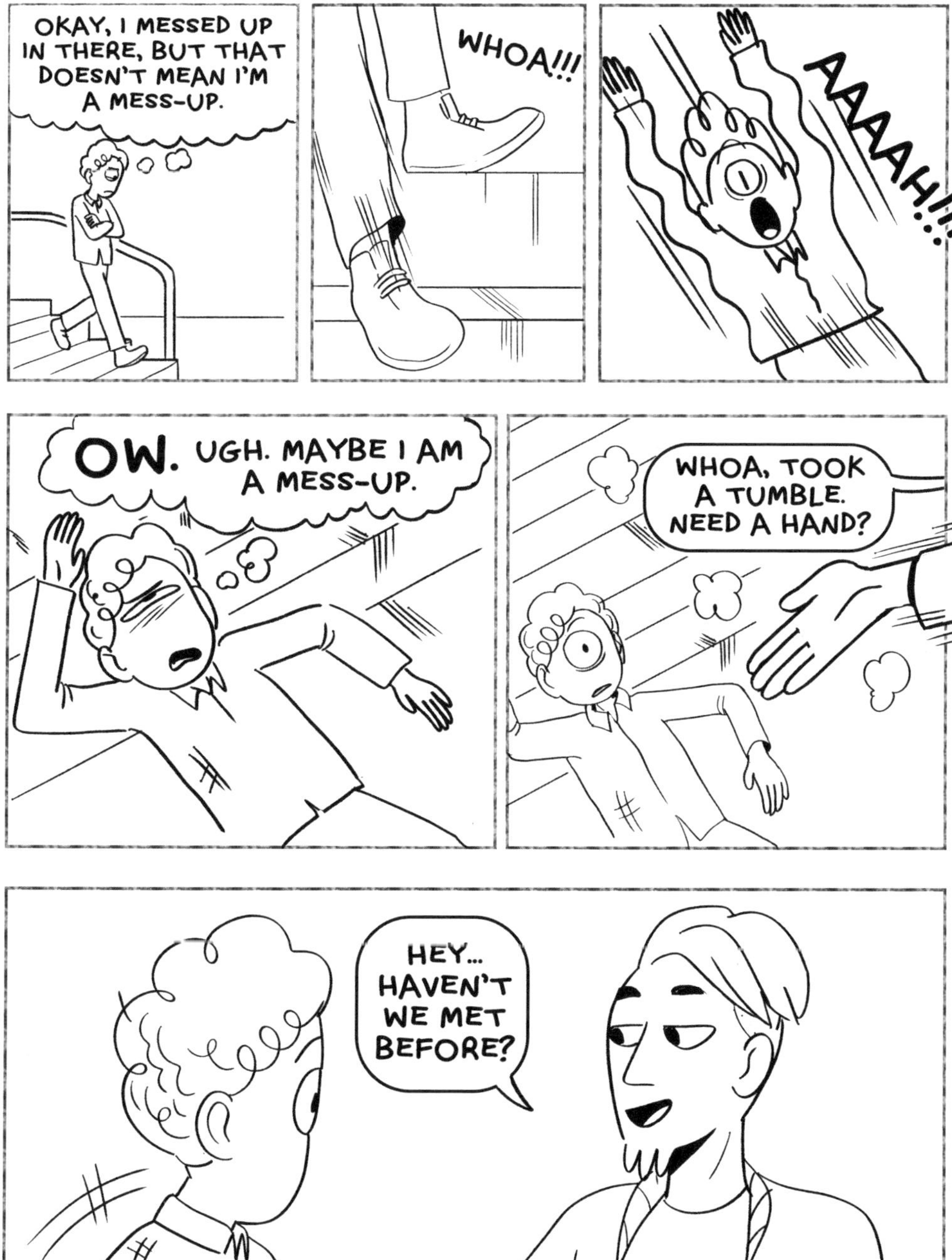
OKAY, I MESSED UP IN THERE, BUT THAT DOESN'T MEAN I'M A MESS-UP.
WHOA!!!
AAAAH!!!!
OW. UGH. MAYBE I AM A MESS-UP.
WHOA, TOOK A TUMBLE. NEED A HAND?
HEY... HAVEN'T WE MET BEFORE?

Conclusions

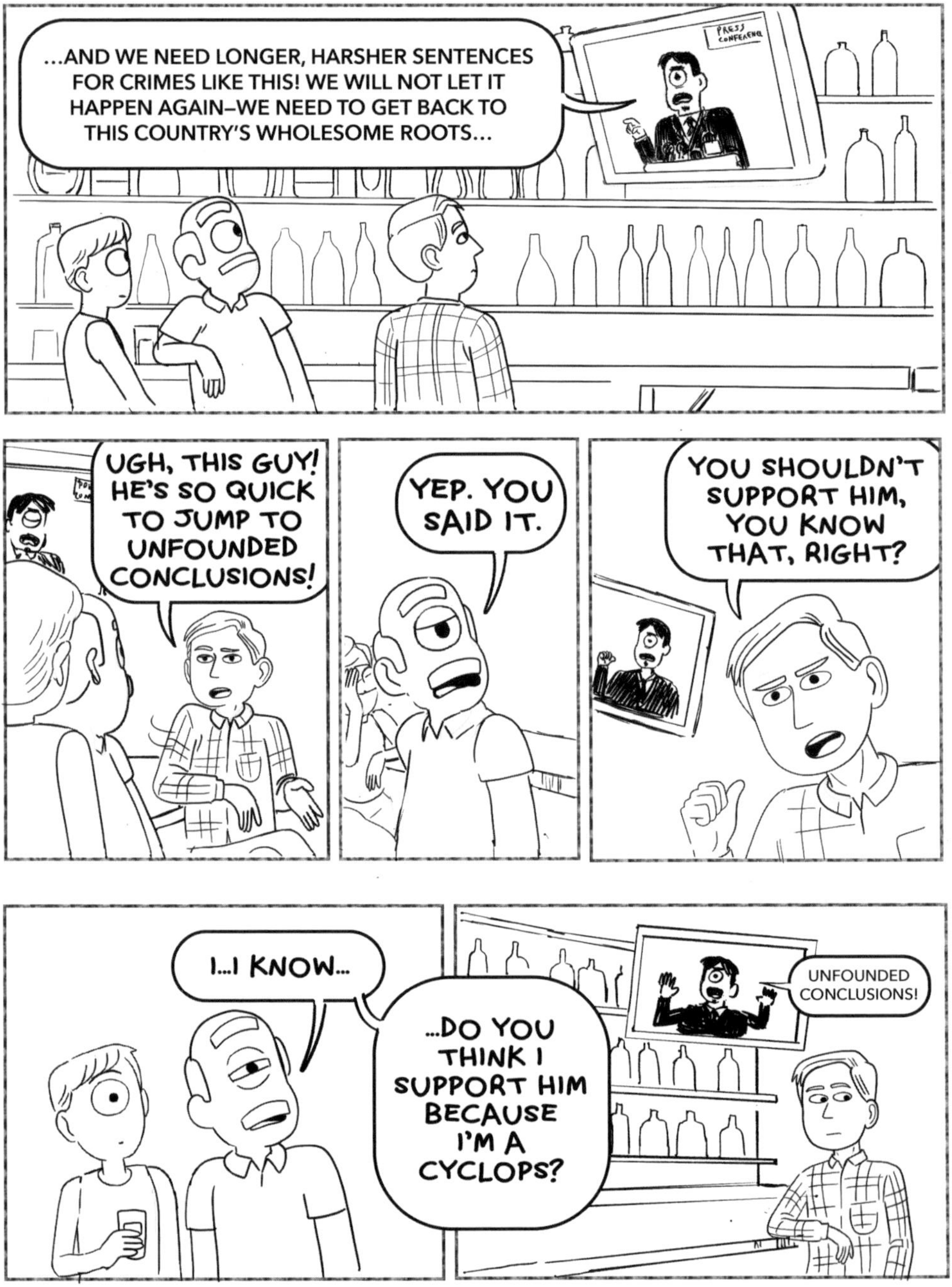
...AND WE NEED LONGER, HARSHER SENTENCES FOR CRIMES LIKE THIS! WE WILL NOT LET IT HAPPEN AGAIN—WE NEED TO GET BACK TO THIS COUNTRY'S WHOLESOME ROOTS...
PRESS CONFERENCE
UGH, THIS GUY! HE'S SO QUICK TO JUMP TO UNFOUNDED CONCLUSIONS!
YEP. YOU SAID IT.
YOU SHOULDN'T SUPPORT HIM, YOU KNOW THAT, RIGHT?
I...I KNOW...
...DO YOU THINK I SUPPORT HIM BECAUSE I'M A CYCLOPS?
UNFOUNDED CONCLUSIONS!

Etna on Etna

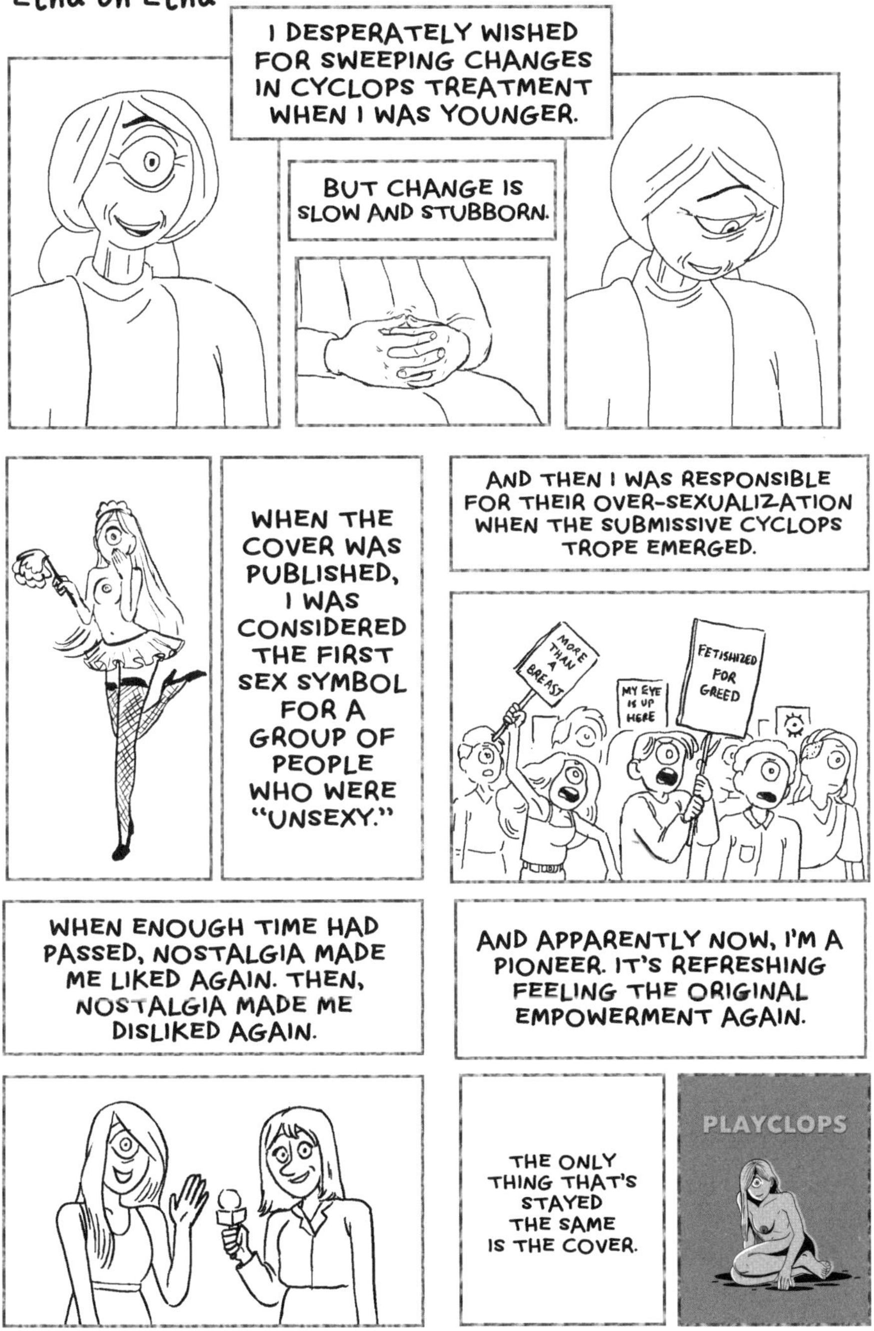
I DESPERATELY WISHED FOR SWEEPING CHANGES IN CYCLOPS TREATMENT WHEN I WAS YOUNGER.
BUT CHANGE IS SLOW AND STUBBORN.
WHEN THE COVER WAS PUBLISHED, I WAS CONSIDERED THE FIRST SEX SYMBOL FOR A GROUP OF PEOPLE WHO WERE "UNSEXY."
AND THEN I WAS RESPONSIBLE FOR THEIR OVER-SEXUALIZATION WHEN THE SUBMISSIVE CYCLOPS TROPE EMERGED.
MORE THAN A BREAST
MY EYE IS UP HERE
FETISHIZED FOR GREED
WHEN ENOUGH TIME HAD PASSED, NOSTALGIA MADE ME LIKED AGAIN. THEN, NOSTALGIA MADE ME DISLIKED AGAIN.
AND APPARENTLY NOW, I'M A PIONEER. IT'S REFRESHING FEELING THE ORIGINAL EMPOWERMENT AGAIN.
THE ONLY THING THAT'S STAYED THE SAME IS THE COVER.
PLAYCLOPS

Moving

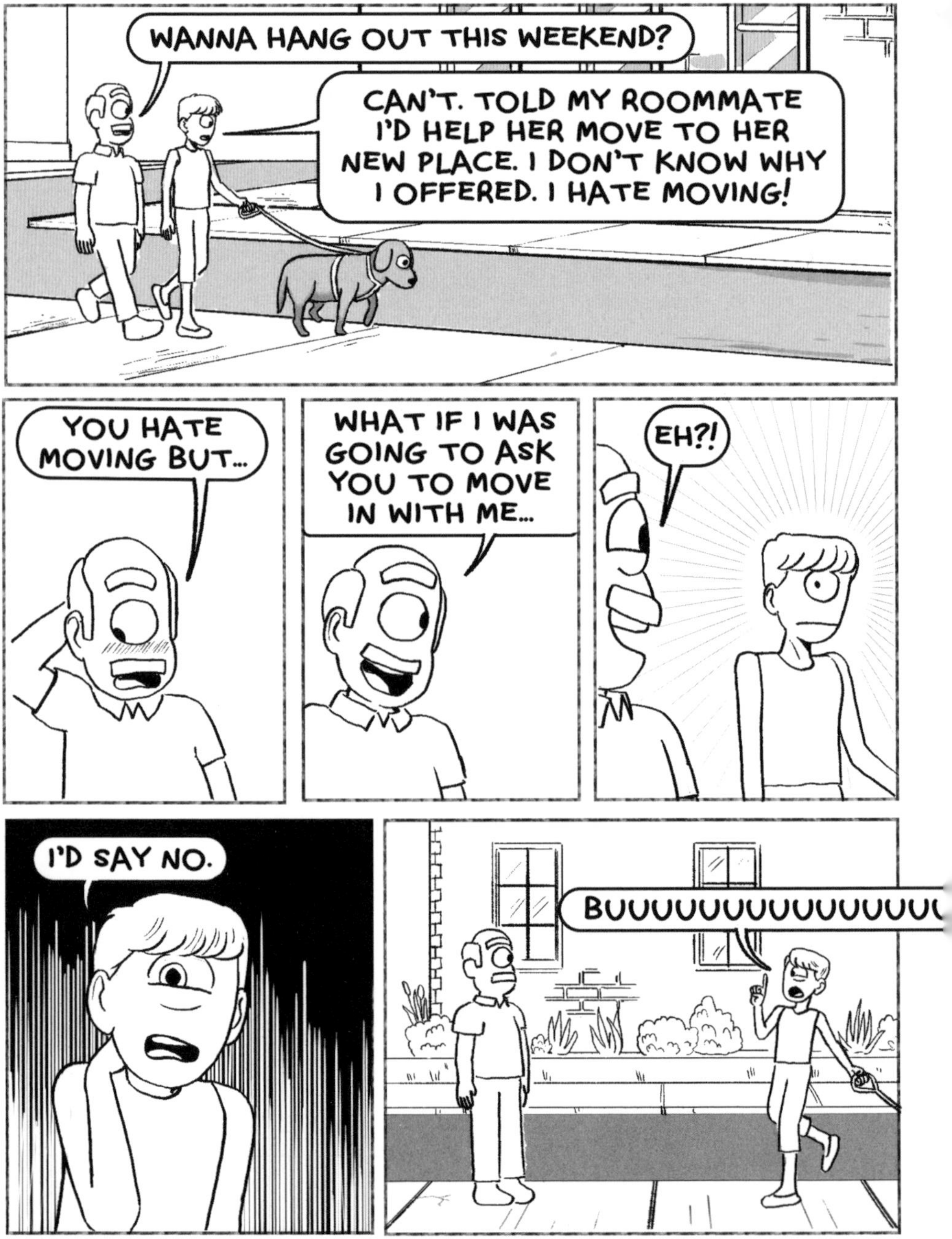
WANNA HANG OUT THIS WEEKEND?
CAN'T. TOLD MY ROOMMATE I'D HELP HER MOVE TO HER NEW PLACE. I DON'T KNOW WHY I OFFERED. I HATE MOVING!
YOU HATE MOVING BUT...
WHAT IF I WAS GOING TO ASK YOU TO MOVE IN WITH ME...
EH?!
I'D SAY NO.
BUUUUUUUUUUUUUU

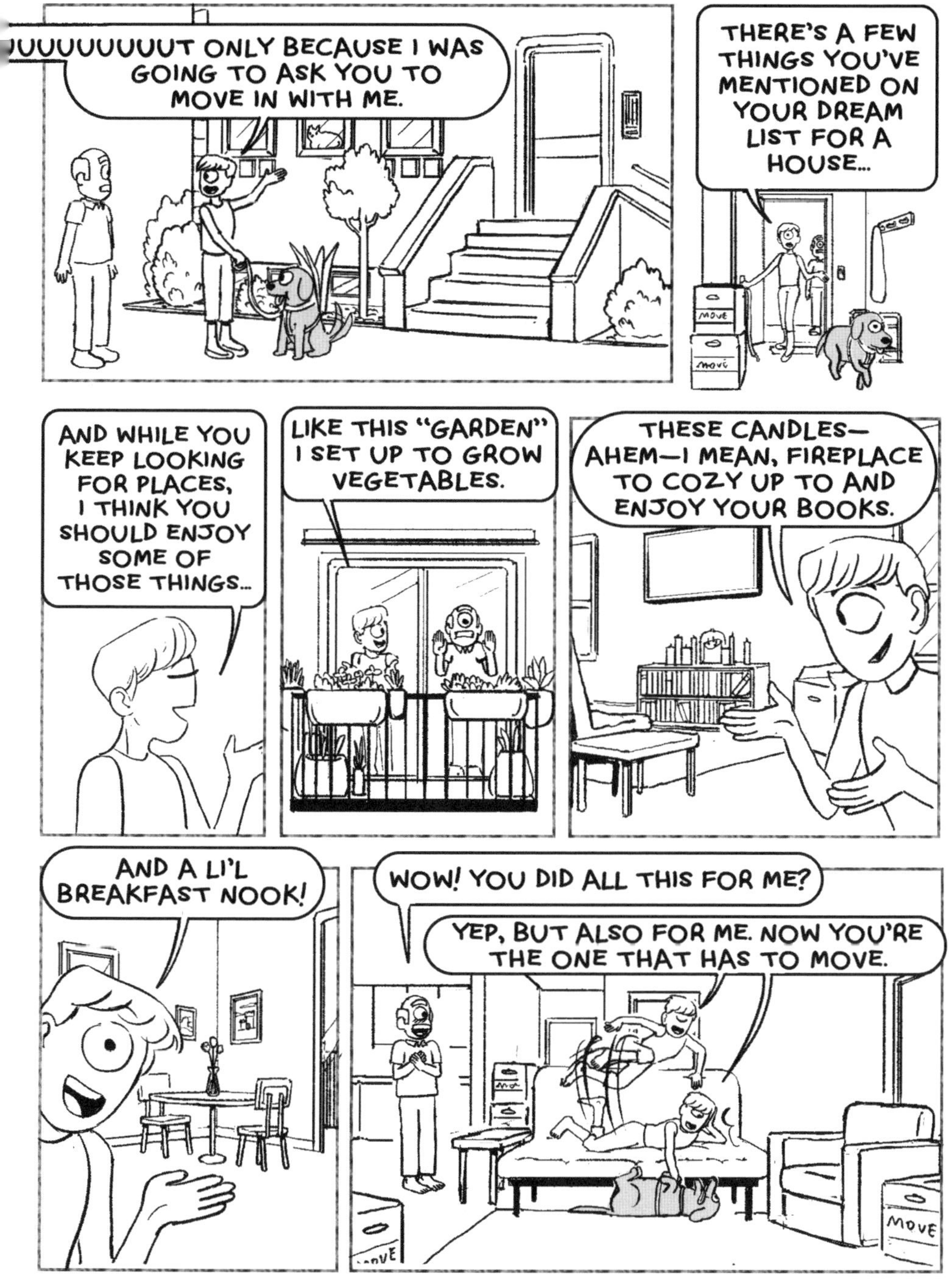
UUUUUUUUUT ONLY BECAUSE I WAS GOING TO ASK YOU TO MOVE IN WITH ME.
THERE'S A FEW THINGS YOU'VE MENTIONED ON YOUR DREAM LIST FOR A HOUSE...
MOVE
MOVE
AND WHILE YOU KEEP LOOKING FOR PLACES, I THINK YOU SHOULD ENJOY SOME OF THOSE THINGS...
LIKE THIS "GARDEN" I SET UP TO GROW VEGETABLES.
THESE CANDLES—AHEM—I MEAN, FIREPLACE TO COZY UP TO AND ENJOY YOUR BOOKS.
AND A LI'L BREAKFAST NOOK!
WOW! YOU DID ALL THIS FOR ME?
YEP, BUT ALSO FOR ME. NOW YOU'RE THE ONE THAT HAS TO MOVE.
MOVE

Five-minute mess

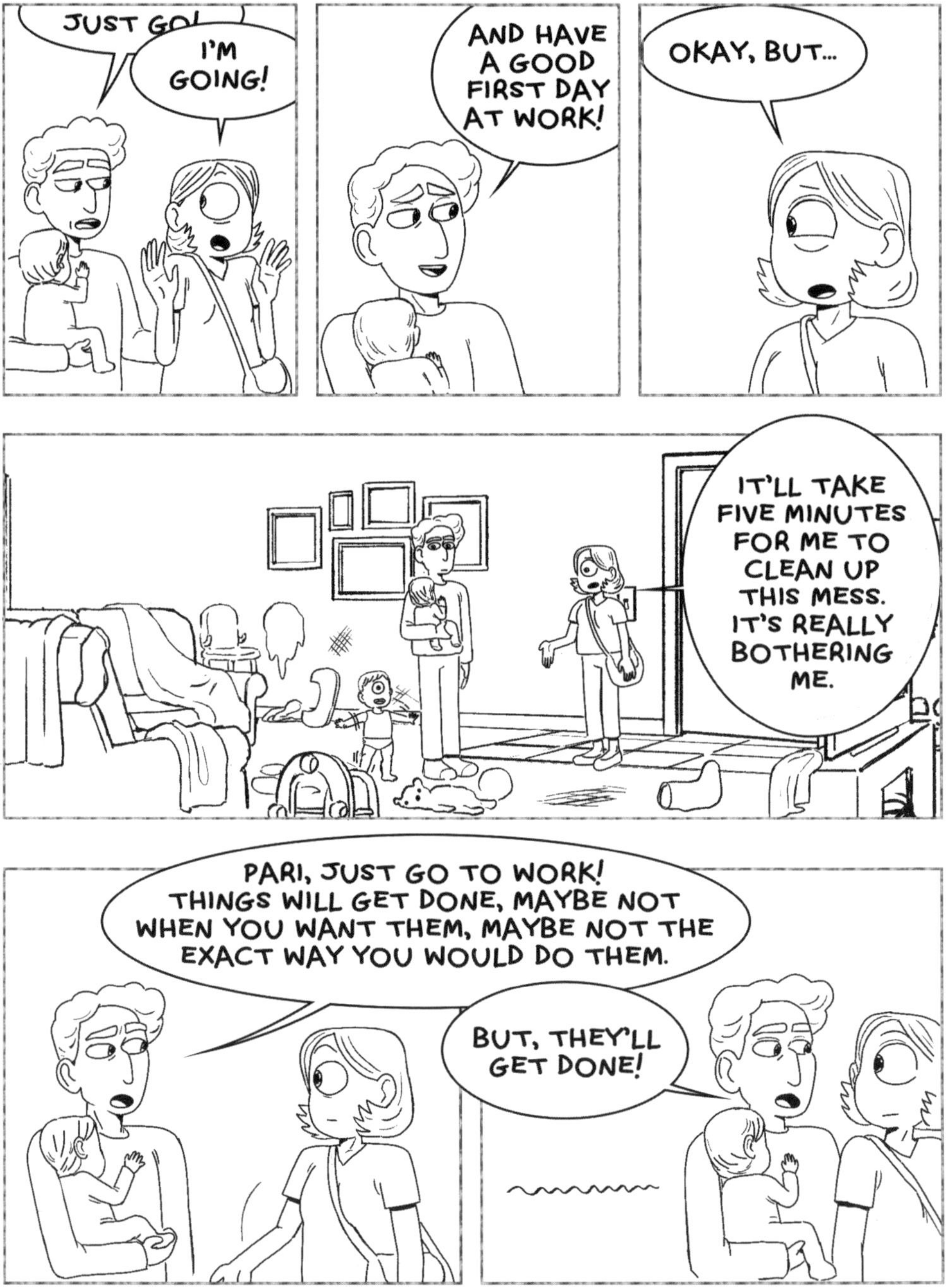
JUST GO!
I'M GOING!
AND HAVE A GOOD FIRST DAY AT WORK!
OKAY, BUT...
IT'LL TAKE FIVE MINUTES FOR ME TO CLEAN UP THIS MESS. IT'S REALLY BOTHERING ME.
PARI, JUST GO TO WORK! THINGS WILL GET DONE, MAYBE NOT WHEN YOU WANT THEM, MAYBE NOT THE EXACT WAY YOU WOULD DO THEM.
BUT, THEY'LL GET DONE!

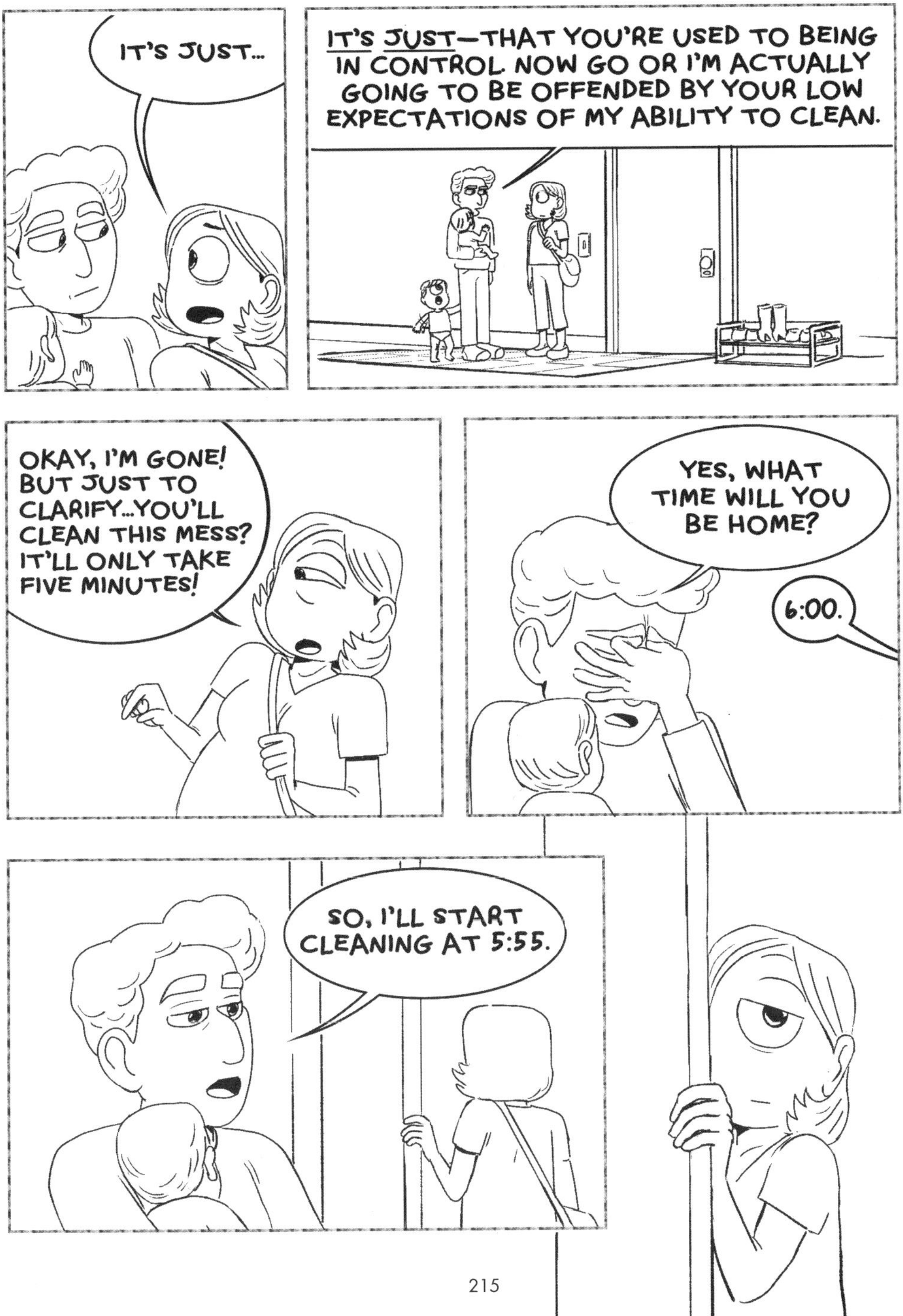
IT'S JUST...
IT'S JUST—THAT YOU'RE USED TO BEING IN CONTROL. NOW GO OR I'M ACTUALLY GOING TO BE OFFENDED BY YOUR LOW EXPECTATIONS OF MY ABILITY TO CLEAN.
OKAY, I'M GONE! BUT JUST TO CLARIFY...YOU'LL CLEAN THIS MESS? IT'LL ONLY TAKE FIVE MINUTES!
YES, WHAT TIME WILL YOU BE HOME?
6:00.
SO, I'LL START CLEANING AT 5:55.

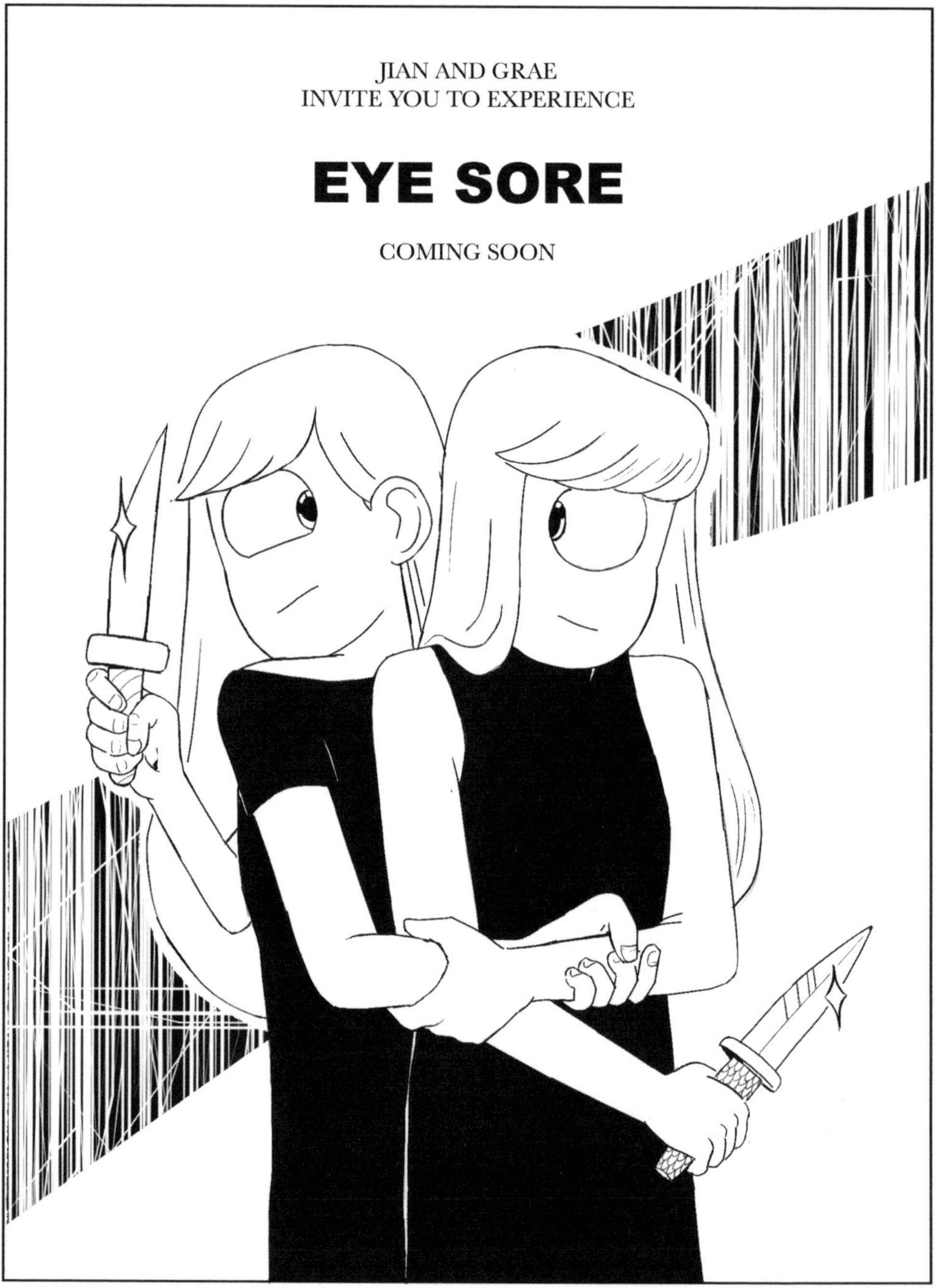
JIAN AND GRAE
INVITE YOU TO EXPERIENCE
EYE SORE
COMING SOON

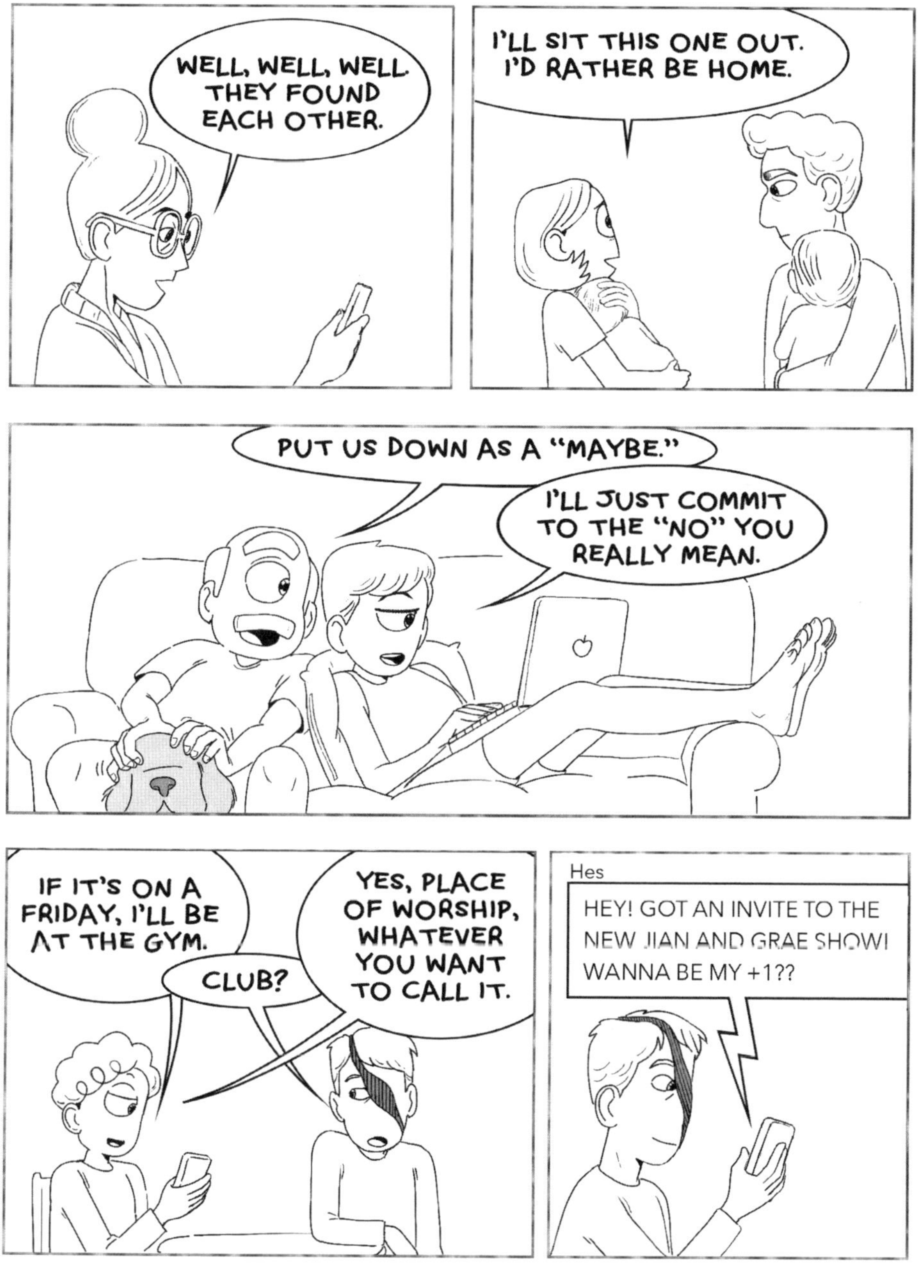
WELL, WELL, WELL. THEY FOUND EACH OTHER.
I'LL SIT THIS ONE OUT. I'D RATHER BE HOME.
PUT US DOWN AS A "MAYBE."
I'LL JUST COMMIT TO THE "NO" YOU REALLY MEAN.
IF IT'S ON A FRIDAY, I'LL BE AT THE GYM.
CLUB?
YES, PLACE OF WORSHIP, WHATEVER YOU WANT TO CALL IT.
Hes
HEY! GOT AN INVITE TO THE NEW JIAN AND GRAE SHOW! WANNA BE MY +1??

Date night

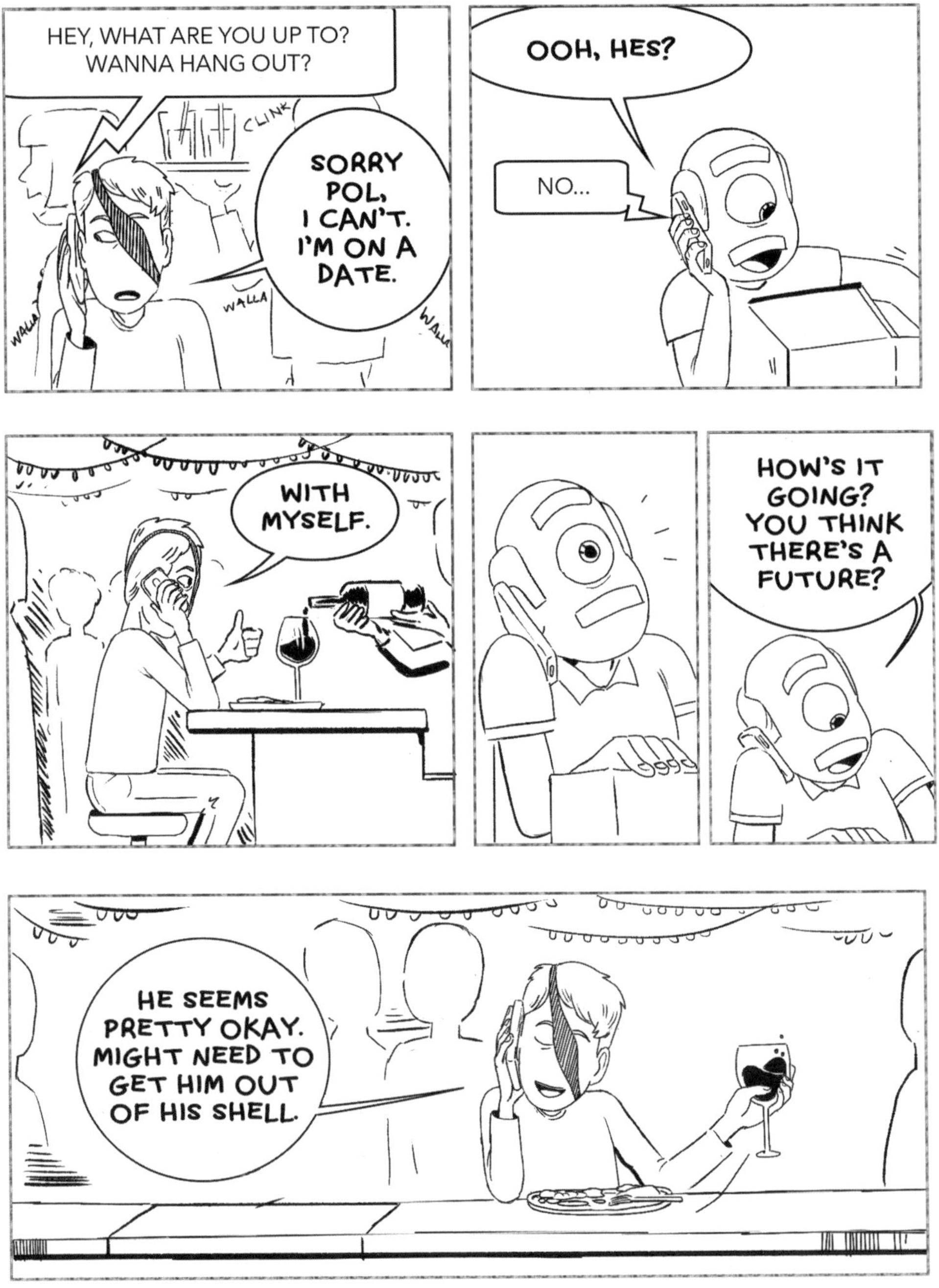
HEY, WHAT ARE YOU UP TO? WANNA HANG OUT?
CLINK
SORRY POL, I CAN'T. I'M ON A DATE.
WALLA
WALLA
WALLA
OOH, HES?
NO...
WITH MYSELF.
HOW'S IT GOING? YOU THINK THERE'S A FUTURE?
HE SEEMS PRETTY OKAY. MIGHT NEED TO GET HIM OUT OF HIS SHELL.

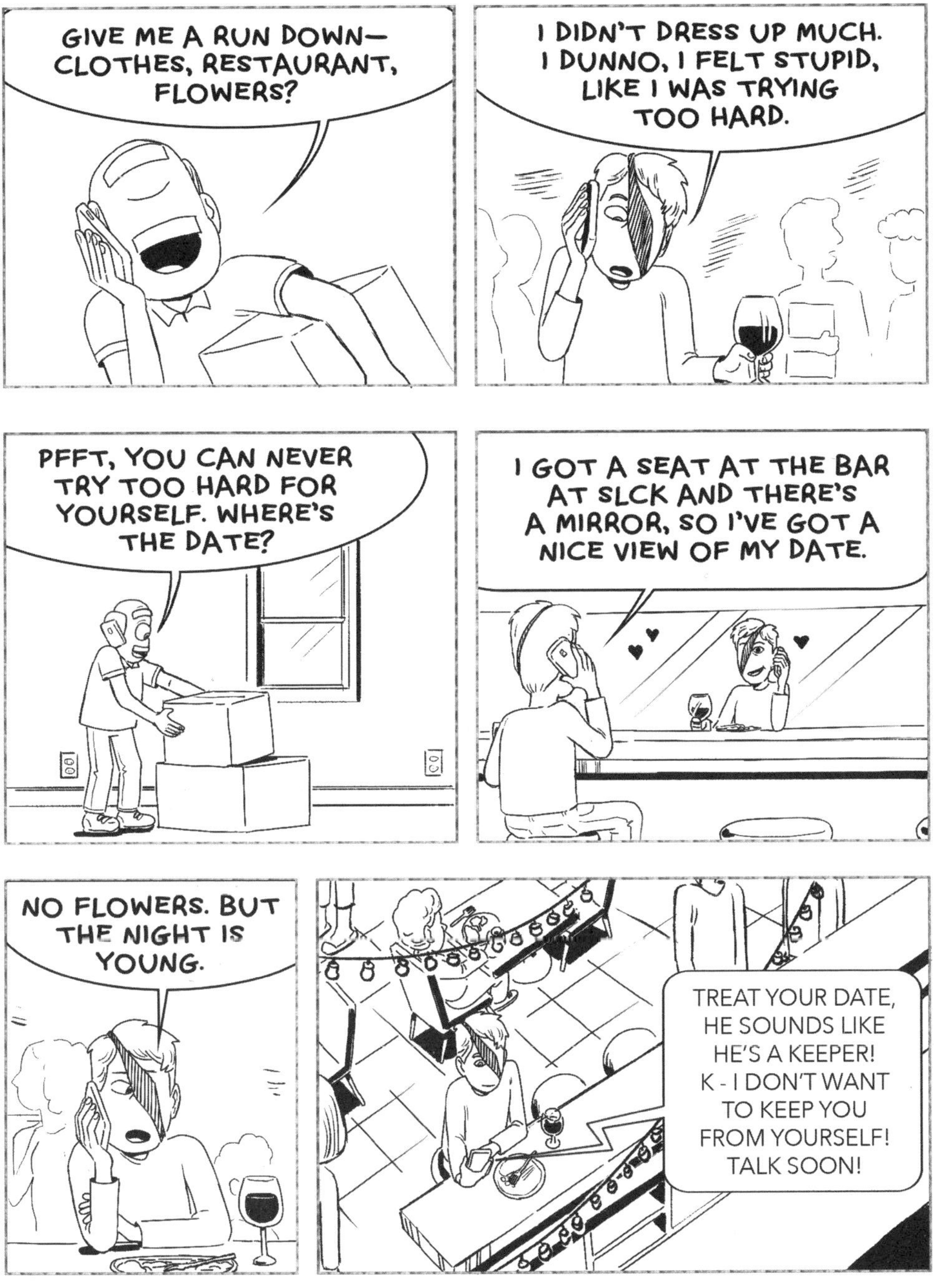
GIVE ME A RUN DOWN—CLOTHES, RESTAURANT, FLOWERS?
I DIDN'T DRESS UP MUCH. I DUNNO, I FELT STUPID, LIKE I WAS TRYING TOO HARD.
PFFT, YOU CAN NEVER TRY TOO HARD FOR YOURSELF. WHERE'S THE DATE?
I GOT A SEAT AT THE BAR AT SLCK AND THERE'S A MIRROR, SO I'VE GOT A NICE VIEW OF MY DATE.
NO FLOWERS. BUT THE NIGHT IS YOUNG.
TREAT YOUR DATE, HE SOUNDS LIKE HE'S A KEEPER! K - I DON'T WANT TO KEEP YOU FROM YOURSELF! TALK SOON!

Pari's inspiration

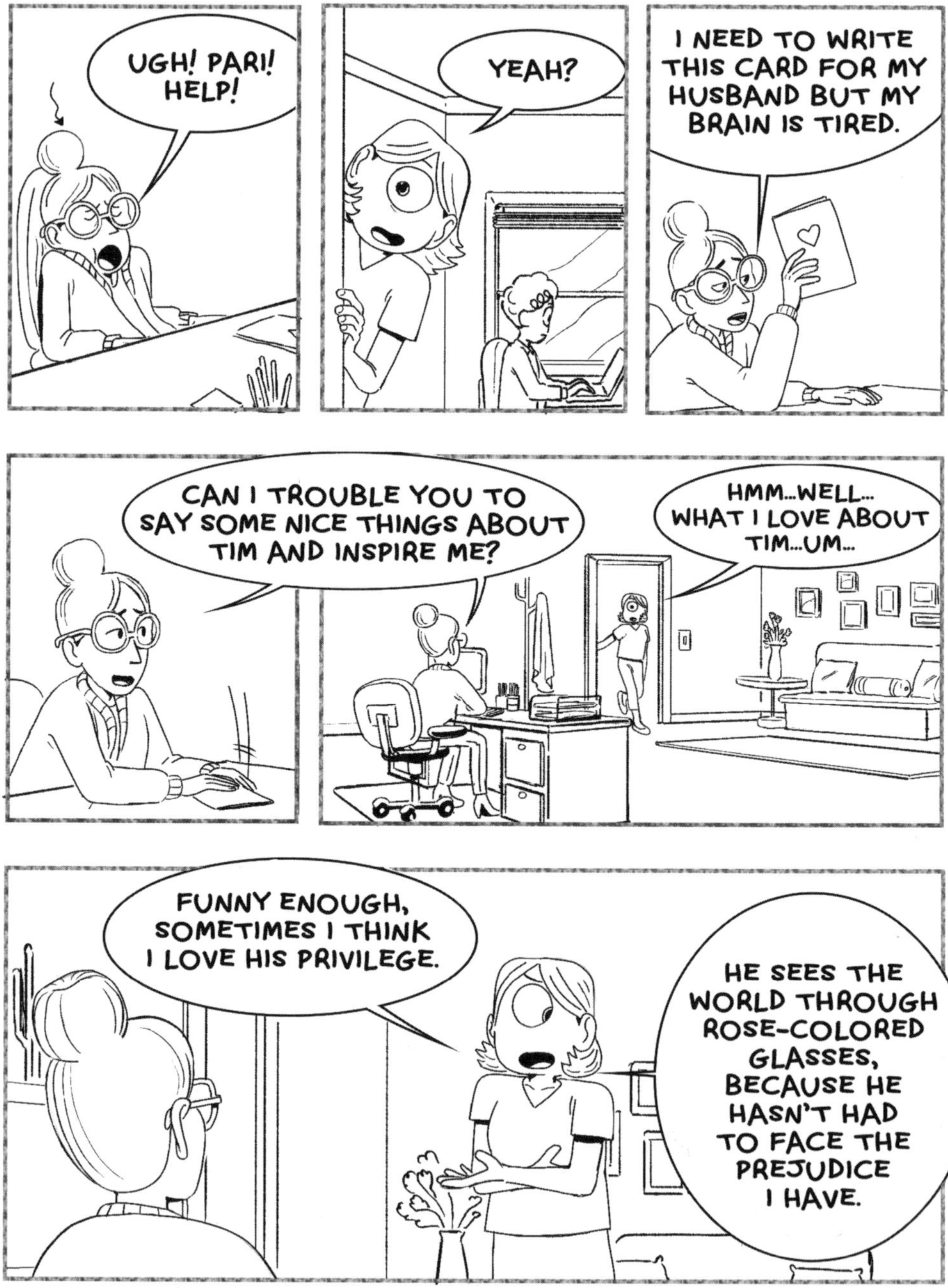

UGH! PARI! HELP!
YEAH?
I NEED TO WRITE THIS CARD FOR MY HUSBAND BUT MY BRAIN IS TIRED.
CAN I TROUBLE YOU TO SAY SOME NICE THINGS ABOUT TIM AND INSPIRE ME?
HMM...WELL... WHAT I LOVE ABOUT TIM...UM...
FUNNY ENOUGH, SOMETIMES I THINK I LOVE HIS PRIVILEGE.
HE SEES THE WORLD THROUGH ROSE-COLORED GLASSES, BECAUSE HE HASN'T HAD TO FACE THE PREJUDICE I HAVE.

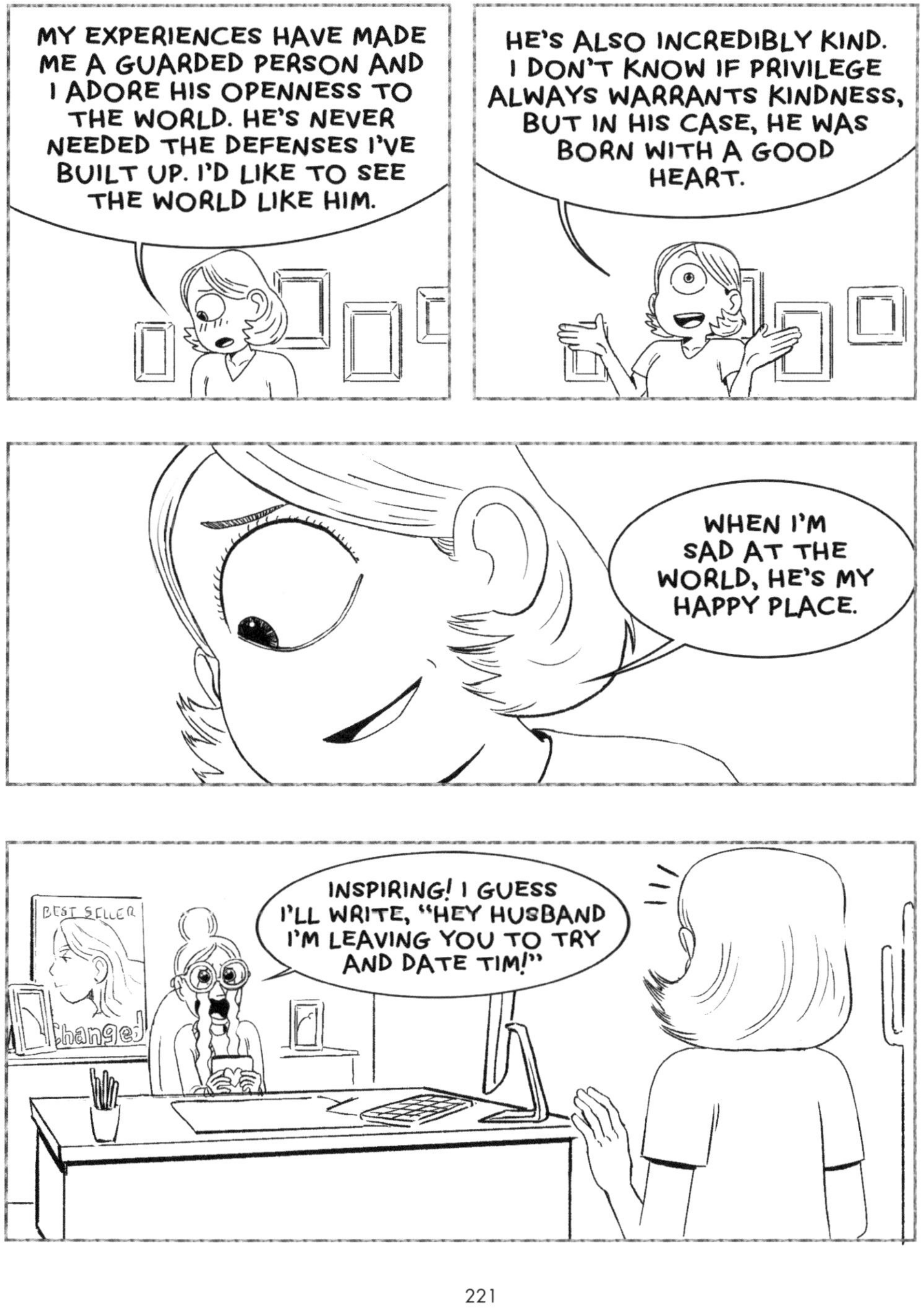
MY EXPERIENCES HAVE MADE ME A GUARDED PERSON AND I ADORE HIS OPENNESS TO THE WORLD. HE'S NEVER NEEDED THE DEFENSES I'VE BUILT UP. I'D LIKE TO SEE THE WORLD LIKE HIM.
HE'S ALSO INCREDIBLY KIND. I DON'T KNOW IF PRIVILEGE ALWAYS WARRANTS KINDNESS, BUT IN HIS CASE, HE WAS BORN WITH A GOOD HEART.
WHEN I'M SAD AT THE WORLD, HE'S MY HAPPY PLACE.
BEST SELLER
Changed
INSPIRING! I GUESS I'LL WRITE, "HEY HUSBAND I'M LEAVING YOU TO TRY AND DATE TIM!"

Eye sore—the experience

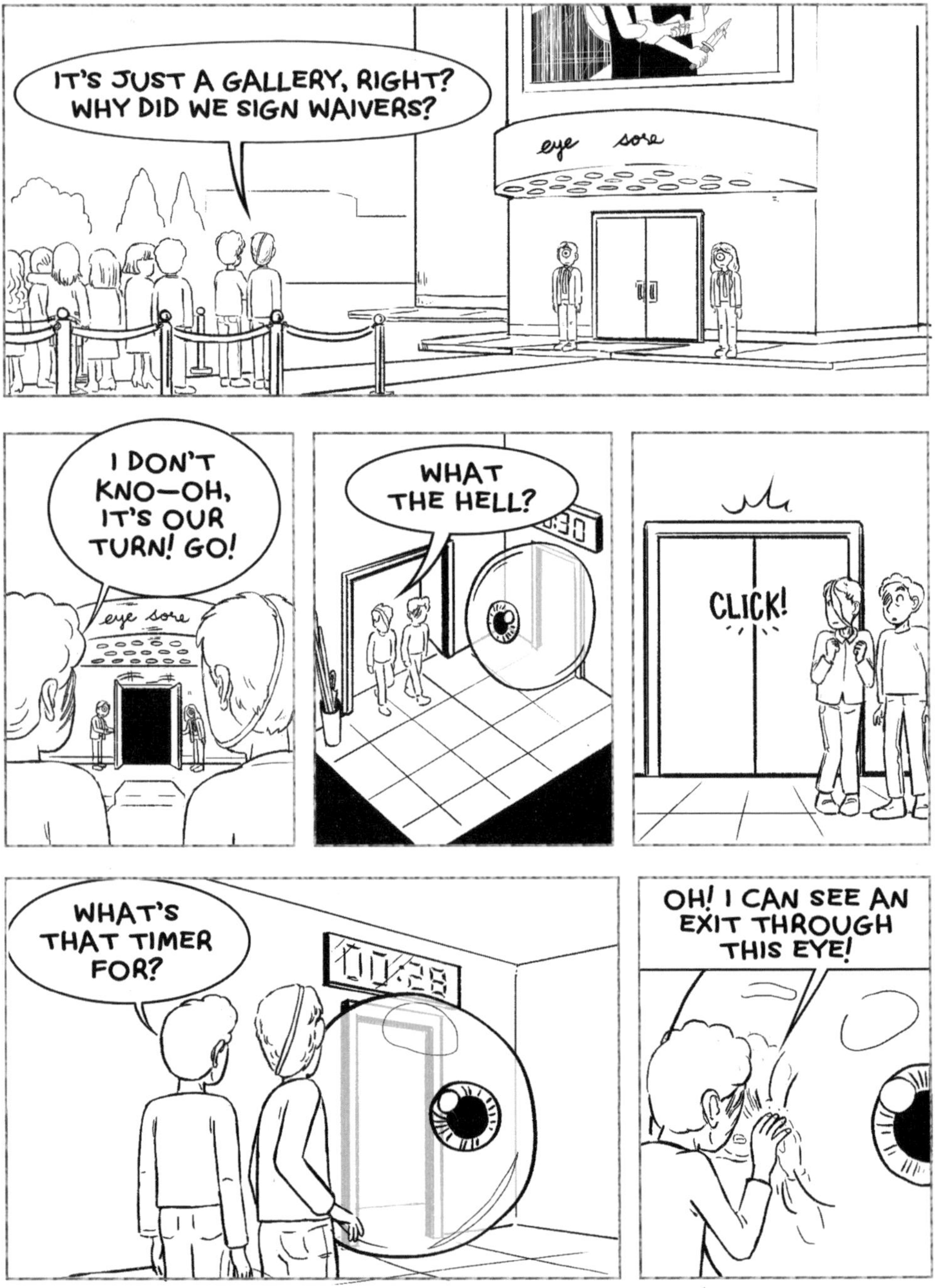
IT'S JUST A GALLERY, RIGHT? WHY DID WE SIGN WAIVERS?
eye sore
I DON'T KNO—OH, IT'S OUR TURN! GO!
eye sore
WHAT THE HELL?
CLICK!
WHAT'S THAT TIMER FOR?
00:28
OH! I CAN SEE AN EXIT THROUGH THIS EYE!

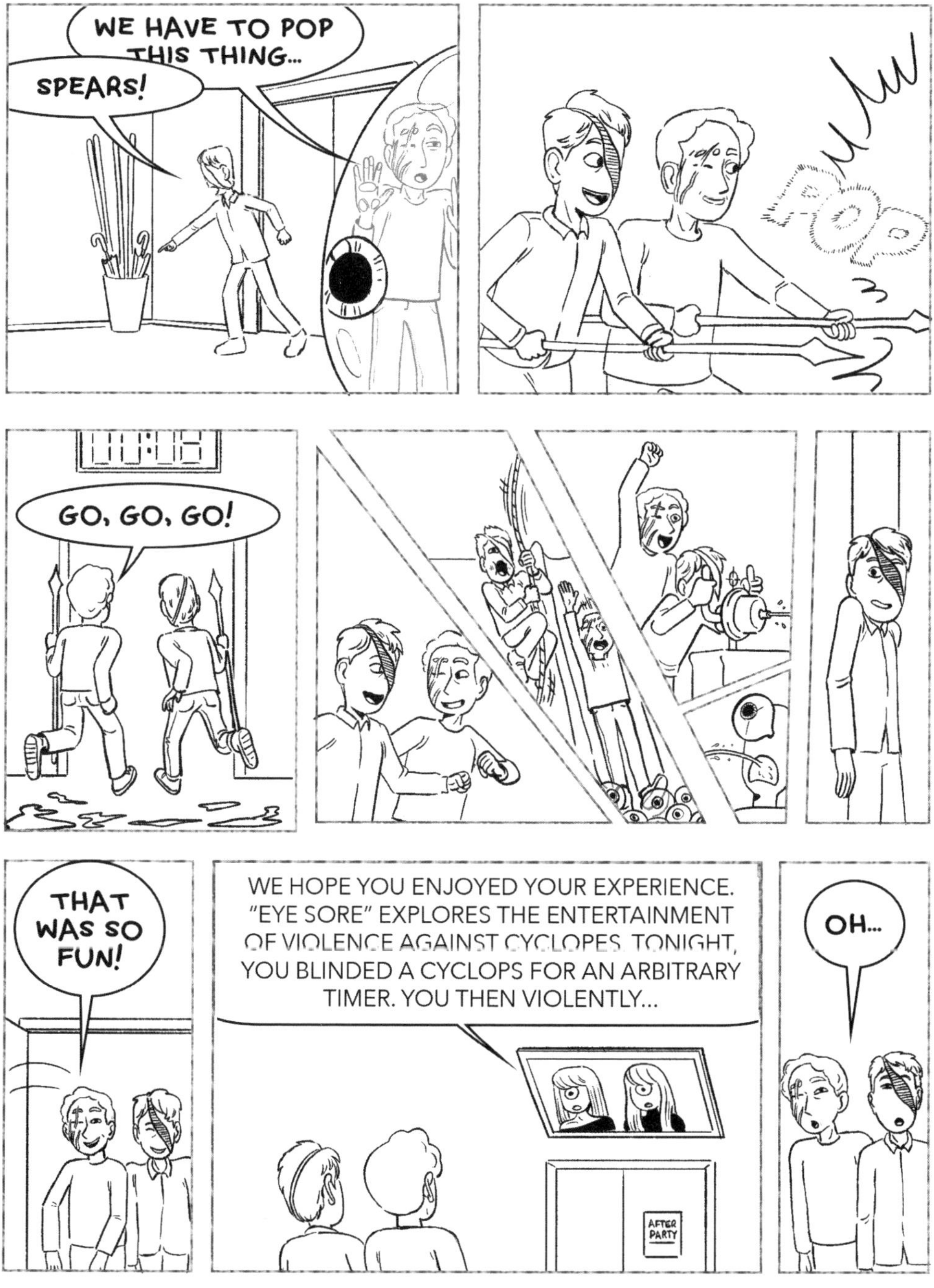
WE HAVE TO POP THIS THING...
SPEARS!
POP
GO, GO, GO!
THAT WAS SO FUN!
WE HOPE YOU ENJOYED YOUR EXPERIENCE. "EYE SORE" EXPLORES THE ENTERTAINMENT OF VIOLENCE AGAINST CYCLOPES. TONIGHT, YOU BLINDED A CYCLOPS FOR AN ARBITRARY TIMER. YOU THEN VIOLENTLY...
AFTER PARTY
OH...

Author Bron

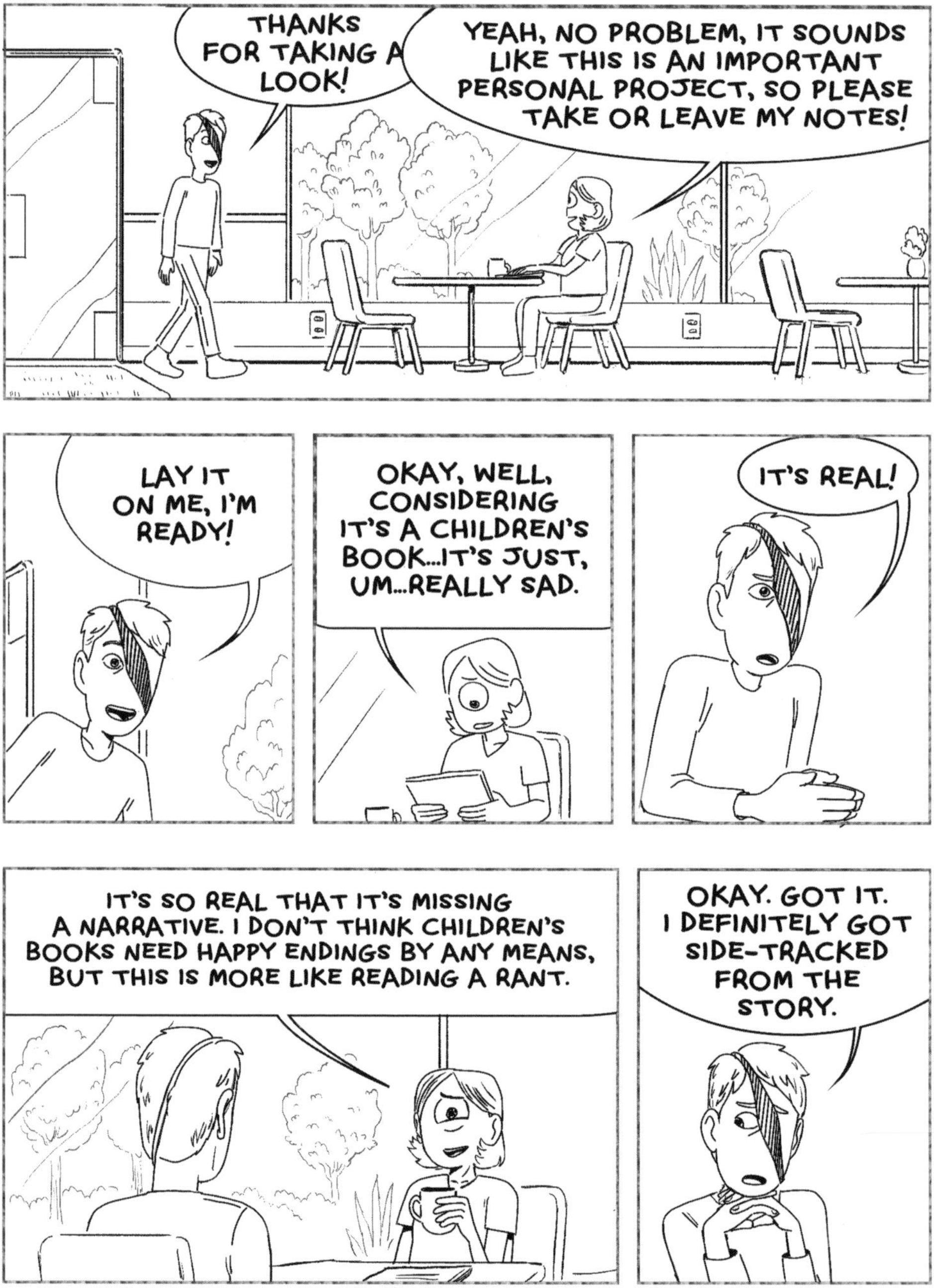
THANKS FOR TAKING A LOOK!
YEAH, NO PROBLEM, IT SOUNDS LIKE THIS IS AN IMPORTANT PERSONAL PROJECT, SO PLEASE TAKE OR LEAVE MY NOTES!
LAY IT ON ME, I'M READY!
OKAY, WELL, CONSIDERING IT'S A CHILDREN'S BOOK...IT'S JUST, UM...REALLY SAD.
IT'S REAL!
IT'S SO REAL THAT IT'S MISSING A NARRATIVE. I DON'T THINK CHILDREN'S BOOKS NEED HAPPY ENDINGS BY ANY MEANS, BUT THIS IS MORE LIKE READING A RANT.
OKAY. GOT IT. I DEFINITELY GOT SIDE-TRACKED FROM THE STORY.

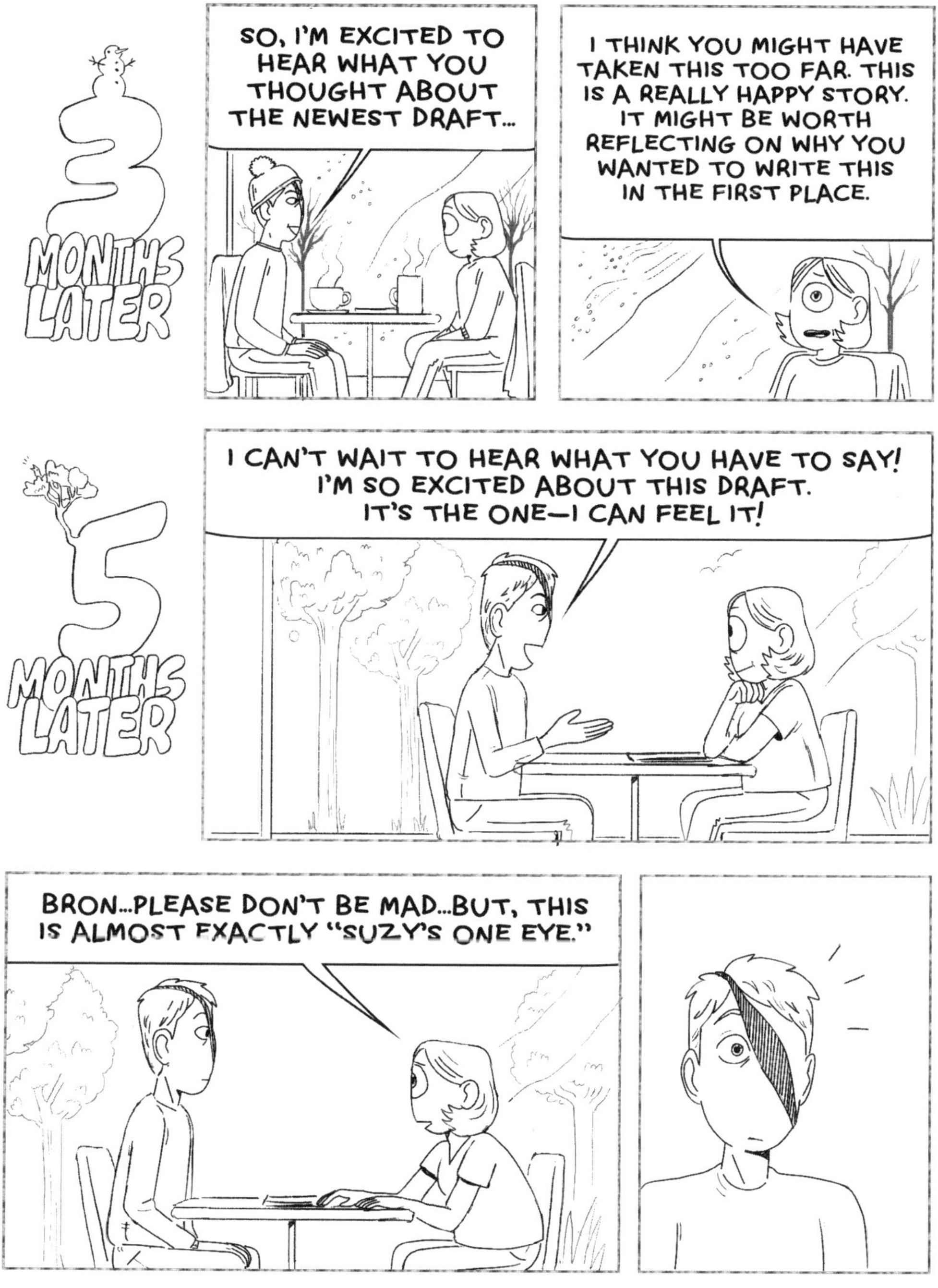
3 MONTHS LATER
SO, I'M EXCITED TO HEAR WHAT YOU THOUGHT ABOUT THE NEWEST DRAFT...
I THINK YOU MIGHT HAVE TAKEN THIS TOO FAR. THIS IS A REALLY HAPPY STORY. IT MIGHT BE WORTH REFLECTING ON WHY YOU WANTED TO WRITE THIS IN THE FIRST PLACE.
5 MONTHS LATER
I CAN'T WAIT TO HEAR WHAT YOU HAVE TO SAY! I'M SO EXCITED ABOUT THIS DRAFT. IT'S THE ONE—I CAN FEEL IT!
BRON...PLEASE DON'T BE MAD...BUT, THIS IS ALMOST EXACTLY "SUZY'S ONE EYE."

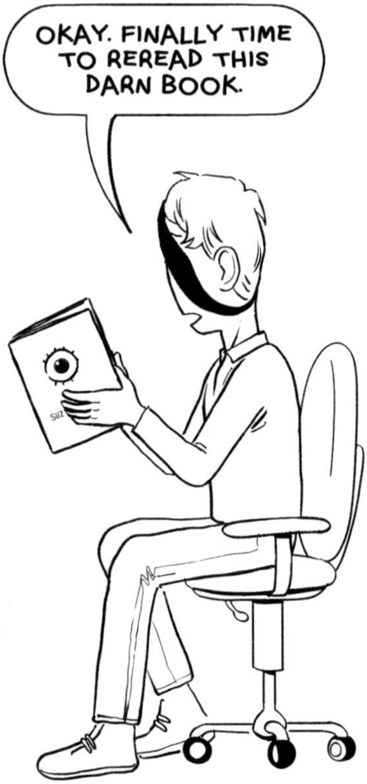
OKAY. FINALLY TIME TO REREAD THIS DARN BOOK.

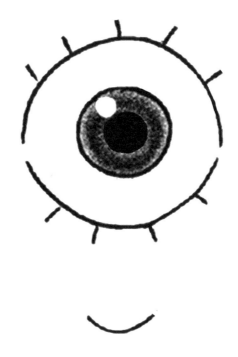

SUZY'S ONE EYE

It was the day before Halloween! And all the children in Northbank were in a frenzy to finish up costumes, hollow out pumpkins, and triple-check their trick-or-treat paths.

Suzy loved Halloween!

She and her friends carefully traced a treat-filled path on their neighborhood map. Mara was in charge and she avoided the scariest house in the neighborhood…the haunted house on Hollyhaven Avenue.

Everyone knew to avoid that house. A monster lived there. Suzy didn't need any convincing. She furiously agreed. She always avoided that house, even when it wasn't Halloween!

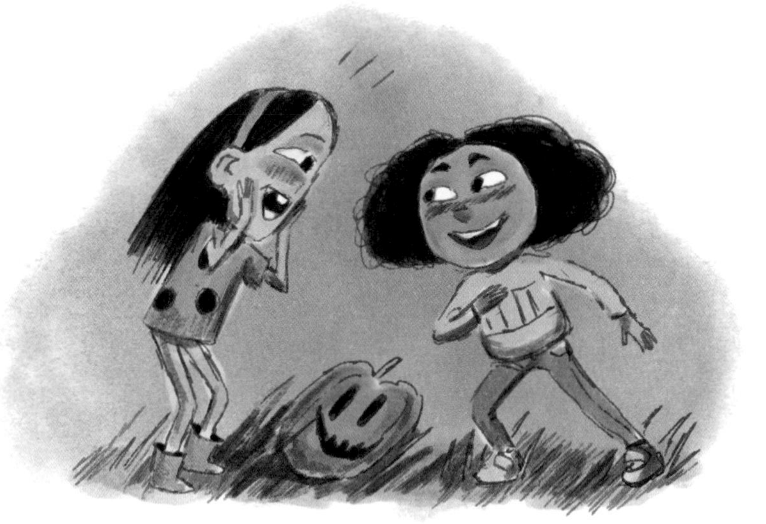

With their plans all set, Mara turned to Suzy, "For Halloween, I'm going as a brave knight, with shiny armor and a horse!"

Suzy couldn't believe it! "I'm going as a knight too!"

"But…you can't be a knight," said Mara, giggling. "You have one eye!"

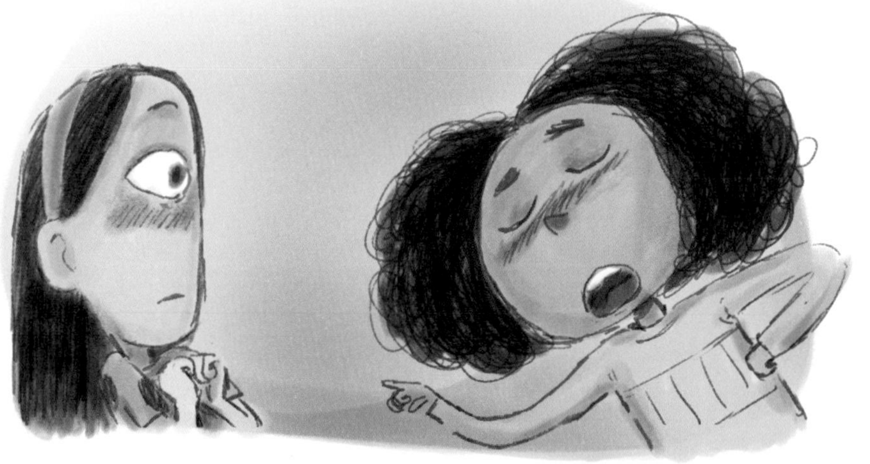

Suzy's smile melted, but Mara didn't notice.

Mara giggled, "Knight? Oh Suzy, you're so funny!"

After Mara left, Suzy stayed out a little longer. She desperately wished she had two eyes. With two eyes, she could be anything for Halloween.

On Halloween, Suzy wanted to stay in. She purposely missed meeting with Mara and the others.

When her mom asked her what was wrong, Suzy wouldn't tell her.

So, her mom insisted Suzy go out and enjoy Halloween. "There's so much candy, Suzy, and I know you'll regret it if you don't!"

Suzy headed out, deciding to avoid Mara and the group at all costs.

Down the street, Suzy noticed a pair of eyes staring at her from the grass. It was a pair of googly eye glasses! Suzy wasn't wearing a costume, especially since she'd learned she couldn't be a knight, so she put on the glasses and went to earn some treats!

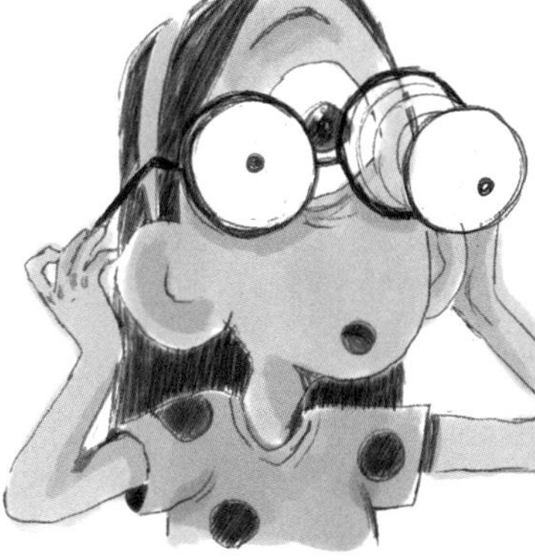

She roamed the street with two eyes!
No more One-Eyed Suzy!!

The problem was, she could barely see a thing. Having two eyes made her see half as much!

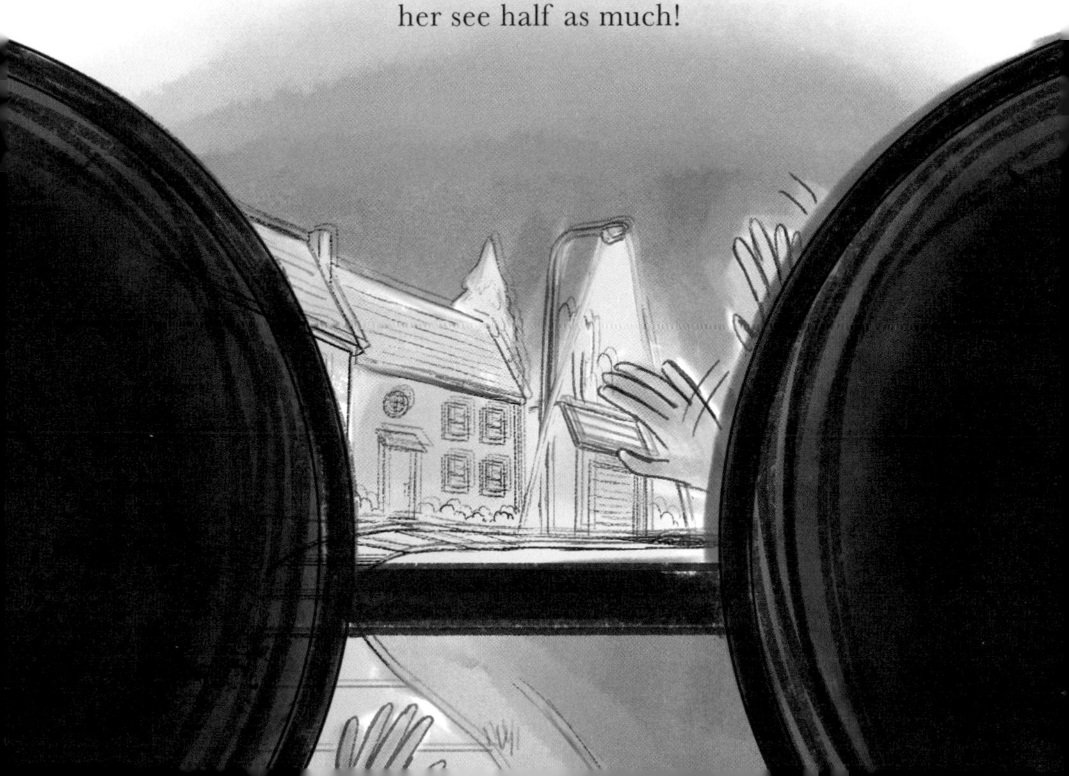

Without a clue, Suzy waltzed up to the front door of the haunted house on Hollyhaven Avenue!

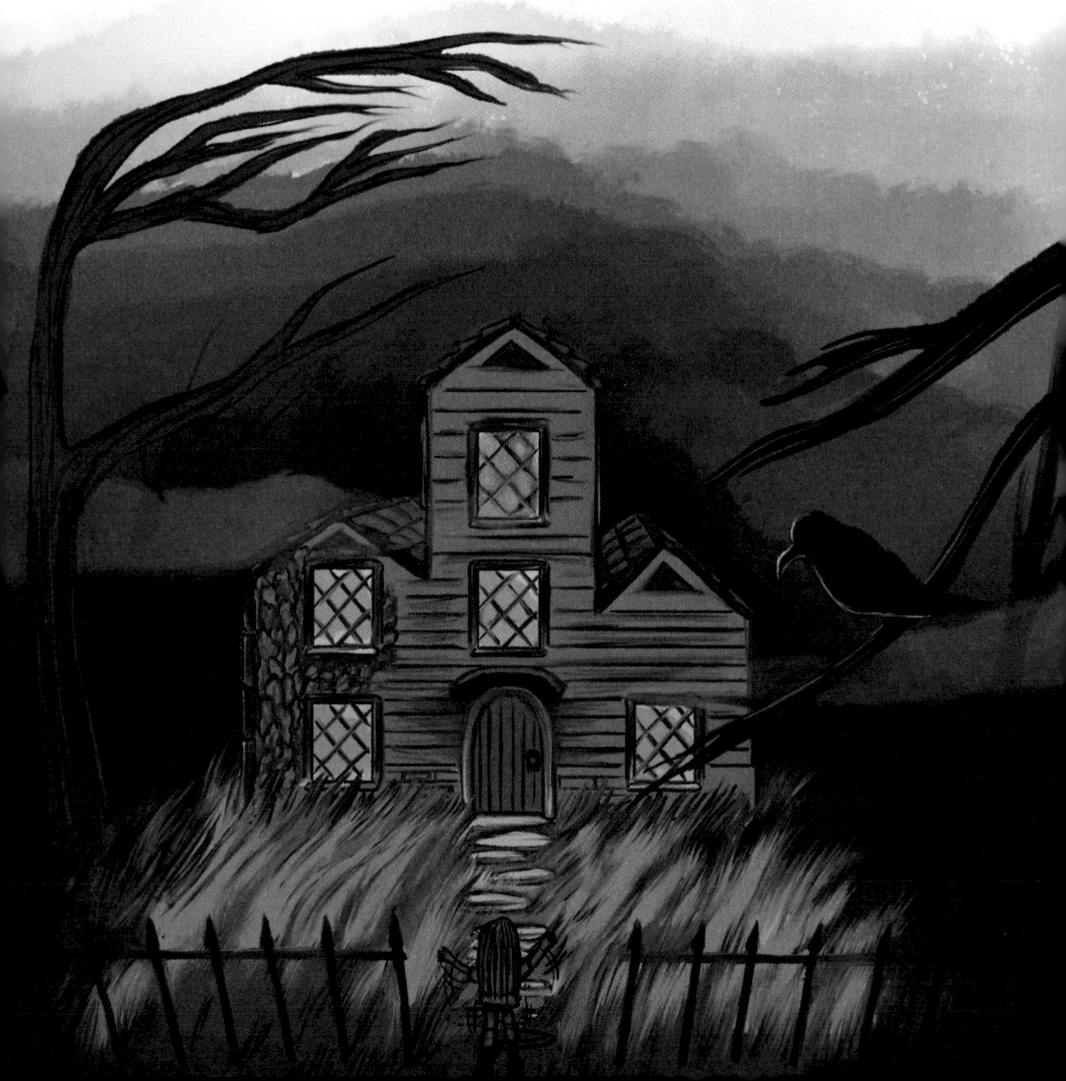

Knock, knock, knock.
"Trick or treat!"
She called, but no
one answered.

Mara and the group were passing by, avoiding the haunted house, when they noticed Suzy standing bravely at the door. She was knocking loudly.

Knock, knock, knock.

Growing impatient, Suzy shouted, "Trick or Treat!"

Mara and the others stopped to watch in awe.

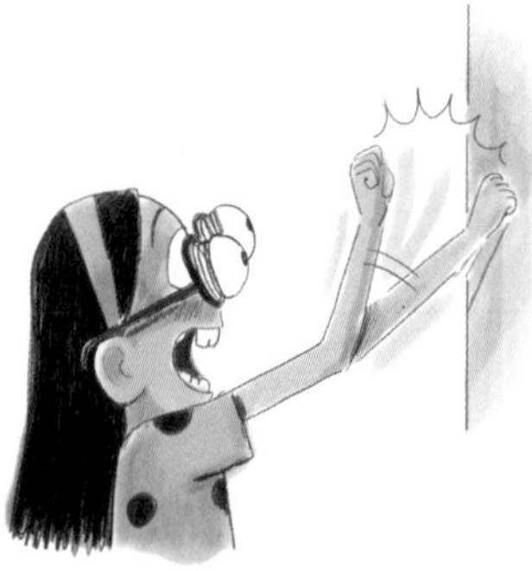

Suzy banged at the door, one last time, yelling, “TRICK OR TRE—”

She took the glasses off to get a better look…

OH NO! The haunted house of Hollyhaven Avenue! There was a dangerous monster on the other side of the door! Suzy turned to run!

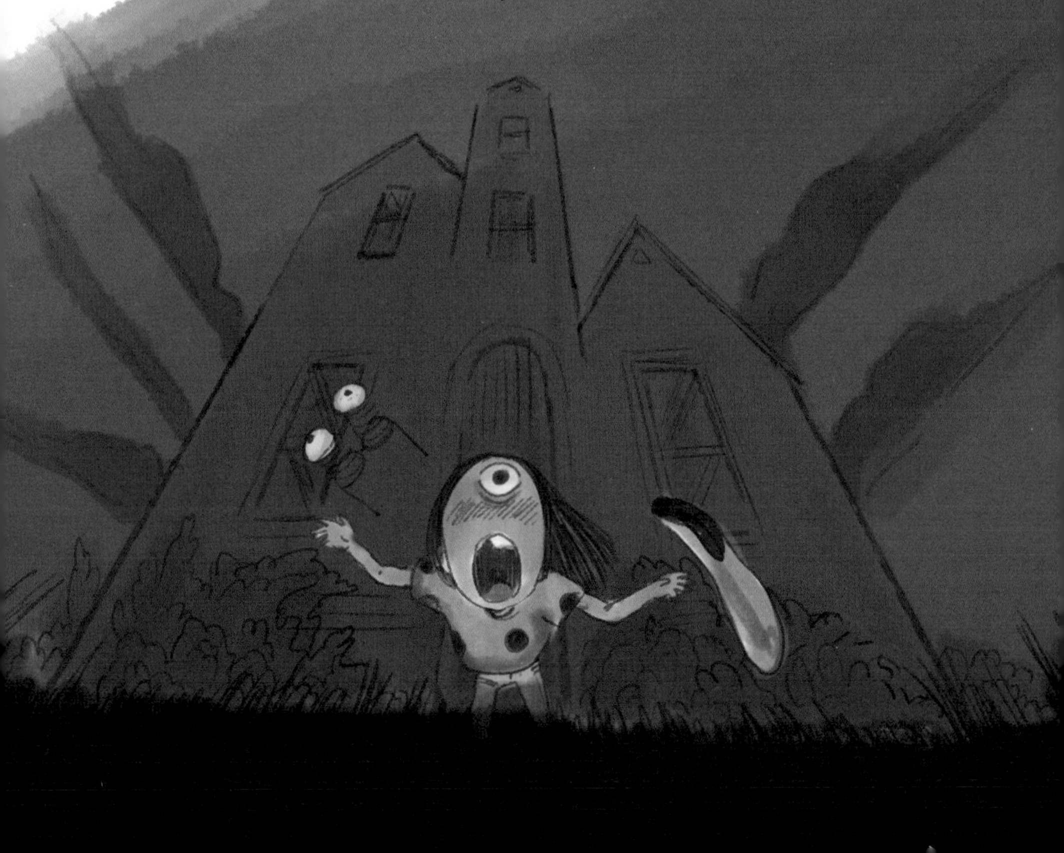

CREEEEAK.

The door opened.

Uh oh.

Suzy stopped in her tracks and
turned to face the monster...

But instead of a monster, stood
a small, old Cyclops.

She popped her head out and
said cheerily, "Hello! I never get
trick-or-treaters, so I couldn't
believe my ears when I heard
knocking. I'm sorry it took me
so long to open the door!"

All the thoughts in Suzy's head vanished.
She stood rooted in place.

The old lady smiled, "Here, have all the candy."
And emptied her bowl into Suzy's pillowcase.
Full-size candy bars and brownies and cookies
poured out of the bowl. These were
the best treats in town!

Suzy finally found some words, "Th-Thank you, but…why don't you get trick-or-treaters? These are the best treats!"

The old Cyclops pondered for a moment before answering. "When I moved into this house, many of the parents thought someone who looked like me couldn't possibly be a good neighbor. They thought a good neighbor has two eyes! So stories spread about me and my house, and those parents told their children to stay away from me, because I scared them. I might not be a monster, but some people fear me like one."

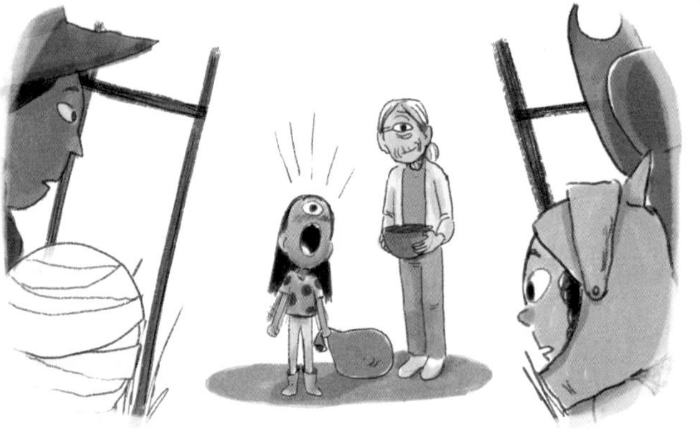

Shocked, Suzy exclaimed, "But a good neighbor can have one eye or two!"

And then thought to herself, *and a knight can too.*

Confidently, Suzy turned to the neighborhood kids and introduced them to the lovely Cyclops of Hollyhaven Avenue! Their newest but oldest neighbor!

Then Suzy ripped open her pillowcase, ready to share the treats.

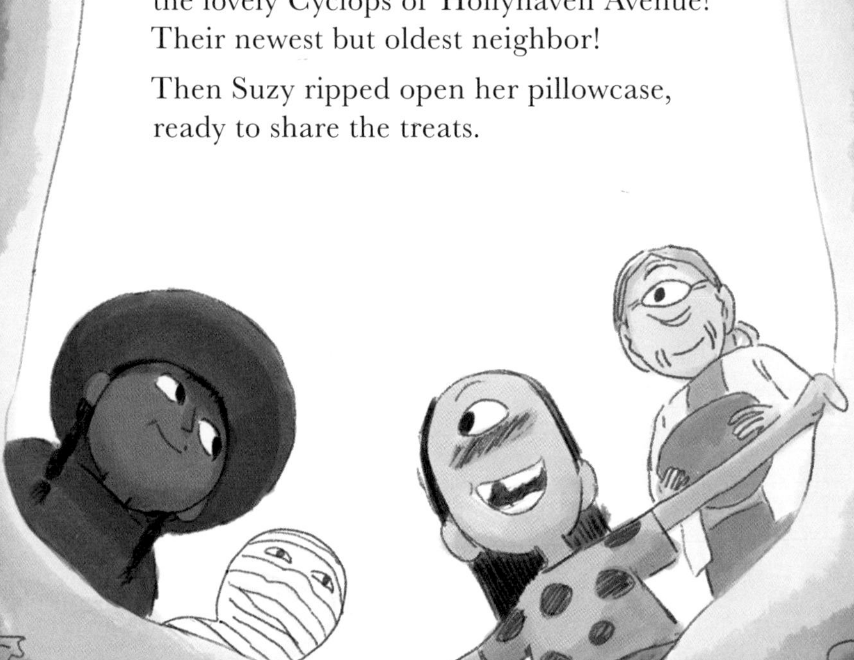

Mara stopped short. First, she had something to say…

"I'm sorry, Suzy! You make a great knight!"

"But you said I couldn't be a knight with one eye!"

Mara shook her head, "I was wrong! I pretended to be a brave knight, but you walked right up to the haunted house and showed us there was no monster. It takes real bravery, like a knight, to do something like that!"

After that, Suzy and Mara made up and ate lots of candy! And after Halloween, the haunted house was just another house on Hollyhaven Avenue. And even farther after that, any kid could dress up as anything on Halloween, no matter how many eyes they had.

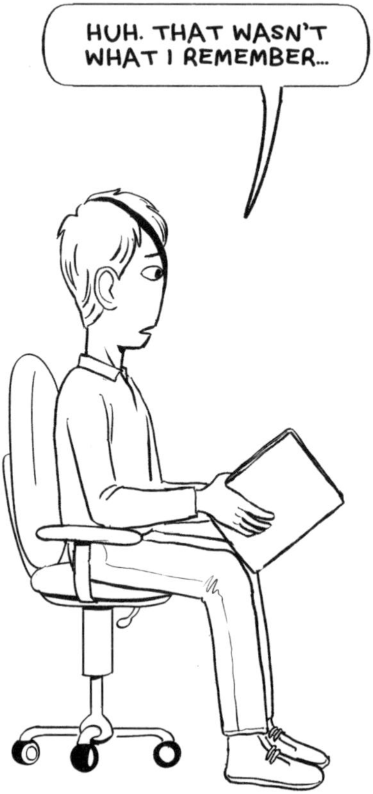
HUH. THAT WASN'T WHAT I REMEMBER...

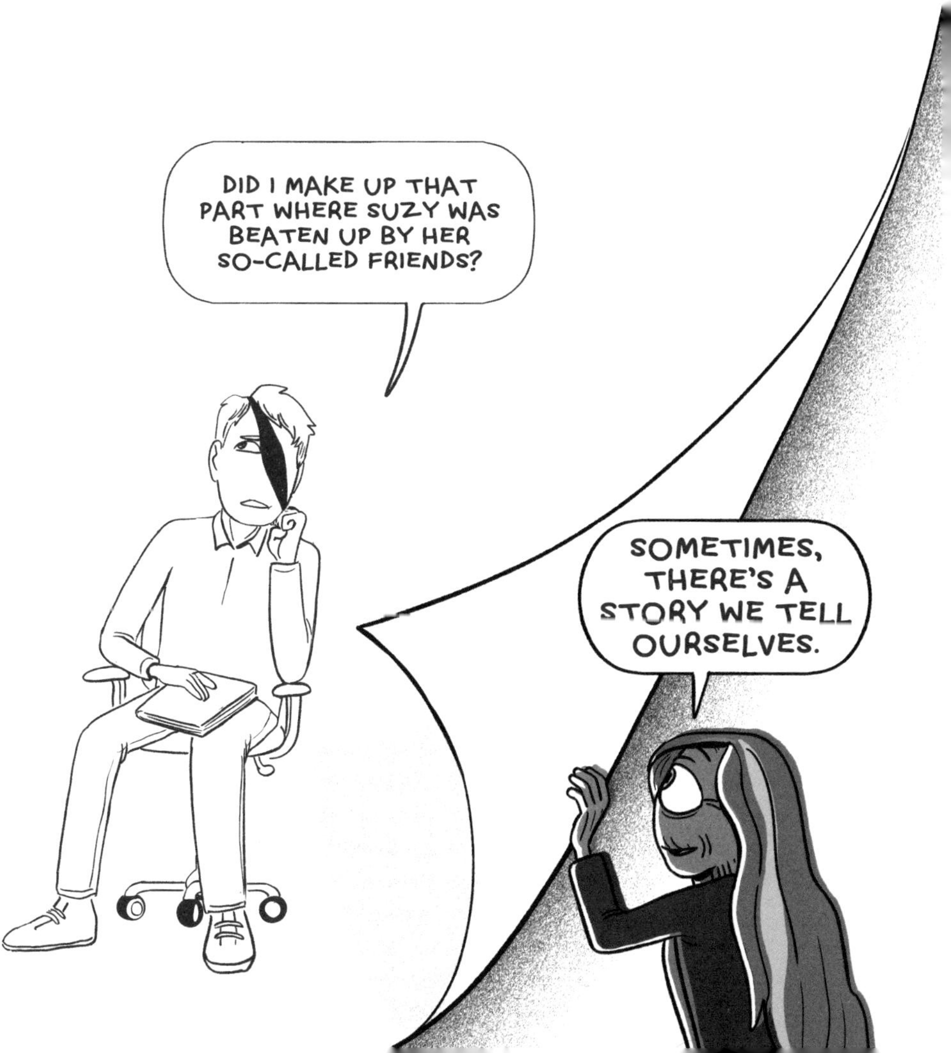
DID I MAKE UP THAT PART WHERE SUZY WAS BEATEN UP BY HER SO-CALLED FRIENDS?
SOMETIMES, THERE'S A STORY WE TELL OURSELVES.

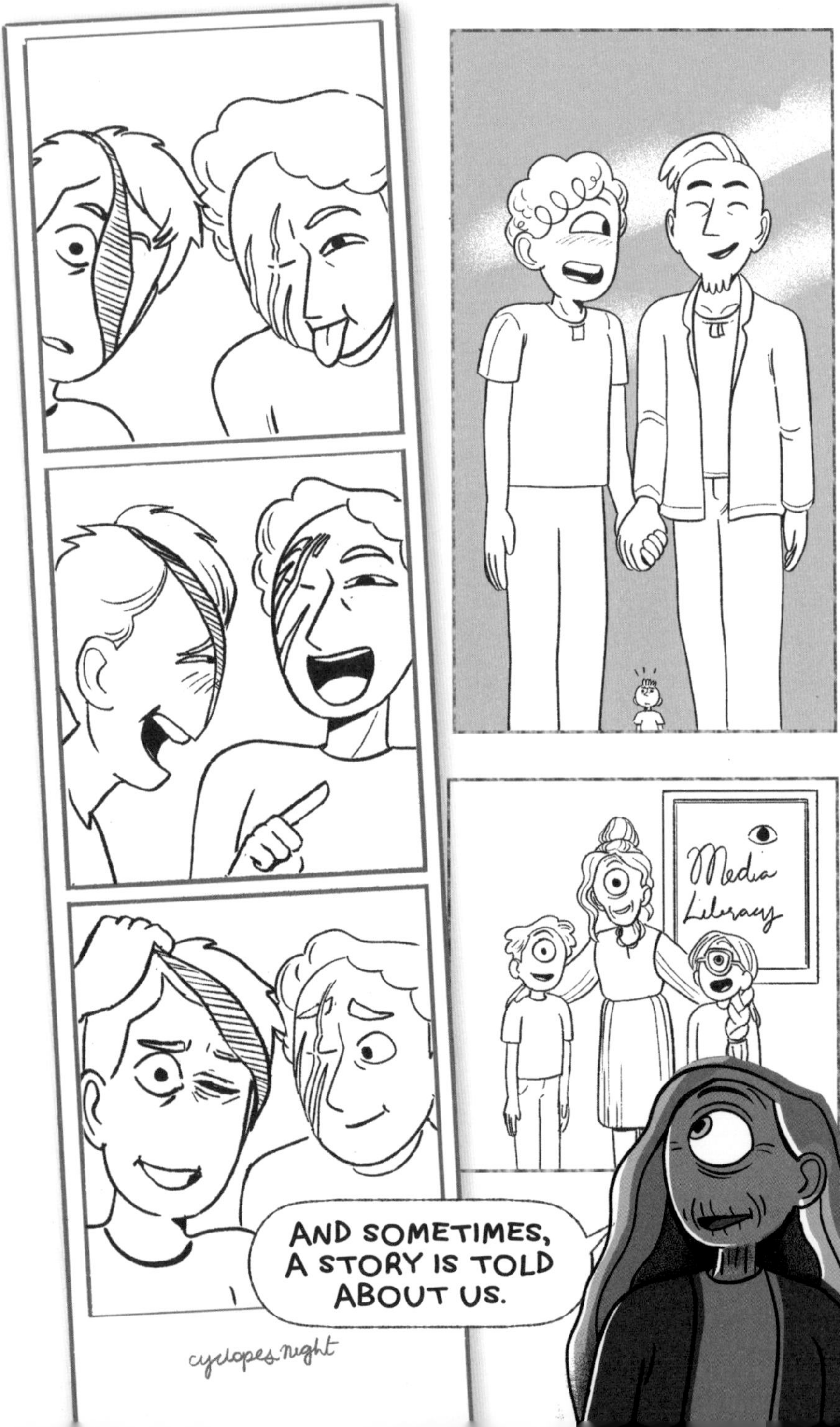
Media Literacy
AND SOMETIMES, A STORY IS TOLD ABOUT US.
cyclopes.night

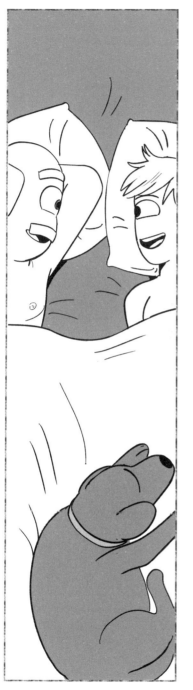

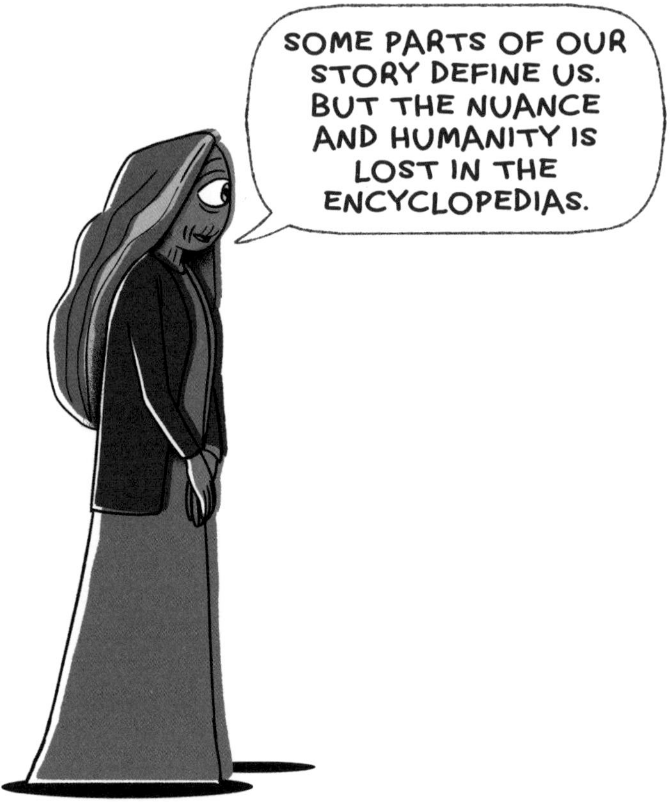
SOME PARTS OF OUR STORY DEFINE US. BUT THE NUANCE AND HUMANITY IS LOST IN THE ENCYCLOPEDIAS.

PLAYCLOPS

ANNIVERSARY EDITION

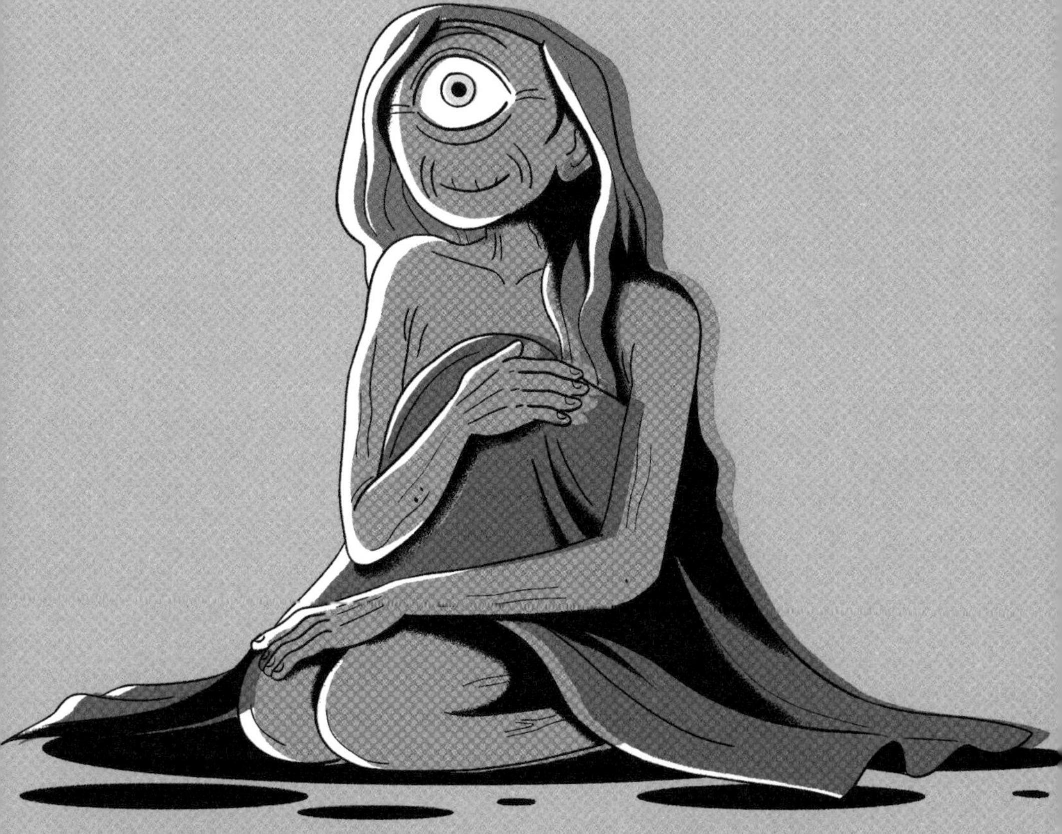

ETNA'S BACK!

FIG. 479. Etna.

Etna
(Figure 479).

Etna was the first Cyclops cover model for a national magazine. Her breakout success on the cover resulted in a short-lived popularity. After her initial acclaim, people demonized her for posing nude. The cover would resurface every decade. Depending on the time, she was a pioneer or a traitor.

As a senior, Etna returned to the *Playclops* cover one more time. In the interim, she devoted her time to help at-risk Cyclopes with her charity, The Etna Project.

AUTHOR'S INTENTIONS

A sketchbook page of Etna drawings is how I started this series. I kind of thought it would be cool to do a drawing of a Cyclops with one eye and one breast. That's the simple truth of how *Cyclopedia Exotica* started.

After one sketchbook page came many more pin-ups of my mysterious Cyclops lady. The original idea with Etna was she would be a beloved sex symbol. And that was it. But the idea morphed into using Etna as an anchoring point for Cyclopean history. I liked the irony of pairing her never-changing *Playclops* cover alongside changing times.

I also thought she could serve as an inspirational role model to Latea, an aspiring model. Early in the graphic novel, she pins up the *Playclops* cover in her apartment. Latea feels her small modeling jobs are meaningless. I imagined her getting home late from a mundane eye-cream shoot, and staring at the cover. Feeling its immensity—the cover that changed everything.

MOUNT ETNA
(Figure 480).

An active volcano on the coast of Sicily, Italy. In Greek mythology, it is where the Cyclopes made their home.

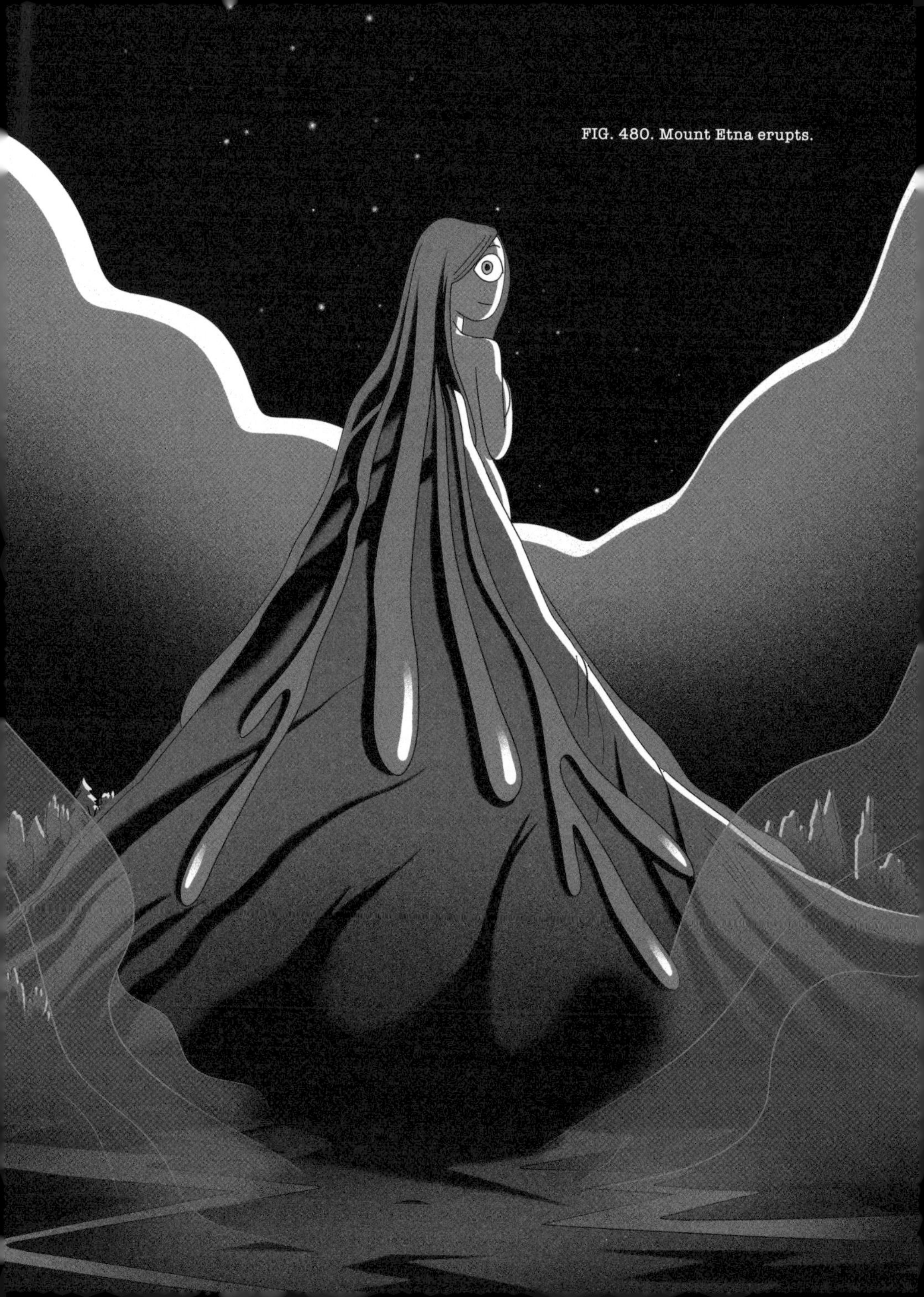

FIG. 480. Mount Etna erupts.

Tim & Pari

(Figure 481).

Tim and Pari met in college and have been together since. Tim grew up in a predominantly Two-Eyed community. Pari did too. And because of that, Pari was certain she would never date a Two-Eyes. Cue rom-com. Cut to the present: Tim and Pari are the parents of two mixed kids. They've come a long way.

Pari struggles with uncertainty about whether she will return to work. She always thought she'd be a stay-at-home mom. With Tim's help, she returns to work.

AUTHOR'S INTENTIONS

With Pari, I wanted to explore being a minority with a good job. She feels pressured to keep working because there aren't many Cyclopes in her position. But she also wants to be a stay-at-home mom.

Although it's never stated, the hidden reason for Pari's indecision is she has few role models. There are few Cyclopes in top positions—her boss is a Two-Eyes. With no role models, she's internalized the idea that there's no position for her. She assumes once she has a family, she'll leave her job.

FIG. 481.
Tim and Pari.

Her desire to keep working creates dissonance. That's where Tim comes in. With him, I wanted to show the power of a supportive spouse. Early on with Tim, I played with making him more of an obstacle in her story. But Pari already had so many struggles, I didn't want to add another. It came out better that he was her biggest cheerleader.

I also had fun including a couple comics where they wonder about the lives of their own kids.

FIG. 482. The island of Lipari.

ISLAND OF LIPARI
(Figure 482).

The largest of the Aeolian
Islands. It is associated with
Homer's *Odyssey* and Cyclopes.

Latea

(Figure 483).

Latea is an aspiring model and actress. Although she's glad to be doing commercial work, she has bigger dreams. Etna is a hero of hers. If it wasn't for Etna's infamous cover, her career options would be even more limited.

Latea spends her day job modeling mundane products. It's not her dream career.

Before meeting Pol, Latea had an active dating life. She'd find herself out every Friday night, on the arm of an impressive man—impressive on paper, boring in real life—a man who needed an exotic escort to make him seem more interesting. Latea was close to giving up on love. Pol was one of the first to see her for more than her looks.

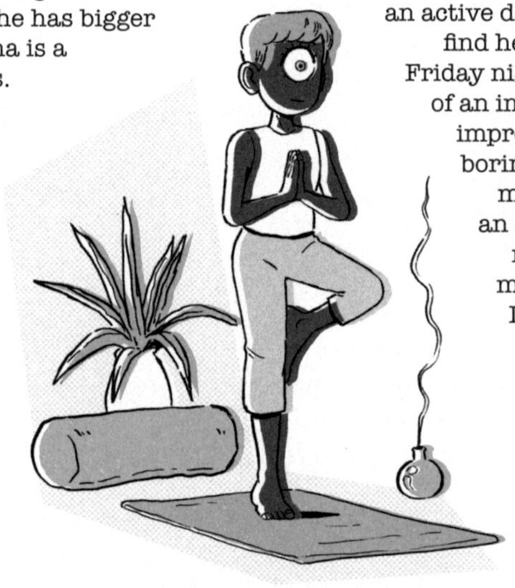

FIG. 483. Latea practices yoga.

AUTHOR'S INTENTIONS

With Latea, I wanted to follow a character who society considers beautiful, but is also from a community society doesn't consider to be conventionally beautiful. I paired her with Pol, who is prematurely bald and overweight, to show how society treats each of them differently. Although I didn't end up exploring this theme further, it popped up in some comics, such as "Rethink things" (see pages 202–203).

GALATEA

(Figure 484).

A sea nymph, Galatea often appears as an object of Polyphemus's love. But in *The Triumph of Galatea*, Raphael chose to center her in a divine pose, riding a shell drawn by dolphins. She is so much more than just a love interest.

FIG. 484.
Galatea the sea nymph.

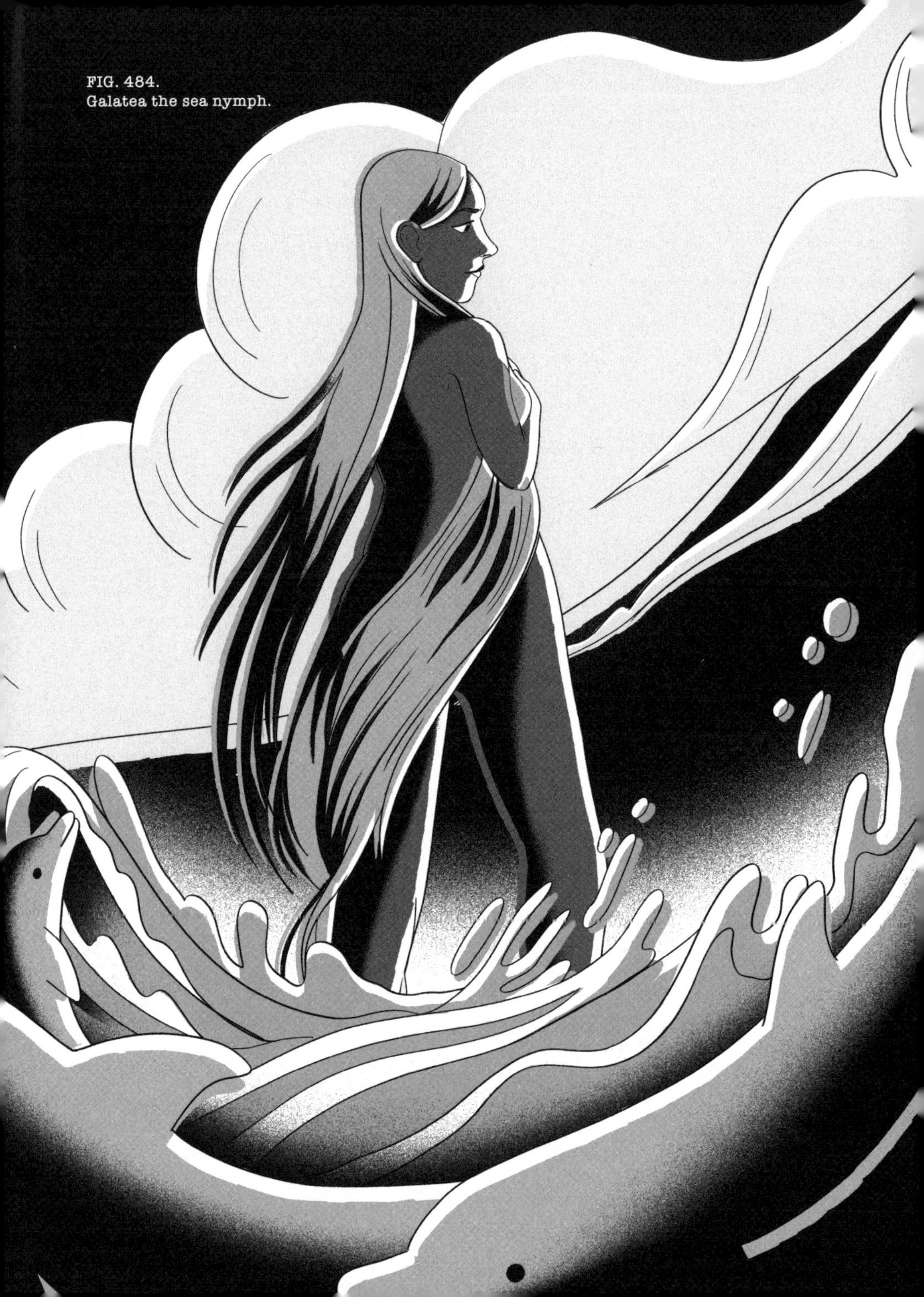

Pol

(Figure 485).

Pol is on the search for love. But love is hard when society tokenizes, fetishizes, and treats Cyclopes differently in general.

When Pol meets Latea, everything changes. He's in love. And with love, it feels like he can start the rest of his life. Like finding a house. But he discovers it to be a long, arduous process. Pol learns life doesn't wait for goals.

AUTHOR'S INTENTIONS

Pol has been at a disadvantage most of his life. In contrast, Latea is "conventionally" beautiful.

Latea gets a "pass" for many things he has struggled with. He's young, balding prematurely, out of shape, and a Cyclops. The world isn't as kind to him. Despite that, Pol has spent a lifetime learning to love himself. In return, he displays a deep, full, reverberating love for his friends and family. With the house storyline, I thought I would push a character who's so "figured out" back into a place of struggle.

POLYPHEMUS

(Figure 486).

The man-eating Cyclops from Homer's *Odyssey*. In later European interpretations, he's a musician pursuing unrequited love.

FIG. 485. Pol's bar and plants.

FIG. 486. Polyphemus tends to his sheep.

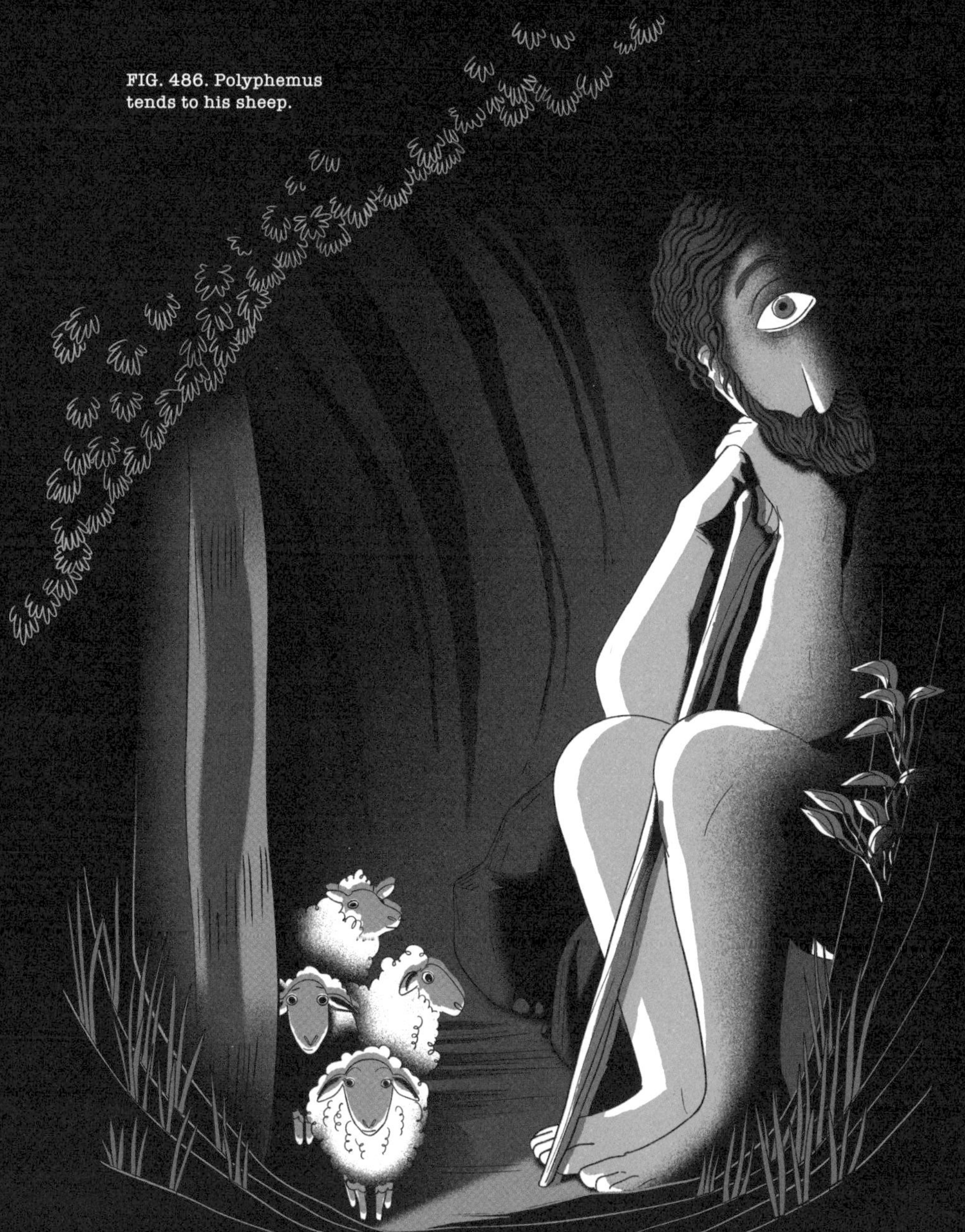

Bron

(Figure 487).

Bron had an unsuccessful surgery to change his appearance from Cyclops to Two-Eyes. The botched surgery resulted in him having to wear an eye patch over a dead eye. For the short time the second eye worked, Bron was happier. His story is one of self-love.

AUTHOR'S INTENTIONS

My intention with Bron was to make a character who struggles with his own identity. For much of his life, being a Cyclops was a disadvantage. So Bron did everything possible to distance himself from it, including a surgery to get two eyes. But when the surgery backfires, he's lost between two worlds. He's not quite a Cyclops, and not quite a Two-Eyes. He went from having an identity he disliked to having no identity at all. I wanted to put him on a journey of self-discovery.

With the *Suzy's One Eye* storyline, I wanted to explore ideas of stories. The stories we tell ourselves, the stories we are told, and the stories that define us. I wanted Bron to hate a book that he read as a child. A book that encouraged kids to be true to themselves. The message was at odds with how the world made him feel. Later in the novel, when he finally reads *Suzy's One Eye*, it's not the story he thought it was. In fighting against the notion "of being true to oneself," he made up parts of the story that were never there.

BRONTES

(Figure 488).

Meaning "thunder." In Hesiod's *Theogony*, the Cyclops Brontes and his brothers craft Zeus's thunderbolts.

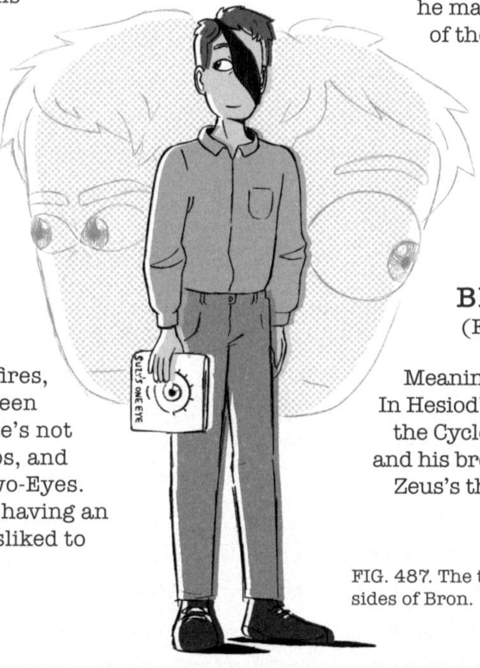
SUZY'S ONE EYE

FIG. 487. The two sides of Bron.

FIG. 488. Brontes crafts a thunderbolt.

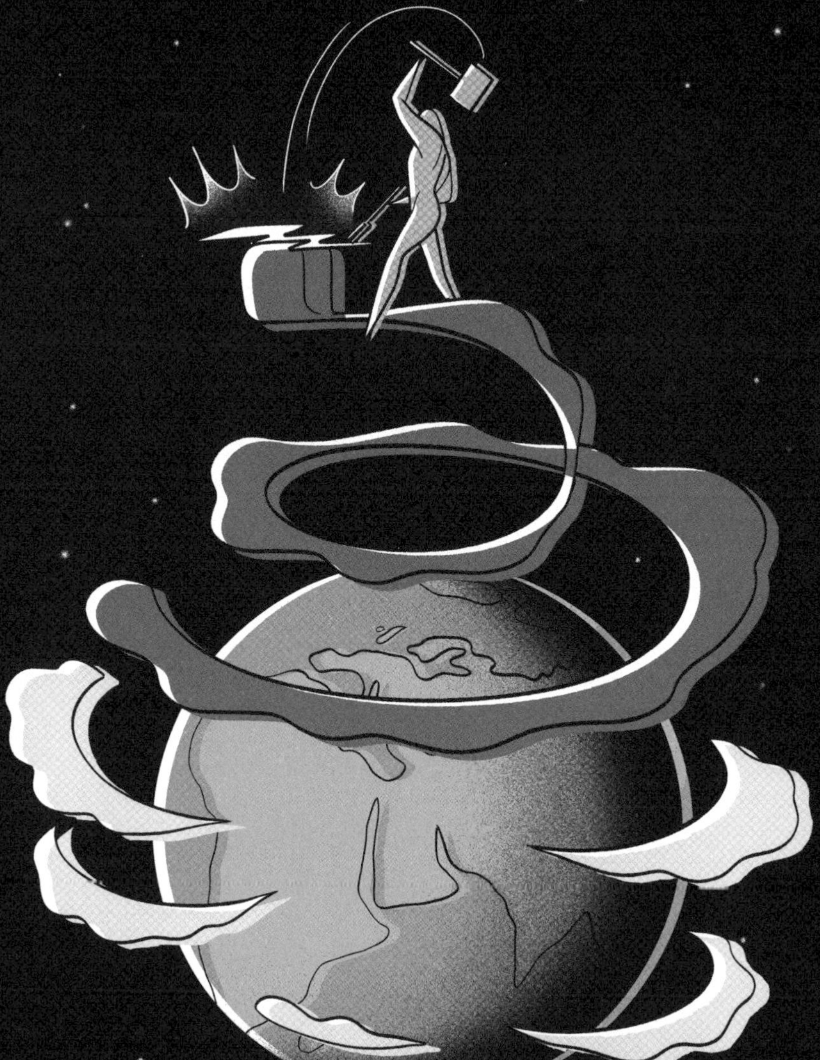

Jian & Grae

(Figure 489).

Jian and Grae are artists who dress alike and explore Cyclopean issues in their art. Later in the novel, they have a falling out, each thinking she doesn't need the other. They later reunite, realizing that sometimes two eyes are better than one.

AUTHOR'S INTENTIONS

My original plan with Jian and Grae was to cut away to a silly drawing, just to have them give it meaningful context. But I fell in love with their whole vibe.

I thought I could explore their passion for meaningful work and struggle with vanity.

With Grae's departure, I explored "selling out." For Jian, I wanted to show the malleability of confidence. Where she once held firm beliefs on the importance of her art as a team, her confidence melts when she's alone.

JIAN AND GRAEAE

(Figure 490 and 491).

Jian are birds from Chinese mythology with one eye and one wing. Two birds depend on each other. Graeae are three witches from Greek mythology that share one eye and see visions.

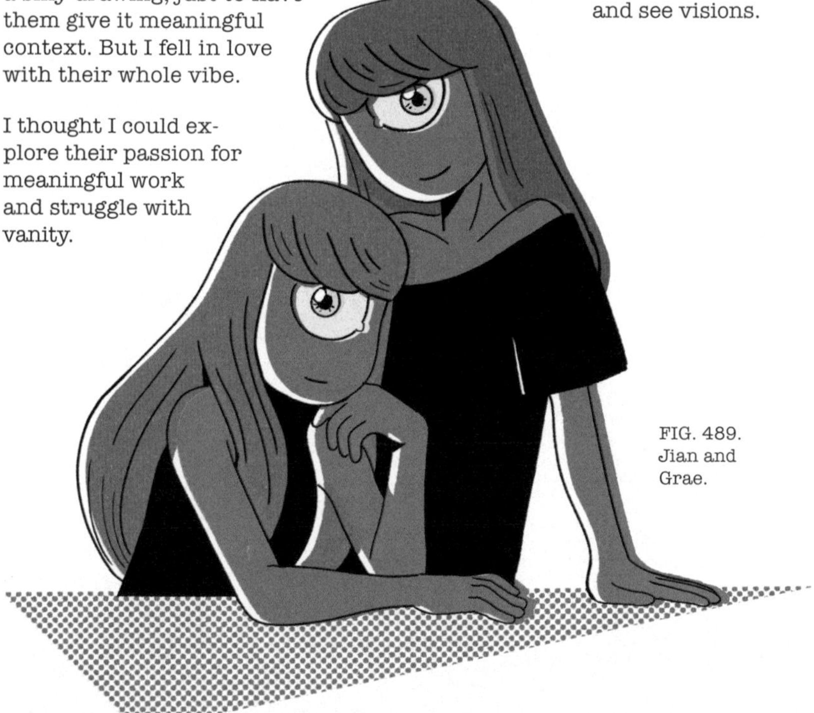

FIG. 489. Jian and Grae.

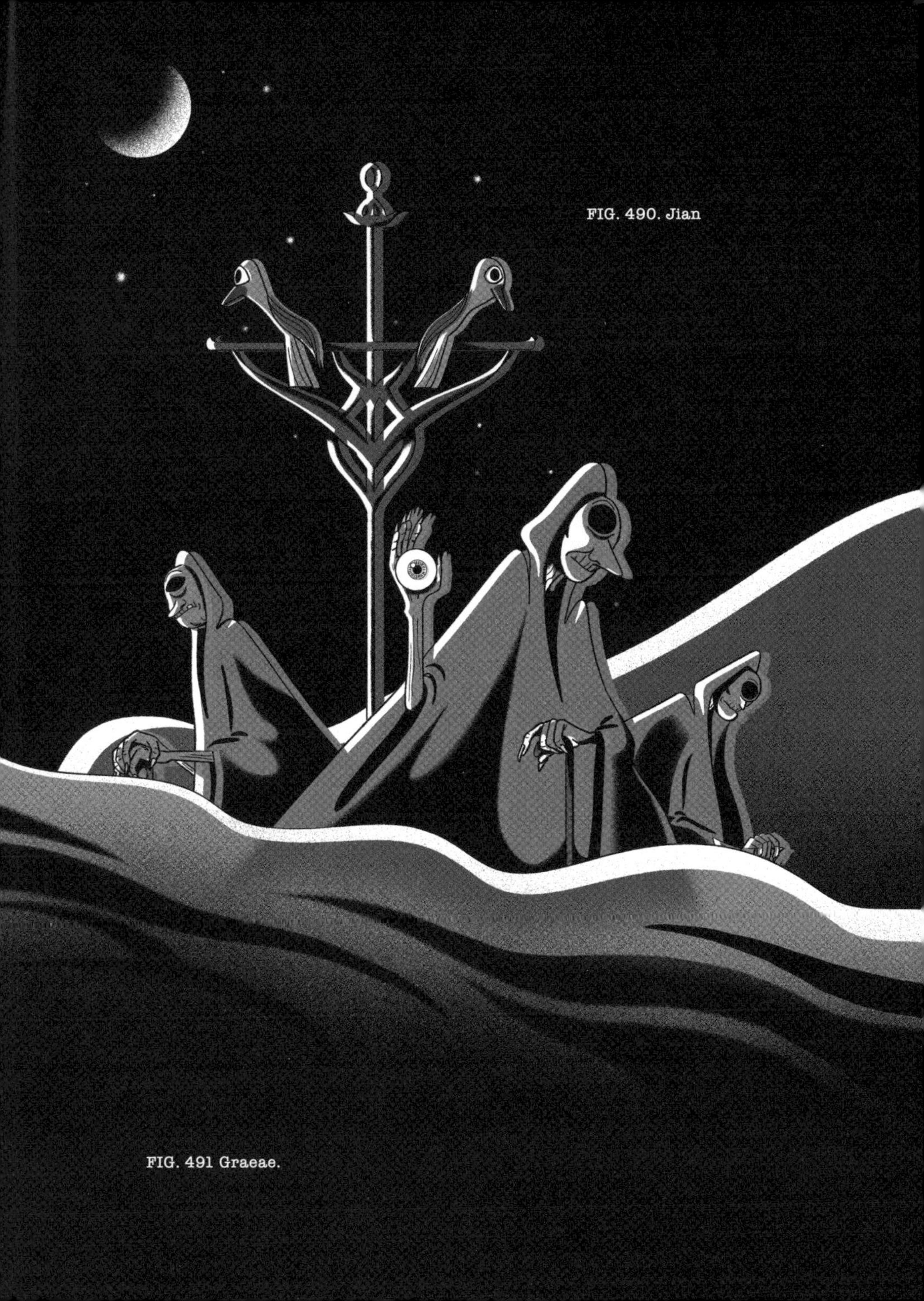

FIG. 490. Jian

FIG. 491 Graeae.

Vy

(Figure 492).

Vy was the face of the Lift and Separator. She later regretted being part of the brand and turned to teaching Media Literacy for Cyclopean youth.

AUTHOR'S INTENTIONS

Young Vy's only modeling opportunities were for problematic products—products that reinforced that Cyclopes should change themselves to be more like Two-Eyes. When the job market is narrow, values fall to the wayside. I wanted to explore Vy's struggle with her own choices and how she spends a lifetime making up for it.

VIRGIL

(Figure 493).

An ancient Roman poet who wrote the Latin epic *Aeneid*, in which the characters revisit Polyphemus and his island.

FIG. 492. Vy.

FIG. 493. A bust of Virgil.

Arj
(Figure 494).

Arj is sweet, adorable, and a little clumsy. The pressure he feels to be perfect (the cause of his clumsiness) stems from a childhood bully.

AUTHOR'S INTENTIONS

When I was a kid, I went to a friend's house for dinner. When her family sat down and said grace, I didn't know what they were doing, but I bowed my head, clasped my hands, and "camouflaged." I feared doing something wrong, and was uncomfortable going to friends' houses for a little while after that. With Arj, I wanted to root his awkwardness in something real. One bully defined Arj. He wouldn't be as clumsy if he didn't overthink things.

ARGES
(Figure 495).

Meaning "bright." One of the Cyclopes, Arges, along with Brontes and Steropes, fashioned lightning bolts for Zeus.

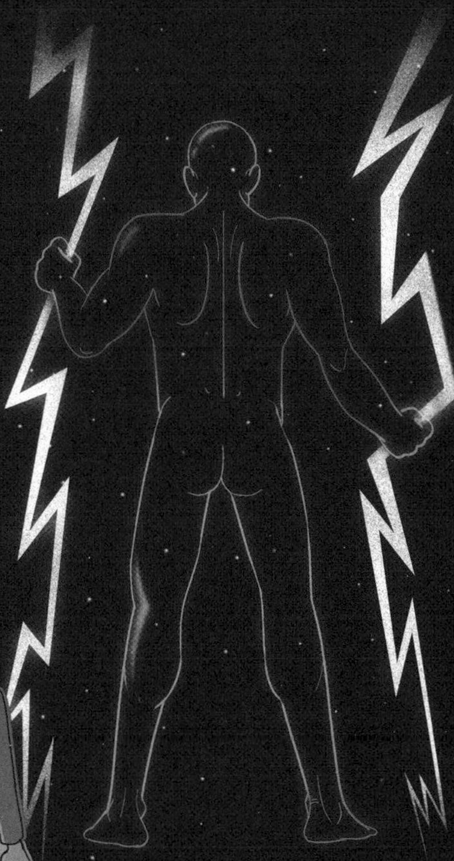

FIG. 495. Arges weilds the bright light of lightning bolts.

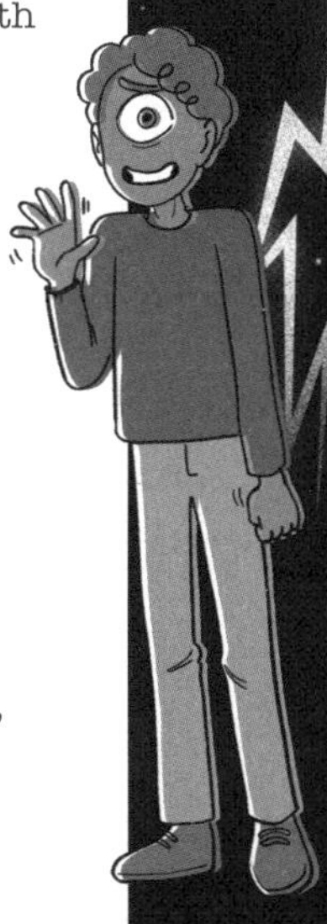

FIG. 494. Arj.

This graphic novel wouldn't be possible without
the following people, thank you...

Nikolas Ilic for more things than I could list here.

Kenneth Hung for proofreading comics at god-awful hours.

Megan Dong and Maha Tabikh for notes.

Peggy, Tom, Tracy, Alison, Megan, Lucia, Trynne, Julia, Kaiya,
Ann, Tomoko, and Jiyeon at Drawn and Quarterly for getting
this book made. Even through a worldwide pandemic.

And finally, you, the readers of the comic.
Thank you for picking up this book.
(Figure 495).

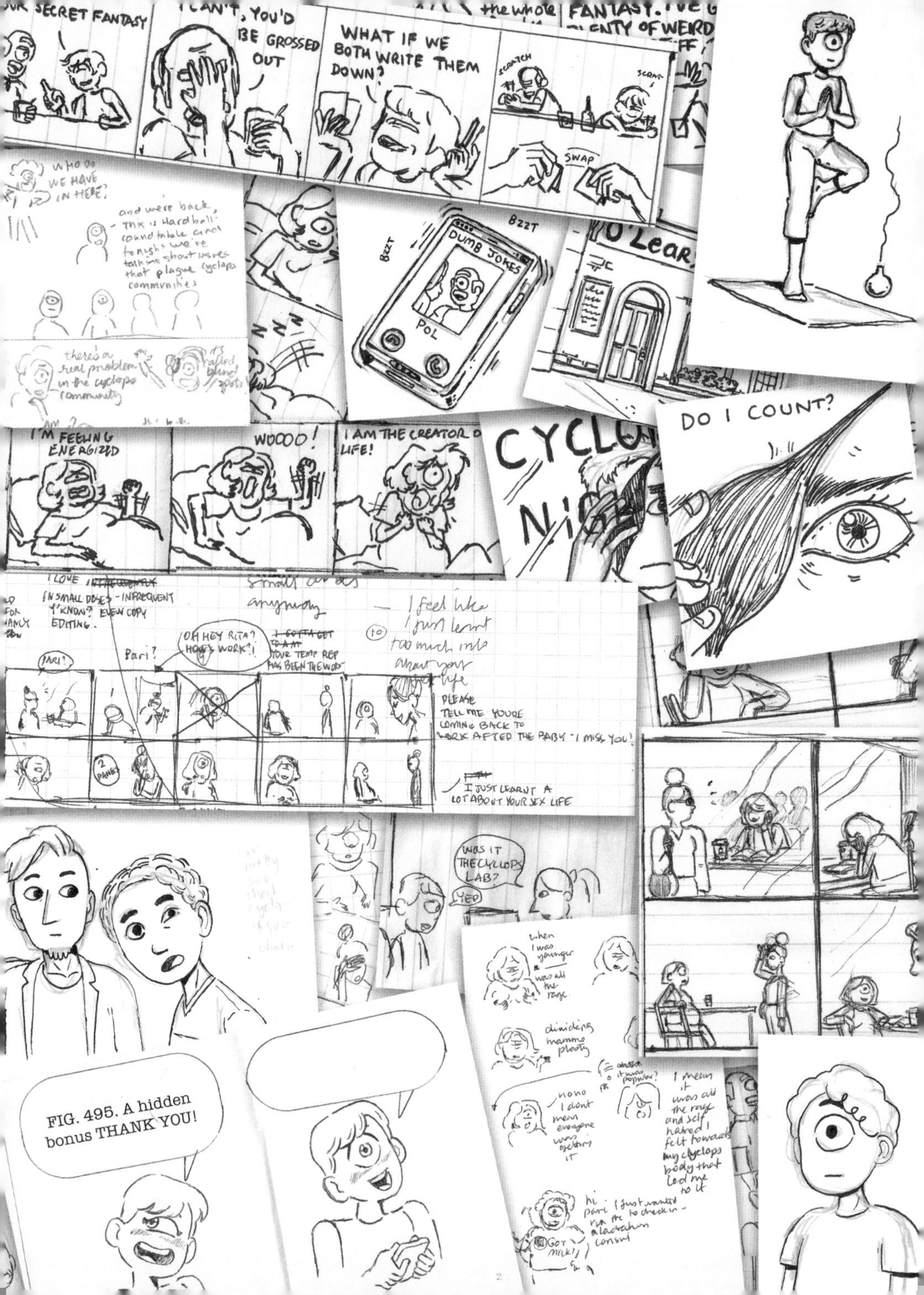

SECRET FANTASY
I CAN'T, YOU'D BE GROSSED OUT
WHAT IF WE BOTH WRITE THEM DOWN?
SCRATCH
SWAP
FANTASY. I'VE
WHO DO WE HAVE IN HERE?
and we're back, this is Hardball roundtable and tonight we're talking about issues that plague cyclops communities
there's a real problem in the cyclops community
it's called blind spots
BZZT
DUMB JOKES
POL
O'LEAR
I'M FEELING ENERGIZED
WOOOO!
I AM THE CREATOR OF LIFE!
CYCLO
DO I COUNT?
I LOVE
IN SMALL DOSES - INFREQUENT
Y'KNOW? EVEN COPY EDITING.
OH HEY RITA? HOW'S WORK?!
Pari?
PARI!
YOUR TEMP REP HAS BEEN THE WORST
I feel like I just learnt too much info about your life
PLEASE TELL ME YOU'RE COMING BACK TO WORK AFTER THE BABY - I MISS YOU!
2 PANEL
I JUST LEARNT A LOT ABOUT YOUR SEX LIFE
WAS IT THE CYCLOPS LAB?
YEP
when I was younger was all the rage
dividing mammoplasty
I mean it was all the rage and self hatred I felt towards my cyclops body that led me to it
hi Pari I just wanted to check in - a lactation consult
GOT MILK?
FIG. 495. A hidden bonus THANK YOU!

FIG. 496.

Aminder Dhaliwal (Figure 496) is
a native of Brampton, Ontario, and
received a Bachelor of Animation from
Sheridan College. She now lives in Los
Angeles, working in animation. She
published her first graphic novel, *Woman
World*, with Drawn and Quarterly in 2018.
She has serialized *Cyclopedia Exotica*
weekly on Instagram since 2019.

FIG. 497.

Nikolas Ilic (Figure 497) is an Emmy award-winning production artist working in animation and children's books. Born and raised in Canada, Nikolas graduated from Sheridan College in 2011, with a bachelor's degree in Animation. He lives in Los Angeles, California.

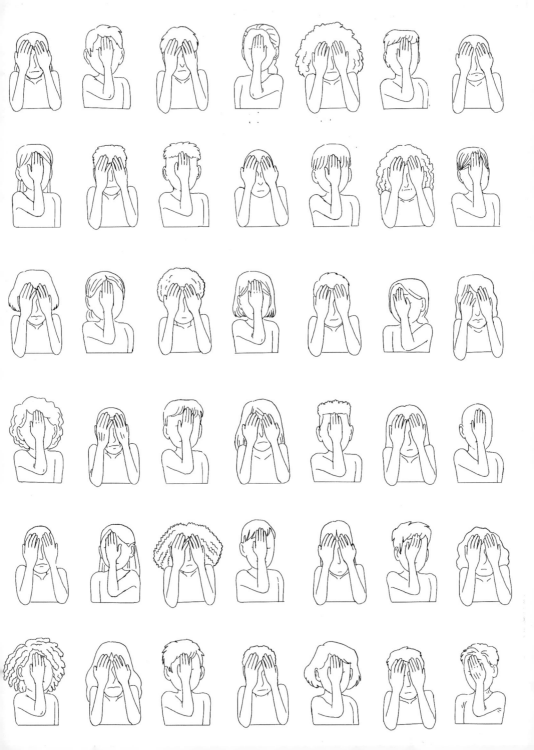